READINGS
FOR WRITING

Elizabeth Cowan
Texas A & M University

Scott, Foresman and Company   Glenview, Illinois

Dallas, Tex.   Oakland, N.J.   Palo Alto, Calif.
Tucker, Ga.   London, England

An Instructor's Manual is available. It may be obtained through your local Scott, Foresman representative or by writing to English Editor, College Division, Scott, Foresman and Company, 1900 E. Lake Avenue, Glenview, IL 60025.

Acknowledgments

All literary credits appear on pages 430–432, which constitute a legal extension of the copyright page.

Cover: Wassily Kandinsky, *Zeichenreihen. 1931*
Kunstmuseum Basel, Kupferstichkabinett.

Library of Congress Cataloging in Publication Data.

Cowan, Elizabeth, 1940–
  Readings for writing.

  Includes Index.
  1. College readers. 2. English language—Rhetoric.
I. Title.
PE1417.C667 1983   808'.0427   82-23083
ISBN 0-673-15845-4

PREFACE

The group must not be defined by the possession of certain characteristics but by the tendency to emphasize them.

—Henri Bergson

What the reader of these genres . . . likes, fundamentally, is the fact that they are all alike yet nevertheless undeniably different. . . . The same thing is true of all the days of our lives. Something identical endlessly returns . . . but this repetition carries with it a constant flow of differences, a variation that is all the more overwhelming because it modulates upon a single register. This vivid contrast, of the different upon a background of sameness, is the strength of genre literature.

—Fernando Savater

Readings for Writing is a college reader.

As a member of that genre, it has the characteristics common to its group. The book is a collection of readings selected to interest and to benefit students who are learning to write.

The book contains more than 80 selections of various types and lengths written by professional, literary, scholarly, and free-lance writers, and by students themselves. Each selection is followed by questions for discussion. These questions not only point to the significance of the ideas in each selection, but they also emphasize the whole situation, the context, in which the selection was written. Writing assignments appear at the end of each chapter. They include discussions of how to write as well as ideas for what to write.

The ways in which *Readings for Writing* contrasts against the background of the characteristics of its genre, however, are what I want to emphasize here. It has these features which you will not find in another college reader:

—Selections that come from the same range of sources students will encounter in real life: books, collections of essays, literature, business and professional writing, sacred writings, magazines for the general reader, trade journals, periodicals for people with special interests, newspapers, and school assignments.

This wide range of sources, because it illustrates the variety of writing that people are required to do or desire to do long after they are out of a classroom, makes an enormously important point to people learning to write: they will *need* to write and they will *want* to write after they leave college.

—A strong balance between subjects of permanence and subjects of immediacy. The selections range from Aristotle to René Dubos; from Helen Keller to Ellen Goodman. The subjects range from topics of the intellect and of the heart—Faulkner, Mann, Virginia Woolf, Martin Luther King, Jr.—to topics of the day—space travel, dolphins, computers, and the Charlie Daniels band.

—Selections written by young and old, rich and poor, learned and not so learned, professional and amateur. Perhaps even more importantly, they are written by people who wrote for many reasons: they make their living that way; they are fascinated by or involved in the area about which they are writing; they are required to write by circumstances and situations; writing gives them a job; writing gives them pleasure. No person learning to write, after reading these selections, could mistakenly suppose that writing is done only by scholars or academicians, or people who live the contemplative life.

—Writing presented as *action*. This is the most significant way that *Readings for Writing* contrasts against its background. The readings are not studied as records; they are not looked at as artifacts. Rather, each reading is presented as an *event*, an event happening as a result of a particular mix at a particular time—of the person writing, the motive for writing, the circumstances and situation, the form the writing needed to take, the emphasis the writer wanted to give, and the place in which the writing was to be presented to the reader.

Each selection, therefore, is studied for its own configuration, its own shape inside the larger shape of the category of writing it represents. This configuration is the result of that combination of time, writer, subject, persons being written to, and place of publication, peculiar to that piece of writing.

Underpinning this concept of *writing as an event, an action*, are interviews with six successful writers. The interviews concentrate on how these writers wrote the examples of their work which adjoin the interviews. The revelations, explanations, and honest admissions that the interviewees make will make any writer—would-be or otherwise—

smile with recognition at the frustration and unpredictability of, and the commitment required by, the act of writing. Annie Dillard, for instance, reveals that *Pilgrim at Tinker Creek* was first a novel set in Maine before it was rewritten; James Dickey tells of 50 revisions or more of his essay on enjoying poetry; Venita VanCaspel admits that it took three books, selling into the hundreds of thousands, before she thought of herself as a writer.

The writers' interviews—as well as the selections by all the writers in the book—also affirm the real and final value of writing: deep satisfaction and genuine pleasure that come from communicating what you see, know, or think to other human beings.

Finally, a word must be said about the relationship of the titles of the parts of *Readings for Writing* to the movement of the book. Here the contrast of the book against its common background of college readers is extremely important. **Writing to Tell**, **Writing to Change**, and **Writing to Express** are not mere renamings of old categories. The titles are not a cosmetic shift. They are not a descriptive shift. The titles actually represent a shift from noun-based distinctions to verb-based. This is a fundamental shift, a shift to seeing writing as an *act*.

If there is writing to tell, there has to be someone who *writes* to tell—a subject for the verb. If there is someone writing to tell there must be *someone* for whom the writing is done. And the scenario could continue. The point is that the titles of the parts of the text are attempts to make an accurate statement about the nature of the writing and to emphasize writing as an act of one person intending to communicate with another.

Further, the order of the parts of *Readings for Writing* suggests an increasing engagement and involvement of the writer with the act of writing and the persons being written to. In **writing to tell** the writer is at a distance and in a position of little personal involvement with the subject matter or the persons being communicated with. **Writing to change** requires more of the writer; to assert with evidence, to evaluate, and to persuade, writers must put more of themselves at risk. They must be more committed to their subjects and more intent upon connecting with the readers. In **writing to express**, writers are at total risk. The subject matter is themselves, how they see the world, what they have experienced, what positions they hold about life. Writing to express, therefore, represents the ultimate personal involvement writers can have with their subjects and the persons they wish to communicate with.

Readings for Writing will be a valuable addition to any classroom. It is a collection people can *enjoy* reading. It is a collection people can *learn* from. And, perhaps more important for students and their teachers, it is a collection that makes writing seem not only useful but worthwhile.

For their reviews of an early draft of this book, I wish to thank Jay Balderson, Western Illinois University; James A. Berlin, University of Cincinnati; Ronald R. Butters, Duke University; Douglas O. Eason, Columbia State Community College; Michael J. Hogan, University of New Mexico; Robert M. Holland, University of Akron; C. Jeriel Howard, Northeastern Illinois University; Clayton Hudnall, University of Hartford; Paul J. Klemp, Oklahoma State University; David Martin, Monmouth College; Jack Moskowitz, Middlesex County College; Donovan J. Ochs, University of Iowa; Peter Page, University of New Mexico; Martha Reid, Moravian College; John J. Ruszkiewicz, University of Texas; Charles I. Schuster, University of Washington; Jack Selzer, Pennsylvania State University; and James C. Work, Colorado State University.

And to Tom Waldrep for conducting a preliminary interview with James Dickey, I want to say a special thanks.

Jerele Don Neeld assisted in the formulation and refinement of the central idea of this book—categories and configurations—and did all of the early research on categories and representations of these categories. In fact, many of the best pieces in this book were discovered by Jerele Neeld. It was a real pleasure to learn from his writing and his discussions.

I would not have done this book without the assistance of my partners at Scott, Foresman: Amanda Clark, Jane Steinmann, Andrea Coens, Lydia Webster, and Lucy Lesiak. Anyone who has ever written a book knows the value of people who not only understand but also enable you to refine your concepts. With deep gratitude I thank them.

I want to thank Nancy Foushée for being the kind of friend who makes it possible for a book to be written.

To my family, Miss Rachel, Mr. T., Frank, Sheri, and Sarah, Barbara and Will, Pearl, and Rita: Thanks.

Elizabeth Cowan

CONTENTS

INTRODUCTION

CATEGORIES AND CONFIGURATIONS 1

PART 1

WRITING TO TELL 12

THE HOW-TO ESSAY 16

The writer breaks down the process or activity so that readers can follow it easily, seeing exactly how one step leads to the next. After determining the needs of the audience, the writer chooses the kind of instructions or directions and details to include.

JOAN K. DAVIDSON *A Beach Cure That Works in Mysterious Ways and Lasts Forever* 18

NOEL PERRIN *Buying a Pickup Truck* 20

SUE LUCKSTED *How to Bake on a Boat* 28

JOHN VON RHEIN *Listen, and Listen Good: How to Attend a Concert* 32

RUTH RUDNER *Body Surfing* 36

PAUL MERRIMAN *How to Catch Speckled Trout* 38

Writing Your Own: The How-To Essay 41

THE PROBLEM/SOLUTION ESSAY 46

The writer emphasizes the problem, the solution, or both, depending on the purpose in writing the essay. Examples and illustrations should have meaning for the particular readers to whom the writing is directed.

MARGARET MEAD *How We Can Help Children Learn to Write* 48

ERIC PERLMAN *Friends Between a Rock and a Hard Place* 53

RENÉ DUBOS *Beyond the Garden Wall* 56

CAROLINE DREWES *Is Honesty Still the Best Policy?* 63

ELLEN GOODMAN *Being a Secretary Can Be Hazardous to Your Health* 67

VICKI WHITE *Solving the Problem at Dettmers' Greenery* 70

Writing Your Own: The Problem/Solution Essay 73

THE INFORMATION ESSAY 78

The writer places the information at the center of attention. But the reader will still know that a <u>person</u> wrote the essay because the writer's voice can be "heard."

LOREN EISELEY *How Flowers Changed the World* 80

CAROL TAVRIS AND LEONORE TIEFER *The Meanings of the Kiss* 84

E. B. WHITE *What Is an Essayist?* 86

DOUGLAS COLLIGAN *Life in Zero Gravity* 88

ARISTOTLE *The Three Stages of Man* 93

RICHARD BULLIET *Let's Hear It for the Camel!* 97

JOAN DIDION *Georgia O'Keeffe* 102

BUSINESS LETTER (H. J. Hays) *106*

BUSINESS REPORT (Linda Reed) *107*

Writing Your Own: The Information Essay 110

JAMES DICKEY TALKS ABOUT WRITING   114

James Dickey, novelist and poet, talks about the way his writing happened when he wrote an essay on enjoying poetry.

How to Enjoy Poetry   *114*

Interview   116

VENITA VANCASPEL TALKS ABOUT WRITING   120

Venita VanCaspel, author of several books on managing money, talks about becoming a writer even though she "knew" she had no writing ability.

You Can Become a Millionaire   *120*

Interview   124

PART 2

WRITING TO CHANGE   128

THE ASSERTION-WITH-EVIDENCE ESSAY   132

The writer makes the assertion early in the essay. The evidence—facts, examples, and illustrations—is relevant to the assertion and sufficient to convince the intended audience.

BARBARA LANG STERN   *Tears Can Be Crucial to Your Physical and Emotional Health*   *134*

DANIEL YANKELOVICH   *The Work Ethic Is Underemployed*   *136*

KEVIN STREHLO *Talk to the Animals*   142

BOOTH FOWLER AND SAUL BRENNER *In Defense of Optimism*   147

EDWARD SADALLA AND JEFFERY BURROUGHS *Profiles in Eating: Sexy Vegetarians and Other Diet-Based Social Stereotypes*   156

Writing Your Own: The Assertion-With-Evidence Essay   161

THE EVALUATION ESSAY   166

The criteria to be used and how they are appropriate for the evaluation are stated clearly. The writer considers the readers— what they know, believe, already agree with—in providing support for the evaluation.

YI-FU TUAN *American Space, Chinese Place*   169

E. M. FORSTER *Tribute to Mahatma Gandhi*   171

WENDEL BERRY *A Good Scythe*   173

RUSSELL BAKER *The Two Ismo's*   177

STEPHEN KIMMEL *I Sing the Editor Electric*   179

BOOK REVIEWS   184

BRUCE COLMAN *A Disagreeable Defender of the Prairie*   184

HENRY MAYER *Digging into the Past: Seventeenth Century Virginia*   186

JOHN MARLOWE *Schools, Learning, and the Quality of Life*   188

MUSIC REVIEWS   191

GARY GIDDINS *High Notes: The Five Best Recent Releases*   191

MICHAEL BANE *Charlie Daniels: In Celebration of the Things We'd All Like to Believe In*   194

JOEL SELVIN *Capturing the Beat of the Beach*   199

Writing Your Own: The Evaluation Essay   201

THE PERSUASION ESSAY   207

The writer establishes his or her authority by showing sufficient knowledge of the subject. The readers will know exactly what the writer wants them to believe or to do.

MARTIN LUTHER KING, JR. *Letter from Birmingham Jail* 209

PLATO *Socrates' Defense* 222

PAUL MCBREARTY *We Should Abolish Anonymous Evaluations of Teachers by Their Students* 227

VIRGINIA WOOLF *Professions for Women* 232

THOMAS MANN *A Letter to the Dean of the Philosophical Faculty of the University of Bonn* 237

DON WALL *Lake Maker* 242

WENDELL BERRY *In Defense of Literacy* 246

THOMAS JEFFERSON *Declaration of Independence* 249

Writing Your Own: The Persuasion Essay 253

PETER ROSENWALD TALKS ABOUT WRITING 259

Peter Rosenwald, dance critic for the <u>Wall Street Journal</u> and a businessman, talks about how he writes within the demands of a newspaper column, and why he writes.

Classical vs. Introspective Ballet 259

A Handsome Dance Company Hits Its Stride 261

Swan Lake/Nixon 262

A Beautiful Building Enhanced by Bach 263

Interview 265

CYNTHIA MANDELBERG TALKS ABOUT WRITING 271

Cynthia Mandelberg, dramatist and screenplay writer, talks about how she writes plays and what she hopes to give her audiences.

An Open Letter to the President and Congress 271

Interview 272

PART 3

WRITING TO EXPRESS 276

THE PERSONAL EXPERIENCE ESSAY 280

The writer <u>needs</u> to tell a story, and through that story shares and reveals part of herself or himself. The reader may benefit more from an honestly told story than from kinds of writing intended to profit the reader.

MAYA ANGELOU *Graduation in Stamps* 282

RUSTY CAWLEY *Mentor and Friend: Memory of John Lennon* 292

MARK TWAIN *Uncle's Farm* 295

EDWARD IWATA *Barbed-Wire Memories* 298

JOSHUA SLOCUM *Sailing Alone Around the World* 302

CHUCK ANDERSON *For You, Julie, February 27, 1982* 308

SCOTT MOZISEK *Death* 314

Writing Your Own: The Personal Experience Essay 317

THE PERSONAL PERSPECTIVE ESSAY 321

The writer is saying, without evidence or documentation, "This is how I see the world; this is what I think." And the reader then has the opportunity to see the world through another's eyes.

MAY SARTON *Rewards of Living a Solitary Life* 323

RICHARD RODRIGUEZ from *Hunger of Memory* 325

HELEN KELLER *Three Days to See* 331

ANAÏS NIN *In Favor of the Sensitive Man* 339

H. W. FOWLER *Split Infinitive* 345

MAX LERNER *On Being a Possibilist* 349

Writing Your Own: The Personal Perspective Essay 353

PERSONAL FORMS: A MISCELLANY

Any form can become personal when a writer chooses to make it personal. Writers in—and out of—college find that many different forms can be used to express themselves, depending on the occasion and the opportunity for writing.

SPEECHES   360

OLIVER WENDELL HOLMES   *Excerpt from a Speech at a Dinner of the Harvard Law School Association of New York*   360

WILLIAM FAULKNER   *On Receiving the Nobel Prize*   361

CHIEF SEATTLE   *Reply to the U.S. Government*   362

LETTERS   365

C. C. JONES   *Reverend C. C. Jones to His Son*   365

CARL JUNG   *Carl Jung to His Wife, Emma*   367

E. B. WHITE   *E. B. White to His Brother*   368

LIST   370

STEPHEN KOPP   *An Eschatological Laundry List: A Partial Register of the 927 (or was it 928?) Eternal Truths*   370

JOURNAL   372

LEWIS AND CLARK   from *Journals of Lewis and Clark*   382

DIARY   377

EDITH HOLDEN   from *The Country Diary of an Edwardian Lady*   377

TRAVEL ACCOUNT   378

ISABELLA BIRD   from *A Lady's Life in the Rocky Mountains*   379

OBITUARY   383

High-Society Glamour Girl of the '30s, Brenda Frazier   383

WILL   385

LEONARDO DA VINCI   *Will of Leonardo da Vinci*   386

ADVERTISEMENTS   389

MOBIL OIL   *World Without End*   389

It's What You Do—Not When You Do It   391

UNITED TECHNOLOGIES *Stop Screaming* *391*

This Will Make You Feel Better *392*

Keep It Simple *392*

SPIRITUAL WRITING **393**

SERMON **393**

MEISTER ECKHART *God Laughs and Plays* *393*

MEDITATIONS AND PHILOSOPHICAL WRITING **395**

ST. TERESA *St. Teresa's Bookmark* *395*

U. S. ANDERSEN *Ninth Meditation* *396*

LAO TZU from *Tao Te Ching* *396*

BUDDHIST from *the Metta Sutra* *397*

SENG-TS'AN from *the Hsin-hsin-ming* *397*

HINDU from *the Rig Veda* *398*

CHRISTIAN from *the Bible* *398*

THE GOLDEN RULE **398**

PRAYERS **399**

A JEWISH PRAYER *399*

A NAVAHO PRAYER *399*

A MUSLIM PRAYER *400*

A SIKH PRAYER *401*

A CHRISTIAN PRAYER *401*

POEMS **402**

from *Ecclesiastes* *402*

ANONYMOUS *Spring Scene* *403*

SHAKESPEARE *Sonnet 116* *403*

ROBERT SCHUMANN *Widmung* *403*

WILLIAM WORDSWORTH *I Wandered Lonely As a Cloud* *404*

EMILY DICKINSON *Poem 318* *405*

EDGAR SIMMONS *The Poet* *406*

WOODY GUTHRIE from *Seeds of Man* *406*

JENNY JOSEPH *Warning* *407*

JOHN HARTFORD   *I would not be here*   407

ROLAND PEASE   *Sea Sculpture*   408

Writing Your Own: Personal Forms   410

WILLIAM STAFFORD TALKS ABOUT WRITING   412

William Stafford, poet and teacher, talks about his partnership with the living qualities of words and syllables when he writes.

A Way of Writing   412

Shadows   416

Introduction to Some Poems   416

Vocation   417

B.C.   417

A Family Turn   418

The Stick in the Forest   418

Report from a Far Place   418

Interview   419

ANNIE DILLARD TALKS ABOUT WRITING   423

Annie Dillard, essayist and poet, talks about the importance for writers of constant reading, keeping a journal about that reading, and always writing to a specific audience.

from *Pilgrim at Tinker Creek*   423

Interview   424

INDEX   428

ACKNOWLEDGMENTS   430

Categories and Configurations

Configuration arrangement of parts
form or figure as determined by the arrangement of parts
arrangement
way in which parts of a whole are organized
pattern
to come together into
take the formation of
gestalt: any of the integrated structures or patterns that make up all experience and have specific properties which can neither be derived from the elements of the whole nor considered simply as the sum of these elements

You can divide all the people in the world into two groups:
Those who eat raw oysters and
Those who don't.

Doctor, lawyer, merchant, chief

Democrat, Republican, or Independent

Categories are a paradox.
Categories allow us to group things, to classify according to what is held in common. In other words, categories provide a means of showing how things are alike.

Categories also—and this is the paradox—allow us to recognize individuality, to identify each item as separate from all other items in a category. Categories provide a means of finding out how the things grouped inside them are different, and in fact, how some things in the categories might even be unique.

How can both these things be so? How do categories allow us to see how things are alike at the same time that they allow us to see how they are different?

To look closely at this paradox, let's think about categories of music—religious music, folk music, and rock music. Each of these types of music has a *particular configuration*—an identifiable "shape," an arrangement of parts—based on what the songs in each category share in common. Each category cuts its own "figure," as a skater cuts a figure on the ice.

Let's look first at these configurations—the "shapes"—of the three types of music. When we have identified what the pieces of music in each category have in common, we will be prepared to look at the second part of the paradox of categories—finding out how each piece of music in the category differs from the others.

First, let's identify the elements of music present in all three categories. We will call these the *points* with which we will build or design the *configuration* for each category. All three kinds of music have *sound*. All, when "written," appear as *notes*. Each category of music has a pervasive type of *rhythm*. Each has a typical *way* or *means of being performed*. Each has typical *subject matter* covered in its lyrics. There is a typical *place* or *environment* in which each type of music is usually heard. Each has a particular relationship to the *listeners* or *the audience*. Each has a typical *length*.

So the *points* for each of the three *configurations* of music are these:

Sound:
  Notes
  Rhythm   Points appearing in the *general*
  Way of being performed   configuration of all three cate-
Subject matter   gories of music
Place performed
Relationship to listener/audience
Length

Let's see now how these points arrange themselves in the configurations that are religious music, folk music, and rock music.

Religious Music

Rock of ages
cleft for me,
Let me hide
myself in thee. . .

The *sound* of religious music is usually serious and rather slow, with a steady simple *rhythm*. It is most often performed by a choir, a soloist, a small group, a chorale, or a congregation in unison. Of these, the choir and the congregation are the two most common. The performers usually use a piano or organ as accompaniment.

The *subject* of religious music is God, the spiritual journey, love, service, thanksgiving—and human beings' relationships to these.

The usual *place* of performance is a church, a temple, or some other place of worship.

A choir performs for the *listeners'* edification and enjoyment; in congregational singing the relationship is one of community—sharing and participating with each other.

The typical *length* of a piece of religious music is five to fifteen minutes; most hymns can be sung in five to ten.

That is religious music, in general.

Folk Music

My bonnie lies over the ocean
My bonnie lies over the sea
My bonnie lies over the ocean
Oh, bring back my bonnie to me

Now, let's look at how the *points* would arrange themselves in a configuration called folk music.

The *sound* of folk music is usually soft, gliding, drifting, mournful, poignant. The melody and the *rhythm* are simple. Folk music is usually performed with a guitar, banjo, dulcimer, or without accompaniment. It is most often sung by a single person (like Pete Seeger), a group of three or four (Peter, Paul, and Mary), a small chorale (Back Porch Majority), or everyone who is present.

The *subject* of folk music is the basics of life—birth, death, working, love, injustice, the celebration of daily chores. (Think of "Oh, Susanna" or "Scarborough Fair" or "If I Had a Hammer.")

Folk music is most often sung in the open air, around a campfire, in a car, around a kitchen table, and, in the last few decades, in concert halls.

The *audience/listener* is often also a participant; folk singing is "singing of the folk." It is community in a very personal way.

The typical *length* is short; folk songs sometimes grow long by virtue of repetition of the same tune with different verses or refrains. (But folk songs do not flow into different movements or sections the way, for instance, a symphony does.)

That is the way folk music goes.

Rock Music

I had skin like leather, and the diamond-hard look of a cobra
I was born blue and weathered but I burst just like a supernova
I could walk like Brando right into the sun
Then dance just like a Casanova
With my blackjack and jacket and hair slicked sweet
Silver star studs on my duds just like a Harley in heat
. . . It's so hard to be a saint in the city.

—Bruce Springsteen, "It's Hard to be a Saint in the City"

What about rock? What is the configuration that the points fall into for this category of music?

The *sound* is loud. The *rhythm* is quick, marked, bold, and strong. Rock music is performed by a band, a group of singers, and/or a lead singer.

The *subject* of rock is anything—often issues of society, freedom of the individual, assertions of independence, love, relationships, alienation, rebellion, loneliness, and life as experienced by the young.

The usual *place* of performance is a concert hall.

The *listener/audience* is "performed to" for its enjoyment. There is almost never any sing-along. The audience usually participates in rock music through movement rather than sound.

The typical *length* of a piece is three to six minutes, although length in concert will depend upon the dynamics between the band and the audience.

That, basically, is the configuration of rock music.

These overall configurations show us how songs in each category are alike. Once we identify the category of a song, however, the category recedes into the background—rather, the category becomes the background against which we look at the individual song.

But—and here is that paradox again—only when a song is placed firmly against the background that the category provides can it stand out in relief. The background provided by the category tells us what kinds of questions to ask, lets us know what is usually expected (allowing us to be surprised or to notice when that usual expectation is not fulfilled), actually sets us up to recognize originality, talent, skill, experimentation, accomplishment, and uniqueness *inside* the category. Without the general configuration of the category we would have no way to recognize or identify these individual achievements or actions.

It is only, for instance, after you know the general configurations of religious, folk, and rock music that you can notice variations and appreciate unique accomplishments made inside the categories. If you are aware of the categories, then you can speculate about how and why these variations come to exist, and you can recognize the individual genius that produced the variations.

If you paid attention only to the *general* configurations of religious music—if you kept the category in the foreground instead of letting it become the background against which you looked at individual pieces of religious music—you would not think about folk singing at mass, be aware of the new sound called "Christian rock," hear those rhythmic and jaunty spirituals sung in Pentecostal churches, or include those long, long pieces of religious music like Handel's *Messiah*.

Or, if you concentrated only on the *general* configuration of folk music, you would miss particular kinds of folk music like railroad songs or sea chanties or field workers' laments which put together their own configurations inside the larger one.

Likewise, if you hold tight only to the *general* configuration of rock, you will miss the particular kind of rock music sung by Neil Diamond when he recorded his Greek Theatre Album in San Francisco; the quietness, even softness, of some of the great songs of the Beatles; the unique style of a group like Blondie or a performer like Elton John.

With the category as background you can put your emphasis on a question like this: What was the *action* that resulted from the "mix" of this particular music maker with the time in which she or he lived, the demands of the music world, and all the other elements affecting the music as it was being written?

It is knowing these general configurations, however, that lets you recognize and appreciate the individual approaches, styles, the changes, the experiments, and the accomplishments *inside* the categories.

CONFIGURATIONS IN WRITING

The selections in this book have been grouped—like the music we just discussed—into three categories. These categories, like all categories, illustrate that paradox described earlier: they allow us to identify how pieces of writing are alike, yet they also are the sole means by which we can see how things are different.

The three categories are *writing to tell, writing to change,* and *writing to express.* Just as we did with music, let's identify first the elements common to all three categories. These elements will be the *points* that are used to make up the design, the "shape," of each configuration.

Points

A piece of writing always has a main *emphasis*: most of the attention is given either to the content of the writing, to the reader's response to the writing, or to the writer's involvement with the writing.

Writers always have some *motive* for writing, something that spurred them on to do the piece.

There is always a *particular situation*, a *set of circumstances*, in and under which the writing is done: a time available to get the writing done, an appropriate or a prescribed length, a particular place in which the writing will appear.

Every piece of writing has some kind of *form*.

Every piece of writing has an *audience* and reveals the *writer's relationship* to that *audience*.

Finally, every piece of writing results from a specific *intention* of the writer.

So, the points for each of the three configurations of writing are these:

Emphasis
Motivation for writing
Circumstance and Situation
   Time
   Length
   Place of presentation
Form
Audience
Writer's Relationship to Reader
Writer's Intention

Points in the General Configurations of all Three Categories of Writing.

Let's look now at how these points arrange themselves to make the configurations of **writing to tell, writing to change,** and **writing to express.**

WRITING TO TELL

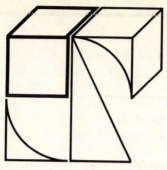

The surface is fine and powdery, it adheres in fine layers, like powdered charcoal, to the soles and sides of my foot. I can see the footprints of my boots and the treads in the fine, sandy particles. . . . It's a very soft surface. . . . It has a stark beauty all its own. It's like much of the high desert of the United States. It's different, but it's very pretty out here.

> —Neil Armstrong, on first walking on the moon

Writing to tell has as its emphasis the content of the writing itself. **Writing to tell** reports, informs, conveys facts or details, announces, instructs, makes known, makes available. The *content* of the writing, not the personality or views of the writer, nor the form that the writing takes, nor the responses of the readers, gets the *emphasis* in **writing to tell**.

The *motivation* for doing this type of writing is varied: to educate the reader, to share one's expertise, to relate a breakthrough or new development in one's field, to meet a demand of a job or an employer, to make money, to tell facts about something. The writer may be interested in airing a problem and providing a solution.

The *circumstance* and *situation* in which **writing to tell** is usually done is upon request, upon demand, with a *time* deadline, and with a prescribed *length*. **Writing to tell** is most often presented in work situations—as memos, reports, analyses, and letters; in magazine and newspaper articles; in text and other educational books; in manuals; and in essays for college courses. The information may have a "shelf life" that determines how soon it must be conveyed; for instance, it might become outdated or someone else might tell it first.

The *form* that **writing to tell** takes is usually predictable—an essay, a memo, article, report, or newspaper format, for example. The form does not contain a lot of surprises. And the form does not get attention for its own sake; it never gets in the way of the information conveyed.

The *audience* for **writing to tell** can usually be well identified by the writer: one's boss or peers on the job, the readers of a particular magazine or newspaper, people in charge of certain organizations, experts in certain fields, members of a particular group, workers who share an occupation, for example. The writer can do a fairly good job of pinpointing the people she or he wants to reach with the writing, can describe them, and can anticipate what they might expect.

The *relationship between the writer and the reader* is of "person informed" giving information to "persons not informed." The writer shares information and expertise with the reader. The writer assumes that he or she knows something that the reader does not know and is (or can be made) interested in finding out.

The writer's *intention* is to present to the audience some particular facts, information, or insight, and these are dictated by the subject and approach of the writing itself as well as the writer's expressed and unexpressed interests.

This, then, in condensed form, is the configuration of **writing to tell.**

WRITING TO CHANGE

Ask not what your country can do for you, but what you can do for your country.

—John F. Kennedy

Writing to change has as its *emphasis* a combination: the content of the writing itself and the intention of the writer. In **writing to change** the writer sees the reader as a person to be moved from one stance to another; to be directed, balanced, or guided in what to think; to be persuaded or convinced. This *emphasis* is dynamic: if the writing is effective the reader will think differently, will believe strongly, or will act in a particular way. In other words, there will be a change in the reader.

A writer is most often *motivated* to write in this category by his or her own interests, commitments, and passions.

The *circumstance* and *situation* are usually immediate and pressing. **Writing to change** is often closely related to current events, cultural happenings, and movements and developments in society. The writer would like the change *now,* the realization *now,* the action *now.* The *length* is less prescribed than in **writing to tell**, because it depends more on the message being communicated and on the emotions and commitments of the writer. The *place of presentation* may be public—newspapers, magazines, books—or it may be private—letters, journals, personal papers (which may then be made public).

The *form* of **writing to change** is usually the article, the essay, the letter, the review, the critique, the tract, the manifesto, and the book. The form exists to serve the writer's intention and the message to be communicated. The form makes no demands on the readers.

The *audience* may be the general public, a particular group that has the same or even different interests, or persons committed to particular causes.

The *relationship of the writer to the reader* is defined by the ways in which the writer's vision, experience, work, insights, expertise, and awareness are different from (and often greater than) that of the reader.

And the writer's *intention* is to have the reader know, accept, act upon, talk from, believe, or make decisions on the basis of what the writer has conveyed.

WRITING TO EXPRESS

Whenever I find myself growing grim about the mouth; whenever it is a damp, drizzly November in my soul . . . then, I account it high time to get to sea as soon as I can.

—Herman Melville, *Moby Dick*

Writing to express has as its *emphasis* the writer. The writer is the center of the writing. Not the center of attention, but at the center of the writing. The reader always leaves **writing to express** knowing the writer first and foremost—through the facts, narratives, ideas that have been presented in the piece.

The *motivation* for **writing to express** lies in a writer's wish to state thoughts, share thoughts, reveal her- or himself, or give form to feelings, imagination, creativity, sensitivities, and experience. The *motivation,* therefore, is usually internal.

The *circumstance* and *situation* are not usually constrained by time. A writer takes whatever time he or she must—even if there is a deadline, it must "wait" for the expression emerging from inside the writer. The *length* is an integral, organic part of the expression the writing takes. The *place of presentation* is rarely a primary concern in **writing to express;** this writing will occur even if it never appears in public. But, paradoxically, in many cases the writing act is not complete for the writer until the writing has an audience, until it is shared with other human beings.

The *form* of **writing to express** is totally unpredictable. Since this writing is the expression of the person writing it, its forms are as personal as that individual—sometimes unique. Familiar forms are the essay, editorial, article, poem, play, meditation, prayer, note, journal, travel account, personal document, and diary.

The *audience* is first the writer herself or himself and then the community with whom the writer wishes to share.

The *relationship of the writer to the reader* is one of risk-taker, because in **writing to express** a person reveals how she or he sees—or is—in the world. But the relationship is also one of community; the readers are privy to the working of another human mind, and see, for the moment, with another person's eyes.

The writer's *intention* is to give external form to something from inside.

Configurations as Background

These configurations are the background against which we will look at each selection in this book. The categories will provide us the content by which we can recognize—and appreciate—the approaches, skills, accomplishments, intentions, experiments, even the genius on some occasions, of the individual writers. We will look at individual selections to see how all the *points* work that make up the configuration of a particular piece of writing. We will look for variety inside sameness, for explanations for particular, specific configurations made from the larger, general ones.

A piece of writing is not a fossil. It is not an artifact.

A piece of writing is an *act* caught for reading in its particular configuration—an act resulting from one live person intending to communicate, often against great odds, to other live people across space and time.

No mean accomplishment. And well worth our commitment to study—and to learn to do ourselves.

PART 1

Writing to Tell

THE CATEGORY AND ITS CONFIGURATION

To Tell	to report, announce
	to reveal, disclose
	to make known
	to distinguish
	to let know
	to inform
	to acquaint
	to give an account or description of
	to produce a result
	to be effective
	to convey the facts or details of some circumstance or occurrence
Tellable	that which can be told
	worth being told
Telling	having an effect, forceful
	striking

You read a brief description of **writing to tell** in the opening introduction, but let's look now at this category in more detail.

How can you recognize **writing that tells?** What is the pattern of the *points* in this configuration of writing?

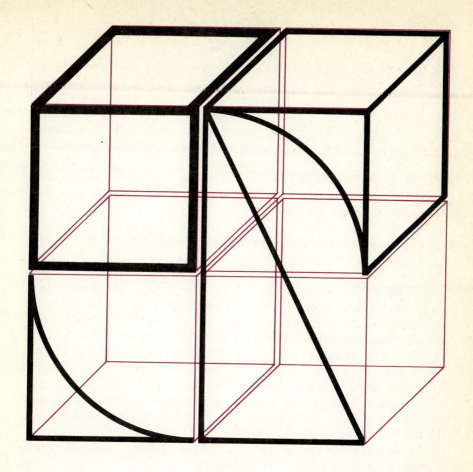

Points

The *emphasis* in **writing to tell** is the information itself. You read to learn something, to find out, to be educated, to know the facts. This means that the writer himself or herself will not be the center of attention. You don't read **writing that tells** for the personality of the writer, to explore the life of the writer, to share the vision of the writer—in fact, you hardly *see* the writer at all.

Now, it is true that if the writing is effective, the writer is present—has marshalled the facts, selected the information, arranged the parts, shuffled, sifted, organized, focused—and that means that in no way can the writer's sensibilities not be present.

But the writer's *intention* in **writing to tell** is that the *content* of the writing be the focus. So the writer doesn't draw attention to herself or himself. The writer, instead, gets down to the matter at hand—what there is to tell. (A writer may begin the piece with a personal experience, but it will always be for getting the reader into the writing.

The *forms* of **writing to tell** are more predictable than they are for other kinds of writing. The purpose of this category of writing is to get the work of the world done or to give accurate information or to tell people something they probably don't know. **Writing to tell** is useful, clear, and to the point. Therefore, the writing has no reason to be unusual in its format. The writer does not usually experiment with shape or arrangement or presentation. Most **writing to tell** appears in the traditional formats such as the article, the memo, the report, and the essay. The writing is fairly predictable in its movement—logical, orderly, straightforward. This, too, serves the purpose of the writing. If a writer means to give information to a reader, the writer wants nothing to interfere with that.

The writer of a selection **to tell** can probably count on the reader's interest because the writing is of immediate importance to the reader. For instance, readers may actually need to know a certain thing—on the job, perhaps—or may clearly find the information useful. Readers may also realize the information is something they will benefit from knowing. So there is often a motivation to read that is more pressing than that for some other kinds of writing, some motivation outside the readers themselves that will also work to the writer's benefit.

The tone of **writing to tell** is crisp, straightforward, sometimes quite conversational in spite of its factual and informative subject matter. The voice of the writer is appropriate to the situation, the subject, the purpose, and the intention. But what is interesting—and encouraging—is that you can hear the voice of the writer in **writing to tell** even though it is the content of the writing that is important. Even in giving straightforward information, the voice of one person actually communicating with other people can be heard.

The *circumstance* and *situation* in which **writing to tell** occurs usually include a time deadline, a length dictated by something other than the writer's personal inclination, and a place of presentation that is known or at least anticipated in advance. Writers who use this configuration are not usually free to take as long as they like; the writing needs to be done for a particular meeting at work, for a magazine or newspaper that goes to the printer at a certain time, or for people who need or want to know *now*. The length is usually a function of the form of writing: memo, article (usually determined by restrictions of newspaper or magazine), report. It is often short. **Writing to tell** is written for outside presentation, not just for the writer's satisfactions.

A person might think that **writing to tell** will be boring, or at best dependable and drab—like the workhorse pulling the plow instead of the thoroughbred winning the race. After all, reports? Facts? Information? Who reads all these unless they have to—or who gets excited about writing it?

But this section of the book will prove that reaction hasty, because you are going to find that information can be interesting, facts can be fascinating, and even standard formats and essay discussions can be lively and pleasurable to read, all the while that they are educational, instructive, and informative. The writers of these selections have made their own individual configurations inside the general configurations of **writing to tell.** It is the presence of a real person writing for other real people that informs all the selections in this section. It is fascinating to see how—in each selection—the "mix" of the person writing, the place of publication, the person written to, and the content result in a form and a voice particular to that writing.

In summary, then, here are the configuration points of **writing to tell:**

Emphasis	the content of the writing itself
Motivation for Writing	to meet some demand or requirement of work
	to make money
	to share expertise
	to share the writer's fascination with the facts
	to relate new developments or breakthroughs
	to educate
	to instruct
	to tell about something of interest to the writer
Circumstance and Situation	time deadlines present
	length inherent in the form
	place of presentation known or anticipated
	place of presentation public
Form	essay
	article
	memo
	report
	manual
Audience	people who will benefit from knowing
	people who want to know
	people who need to know
	people of a particular occupation/interest
Writer's Relationship to Reader	knower to not-knower
	expert to not-expert
	teacher to student
	experienced to not-experienced
	investigator/researcher to not-informed
Writer's Intention	to have the reader know specifically *this*

In this part of the text you will find three kinds of writing to tell:

Essays that tell you *how to do something.*
Essays that tell you about a *problem, solution, or both.*
Essays that tell you *information.*

The How-To Essay

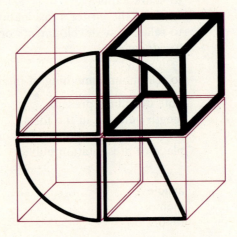

A how-to essay tells readers how to do a certain thing. A good how-to essay has these characteristics:

The content of the essay is directly related to the audience. Knowing who the readers will be, a writer makes decisions about just what kind of information to include and how much to include. Judging from how much the readers already know and how likely they are to be interested already, a writer can determine what kind of instructions or directions are needed and what details should be included.

The process or activity being described in the essay is divided into clear, logical steps. The writer is careful to break the process or activity down so that the readers can follow it easily, seeing exactly how one step leads to the next. The writer works to be certain there are no gaps in the directions, no faulty assumptions about what the readers will "automatically understand."

The essay is full of vivid, concrete details so that the reader can see exactly how to do the thing the writer is describing. The writer realizes that words have to do all the teaching in a how-to essay. These words must be as clear and sharp in detail as possible.

The information in the essay is presented in an interesting framework rather than just as cut-and-dried directions. The opening of a good how-to essay must get the reader's attention. It will have an interesting lead-in to or a frame around the information itself—something to move the reader into the subject. No writer expects anyone to be interested in a set of dull instructions.

The essay sounds as though a human being, not a mechanical robot, wrote it. A good how-to essay is more than a list of directions; it is a *piece of communication* from one *person* to other *people*. The writer takes into account the fact that readers like to hear a "voice" behind the words, like to think someone alive and enthusiastic wrote the essay.

On the following pages are examples of how-to essays written by professional writers and one by a freshman student. As you read these essays ask yourself these questions:

What has the writer done to adapt the *information* to this particular audience?

What does the writer do to get the reader interested? Place the information in a framework at the opening of the essay? Introduce the subject *before* the directions begin?

Is the process divided into clear, logical steps? How many? What are they?

What examples can you find of vivid details that let the reader see exactly how to do what the writer is describing?

What does the writer do to put a "voice" behind the words, to make it sound as though a *person* wrote the essay?

How does the place of presentation relate to the form of the writing? the tone? the approach the writer took?

What would you guess was the writer's motive for writing the essay?

What was the writer's intention?

Is there anything unusual about the form?

JOAN K. DAVIDSON

Joan K. Davidson wrote this entertaining essay on how to go to the beach for the New York Times *Leisure Section. Her explicit instructions tell how to make a trip to the beach healing, rejuvenating, and fun.*

A Beach Cure That Works
in Mysterious Ways and Lasts Forever

Morning Instructions

1 Early, while the rest of the world is still getting organized, hastily dispatch or ignore household chores; hop in car or on bicycle, and head for a saltwater bay. Leave before high noon, when the cars full of mothers, babies, nannies, umbrellas, blankets, floating rubber animals and suitcases of lunch begin rolling up.

2 For best results, choose a large bay with the following healthful properties: a long curving shoreline, white sand, cliffs, beach grass, seashells, sea gulls in conference, fishtraps on wood stakes and sailboats in the middle distance, and a pale island on the horizon.

What to bring

3 Beach towel, shirt, hat, and a totebag with sunstuff and a few other necessities:

4 (a) The Ideal Book. Must have paper covers and be small, to provide easy hefting in odd positions. Should be interesting to read, but not that interesting, so as not to foreclose essential napping. Leave the *New York Times*, especially Sunday's, at home—trying to turn newspaper pages in the wind causes hives. No yellow legal pads either; they curl at the corners and bring sand into the house. A small notebook and pen are all right, for beginning a journal at last. Leave behind "The History of Serbia."

5 (b) Food. It is wise to recognize that hunger symptoms are automatically induced by beaches of any sort. Possible treatments: The *oeuf-en-gelée* dream picnic (too much bother); mass-produced peanut butter and jelly sandwiches (boring but good!); a peach or orange from the

18

kitchen table, an honest tomato and/or a package of Pepperidge Farm Bordeaux cookies (recommended).

Who to Bring

(a) Someone one has been looking for a chance for a conversation with. 6 Spouse? Friend? Adolescent child? A still-deserted beach on a lazy morning is (with the possible exception of the long car ride) modern time's best setting for a Real Talk.

(b) Small or middle-range children, but only of the independent and 7 cheerful sort. Whiners and naggers-for-attention impede the cure. Contributions of good children: ecstasy of the water squeal; the high seriousness of channel building and other sand construction; excitement (slightly nervous) in the presence of tiny sea animals; shining hair, smooth skin, the salt-white outline on tanned arms and legs.

(c) No one. A few hours at the beach alone is luxury, a gift. Do a 8 long bay swim in clear water sweeter than the cold of a mountain lake and the chlorine of swimming pools; sweeter even than the warm blue of the Mediterranean and Caribbean. Think, walk, make a pass at collecting driftwood and pebbles, think some more, give up thinking, zzzz. . . .

Afternoon Instructions

Arrive at an ocean beach toward the end of the day, the most beautiful 9 moment, just as everybody else is packing up to leave. Breathe deeply, gaze at the sea in awe, contemplate the insignificance of human problems, the meaning of life, etc. Walk (jog if you must) along the water's edge, calling up the charging white horses of Virginia Woolf and feeling literary. Tick off the ancient beach markings: rock jetties, wind fences, a windmill, gray shingle roofs, Mr. Clean plastic bottles, logs, the distant mist, the curve of earth. Cry hosannah for one last beach still safe from hotels and condominiums and statement architects. Stumble across people it is pleasant to see, and note the curious fact that ocean beaches are improved by human noises—rumor and gossip, movies talk, politics talk—with or without something refreshing from a thermos. This is probably nature's answer to the cocktail party.

At sundown, assuming plenty of hands to divide up the work, take 10 supper over coals that have been dug into the sand—clams, seaweed-flavored corn, bluefish. . . . thus completing the perfect happiness prescription.

The beach cure works in mysterious ways and lasts forever. Neither 11 peeling skin, nor suntan sicklied o'er and yellowing hideously, nor even car keys and contact lenses lost in the sand can take it away.

FOR DISCUSSION

1. Without looking back at the essay, make a list of four specific details you remember. What made *those specific details* stick in your mind?

2. Go back and read the section on the Ideal Book. What is Davidson actually saying about reading at the beach?

3. What makes this beach cure work for either a male or female reader? What does the author do specifically to include both women and men in her audience?

4. Identify at least three aspects of the writing that could have been determined by the fact that the essay was written for the *New York Times* Leisure Section.

5. In the first part of the article, "Morning Instructions," the author divides the how-to instructions into three categories. What is the logic of the three steps? Are the steps in the order in which they would probably occur?

6. In the second part of the article, "Afternoon Instructions," Davidson does not divide the information into parts. Is this a mistake? Why? What is different about the two sections of the essay?

7. While this essay is *not* about the author's own trip to the beach, the voice and particularly the personality of a *person* are present in the writing. What characteristics of the person whose voice you hear in the essay can you list?

8. Are the instructions in this how-to essay actually practical? Did *you* learn anything about going to the beach when you read the essay?

NOEL PERRIN

In the following selection Noel Perrin, a professor at Dartmouth University, describes the value of owning a pickup truck in the country—and then tells how to buy one. This essay is taken from First Person Rural *(1978), his personal account of learning to live on a farm.*

Buying a Pickup Truck

1 One of the ways a newcomer to the country knows he's getting acclimated is when he begins to notice trucks. (I say "he" strictly through obedience to grammar. The phenomenon happens to women almost as much as to men. Under age twenty-five, I'd say just as much.)

Back in his other life, back when he was urban or suburban, it may 2
have been sports cars that caught the newcomer's eye. Or maybe a
showroom full of compacts, fresh and glittering from the factory. Now
he finds himself eyeing some neighbor's sturdy green pickup with a big
load of brush in the back and wondering how much one like it would
cost. Welcome to the club.

Pickups aren't necessary in the country, but they are certainly 3
handy. Any rural family that can afford two vehicles should probably
make one of them a truck. And it is quite possible to have a truck as a
family's sole transportation. It is also quite economical, since pickups
begin almost as cheap as the cheapest cars, and go up in price, size,
and quality at the same rate cars do—except that about halfway up the
car price range, you have reached the most expensive pickups there
are.

What's handiest about pickups is their versatility. First, obviously, 4
in load. Because of that big open space in back, you can carry almost
anything. Two beef cattle. Two full-length sofas that you're donating to
the rummage. All the apples in a small orchard. With the tailgate down,
a load of sixteen-foot boards. About forty bales of hay. A full cord of
firewood (provided it's dry). All your fence posts, your wire, and your
tools, when you're building a fence. It's possible to get a little drunk
with power, just thinking what a pickup can do.

Second, in range. Even without four-wheel drive, a pickup is a great 5
deal freer than most cars to leave roads and drive over fields. Picking
up hay bales, for example. Or to squeeze along homemade woods
roads. This freedom comes partly because pickups are designed to
have fairly high road clearance, even when loaded. Partly because they
can take tires that will walk you right through a wet spot or over a (not-
too-big) rock. Most pickup owners in rural New England keep a pair of
oversize snow tires mounted on the rear wheels all year round. And
partly because you can shift weight around in a truck to get maximum
traction in a way that would cause the average car to collapse on its fat
Detroit springs.

Third, a pickup is versatile in function. Besides its truck role, a 6
pickup can do anything a car can do, with one exception—about
which, more later. It can drive you to work, for example, using no
more gas than a car, and when you arrive, it will not only park in the
regular lot, it will do so in a smaller space than a Cadillac or an
Oldsmobile.

Nor are you going to complain on the way that it drives like a truck, 7
because it doesn't. It drives like a car. The ride is reasonably smooth,
the surreptitious U-turn reasonably easy. Drivers of big highway
trucks have ten gears to shift, and air brakes to worry about. Drivers of
pickups have a standard shift and regular car brakes. And if they hate
shifting, most pickups can be had with automatic transmission. For
that matter, most can be equipped with a stereo tape deck, so that you

barrel out to the woods playing Beethoven. I admit that a fully loaded pickup—say, a Chevrolet C-10 with a ton of rocks in the back, or a six-barrel gathering tank full of maple sap—doesn't corner quite so neatly as an MG, but it still drives essentially like a car.

8   The one exception is that a pickup is not much good for carrying a big load of people. At least, not in the winter or in wet weather. On a sunny summer day, its capacity is something else. Giving hayrides at our local fair, I once had fifteen children and two mothers back there in the hay, plus myself and a friend in the cab. I make that eighteen passengers.

9   Even if two couples are going out to dinner, a pickup is not handy. Four adults will fit not too uncomfortably in the cab of an American (though not a Japanese) pickup—but the law says three. The other husband may or may not want to crouch in back. Furthermore, it doesn't take many bags of groceries to produce a sense of claustrophobia in a pickup cab. A mother taking two children shopping on a rainy day in a pickup generally wishes she had a car.

10   There *is* a solution, to be sure. People who go out to dinner a lot, or mothers with four children, can get a crew-cab pickup. This is not what you'd call a glamour vehicle. It has two cabs, one behind the other, and looks something like a centipede dragging a large box. But it does seat six people. The only problem is that you now have a truck not only so ugly but so big that it is no longer versatile in the woods. I do not recommend it.

11   One last advantage of pickups should be mentioned. They never make hideous noises or refuse to start because you haven't fastened the seat belt. Like other trucks, they are exempt from that law. You can use the belts when you're roaring down the highway and skip them when you're going one mile an hour in the woods. Handy.

12   So much for pickups and their virtues. The time has now come to discuss the art of buying one. It *is* an art, incidentally, unlike car buying. A few wrong decisions on options can cut a farm pickup's usefulness by fifty percent.

13   The first decision, of course, is new or used. A really old pickup, small and square and no-nonsense, is about the most charming vehicle there is. Also one of the cheapest. You can get one for $200. Any children you know will adore the running boards and—if you have an old enough one—the windshield that pushes open for ventilation.

14   On the other hand, old pickups tend to have unreliable brakes and not notably reliable anything else. The 1947 Dodge I once owned—from its nineteenth to its twenty-first years—couldn't be counted on to start at any temperature much below freezing. That meant a long period of parking on hills and losing my temper, each October and November, until I finally gave up and put it in the barn until spring. One year I waited a week too late and had it frozen in the barnyard, in the way of practically everything, for three and a half months.

Even much newer pickups have generally led hard lives. (Little old 15 ladies seldom own pickups.) Furthermore, it's difficult and expensive to have heavy-duty springs and other desirable country equipment installed in an existing truck. Probably only people with real mechanical ability should consider getting one.

But one last word. If you do get one, take a nice winter vacation and 16 get it in some place like South Carolina. South Carolina pickups have never experienced road salt. At least the body won't rust out on you in a few years.

Now let's turn to new pickups. They come, basically, in three sizes 17 and three styles. The sizes are called half-ton, three-quarter-ton, and one-ton. Not one of these names means what it says. Which is a good thing, because a bunch of trucks that could carry only 1,000 to 2,000 pounds wouldn't be worth much.

Let me define the three. A half-ton is the basic pickup: what you find 18 at a car dealer, what people mean when they speak of a pickup. At the moment it comes in two avatars. It is a small Japanese-made truck that can carry almost a ton of cargo. Or it is a somewhat larger American-made truck that, with proper springs and tires, can manage a ton and a half.

A three-quarter-ton looks much the same, but has a much larger, 19 truck-type rear axle. It costs more, gives a rougher ride, and carries loads of up to about three tons. People with campers put them on three-quarter-ton pickups—and then usually get about six miles to the gallon.

A one-ton has an even bigger rear axle. With dual rear wheels, it can 20 carry up to near five tons. Neither it nor a three-quarter is what most people need for use on a country place. Not unless they plan to get into the lumber-delivery business, or maybe have always wanted, since they were kids, to have their own personal dump truck. (No fooling. There are truck shops in every New England state that will put a dump body on a three-quarter or a one-ton. The cost runs around $1,200. I have sometimes played with the notion.) But for general country use a half-ton is right; and for the rest of this article I shall talk about half-tons only.

Of the three styles, one can be dismissed right off. This is the tarted- 21 up and chromed-up half-ton which attempts to pass itself off as a car. Chevrolet calls its El Camino; other makes have equally foolish names.

For families that are sincerely embarrassed at having to own a truck 22 and that really think it would be preferable to drive something that looks like a scooped-out car, spending the extra money for an El Camino may make sense. Especially in those flat and treeless parts of the country where taking your truck out to the back forty must be something like driving across a very large football field. But to get one as a working truck on a rocky, hilly, wooded New England farm would be an act of insanity.

23   The other two styles are narrow-bed and wide-bed. Just as the half-ton is the classic American pickup, the narrow-bed is the classic half-ton. The design has been stable for fifty years now. Behind the cab you have—in most makes—a wooden-floored metal box four feet wide and six or eight feet long. (You get to pick.) This sits inside the rear wheels. Because it doesn't rust, and because it gives surer footing to any livestock you happen to be transporting, the wooden floor is a considerable advantage.

24   Until a few years ago, the narrow-bed was the cheapest of all pickups: now it costs exactly the same as a wide-bed. It retains two other advantages. Since the rear wheels don't stick up into the bed, you can slide slidable cargo in and out with great ease. And because this is the classic model, the tailgate in most makes is still the traditional kind that you hook with a chain on each side. That matters. You are able either to put such a tailgate down level, as an extension of the bed, if you are carrying a load of long boards, or to let it drop all the way down for ease in loading. Now that I no longer have one, I miss it.

25   All the Japanese-made pickups and most of the current American ones are wide-bed. These have a cargo space five and a half feet wide (American) or four and a half feet (Japanese). Obviously you can carry a lot more cargo. On the other hand, the rear wheel housings stick in on each side, which is sometimes inconvenient. (I will say they are handy for children to sit on.) And on many wide-beds you get a fancy one-handed tailgate, like a station wagon's, which won't drop down unless you disconnect the hinges. It's not difficult, it's just tedious. And when you want to close the tailgate, you have to reconnect them.

26   Which style is better? Myself, I used to have a narrow-bed and now have a wide-bed. I think the advantages and disadvantages of the two models just about balance. So on my current truck, I made the choice on esthetic grounds. The narrow-bed lost. Properly designed, it is the truest of trucks, the very platonic essence of a truck. But in the last five years Ford, Dodge, Chevrolet, Jeep, and International Harvester (a GMC pickup is just a relabeled Chevrolet)—all have moved to such enormously wide cabs that a new narrow-bed looks hydrocephalic. Wide-bed is now the handsomer truck.

27   As to whether Toyota, Datsun, LUV, or an American make, the decision really rests on how much highway driving you're going to do. The Japanese trucks, with their four-cylinder engines, get far better gas mileage. According to *Consumer Reports,* they average about twenty mpg, while American half-tons average fifteen. My own experience suggests that Japanese pickups do a little better than twenty, and American pickups a little worse than fifteen. For a vehicle that I was going to commute to work in, and just use as a truck on the occasional weekend, I would probably choose to save gas (plus about $300 in purchase price) and get a Japanese.

But for a truck that was to be mainly or even considerably a working 28 farm vehicle, I still prefer the larger and more versatile American pickup. It's not just that you can carry more weight, it's that you can get a specially adapted country model. The Japanese trucks tend to be unadaptable, the same for an appliance dealer in New York City as for a family with sixty acres of woods in Colebrook, Connecticut.

The man delivering refrigerators in the Bronx doesn't need any 29 special traction. He never leaves the pavement. But the family in Colebrook does. And one of the most humiliating things that can happen is to get stuck in your own truck on your own place. Especially since you're so unlikely to be able to jack, or rock, or bull your way out.

The trick is not to get stuck. Which means that you may want the 30 four-wheel drive available as an option (a very expensive one) on all the American but none of the little Japanese trucks. Otherwise, you will certainly want limited-slip differential. This inexpensive ($75 to $100) option means a special rear axle designed so that when one rear wheel starts to spin, all the power goes to the other wheel. Normally when one wheel starts to spin, all the power goes to *it,* and that's why you get stuck. Limited-slip differential is said to have its dangers, especially in very fast highway driving, where you may fishtail in a skid, but it is highly desirable in a farm pickup. I would rate it, quite impressionistically, as making about a third of the difference between regular two-wheel drive and four-wheel drive. You can get it on American pickups, but not Japanese. It's only fair to add that I know farmers with Datsun pickups who say they have no trouble at all zipping up and down their rolling fields, even on dewy mornings, but I still commend limited-slip differential.

If you decide on a Japanese truck anyway, about all you have to do 31 is go get it. Maybe settle whether or not you want a radio. But if you opt for an American truck, you still have to pick your engine, with at least six more country options to consider.

The engine is easy. Get a six-cylinder. Almost all pickups—includ- 32 ing three-quarter and one-tons—can be had either six or eight cylinders. A six has all the power you will ever need, and wastes less gas. As to options, the first and most important is to specify heavy-duty springs in the rear, and heavy-duty shock absorbers front and rear. All this costs about forty dollars; its value in increased usefulness must be about fifty times that much.

Second, for any pickup that's going to leave roads, either a four- 33 speed shift or automatic transmission is a great asset. Why? Because going through a field with long grass (and hidden rocks), or up into the woods, you need to be able to creep along, almost literally feeling your way, and still not lose momentum. Low speed in a three-speed shift will not let you go slowly enough.

34   Here the Japanese trucks have an advantage, since all of them come
with a four-speed shift. It costs an extra $125 on an American pickup.
But even better than four-speed is an automatic transmission. You can
creep with astonishing slowness, and still have power. I have never
owned a car with automatic transmission and never plan to, but on my
sturdy green pickup I find it marvelous. It does, of course, use too
much gas, and my next truck will be four-speed manual.

35   Third, you ought to get a step-and-tow bumper. Unlike cars, trucks
are sold with no rear bumper at all. (How much rear bumper have you
ever seen on a tractor-trailer or on a gasoline truck?) But a step-and-
tow—which is a broad bumper covered with sheet steel—really is
handy for pulling, and as a rear step. The ones you get factory installed, for about $50, are not nearly as sturdy as they look, but are still
worth having. The ideal is to have one made by a local welder. Rodney
Palmer, the man who owns the garage in Thetford Center, is a superb
welder; and for $101.50 I have a rear bumper that will fend off anything
short of a Centurion tank, that is heavy enough to give me good
traction with no load in the truck, and that will last for a hundred years.
(Rodney designed it so that I can move it from pickup to pickup for the
rest of my life. Then I'll will it to my daughters.) Incidentally, if you
don't get a bumper like that, you should plan to keep a couple of large
flat rocks or about four cement blocks in the back each winter. Way
back. Otherwise you'll find yourself spinning to a halt halfway up icy
hills. Better anchor them too, so that if you have to slam the brakes on
hard they won't come hurtling through the back of the cab and kill you.

36   Fourth, for a family truck it is worth getting extra padding in the
seat. A pickup has a reasonably smooth ride, but not so smooth that
additional cushioning won't be pleasing to visiting grandparents, people with bad backs, and so on. If you're going to get stereo tapes, you
might even want to pad the whole cab, so as to reduce road noise.

37   Fifth, if you can talk the dealer into it, get him to remove the four
automobile tires the truck comes equipped with, and have him put on
four truck tires. They should be not merely heavier ply, but if possible
an inch larger in diameter. And as I said earlier, the rear ones should
probably be snow tires, even if you get the truck in May. (Come
winter, put snow tires on the front, too. They won't improve traction
unless you have four-wheel drive, but they will help astonishingly in
preventing sideslipping.)

38   If you can't talk the dealer into it, you're no horsetrader. In that
case, resign yourself to your helpless condition, and pay extra for big
tires. Or go to another dealer. Or hurry home and read Faulkner's *The
Hamlet*. Then you will learn—from a master—how to trade.

39   Sixth, get the truck undercoated. Presumably any New Englander
knows about undercoating anyway—but it's even more important on
pickups than cars, since people usually keep pickups longer. The

process called Ziebarting is probably the best and certainly the most expensive. If you can stand having your truck smell like fish oil for a month or so, I recommend it. If not, a grease undercoating is said to be adequate. But the full mysteries of Duracoat (acrylic resin), asphalt and all the other undercoatings, I do not pretend to be a master of.

There are all sorts of other machismo things one can get with a 40 pickup. You can have a snowplow mounted—in which case be sure to get four-wheel drive. Plan also to have the front end realigned frequently, because plowing will spoil the wheel alignment with surprising speed. You can have an electric winch put on the front, and thus be sure of freeing yourself ninety-nine percent of the time when you get stuck. (Though a two-ton manual winch of the kind called a come-along will do nearly as well. You can get one for about forty-five dollars, and keep it under the seat.) You can have a power take-off on most larger pickups, and run your own sawmill. You can merely buy a logging chain, keep that under the seat, too, and then when you find eight-foot poplars growing in the corners of your best field, you hook the chain on your step-and-tow bumper and pull them out by the roots. They don't grow back next year *that* way.

But just a basic pickup is machismo (or feminismo) enough. In fact, I 41 can think of just one problem. Someday when you're going past the post office with a big load of brush, you'll glance up and see a whole row of summer people staring at you. With naked envy in their eyes.

FOR DISCUSSION

1. How is this essay an education about pickup trucks as well as information on how to buy one?

2. Identify points in the essay where the voice of the writer is heard.

3. Since the essay was written for a book, what kind of leeway for writing the essay did Mr. Perrin have that he might not have had if the essay were going to be in, say, *Road and Track*.

4. What would make this essay interesting to someone who was not even anticipating buying a truck?

5. Identify the different parts of this essay. How does Perrin connect these parts?

6. Locate at least four concrete descriptions or vivid examples. What specifically do these add to the essay?

SUE LUCKSTED

In the following article Sue Lucksted, a freelance writer, gives step-by-step instructions for creating a makeshift oven for a boat—and describes how to use it to bake cookies and bread. The article originally appeared in Multihulls, *a monthly boating magazine.*

How to Bake on a Boat

1 Sailing over the horizon, away from the supermarket and the electric four-burner stove with an oven, is certainly stimulating for creative cooking. . . . By far, the most challenging aspect is baking without an oven. There have been several methods which I have used with varying degrees of success. Baking yeast bread has always been a favorite, so I started the "dutch oven experiment." Use a large heavy dutch oven; set three metal rings (canning jar lids) on the bottom of it, and place your baking dish on top of them. Place two flame tamers on the burner (these can be purchased, but I went to my local junk man and bought aluminum disks, 6–8″ in diameter and about ¼–½″ thick). These and the rings in the oven spread the heat and prevent burning; in addition the flame tamers can be arranged to control the heat. Be certain to preheat the empty oven least 10 minutes prior to cooking. Baking in the dutch oven takes about 15–20 minutes longer than the recipes call for, and you cannot regulate the temperature exactly. Also, watch that the contact between the dutch oven and the flame tamers is good and that the lid is tight, or you will waste a lot of heat and greatly lengthen the cooking time. Caution: don't try any fussy French breads, try basic ones. When I put the first yeast bread I tried in the oven, all was well until the galley became perfumed with a faint burnt incense.

Homemade aluminum "flame tamers."

Alas, I had filled the pan too full; the dough rose right up out of the pan, sticking to the top of the lid. So, watch your recipe and pan size. Later I successfully used 4 coffee cans to bake in; 2 cans equal 1 loaf pan. These are great for storage and slicing; just cool and cover.

The second method proved more heat efficient and quicker. Use a heavy 4-quart pressure cooker, grease the bottom and sides and coat heavily with cornmeal. It acts as an insulator and burns instead of the bread. Preheat and bake as before, using flame tamers. Do not use the pressure valve or the gasket on the cooker.

Dutch oven with 3 metal rings on the bottom of the inside.

Pressure cooker, without pressure valve.

Poor Man's Yeast Bread

½ tsp. salt	1 tsp. honey
2 cup whole wheat flour	Optional:
½ cup dry milk	½ cup sprouts
1½–2 cup **warm** water	½ cup nuts/raisins
2 T. (2 pkg.) yeast	

3   The flour that we use is 100% whole wheat. We grind our own fresh flour in a simple hand mill, sometimes mixing it with store-ground.

4   Dissolve yeast and honey in ½ cup warm water; cover; let rise 5 minutes. Put dry ingredients in a bowl; stir in 1 cup warm water and yeast mixture. Add enough of the remaining water to make dough thick, sticky, and stirable. Put mixture directly into the pressure cooker that has been previously prepared. Let rise 45 minutes, until double in bulk. The best way to do this is to cover with a dark towel and set in the sun, out of the wind. Cook as stated; when 25 minutes have passed, loosen from sides of the cooker and turn over for the remaining 15 minutes; this helps both sides brown, but is optional.

5   Crunchy food is very appealing at sea and so the third type of oven is especially adapted for baking cookies. Use the same dutch oven and flame tamers which we will rig for the cookies. First, go back to your junk man and purchase 3 round flat pieces of aluminum (the weight of a pie pan) making certain they fit in the oven; ideally they should be graded, each smaller, though equal sizes will work. Next, bend 12 pieces of aluminum, ½ by 3'', drill and screw one to the center top of each circle and three on the bottom for legs. Now you are ready to stack your favorite recipe onto the greased tins.

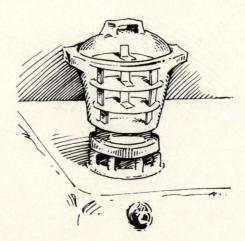

Dutch oven fitted with 3 tiered aluminum cookie "sheets."

Aggression Cookies

1 cup brown sugar   ½ tsp. soda
1 cup whole wheat flour   ½ tsp. baking powder
1 cup uncooked rolled oats   ½ tsp. salt

Mix thoroughly in a bowl; make a well in the center and add: ½ cup   6
Crisco (use very soft; don't use butter as it causes runny cookies), 1
egg and ½ tsp. vanilla. The easiest way is to dig in with your hands and
mix away all those aggressions.

Add: ¾ cup chocolate chips, ½ cup raisins, ½ cup nuts and bake 10   7
minutes.

I have found that you can use the baking times as specified in the   8
given cookie recipes. After the time has elapsed, lift out the bottom
layer; refill; place it on the top; repeat until the batch is done. The
bottom layer always finishes first.

Modern ovens certainly are marvelous devices, but despair not, "O   9
fair galley slave," for you can bake almost anything in those ovens and
be a true galley gourmet. With patience, time, experimentation, and
inventiveness your 'one burner' will reap bushels of praise from your
fit and happy crew.

FOR DISCUSSION

1. What makes this article interesting to someone who has never
   been on a boat?

2. How does the author establish her relationship with you, the
   reader? How would you describe that relationship?

3. What do you know about this writer from reading the essay?

4. What do the recipes add to the article? Why do you suppose the
   author included them? What do the drawings add? Are they
   necessary?

5. What are some possible motives the author might have had for
   writing this piece?

6. Find the places in the selection where the writer establishes a
   "voice." What does this voice add to the effect of the instructions?

JOHN VON RHEIN

This selection, written for the Chicago Tribune *by its music critic John Von Rhein, gives advice on how to enjoy a classical music concert. With its sympathetic and encouraging tone, this article is particularly aimed at those listeners who find classical music puzzling, intimidating, and hard to enjoy.*

Listen, and Listen Good:
How to Attend a Concert

1 The cards seem to be stacked against our enjoyment of great music. Sitting in a concert hall cheek to jowl with people we are convinced are having the time of their cultural lives, we are equally convinced we'll never understand the nuances of serious music.

2 And we may go home feeling that the concert *was* over our heads. Everything, that is, but "The Star-Spangled Banner," which we are proud to say we recognized almost immediately. It was all that noisy stuff that came afterward that gave us trouble.

3 To make matters worse, the learned program annotator intoned that all that noisy stuff consisted of great music. The man on the podium conducted it in a manner befitting great music. To judge by their jubilant applause, everyone else in the hall embraced it as great music. So how dare we doubt the general judgment?

4 Relax. This is a case of nothing more than a musical inferiority complex. It's a widespread malady, socially embarrassing but curable in most cases. The following handy hints, if diligently applied, should relieve those nagging doubts and make you a better listener.

5 You still might not be able to tell the difference between the "Hammerklavier" Sonata and the "Anvil Chorus," but now, while the orchestra is playing, you will be able to affect an expression of such knowing contentment that everyone seated in your vicinity will marvel at your obvious connoisseurship.

6 First of all, you must rid yourself of the "great music is too great for me" syndrome. So much of the orchestral music that forms the bulk of our listening diet comes salted with such a formidable reputation that it can only be swallowed with the greatest of awe. Many people who attend concerts regularly are convinced high art by its very nature must be forbidding, unapproachable except by those having special knowledge.

Who or what perpetuates such nonsense? The overly technical   7
jargon that oozes from most orchestra program books certainly does its
best to intimidate, puzzle or simply alienate the average listener. Others may be frightened off by lingering memories of a childhood spent
trudging wearily through finger exercises on the violin or piano.

Before you can understand serious music, you must learn how to   8
make the initial approach—directly and simply, without fear or reverence. And, yes, without special preparation. The only way to learn
how to listen is by listening.

Unfortunately, true listening—an active rather than passive pur-   9
suit—is impossible if you regard music as aural bathwater, something
warm and lulling in which you can float yourself away from reality.
"What most people relish is hardly music," wrote George Santayana.
"It is rather a drowsy reverie interrupted by nervous thrills." Wandering attention is the great enemy of experiencing music to its fullest.

Come on, now, confess. You *are* a habitual wanderer, aren't you?   10
The climaxes, the loud and fast passages—these things send nervous
thrills up and down your vertebrae. But let the music turn soft and
slow, and you start to float. You hear but you no longer listen. Before
you know it, you have forgotten all about the music and the performance.

There is nothing inherently wrong, of course, with listening for the   11
sheer pleasure of the musical sound itself. The danger, as noted above,
comes when you regard music *only* as a sensuous experience, something you don't have to think about or bring any conscious effort to;
then it becomes classical Muzak. Shoving symphonic music into the
background may be all right when you are at home washing dishes to
the Pachelbel Canon, but it insults those ninety hardworking musicians
up there on stage—not to mention the composer.

Concentration is not really all that difficult to achieve. It comes with   12
experience and repeated hearing. But if you're going to really flex your
listening muscles, you must learn how to listen on more than one plane.
The composer Aaron Copland has identified two of these: the expressive plane and the purely musical plane.

First, a caveat about the expressive plane. For the novice the danger   13
lies in trying to read extramusical meaning into each and every opus.
Most of us, when we first start out going to concerts of classical music,
search for specific word pictures on which to hang our reactions to
hearing a given work. When listening to the Fifth Symphony, for
example, we like to fall back on the image of Fate knocking on Beethoven's door. Why? Because Beethoven himself suggested the metaphor.
But also because it seems to give the music a tangible reality that is far
more "real" to us than a purely musical analysis. In other words, we
are only too anxious to hang onto any explanation that seems to bring
us closer to the music's meaning.

14   Music expresses, at different moments, joy or sadness, triumph or tragedy, serenity or unrest. It may express each of these moods, and any number of others, in an infinite variety of shadings. Or, depending on your stance, it may express nothing but the notes themselves. Arnold Bennett once observed: "What makes music the greatest of all the arts is that it can express emotion without ideas. Literature can appeal to the soul only through the mind. Music goes direct."

15   Useful as it may sometimes be for the beginning listener to assign expressive associations to the scores you hear, you can greatly profit from approaching them purely and simply *as music*. Listen for the melody, which is perhaps the simplest element to follow. Try to follow its journey through the musical structure. It is the development of melodies as themes, whether in a symphony, concerto, overture or tone poem, that forms the basis of most symphonic works the average listener encounters. Think of a melodic theme as a river: Following its path may prevent you from losing your bearings.

16   Once a theme has stuck in your ears, its musical adventures become more interesting, as it is supported by different harmonies, chased into various keys and through various expressive modes, broken into pieces and put back together, tossed back and forth between various instruments and instrumental choirs.

17   As you proceed to search through symphonic music for more than melody, you will become aware of beauties of structure, of contrasts of tone color and musical texture, of dynamic and rhythmic influences, of the logic and cohesiveness of a score. The greater the music, the more pronounced those qualities.

18   You will soon begin to discern differences of style by the shape of a composer's melodies. A composer's grammar can be as individual as an author's prose. Just as we speak of a Dickensian figure or a Dostoevsky character, so can we identify a typical Verdi melody or Beethoven theme. It is part of each composer's musical fingerprints. Recognizing them gives you the satisfying feeling of "knowing" Verdi or Beethoven or Brahms, even if you may never plunge any deeper into their works.

19   To find out for yourself—rather than being told by a teacher or program annotator—how all these things work simultaneously to produce a work of art is one of the more delicious discoveries available to the neophyte music lover.

20   To explain symphonic form in any detail here would require twice as much time as it takes to listen to the entire "Jupiter" Symphony of Mozart. Any music appreciation text will give you the basic information. Suffice it to say that the classic symphony has four contrasting movements, each with a different mood, pace. The form of each movement varies—sonata form, three part song form, minuet-and-trio, scherzo, theme and variations, etc.—according to the work's overall structural and expressive scheme. There is, however, a certain themat-

ic unity that links one movement to the next. Often, particularly in much nineteenth-century Romantic music, the unity also may derive from key, tone color, style or programmatic content.

Do not expect every symphony you hear to conform to such a baby- 21 simple schemata, however. Part of the excitement of experiencing the symphonic masterworks of the last 200 years lies in discovering how composers departed from the prescribed forms and content of the Viennese classical composers. If Mahler could write a symphony in six movements, Stravinsky a symphony in three parts, and Sibelius a symphony in a single movement, anything goes.

The pleasure you take from listening to a symphony performance 22 will derive from many things. It will depend first of all on your ability to grasp and enjoy the melodic materials and the musical and sonorous quality with which they are combined. Out of this should grow naturally an understanding of musical design. This, of course, will not be the understanding of a professional musician. It need not be as broad or deep as that. Intricacies of structure and harmonic nuance can be sensed, you don't have to be armed with all sorts of technical knowledge to feel these things operating in the music. The powerful effect of the finale to Beethoven's Symphony No. 5 is unmistakable even if you do not know that, for the reappearance of the theme, Beethoven adds a bassoon under the strings.

Virgil Thomson, the composer and critic, once described the ideal 23 listener as "a person who applauds vigorously." By that witticism he no doubt meant to imply that only a listener who really involves himself is of importance to music or the matters of music. Are you aware of the interpreter's part in the performance you are hearing? Music, after all, does not live in isolation. It must be created anew every time.

Hearing a lot of symphonic music over and over again by different 24 conductors and orchestras will give you, among other things, a most useful frame of reference. You will eventually adopt for yourself a more or less ideal conception of the style that applies to a given composer. You will then be able to sense to what degree the conductor and orchestra are reproducing that style within the bounds of their musical personalities. This is no more or no less than what a music critic is paid to do professionally. You, however, will have the chance to practice the art in a less conspicuous fashion.

By now you must be pretty tired of being lectured on your responsi- 25 bility as an informed and diligent listener. But it is true, as Copland pointed out, that "music can only be really alive when there are listeners who are really alive." That means listeners with taste and sensitivity, listeners who are willing to listen to music of all schools and periods with an open mind. The combined efforts of the composer and the performer have meaning only insofar as they find an intelligent audience.

FOR DISCUSSION

1. What do such words and phrases as "our listening diet comes salted with . . . ," "who . . . perpetuates such nonsense," "come on, now," and "baby-simple," disclose about the relationship Von Rhein wants to establish with his audience?

2. The how-to instructions in this essay are not sharply delineated—for instance, they don't have numbers; they aren't prefaced by "first," "second," "third," etc. First make a list of all the instructions the writer gives for how to listen to a concert. Then make an educated guess why he did not make these stand out in outline form in the essay.

3. If you were going to a concert tonight, after having read this essay, how would you listen differently? What would you remember specifically from the essay?

4. Make a list of at least four things that make the essay appropriate for a newspaper reader. Then make a list of four things that probably would have been different if Von Rhein had been writing this for a serious music magazine.

5. Correct grammar would dictate that the title of this essay be "Listen, and Listen well," instead of "Listen, and Listen Good." Why do you suppose the headline writer used unconventional grammar?

6. This essay's tone is very conversational. Since the writer could have used any tone he wished, what is gained by his sounding as though he is talking to the reader? And what *specifically* does he do that establishes that tone? Find examples of the conversational tone.

7. Von Rhein's main job as music critic for the *Chicago Tribune* is to review musical programs, artists, recordings, and so on. What would you guess motivated him to write this article?

RUTH RUDNER

The following selection is taken from Ruth Rudner's Forgotten Pleasures *(1978), a guide to outdoor activities and adventures. Here she gives instructions on how to "catch a wave"—without the aid of a surfboard.*

Body Surfing

There is hardly a pleasure more elemental than body surfing. For a willingness to be carried by the sea you get your own personal chance to emerge from it. It seems downright primordial . . . the beginning of life. 1

Body surfing is simply making a surfboard out of your body to ride the crest of a wave as it breaks and rolls onto the sand. You must catch the wave at just the right moment for a real ride. If you are too early the wave breaks over you, or just behind you and then all you get is a shove and a dousing. If you are too late you are *in* the crest just after it releases itself and its power, and you get left behind while it rolls on to the shore without you. 2

The right moment is the whole thing. It is a moment most apt to happen in the Pacific where the waves are big, slow, powerful and even. They are easy to predict since they come in a regular series. But other seas will do, if the Pacific isn't immediately available. 3

Stand, or tread water, until you see the right wave far out, gathering momentum. Then position yourself—swim farther out or farther in if necessary—so that you are ready to plunge toward shore in the trough created in front of the cresting wave. Once you are in the trough, swim as hard as you can. Ideally, you will be sucked down into the trough. Suddenly the cresting water above you lifts you, holds you, shoots you forward. At this moment, arch, point your body with your arms like tensed wings down at your sides, flat and bulletlike. You become a missile projected by the churning, breaking wave. If it works, if you are *in*, if you *catch* the wave, you become a part of it, the forward part of the cresting wave, like the prow of a boat made somehow of churning foam, and you can ride all the way home to the sand, and come home *into* the sand like a wedge, grinding into the shore like the wave itself. 4

The ultimate ride sends you all the way up onto the beach, stinging from the grinding into the sand, dazed perhaps—for the space of a wave or two. 5

The perfect catch, the ultimate ride, the pure moment of release, of flying—it's to feel at one with the wave, in it, of it, connected to its rhythm, yet *using* its power, its locomotion, to give you the ride. 6

A lot of time is spent waiting for the right wave, making false starts, getting half-rides, bad rides, so-so rides. These are the ones that leave you bobbing somewhere just off shore, or the ones in which the wave chops at another wave and you get battered in between. These, of course, are part of it, part of the fun, but not the experience you dream of, that you're willing to spend an hour shivering and treading water for. 7

Atlantic body surfing is less dependable and less exciting—unless it's a wild surf and you really like being tossed and battered and turned 8 upside down. Usually it's too mild for long, rushing, rolling rides, or too wild for anything but a series of dunkings.

9   Even so, wherever you find a wave, try it. All of it can be good practice for that day when you will get to the ultimate Pacific wave.

FOR DISCUSSION

1. The book this selection is taken from was written for outdoor enthusiasts. What bearing does that fact have on Rudner's tone? How is her tone different from that of, say, a first aid manual's instructions for rescuing a drowning swimmer?

2. Body surfing is an activity foreign to most people—even to many people who are fond of the outdoors. Identify at least three vivid analogies the author uses to convey what body surfing is like.

3. Rudner gives straightforward, step-by-step instructions on how to body surf. But she also seems to imply that more than the mere ability to ride a wave will be gained by learning the process. List all the benefits the author claims are to be gained from body surfing.

PAUL MERRIMAN

Paul Merriman, a student, wrote this essay for an assignment in his freshman English class. In writing the essay, Paul assumed the persona of the owner of a bait stand, who would use the essay as a free brochure. Paul's hypothetical audience consisted of customers buying bait before going fishing—especially those in pursuit of the wily and elusive speckled trout. The actual audience, of course, was the rest of his English class.

How to Catch Speckled Trout

1 The young boy pulled in his tenth speckled trout within the hour. A few yards away from him, you sit in your boat with just one fish to show for your two hours' work. Convinced that the fishing gods are frowning on

you, you rev up your motor and head for home. Actually, if you had just planned ahead and had used a few specific techniques, you could have had an ice chest full of specks just like that young boy did.

Planning ahead before you start fishing for speckled trout will set 2 you up to achieve success. This planning involves four areas, the weather, the fishing location, the time, and the bait. The first thing you should do is check to see that the weather conditions are right before starting out. If it is a windy day, stay home. Wind will cause the water to churn up, and specks do not stay in cloudy water. They always head for clearer water if the wind is up.

The second thing you must do in this preparation stage is go where 3 the fish are. This usually means taking a boat or a four-wheel drive vehicle. Speckled trout are found in large numbers almost always in back bays or other unpopulated areas. Sure, you could probably stand at a dock all day and catch, maybe, one, but to really get into the action, you must go where they live. That means taking the trouble to get there to those out-of-the-way fishing sites.

Planning ahead also means going fishing at the right time. The best 4 time to catch specks is from just about an hour before dawn to around nine o'clock. This is when the trout is feeding on the small baitfish which swim on the surface. If you wait much later than nine o'clock, you will be wasting your time. Much earlier than a hour before dawn and you can't see what you are doing.

Finally, prepare by checking local reports to see how supplies of 5 fresh shrimp are holding out. You must have live shrimp for bait. You could use lures, but nothing is as sure-fire as the frisky live bait. To put it in perspective, a live shrimp to a speck is like a filet mignon to a hungry football player. Live shrimp are not always available, so check before you head out.

This planning ahead must be followed up by some specific tech- 6 niques at the fishing site. Once out on the bay, you are now ready to rig a bait so that it is most enticing to the fish. Here is what I have found to be the best method. Cut about a four foot section of line off your reel and set it aside for a moment. Now tie a small bobber on the end of the line on your reel. Then take the four-foot section and tie it under the bobber. Under this, tie a small treble hook. This hook is then baited with the live shrimp.

The next step is to cast the rig. When you cast, the bobber will float 7 on top and the shrimp will swim for the bottom. This is when the fish will hit it. If the bobber just jumps and jiggles a little, then the fish is just lipping it. But when the bobber drops under water like a bullet shot out of a gun, that is when you should set your hook.

But be careful! Specks get off a hook very easily, so bring the fish in 8 gingerly. When the fish is close enough, use a landing net. There is no sense in losing a fine fish because the line broke or the hook fell out just as you were lifting the trout on board.

9   It is true that speckled trout fishing is not something everybody excels in doing. It is something, however, that everybody can learn to do. By planning ahead—checking the wind, going to where the fish are and at the right time, and using the right bait—and using the right techniques when on the spot—rigging the bait and casting properly and using skill in bringing the fish into the boat—anyone can be successful at catching the specks. Once the skill is acquired, it can lead to many fun days and many fine fish.

FOR DISCUSSION

1. Although Paul Merriman was in a freshman English class when he wrote this essay, he did not want to write for an anonymous audience or just for his teacher. So he "made up" a reason he was writing. Can you make a list of reasons why this essay assignment was not only more enjoyable but more valuable to Paul because he set up a "real life situation" for it? What did he do that he would not have done in a conventional "classroom essay"?

2. Make a list of the steps Paul gives for catching the fish. What can you say about the order in which these appear? What can you say about the order?

3. How prominent is the "speaker" in this essay? What can you say about the voice of the speaker?

4. What details do you remember from the essay? What makes them stand out for you?

5. Turn this essay into a list of instructions on how to catch speckled trout. What is the difference between this list and the essay? Can you describe how Paul has tailored the basic instructions in his essay to make them appealing to a particular audience—the customers of a bait stand?

WRITING YOUR OWN
The How-To Essay

Before you write your own how-to essay, let's review the individual configurations made by Joan Davidson for her essay, "A Beach Cure That Works in Mysterious Ways and Lasts Forever":

Motivation (an educated guess): to sell an article and/or to see her writing in print.

Circumstance/Situation: New York Times Leisure Section, which prints pieces that do not follow the usual newspaper-column format.

Audience: general reader of newspapers; people who go to the beach.

Writer's Relationship to Audience: friendly instructions to persons who probably need only a gentle nudge to remind them of how to do something they used to do or that they plan to do.

Emphasis: details, not general instructions.

Form: newspaper special-interest column.

Intention (an educated guess): to celebrate quietness, companionship, being good to oneself, and the simple truths about the good things in life.

You may find it helpful to spell out the configurations of some of the other essays in this chapter.

DESIGNING YOUR OWN CONFIGURATION

Since classroom writing often has the characteristic and opportunity of a laboratory experiment (take this subject and discuss it for that audience to learn what you can do to be the most effective . . .) you can approach writing your own how-to essay as though you were setting up an experiment. You can think like this:

"If I decide to write a how-to essay on how to water ski . . . and if I decide to write this for people who have never done the sport . . . and if I pretend that this essay has been commissioned by a boat magazine . . . and if the deadline is within 10 days . . . and if the length required by the magazine is no more than 500 words . . . and if my motive is that I need the money and that I love to write about all sports . . . and if the form is to be clear instructions with some commentary . . . and if I want my relationship to the reader to be instructor to eager student . . . and if my emphasis is going to be on the instructions themselves . . . and if my intention is that the readers *want* to water ski and feel confident about water skiing when they finish the article . . . then what will I do when I write?"

Here are some examples of *configurations* for **how-to** essays that students have designed:

Example 1

The local Community Crime Prevention Center needs money. After seeing that a citizens' club had published a cookbook, the Center decides to publish a book itself—a survival kit for people in the city to be sold to the public to raise money for the Center. The book will contain articles which will cover topics like "how to find an apartment," "how to be safe on the streets at night," "how to find good restaurants," and "how to find a place to park your car." Your motive, then, is to help raise money for the Center by contributing an essay on some aspect of how to live in the city.

The deadline is in two weeks, and the length is to be around 500 words. The audience is people like you who live in the city, and the relationship you want with the reader is of friend to friend, sharing information that helps you live easier and safer.

Your emphasis is on the information itself; the form is typical essay form, and your intention is to give very clear instructions that people can follow when they have finished the essay.

Example 2

You have gotten another job. But before you leave the place where you now work your employer requests that you write a report that will help someone else do your job. The boss says you have done a very good job in your work, so your expertise will be valuable to the people in the future who are hired to do the same kind of work.

There is a deadline, the day you are going to leave work. The form is determined by the training manual that is already in existence—you will need to write in that same style.

The emphasis, of course, is on the specific instructions for how to do your job.

Your intention is to assist the next person doing your work to carry on the innovations and improvements you have brought to the job. Your motive is to comply with your employer's wishes and to complete the job for yourself. Your relationship to your reader will be assistant to person being helped.

You can probably choose a topic to write about from your own life—school, work, home, for instance. Use your imagination. If you are having trouble finding a topic, here are a few suggestions:

1. You might write an essay on how to manage your time to do all the things you want to do in one day.
2. You might be interested in telling people how to buy a motorbike. What should they look for? How should they test it? And so on.
3. Write a piece on how to watch a movie to review for your college newspaper.
4. Write instructions on washing a new car for the owner's manual.
5. Give advice on how to attend a service at your church or synagogue.
6. Write an orientation bulletin for college freshmen.

And if you don't immediately think of a configuration you would like to use for your own how-to essay, let this chart suggest points you might choose.

Designing Your Own Configuration for a How-To Essay

MOTIVE	CIRCUMSTANCE/ SITUATION	AUDIENCE	RELATIONSHIP TO AUDIENCE
To sell an article	For x magazine or newspaper with x deadline and x length required	People who have never done this	Instructor/student
To educate people about something they don't know	For a class assignment due x with x words required	People who know about this but who would like more information	Friend/friend
To meet a classroom assignment	For x club's money-making-project book with x requirements	People who think they aren't interested in this	Expert/novice
To make a speech at a local club	For company that wants more business/good public opinion	People who like to read about unusual things	Confidence builder/insecure
To teach someone how to do something		People who could benefit from knowing this	Experienced/inexperienced
To share your own expertise			
To give away for publicity			

EMPHASIS	FORM	INTENTION
On the instructions themselves	Newspaper article	To interest the reader
On the subject itself	Magazine article	To inspire the reader to think about this
General instructions	Essay in a book	To be certain the reader can do this after reading about it
Very specific, detailed instructions	List	To take the mystique out of the subject
Using personal experience as background	Manual instructions	To win supporters
On making reader feel secure		To increase the number of people who do this
		To make a hard thing easier

RULES FOR A HOW-TO ESSAY

1. Be sure to choose a process that you know thoroughly.
2. Be certain that your essay will give value to the reader.
3. Know exactly what audience you are writing for, and tailor your discussion of the process to that particular group of people.
4. Anticipate anything the reader might not know; make every step clear and in order.
5. Use vivid details.
6. Put the information into an interesting framework.

RHETORICAL PATTERNS OFTEN APPEARING IN HOW-TO ESSAYS

Analysis by Division: How to Be Clear and Orderly.

1. Divide the process into distinct steps.
2. Discuss these steps in the *exact order* in which they occur when the process is done.
3. If there is a large number of steps in the process, group the steps into categories and then discuss them.
4. Define all terms and procedures that might be unfamiliar.
5. Do not omit *any* step in the procedure.

Details: How to Be Specific

1. Details are individual or minute parts of a whole. When included in a piece of writing, details give the reader a much clearer picture of what is being discussed.
2. Select details that are relevant to the point you are making. Don't try to include everything.
3. Among those relevant details, select only the most important ones to include.
4. Make the details as specific and concise as possible.

The Problem/Solution Essay

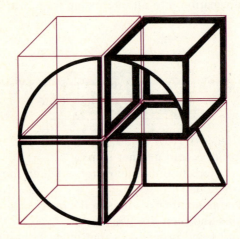

A good problem/solution essay will have these characteristics:

The writer will thoroughly discuss (a) the problem, (b) the solution, or (c) both. Problem/solution writing does not always cover both the problem and the solution with equal thoroughness. Sometimes a writer's purpose is to emphasize the problem so that people will think more about it. Perhaps the writer isn't even sure of the solution. Other times a writer's purpose will be to present the solution to a problem, and the problem itself will be mentioned only briefly. The writer will assume that the problem is evident to and agreed upon by the reader. At still other times the problem and the solution will be given equal space. The emphasis in problem/solution writing—on the problem, on the solution, or on both—depends on the purpose of the writer.

Examples and illustrations will be used in abundance. The writer cannot expect the reader to understand the problem or to agree with the solution unless they are really *discussed* in the essay. The best way to help the reader see the situation as the writer sees it is to use many examples and illustrations. A problem/solution essay, then, will be filled with phrases like, "For instance . . . ," "An example of what I mean is . . . ," "To illustrate my point. . . ."

The writer will choose examples and illustrations that will have meaning for the particular audience to whom she or he is writing. Just the presence of examples and illustrations won't get the problem and solution across. The examples must mean something to the people who will be reading the essay. They should, then, be about things, people, places familiar to the audience and preferably be examples that have a direct bearing on the readers' lives.

The writer will not assume that she or he has a captive audience, but will aim to engage the reader in the issue with the subject of the essay.

The essays that follow have been written by both professional writers and by students. As you go through the essays, ask yourself these questions:

Does this essay emphasize the problem, the solution, or both?
Does the writer make the problem/solution real *to me?* If so, how? If not, why?
Does the writer use enough examples and illustrations? What kind does she or he use?
Do I leave the essay convinced that the problem is real? The solution workable?
What made me feel this way when I finished the essay?
What are possible motives for the writing of the essay?
What were the circumstances and situations which provided certain constraints for the writers?
Do the essays vary in how the writer relates to the reader?
Are some essays for people who have not thought about the problem and some for people who already know quite a bit about how the problem might be solved?
Is there anything unusual about any of the forms the essays take?
Where do the writers put the emphasis?

MARGARET MEAD

Margaret Mead (1901–1978), the anthropologist, discusses solutions to the problem of illiteracy in this essay, which appeared in Redbook *magazine in 1976.* Redbook *is aimed at parents, the primary audience for this essay on teaching children to read and write.*

How We Can Help Children Learn to Write

1 Children *can* be taught to read and write, and to do both with some measure of ease and competence. In spite of all the evidence today to the contrary, that is one thing we must keep in mind. Now more than ever before, the ability to understand what others have written and to express oneself clearly are necessary adult skills. They are skills no one is born with and that everyone who is to become literate must learn.

2 Given a chance, children can learn to use words exactly and vividly to write about the world they are so busy discovering, as well as to express their thoughts and feelings. They can learn how to tell a story, how to describe accurately an event they have watched or taken part in, how to give directions to another person who wants to go somewhere or make something, how to organize an argument, and how to share with others their moods of pleased excitement, anger, fright and happiness. This much is within the reach not of just a few especially talented or privileged children but of every child—or it should be. Given a proper chance to learn how to write, children can even learn to enjoy the process of discovering how to communicate more and more meaningfully.

3 An English philosopher, R. G. Collingwood, once said that you cannot fully know what the poem you are writing is about until you have finished writing it. It is equally true, I think, that you cannot fully know your own thought until you have succeeded in expressing it clearly, either orally or by writing it down. Learning to use words is not only a way of reaching out to others; it is also a way of finding yourself.

4 But the evidence cannot be dodged. Our children are not becoming competently literate. Great numbers of elementary-school children fail to grasp the basic elements of reading and writing and each year fall further behind. The majority of adolescents are incapable of expressing themselves in good, clear English. And the average adult has little confidence in her own ability to read rapidly and with understanding.

to conceptualize what she wants to say and to say readily what she has in mind.

The facts are well known. The question is what we are to do.   5

First of all, I believe, we must scrap most of the current theories as 6 to why our children are not learning. They are simply poor excuses for our own failures. It is said, for example, that television is so attractive to children that it is keeping them from reading. But watching television—for reasonable periods of time and with some attention paid by parents to the quality of the programs—is at least as useful in learning to read as the same number of hours spent roller skating or playing ball. It is certainly true that many children would benefit by more active play out of doors—but this would not turn them into readers. Just because children learned to read in the past does not mean that they spent all their free time reading or keeping diaries or writing stories. For one child who was a delighted bookworm or a precocious author, there were thousands who read no further than their school lessons required. But it is also true that children today who do learn to read and write do not treat television as their *only* resource.

We must also realize the pernicious effect on almost everyone of our 7 continually rising anxiety about our children's education. Two generations ago the young adult who for some reason had not learned to read and write English could still get a job. Today this is not so; the illiterate person is a social cripple. And as we have raised our standards our ability to teach the necessary skills has diminished.

This is not the paradox it seems. For high standards can be used, not 8 only to increase care and to provide timely warnings about things that may be going wrong, but also to frighten people with the specter of failure. And anxiety of this kind is paralyzing both to parents, who fear for their children's future, and to teachers in school systems where no one suggests workable remedies. In the end, of course, this adult anxiety paralyzes the children most of all, and they cannot learn.

Concern is legitimate in some cases. Parents and teachers must be 9 alert to the needs of handicapped children and the special kinds of help they must have. But what I am speaking of here is the vague, unplaced worry that is extended to all children and that serves only to aggravate the difficulties along the way without providing remedies. In many schools, teachers, uncertain about the effectiveness of their methods, discourage any efforts made by parents—even though we know that the best way for a child to learn basic literacy is in the natural, everyday give-and-take with literate parents who are close to each child's interests and learning habits. Deprived of help, healthy children become handicapped, deprived of the ability to learn through no lack or failure of their own.

The children of illiterate parents need more help, and in the past we 10 used to give it to many of them. And elsewhere in the world today, in new countries and postrevolutionary countries, whole adult populations have become literate almost overnight—because educational planners and teachers and students alike believed in the importance of reading and writing and had no doubt that these skills could be put within everyone's reach.

11   In our own country, in fact, during World War II, we had a splendid literacy program in the armed forces that was designed, not by educators who had given up on half the children it was their responsibility to teach, but by highly sophisticated people who respected their students as adults interested in adult things, who happened not to have learned to read and write but were perfectly capable of doing so. And they learned. Somehow we have forgotten what we have done and have not observed what others are doing.

12   Our most immediate task, then, is to change the level of our expectations. Instead of indulging in worry that carries with it the expectation of failure—and our contempt for those who fail—we must be convinced that what other children have done and are doing, all our children can do. We must establish a nationwide expectation that *all* children can and will be taught to be literate. And we must not be deterred by educators' quarrels over the methods of teaching or by shibboleths about such things as the McGuffey Readers or the dangers of permissiveness. Children have learned to read by being beaten—and also by learning their letters from cookies coated with honey. As long as the society—and so the teachers and parents—expect children to be able to learn, they will learn.

13   It is when that expectation falters, when a society believes that any group of children is incapable of learning—whether they are physically handicapped or the children of mountain people, whether they come from rural or urban slums or are Black or foreign-speaking, whether they are barefooted, or girls, or twitchy and unused to sitting still— then such children will become "social dyslectics," children who suffer from an impairment in the ability to learn to read that is social in origin.

14   Expectations have to change equally in the minds of educated, anxious parents who have accepted uncritically their children's failure to learn for complex psychiatric reasons. As I began by saying, we must keep firmly in mind that children *can* learn to read and write.

15   Our second task is to recognize the fact that education is costly as we now define it in a very complex world. And it is costly as it applies not only to beginners but also to all those in search of higher education—indeed, to everyone who wants to learn. There are those who say we should not raise our level of expectations until we are ready to pay for what we will need. Certainly the two go together. But on the whole, Americans are willing to commit themselves only to working hard for and spending money (especially tax money) on activities they accept as necessary and good and likely to succeed.

And in making plans for education and budgets to implement those 16 plans, we must provide not only for children, adolescents and college students, but also for adults who want to advance and for the drop-outs—the neglected, the deprived and the damaged—who want to enter the mainstream of living. As Americans we have never believed in penalizing people for their past, and any plan we make and advocate broadly must take into account those who have suffered. Today we have a vast number of parents who have been marred by the experience of their schooling. If we do not realistically give them a chance, we shall endanger the chances of their children, and so the well-being of still another generation.

But what about time? What about *my* children—now? Isn't there 17 something we can begin to do now, immediately, for the children who are already in school and the still smaller ones who will come streaming into schools next spring and next fall? This is a legitimate demand. For every child, childhood happens only once and is always now.

There is, of course, a great deal we can do—parents and teachers 18 and everyone involved in the teaching side of the educational process. We can begin by drawing on what we know worked in the past and adapt it intelligently to the kind of children we hope, at best, to bring up for tomorrow's world.

And we are not without help in the matter. Here and there in the 19 country some children—a few—*are* learning to use their language very well. They are learning to write correctly and much more individually than the best-taught children did in the past. And there are teachers—not only very young teachers, and many more than we know about—who are struggling successfully with the problems of how to teach children the kind of literacy they will need and can take pride in as they are learning it. I have talked with some of these teachers and I have read some of the lively and interesting work that their pupils are producing.

One thing we have to realize is that the ability to read and to 20 comprehend the meaning of written material does not give a child proficiency in writing. It is true that reading and writing are linked tightly together, so that unless a child understands that someone has written the words she is asked to read, and learns to write those words herself, reading remains a kind of mumbo jumbo. The child needs to see the teacher (or the parent as teacher) write the words that the child then reads. And then the child herself must write what she has read.

And she needs to practice writing all the time in order to begin to do 21 it well—and better still as she goes along. We don't object to tennis players' or skaters' or jazz musicians' or ballet dancers' practicing incessantly, or to their knowing the technical names of the tools they use and how exactly to produce their formal, highly stylized actions. Why, then, should we let our old rebellions against admittedly outmoded disciplinary forms dominate us so that we call all practice and memorizing and technical study "dull drill"—and throw it out? Surely children have as much right to gain proficiency in a most basic skill as they do in learning a sport. And certainly they have as great a need to know how the language works and to have an accurate, specific way of talking about what they and others have tried to do in their writing.

22 In fact, children need to understand the whole wonderful literary process, from the first struggle with an idea, a fantasy or a muddled bunch of "facts" to printing and publication and reading and criticizing and weaving new patterns of ideas out of ones that have become familiar. And it can be done.

23 What is different now, I believe, and what differentiates the best of modern teaching and learning from the best of the past is that we recognize the fact that learning is a social process in which every participant plays a crucial role. The teacher respects the child, knows where the class is headed and how her students will proceed. But at the same time the teacher, like every child in the class, is a participant in the learning that is taking place for each child and for all the children together.

24 This is the true beginning, I believe, and it depends on a mutuality of trust and respect between teacher and pupil and among all the pupils. It depends on a belief shared within and outside the school that what the student learns is valuable to herself and her whole society. Learning to write takes time and much effort, but it can be done. And the joy of writing well is that this skill, learned early, stays with you and continues to grow through the whole of your life.

FOR DISCUSSION

1. Margaret Mead was an anthropologist. What qualifications, then, did she bring to an article about children and writing?

2. Who is Mead's audience? How can you tell?

3. What are the two tasks the author suggests will solve the problem?

4. Make a list of five examples or illustrations Mead uses to support her solution. What makes them valuable? What makes them effective?

5. What is the ratio of statement of the problem to statement of the solution in this essay?

6. How does Mead bring the pieces of her analysis together to conclude the essay?

7. The ability to read and to comprehend the meaning of written materials does not give children proficiency in writing. According to Mead, what does?

8. According to this essay, what differentiates the best of modern learning and teaching from the past?

ERIC PERLMAN

This essay is about the solution to a perennial problem for rock climbers: how to stay alive when one falls. Eric Perlman, writing for Science 81, *describes the equipment that has solved this critical problem for rock climbers for all time.*

Friends Between a Rock and a Hard Place

1931—A mountain climber grips the steep rock with waning strength. His hobnail boots scrape at the granite. He screams for help to his partner who tends the frayed hemp rope from around a rocky corner. The screams go unheard in the high wind. Desperately, the climber pulls out a soft iron piton, stuffs it into a crack, and pounds it with his alpine hammer. He attaches a quarter-pound iron snap-link, called a carabiner, into the eye of the piton and clips his rope into the carabiner.

Safe at last, he tells himself. Then he slips, dislodges a piton, snaps the rope, and tumbles to the ground 1,000 feet below. In 1931 climbing was not a very popular sport.

1981—A mountain climber steps delicately onto a rock edge the thickness of a dime. His high friction shoes do not slip. He whispers into his walkie-talkie wired climbing rope and, despite the howling wind, calmly informs his partner that the next section of rock looks severe and deserves some protective hardware. He grabs a spring-loaded camming device, called a Friend, and wedges it with one hand into a two-inch-wide crack, then clips his rope into it with a one-and-a-half-ounce chrome-molybdenum alloy carabiner.

His finger strength fails, and he falls. No problem. The Friend and carabiner can withstand more than 3,500 pounds of impact. The rope easily handles 4,000 pounds with a gentle, shock absorbent strength.

5   Advances in equipment have improved climbing capability and safety so greatly that despite nerve-wracking exposure to falling rocks and weather and the ever present danger of falling, climbing has become one of the fastest growing sports in America. In 1958, for example, 388 climbers reached the 14,410-foot summit of Mt. Rainier in Washington. Last year almost 4,000 climbers made it to the top.

6   The most radical advance in climbing hardware since the nylon rope is the Friend, developed by Ray Jardine, a master rock climber and former space flight mechanic in Colorado. Jardine was frustrated with the awkwardness, weight, and marginal safety of conventional climbing hardware, which consisted of iron pitons that were driven into cracks with a hammer (often a two-handed operation) and nuts, wedge-shaped chunks of metal that were slotted into cracks like nickels into a vending machine. "Finding the right nut to fit a crack can be time-consuming," Jardine says, "especially if you're hanging on for dear life."

7   "We were looking for material that produced a lot of friction between metal and rock but was also incompressible," Jardine says. He chose an aluminum alloy that held against rock ten times better than iron or steel.

8   With the help of a computer, Jardine worked out the best shape of the comma-shaped cams that would grip and hold with a constant force regardless of their orientation. Each Friend has four cams that are independently suspended so they can flare out to adjust to widely different cracks. Unlike the nuts, which can only be used on cracks that widen and then narrow, the Friends can hold in cracks that open out as much as thirty degrees. And Friends come out of a crack as easily as they go in—a "trigger" on the stem pulls in the cams to their narrowest setting releasing their grip.

9   The heart of a climber's safety system is the rope. It must be strong enough to hold a 180-pound climber for a fall of more than 50 feet, yet it must stretch and absorb the shock of impact. Thin steel cable is lighter, stronger, and more resistant to cutting than nylon, but it does not stretch at all. The poor climber whose fall was stopped by steel cable would probably snap his spine. A rubber rope on the other hand would be virtually shock free, but the stretch would be so great that a falling climber would probably slam into a ledge or other rock outcrop even while the rubber rope was saving him from the shock of the fall.

10   Climbing ropes were made first from the hemp plant, then natural silk, then twisted nylon. Modern ropes are made of Perlon, a synthetic material close to nylon that combines both strength and elasticity. The ropes are constructed in two parts—an exterior sheath, woven to resist cuts and abrasion, and an inner core made of thousands of braided filaments that run the length of the rope.

Edelrid of West Germany, the world's leading climbing rope manu- 11
facturer, weaves its rope cores with 50,400 threads, each with a diameter of 1/100,000 of an inch. There are more than 2,500 miles of Perlon
thread in a standard 165-foot climbing rope with a diameter of a little
less than half an inch. This microscopic distribution of impact is the
key to the climbing rope's lifesaving strength and resiliency.

The most exotic development in rope technology is the "talking 12
rope" with a built-in, battery-powered intercom. The communication
line is coiled through the interior of the rope and stretches out with the
impact of a fall. Talking ropes are especially useful in high winds,
inside rock chimneys, and next to thundering waterfalls.

Modern rock climbing shoes look and perform more like ballet 13
slippers than mountain boots. They are tight fitting for extra leverage
and control. The toes of the shoes are narrow and tapered for slotting
into inch-wide cracks. The sole is smooth and pliable and resists
slipping on climbing surfaces that may consist of nothing more than a
few hundredths of an inch of crystalline bumps on a slab of granite.

The composition of the sole is the key to modern rock climbing 14
technique. While most shoe manufacturers spend research money to
find ways to harden the rubber and increase sole longevity, climbing
shoemakers have refined the science of softening the rubber. By jug-
gling the recipe for compounding rubber, they've made it almost
sticky.

A few European rubber makers dominate the market and zealously 15
guard their high friction recipes. The profit margin is huge, and the
turnover is rapid—sticky-soled climbing shoes wear out with about a
month of daily use. An average pair retails for $80 to $100. Not that
there is much of an alternative. To climb the severe routes that were
unthinkable thirty years ago but are well-travelled now, even the best
climbers could not get off the ground without their high friction shoes.

FOR DISCUSSION

1. There's an organizational pattern called Borden's Formula that is
   often used by writers as a guide to the development of their
   essay. Borden's Formula goes like this:
   Step One: "Ho Hum!" This step aims to "build a fire."
   Step Two: "Why bring that up?" This step builds a bridge
                  between the reader's needs and the writer's thesis.
   Step Three: "For instance." Specific examples, etc., are cited
                  in this step.

Step Four: "So what?" This step appeals for the desired action.

How does this essay match Borden's Formula as a pattern for development. Is there any step *not* present in the essay?

2. This essay has some history, some technical information, some serious details. What keeps the writing from being boring? How did the writer accomplish this liveliness?

3. How did Ray Jardine solve a serious problem for rock climbers?

4. Perlman states the problem in an unusual format. Where is the problem located in the essay? What reasons can you imagine were behind the writer's decision to state the problem this way?

5. Examples always help a reader understand. Identify three different kinds of examples the writer uses in this essay that assist even a non-rock-climbing reader in knowing what the writer is talking about.

6. What makes the essay appropriate for the magazine in which it was published?

7. What is the voice of the writer in this selection?

RENÉ DUBOS

In this essay which appeared in The Sciences, *April 1982, René Dubos (1901–1982) states that botanists, besides satisfying their scientific curiosities, should search for solutions to urgent world problems. This essay provides a discussion of a solution to a problem at the same time that the content of the essay itself is* about *problems and solutions.*

Beyond the Garden Wall

1 Botanical gardens and arboreta once wielded enormous influence in the world. At the end of the eighteenth century, the Swiss physician and botanist Jean Gesner estimated that there were more than sixteen hundred botanical gardens and arboreta in Europe. A few of these were on estates of the rich, but most had been created for the cultivation of medicinal plants. Until our day, plants were practically the only sources of drugs, and, as a result, professors of medicine like Gesner

were also botanists who used university gardens under their supervision for the training of medical students.

Nor were medicines the only product of these gardens. Some botanists also made it a practice to cultivate, disseminate, and study exotic plants received from explorers around the world, and many of these plants later assumed enormous economic importance. The tulip, now considered the most typical flower of Holland and one of its chief exports, was introduced to the botanical garden of Leiden from the Near East, in the sixteenth century. And in the 1850s, cinchona seeds sent from the Amazon to the botanical garden of Java enabled Dutch colonists there to create plantations that became the world's chief source of cinchona bark, from which quinine is derived.   2

Natural rubber is one of the most spectacular examples of the influence that botanical gardens can exert on the fate of an industry and of a region. The tree *Hevea brasiliensis* grows naturally in several parts of the Amazonian valley, and the rubber obtained from it was shipped to industrial nations through the Brazilian port of Manaus. Although Manaus lies in the heart of the Amazonian rain forest, the rubber trade was so intense between 1890 and 1920 that this relatively small city became one of the richest and most highly developed in the world. It was the first Latin American city to have electric light. Majestic buildings and homes, churches and cathedrals, and a complex system of sewers and floating docks were built there nearly overnight. The year 1896 saw the dedication of a large, ornate opera house built of Italian marble and crowned with a dome of polychromatic tiles imported from Alsace. And on its opening night, the Italian tenor Enrico Caruso sang before a full house of fourteen hundred spectators.   3

In the meantime, English botanists learned to cultivate *H. brasiliensis* in greenhouses and began distributing seeds and seedlings to several Southeast Asian countries through the Kew Gardens of London (officially known as the Royal Botanic Gardens). Plantation rubber was so readily produced in Malaysia that large quantities of it could be exported as early as 1910. Shortly after, it completely displaced the natural rubber of Brazil, and Manaus became a ghost town.   4

Today, directors of botanical gardens and arboreta no longer engage in activities so economically urgent as the preparation of medicinal drugs, the propagation of tulips, and the transfer of cinchona and hevea trees from one tropical country to another were in their times. In our era, their contributions could never make or break the fates of cities or countries. These days, the gardens simply try to appeal to the general public by displaying plant species under the most attractive conditions at suitable times of year.   5

While these traditional contributions to science and to the public are important—and deserve appreciation—botanical gardens and arboreta could serve an even more essential purpose by involving themselves   6 more directly in solving certain contemporary problems, a task for which they have unique qualifications. Indeed, they could yet become as vital to the world as they were in the time of Gesner, or in the heyday of Manaus.

7   There are clear signs that several botanical gardens and arboreta have already begun to evolve in this way. At the Kew Gardens, for example, the emphasis has long been on the collection of wild plant species (Kew boasts the world's largest herbarium) and on taxonomy. But the new director of Kew, Arthur Bell, is a biochemist who has stated that one of his main concerns will be to use the garden's facilities for improving patterns of agriculture in developing countries. Again, at the New York Botanical Garden, the traditional herb garden is now being complemented by what has been called a "chemurgic" garden, the beds of which display economically important plants—those of industrial, medicinal, and cosmetic value, as well as those used for fuel, dyes, and flavorings. And in Washington, D.C., the Herb Society of America is helping to develop, at the U.S. National Arboretum, a national herb garden that will include not only herbs used in the home but also those used in agriculture and industry.

8   Ever since neolithic times, humans have cultivated plants with a few very practical purposes in mind—for production of food, lumber, textile fiber, drugs, and ornament. Plants that do not fit these categories generally have been regarded as weeds. (It is rather shocking to realize, for example, that just thirty plant species provide eighty percent of the world's food supplies, even though many thousands of other species possess desirable nutritional properties.) Botanists have searched for new plant varieties mainly out of scientific curiosity. This scientific policy must of course be continued, but botanical gardens might supplement it with a more utilitarian motive: the search for socially useful species. For such an approach to succeed, techniques must be developed to evaluate (or at least to detect) not only a plant's properties in its natural habitat, but also its potentialities under other conditions. The search for plants with desirable properties always involves two independent considerations: proper genetic endowment and the environmental conditions required for its phenotypic expression.

9   The second consideration can be almost as significant as the first. For example, most herb gardens in this country and in Western Europe consist of a few aromatic species, almost everywhere the same. But the aromatic characteristics of the plants of a particular species or variety differ markedly from garden to garden, even under the same climatic conditions. I know from simple "nose tests" of crushed leaves that plants grown in the herb garden of the New York Botanical Garden differ aromatically from those grown in Central Park, or in the Brooklyn Botanic Garden—all in New York City. On many occasions

in the 1920s and 1930s, I visited villages of southeastern France, near Grasse, the capital of the French perfume industry. Three of these villages specialized in the cultivation of jasmine because, according to specialists, jasmine plants grown there have qualities most desirable for the manufacture of perfumes. Similarly, while roses grow readily in many parts of the world, certain limited regions of Asia and eastern and southern Europe seem to be best suited for the production of attar of rose. It is also known that the yield of a particular medicinal drug by a given plant species is profoundly influenced by methods of cultivation, as well as by environmental conditions.

Clearly, if Earth's biomass is to be used either as fuel, or in the chemical industries, the criteria for selection of plant varieties should be very different from those that apply to the production of food, lumber, or fiber. For example, we should search out plants with the highest possible photosynthetic activity, as well as those capable of growing on soil or in waters not suitable for the production of food or for other valuable crops. Many plant species currently ignored should be investigated for their ability to produce hydrocarbons or other substances that could be put to use in the chemical and pharmaceutical industries.

There are many other fields of endeavor for the new botany, and one of the most urgent is the study of injured ecosystems. While much ecological damage is taking place all over the earth, it is also true that ecological recovery can often occur spontaneously when insults to the ecosystem are ended. After the First World War, the Verdun region of France was a wasteland; now its indigenous vegetation has returned, along with its birds, rabbits, deer, and even boars. Spontaneous ecological recovery can take place under seemingly unfavorable conditions provided the areas are protected from grazing animals. Little is known of these natural recovery processes, though such knowledge would greatly help in the formulation of ecologically sound policies of land use and reclamation.

In most cases, however, damaged ecosystems will require more direct human intervention for their successful recovery. This is already happening in Israel; but the reclamation of strip-mined areas in this country will certainly present problems of greater complexity and magnitude. As elsewhere, the tendency in such work is to use plant species already well known, even though obscure species might prove more suitable, at least during the early phases of reclamation.

Moreover, it is probably a mistake to assume, as many do, that the "best" environment is an untouched stretch of virgin land and that reclaiming a wasteland necessarily means returning it to its original state. Practically all existing ecosystems that humans find desirable were produced by profound transformations of nature or even by the creation of entirely artificial ecosystems. The eighteenth-century English naturalist William Marshall believed "Nature knows nothing of what we call landscape because this word refers to habitats manipulated by human beings for their own purpose. . . . No spot on this island [England] can be said to be in a state of Nature. There is not a tree, perhaps not a bush, now standing on the face of the country which owes its identical state to Nature alone. Wherever cultivation has set its foot, Nature has become extinct. . . . Those who wish for a Nature in a state of total neglect must take their residence in the woods of America."

14   The expression "total neglect" seems to imply that Nature can achieve perfection, or at least fully develop its potential, only as a result of human management. The truth is, however, that many aspects of human life conflict with natural ecosystems and indeed usually result in their destruction. All farming activities constitute a violent struggle against natural ecological conditions. Farmland had to be created out of wilderness, usually at great cost of energy—to cut down trees, drain wetlands, irrigate dry lands, and also to destroy wild forms of life and their habitats. Successful farming, like flower gardening, is usually incompatible with the kind of ecological equilibrium that would exist under completely natural conditions.

15   In the past, artificial ecosystems like farms, estates, and villages evolved over long periods of time, and this slow development enhanced their chances of success by allowing for the play of corrective forces—natural and human—and thus for the satisfactory orchestration of their different components. As human intervention becomes increasingly rapid and violent, the trial and error of the past must be replaced by scientific knowledge. Studies are needed to determine the amount of energy required for maintaining the ecological stability of artificial ecosystems; the comparative abilities of different types of vegetation to trap solar energy for synthesis of different organic substances and maintenance of soil humus; and the evolution of artificial ecosystems under different geological and climatic conditions—a problem of crucial importance for the utilization of tropical lands.

16   Urban ecosystems present their own special problems. For more than fifty years, I have watched from my windows on the Rockefeller University campus the lawns that we try to maintain, at immense costs of water, energy, and human labor—and usually without much success. Lawns were originated in Great Britain, where the climate is favorable for their development and where labor conditions were once compatible with their maintenance. (Horace Walpole remarked, in a letter upon his return from France, "They can never have as beautiful a landscape as ours till they have as rotten a climate." And half a century earlier the French Prince de Ligne had written of the English, "Their verdure they owe to their fogs.") English lawns are out of place, not only on the Rockefeller campus, or in Central Park, but in

most of the United States. There seems to be a national ambition to create, against all odds, lawns that resemble championship golf courses. Botanical gardens should collaborate with landscape architects in the development of new kinds of ground cover suited to the various climates in this country and to different kinds of human uses as well.

Much also remains to be learned concerning the effects of air and water pollution, as well as of pesticides, on the growth and lives of plants. It seems that fewer and fewer plant species are being used, either for shade, ornament, or the muffling of noise, both in urban and suburban centers. There is need for more knowledge of flowering plants, trees, grasses, and other kinds of ground cover that can thrive under the conditions—natural and social—that prevail in each particular region. Such knowledge might help to correct the monotony and drabness of plant life in cities—and thereby decrease somewhat the desire to escape from the city every weekend. 17

Surprising as it may sound, the time may soon come when certain kinds of foodstuffs will once more be widely grown in urban areas. It is probably true that citrus fruits, artichokes, pineapples, and other such crops with exacting climatic requirements can best be produced on a large scale only in special parts of the country. Food plants less perishable than these also can be produced most economically under special climatic and soil conditions: Why grow apples, tomatoes, and carrots in New York State if they can be obtained at low cost from Washington, California, or Texas? However, there are great ecological and social dangers inherent in such excessive concentration and specialization of food production. Complete dependence on food that must be hauled over long distances is probably not a wise policy. Rather, each urban area should strive once more toward partial self-sufficiency, especially in the case of perishable foodstuffs. The phenomenal increase in the price of vegetables and fruits, as well as the lamentable deterioration of their taste, may spur a renewal of food production in urban areas—if only to make fresh and tasty fruits and vegetables once more available to the city dweller. 18

There exist in many cities examples of successful gardening and farming, even in environments that appear extremely uninviting. Local children from Manhattan public schools, organized under the Dome Project, have turned a rubble-strewn lot on West Eighty-fourth Street into a very attractive vest-pocket vegetable garden. In San Francisco, unused land under a city freeway exchange has been transformed into a farm where urban children have the opportunity to raise animals and learn gardening. This project has been so successful that the city has purchased five adjoining acres to enlarge the farm. 19

I myself have done enough old-fashioned gardening to know the ordeals and frustrations of trying to produce significant amounts of 20 food on a small patch of soil, using only conventional methods. On the other hand, it appears that more convenient methods of cultivation can be developed scientifically for the production of many different kinds of valuable foodstuffs, at least on a small scale, under completely controlled conditions.

21   Clearly, botanical gardens and arboreta have missions that transcend their traditional scientific concerns. The availability of plant collections, and more precise knowledge of the properties of plants, will be increasingly needed in the management of environmental and social problems. Botanists, ecologists, and environmentalists may criticize these proposals for being almost completely human-centered but, while acknowledging the truth of this, I do not think it is a valid criticism. Even when we attempt to look at the external world objectively, we see it with human eyes, evaluating it and using it on the basis of human needs, values, and aspirations. As Ralph Waldo Emerson wrote long ago, we call a plant a weed only when we have not yet discovered a way to use it to our own ends.

FOR DISCUSSION

1. What evidence does René Dubos use to support the solution he offers in this essay?

2. What is the problem for which Dubos is offering a solution?

3. What are some of the specific areas that botanists need to put their energies and attention to, according to Dubos?

4. Even though this is a serious article about a serious situation, you can still hear the voice of the writer in it. Find specific places in the essay where personal experience or illustration is used. What value do these provide for the essay?

5. Even though this essay is longer than some in this book, and it appeared in a science magazine published by the New York Academy of Science, the essay is still readable. It is not beyond the grasp of a person who is not a botanist. What were some of the things you specifically learned from this essay? Was there anything you had difficulty understanding in the essay? Is there any evidence that the author was concerned about his readers understanding what he was writing? Discuss these questions in detail.

CAROLINE DREWES

Caroline Drewes, a reporter for the San Francisco Examiner, *uses this essay as a way to* question *her own perspective on the subject of honesty. She leaves it to the reader to decide his or her own answer to the question, is honesty still the best policy?*

Is Honesty Still the Best Policy?

Dishonesty is never an accident. Good men, like good women, never see temptation when they meet it.

—Old English proverb

On the other hand:

Many of us believe that wrongs aren't wrong if it's done by nice people like ourselves.

—A thought from John Peers' "1001 Logical Laws"

1 Late in the afternoon on a dark May day in London, when there were no shadows—in an area near Fleet Street, as I remember—I found myself after payment of a modest entrance fee wandering alone through the many-windowed house once occupied by Charles Dickens, a hero of mine.

2 It was silent in those empty rooms; strangely, I was the only visitor. And at last I stood dreaming by the solitary flat-topped mahogany desk where, in my mind's eye, the writer sat at work, his head bent in concentration.

3 Almost without thinking, I slid open a top drawer, half expecting to find an unfinished chapter of *Nicholas Nickleby*. Instead, in the drawer was a key. A gloved hand—could it have been mine?—reached out and picked up the key. And slipped it quickly in a pocket. My hand, my pocket. I had *lifted* the key belonging to the desk of the great 19th century writer.

4 Well, it *means so much to me,* I said to that still small voice in my head. They can have another key made; besides why would they need the key anyway; I mean what is there to lock up? They might not even miss it. Perhaps they have a whole supply of keys, placed there one at a time for the delight of people like me, who love Dickens. Perhaps it is Supposed To Be Taken. The thoughts were no more substantial than the flicker of a wing, and as fleeting, but they were there. And with a sigh I returned the key to the drawer of the desk of Charles Dickens.

5   No matter how upright in intention, who has not toyed on occasion with the thought of a little larceny? Or committed it, deliberately, in small ways? How far does a minor bit of cheating have to go before it becomes outright dishonesty—in relationships, in the ordinary business of living?

6   What, for instance about ash trays and towels purloined from hotels during travels? Slightly padded expense accounts? What do you do if the computer reverses itself and you are charged $47 for the $74 silk blouse. The former is a reasonable enough price, you tell yourself; the latter is exorbitant. And who would be hurt if I didn't say anything; certainly not the salesperson. It was the *computer* that made the mistake. . . .

7   Is crossing the street against a red light—a practice seemingly on the increase—a risky exercise of sometime common sense? Or is it a slight dishonesty?

8   In any case, are people by and large less honest in today's society than they were a decade or so ago? . . . What is the state of honesty today? When you start listening, you find everyone has a story, an illustration of sorts. What has happened to people's standards? Is it "situation ethics" today—an individual matter, dependent on circumstances? I continue to listen.

9   Here is part of what I heard from Paul, a political commentator who served as an infantry soldier in Vietnam, one of a family of seven children reared in the Deep South, with a strong sense of right and wrong: "There is more anonymity today because of the sheer numbers of people. Also, many of us are transient; the force of family and old friends holding us in check has lessened.

10   "Another factor: less individual contact, isolation between individuals and their institutions. It is more difficult for me to lie to your face.

11   "And there are no more moralists, Billy Graham, for example, is of great religious stature, yet during the high crimes and misdemeanors of the Nixon Administration, he and all the other religious leaders were conspicuous by their silence."

12   In this country, a voice *is* emerging as one of the most powerful, speaking up against hypocrisy, Paul notes, and that belongs to television's Bill Moyers, who also happens to be ordained a Baptist minister.

13   One possible answer to the fact that the small dishonesty, while not a new phenomenon, may be more pervasive: "Our system. Honesty is really not rewarded; the system actually is very cruel, although it is the best we know. Only a certain percentage of people benefit. In close observation of political and industrial leaders, you notice a certain hardness about them. How have they been able to get ahead? What makes them successful? They are willing to say and do things most of us aren't."

We have been forced by the system, Paul says, to accept the fact 14
that we don't dot every *i* and cross every *t*. It is simply a part of the
cultural and survival skills that we have learned. . . .

What *about* the white lie? 15

Playwright Phillip, in his thirties: "My flowering years came in the 16
1960s, the hippie days, when the most important value we had was
honesty. In the sense that we were totally open, we always told the
truth; we grew up with the belief that this was the way the world was. It
took me years to learn that this is *not* the way the world works. People
don't want you to be honest, especially about them.

"I thought I was doing everything right—and look at me, I can't pay 17
my bills. And I have friends who got into the real estate business and
are now slum landlords and go to Europe three months out of every
year. Honesty is a myth. People were never honest. How can you be
honest in business? Game playing is the way business is conducted,
and that's lying. If the government sends me back too much tax, I'll
keep it. On the other hand, I wouldn't defraud a little old lady."

The eloquent churchman takes the positive approach. "Come now, 18
there's a lot of honesty all over the place. Not *everybody* monkeys with
his income tax."

That things may really not have changed much is one of his points, 19
as he muses. "Sometimes we pat ourselves on the back with the
thought that ours is a more virtuous generation than others before us.
For example, we don't burn witches anymore. But may that not be, as
somebody suggested, because we don't believe in witches anymore?"

"Of course there is a lot of honesty around," said my lawyer friend 20
over lunch at the Hunan Village on Kearny Street. "But everyone has
exceptions. Many people consider office supplies an exception. Others
consider shoplifting an exception. There are those who consider that if
the bank makes a large mistake in your favor, *that's* an exception." He
looked wise as he spoke, but he, like everyone else, had only an
opinion. No answer. . . .

And ah, the moral dilemmas. The dilemmas involving situations 21
with murky guidelines: Patti purchased an expensive set of ironware
from a department store. Three months later a store spokesman called
to say her second batch of ironware had arrived. "But I didn't order
any more," she protested. "Yes, you did, and it's marked *Paid*," was
the answer. The argument continued; each party to it adamant. Suddenly Patti remembered the difficulties she had had with her actual
purchase. She decided to accept the extra ironware. Who knows, she
thought, perhaps I *did* pay for it. But she didn't think she had.

"People come here to grapple with difficulties having to do with a 22
multiplicity of value systems crowding in," my red-haired psychologist
friend says. He is a former airline pilot, a fine musician.

23   "There's the old system. Some got it from family, schools, peers, the military, jobs, whatever; and some didn't.

24   "Over and over, I see people being unconsciously trained in ways to behave that are technically dishonest. For example, they spend hundreds of hours watching TV actors in skillfully designed commercials which utilize persuasive, dishonest manipulation to provoke a way of behavior. People learn to act in ways they believe will get them what they want. *'Here's the way I believe I am supposed to behave. It's OK if it's not quite honest.'*"

25   Another thing. "The more pressure, the more pain, the more difficulties, the more negative the thinking, which is a measure of how much people are in trouble. We are so disturbed over the economic, the political, the world picture, and so depressed, that when it comes to small dishonesties, we think, 'It doesn't really matter.'"

26   One night I telephoned Bart, a student, a skier and soccer player who was fourteen on January 20, and I asked him this question: *"What would you do if you bought a hamburger with a five dollar bill and got change back for a ten dollar bill, and the waitress insisted it had been a ten dollar bill but you knew it had been a five dollar bill?"* He said he in turn would insist on taking change for a five dollar bill. Why? Well, because the change for a ten dollar bill wouldn't have been his, it wouldn't have been right. Besides, he said, he might find himself in the waitress's shoes one day.

27   The Golden Rule. Is it still with us? I was reminded of the following mini-maxim among a list compiled in a letter to his godson by a man named Arthur Gordon, thirteen years ago:

28   Keep your eye on the law of the echo.

29   "I remember very well the occasion when I first heard this sharp-edged bit of advice. Coming home from boarding school, some of us youngsters were in the dining car of a train. Somehow the talk got around to the subject of cheating on exams, and one boy readily admitted that he cheated all the time. He said that he found it both easy and profitable.

30   "Suddenly a mild-looking man sitting all alone at a table across the aisle leaned forward and spoke up. 'Yes,' he said to the apostle of cheating. 'All the same—I'd keep one eye on the law of the echo if I were you.'

31   "The law of the echo—is there really such a thing?" asked the godfather of his godson. "Is the universe actually arranged so that whatever you send out—honesty or dishonesty, kindness or cruelty— ultimately comes back to you? It's hard to be sure. And yet, since the beginning of recorded history, mankind has had the conviction, based partly on intuition, partly on observation, that in the long run a man does indeed reap what he sows."

Does mankind in general still hold steadfast to this belief? Maybe 32
yes, maybe no. Some people do, some don't. Maybe an equivocation,
an evasion, is the only honest answer there is to this question. Maybe
just like always.

FOR DISCUSSION

1. How might the experience the author describes at the opening of
   the essay have motivated her to write this article?
2. Summarize the problem which is raised in this essay.
3. What does Caroline Drewes do in this article to reach as large a
   readership as possible?
4. What is the "Law of the Echo"?
5. What is your own response after reading this essay to Drewes'
   question about honesty?
6. How is this article developed? What, in other words, are its
   parts?

ELLEN GOODMAN

*Ellen Goodman, a nationally syndicated columnist, defines a problem
in this short essay. Taken from* At Large *(1981), a collection of some of
her best columns, the essay does not provide a solution to the problem,
but rather highlights the problem itself.*

Being a Secretary Can Be Hazardous to Your Health

They used to say it with flowers or celebrate it with a somewhat liquid 1
lunch. National Secretaries Week was always good for at least a token
of appreciation. But the way the figures add up now, the best thing a
boss can do for a secretary this week is cough up for her cardiogram.

"Stress and the Secretary" has become the hottest new syndrome 2
on the heart circuit.

3   It seems that it isn't those Daring Young Women in their Dress-for-Success Suits who are following men down the cardiovascular trail to ruin. Nor is it the female professionals who are winning their equal place in intensive care units.

4   It is powerlessness and not power that corrupts women's hearts. And clerical workers are the number one victims.

5   In the prestigious Framingham study, Dr. Suzanne Haynes, an epidemiologist with the National Heart, Lung and Blood Institute, found that working women as a whole have no higher rate of heart disease than housewives. But women employed in clerical and sales occupations do. Their coronary disease rates are twice that of other women.

6   "This is not something to ignore," says Dr. Haynes, "since such a high percent of women work at clerical jobs." In fact, 35 percent of all working women, or 18 million of us, hold these jobs.

7   When Dr. Haynes looked into their private lives, she found the women at greatest risk—with a one in five chance of heart disease— were clerical workers with blue-collar husbands, and three or more children. When she then looked at their work lives, she discovered that the ones who actually developed heart disease were those with nonsupportive bosses who hadn't changed jobs very often and who had trouble letting their anger out.

8   In short, being frustrated, dead-ended, without a feeling of control over your life is bad for your health.

9   The irony in all the various and sundry heart statistics is that we now have a weird portrait of the Cardiovascular Fun Couple of the Office: The Type A Boss and his secretary. The male heart disease stereotype is, after all, the Type A aggressive man who always needs to be in control, who lives with a great sense of time urgency . . . and is likely to be a white-collar boss.

10   "The Type A man is trying to be in control. But given the way most businesses are organized there are, in fact, few ways for them to be in control of their jobs," says Dr. Haynes. The only thing the Type A boss can be in control of is his secretary who in turn feels . . . well you get the picture. He's not only getting heart disease, he's giving it.

11   As if all this weren't enough to send you out for the annual three martini lunch, clerical workers are increasingly working for a new Type A boss: the computer.

12   These days fewer women are sitting in front of bosses with notepads and more are sitting in front of Visual Display Terminals. Word processors, data processors, microprocessors . . . these are the demanding, time-conscious, new automatons of automations.

13   There is nothing intrinsically evil about computers. I am writing this on a VDT and if you try to take it away from me, I will break your arm. But as Working Women, the national association of office workers,

puts it in their release this week, automation is increasingly producing clerical jobs that are de-skilled, down-graded, dead-ended and dissatis- fying.

As Karen Nussbaum of the Cleveland office described it, the office 14 of the future may well be the factory of the past. Work on computers is often reduced to simple, repetitive, monotonous tasks. Workers are often expected to produce more for no more pay, and there are also reports of a disturbing trend to processing speed-ups and piece-rate pay, and a feeling among clerical workers that their jobs are computer controlled.

"It's not the machine, but the way it's used by employers," says 15 Working Women's research director, Judith Gregory. Too often, auto- mation's most important product is stress.

Groups, like Working Women, are trying to get clerical workers to 16 organize in what they call "a race against time" so that computers will become their tools instead of their supervisors.

But in the meantime, if you are 1) a female clerical worker, 2) with a 17 blue-collar husband, 3) with three or more children, 4) in a dead-end job, 5) without any way to express anger, 6) with a Type A boss, 7) or a Type A computer controlling your work day. . . . *You better start jogging.*

FOR DISCUSSION

1. What is gained by having this essay be completely about the problem and not about the solution?

2. State in your own words the problem Ellen Goodman discusses.

3. What are some of the ramifications of this problem?

4. This essay, taken from a collection of Goodman's columns, originally appeared in the newspaper she writes for—*The Boston Globe*. What is there in the format of this essay that would make it particularly appropriate for publication in a newspaper?

5. Describe the reader Goodman had in mind when she wrote this column. What in the essay makes it specifically appropriate for those readers?

6. Was the statement of the problem sufficiently discussed to leave you, the reader, feeling satisfied? Discuss your reaction.

7. Was this problem a new one to you? Discuss your answer.

VICKI WHITE

A student, Vicki White, wrote this essay to discuss solutions to the problems at Dettmers' Greenery, the plant store where she worked. Although she wrote this essay as an assignment to be read aloud in her Freshman English class, she used her real-life situation, an employee making a report to her boss, as the background for her paper.

Solving the Problem at Dettmers' Greenery

1   Last week while making out my annual report, I noticed something that has been happening so gradually that I hadn't noticed it before. Over the past year Dettmers' Greenery has been slowly losing business. Each quarter there has been a slight decline. I have taken out time to consider seriously this problem, and I have isolated two factors which I believe explain the loss. These two factors are our low plant sales and the improperly budgeted time of the staff. I have, therefore, several suggestions which could help the company if they are put into action.

2   The first and major concern involves raising the plant sales. These sales have dropped unnecessarily almost 20 percent over the past twelve months. I believe that by underselling certain produce, the greenery would profit in the long run. This would involve a series of special sales offered to our customers on a regular basis.

3   One such sale would be a "White Elephant Sale." In this sale we would separate all of the good plants from the damaged plants and offer the damaged ones at a discount. This would allow the customers to buy the plants they wanted (although slightly damaged) at a very low cost. Dettmers' Greenery, on the other hand, would save money by selling these plants instead of throwing them away, as has been done in the past.

4   A second sale would be the "Plant of the Month" sale. For this sale, a plant would be picked each month to be Plant of the Month. This plant would then be purchased through our wholesalers in mass quantity, resulting in a low price for us. We, in turn, could sell these plants at a reasonably low rate and still increase our income.

5   My last suggestion for raising sales would to be offer a 10 percent discount to our regular customers. For example, last week while visiting the annex store of Dettmers', I ran into one such customer, Miss Schwarer. She comes in on a weekly basis and usually buys a good supply of merchandise. By offering customers such as Miss Schwarer a

"club discount" of 10 percent, we could continue to expect to have her business on a regular—and probably an increased—basis. And as these customers' buying increased, the extra business would overbalance any loss resulting from the discount.

Increased plant sales, however, will not solve our problem at Dettmers'. The staff's use of time must also be studied if we are to return to our healthy financial condition. One problem that arises frequently, and one that wastes an enormous amount of time, is the staff's failure to mark the prices of plants before they are put out to be sold. In the past, plants have been put out and then marked, often resulting in no prices being put on at all because the salesperson forgot to return to do the job. I recall many times when a customer has brought a plant to the cash register to buy it; nobody can find a price and nobody there at that time knows the price. The customer is irritated (sometimes to the point of leaving the plant and walking out of the store), and the staff is frustrated. This problem could be solved easily by a firm policy that *no* plant is to be put on the floor until its price has been marked. 6

Another way the staff time is wasted is in the decoration of pots. It takes more time than is recovered in the price of the flower to cover a pot neatly in colored foil and then tie a ribbon around it or add some other type of decoration. A lot of time could be saved if the company would invest in prefabricated baskets of various styles that the plants could be put directly into without further decoration. Although this would amount to more expense for the company initially, perhaps, the time savings of the staff would, in the long run, outweigh the expense. If hand-decorated pots were still used, they should be offered at an additional cost. 7

The last suggestion concerning the use of the staff's time most efficiently has to do with the assignment of duties to the employees. Just a short while back, when I was visiting our branch stores in the two new shopping centers in town, I noticed that the staff's schedules were in chaos. Both stores had been rotating daily the duties of spraying, watering, and feeding the plants. And at least once a week there was confusion on whose turn it was to feed the plants or give them their spraying, etc. This confusion results often in one of these jobs not getting done and perhaps another of the jobs being done twice in the same day by two different people, one of whom forgot what the exact assignment was for that day. This problem can be avoided by assigning each employee a specific duty, an allotted time to do it, and posting a chart stating each worker's duty. Then, if the plants are neglected, the problem can be pin-pointed very easily. 8

I have put much time and effort into both of the problems discussed here. If my proposals for solutions are put into action, the company will profit greatly. Not only will the earnings increase from the plant 9 sales, but much time will also be saved. Since time is money, this improved budgeting of staff time will also improve the profits of Dettmers' Greenery. Very likely the company would realize the benefits of these changes as soon as the very next quarterly report.

FOR DISCUSSION

1. How many suggestions does Vicki White use to state the solution to the problem at Dettmer's Greenery?

2. Each suggestion she makes has one main sentence that states exactly what the suggestion is. What is the value of the rest of the sentences in each suggestion paragraph? What do these other sentences provide for the reader—and for the writer?

3. What is the ratio in this essay of the statement of the problem to the statement of the solution?

4. What determines the order in which Vicki White lists her suggestions for solving the problem?

5. How does the writer make her own "voice" heard in the essay? What is added specifically because of the presence of that voice?

WRITING YOUR OWN
The Problem/Solution Essay

Before you write your own problem/solution essay, review the individual configurations made by Margaret Mead in her essay, "How We Can Help Children Learn to Write."

Motivation (an educated guess): concern about a social issue of importance.

Circumstance/Situation: had to meet manuscript and editorial constraints of *Redbook* Magazine. Had to conform to length considerations of a regular column.

Audience: general reader, but especially parents with school-age children.

Writer's Relationship to Audience: person who had thought about the problem and come up with possible solutions to suggest to persons who had not perhaps thought about the problem being solved this way.

Emphasis: attitudinal changes that would help solve the problem.

Form: regular column appearing in magazine.

Intention (an educated guess): to inspire in her readers the notion that there is a solution to a perceived problem.

Analyzing the other essays in this section may help you to see how writers solved their own problems in writing their essays.

DESIGNING YOUR OWN CONFIGURATION

Here are some things to think about that may help you design your own configuration.

What problems or solutions am I knowledgeable about? Who would be or could be made to be interested in these problems? Where do I think the written piece should appear?

Here are some possibilities that you might use to stimulate your own creativity:

1. Write a piece for your local paper on a) problems in your neighborhood, b) the lack of places for young people to go in your town, c) the lack of programs for senior citizens.

2. Think about a sport or hobby you enjoy—football, tennis, jogging, cooking. Is there any new equipment that would help solve a problem you have with it or that would make it easier or more enjoyable, such as a portable tape cassette player to wear while jogging or a new kind of racket for tennis? Write an essay discussing these advances for the readers of a magazine specializing in the sport or hobby.

3. Write a report for your employer or co-workers about a solution you suggest for a problem at work.

4. Any annoying problem at your college or university? Crowded parking lots? Noisy rooms or apartments? Not enough sections of a course offered? Write an article for your school paper proposing a solution to one of these problems.

Use the possibilities in these columns to decide on the points in your problem/solution configuration:

Designing Your Own Configuration for a Problem/Solution Essay

MOTIVE	CIRCUMSTANCE/ SITUATION	AUDIENCE	RELATIONSHIP TO AUDIENCE
To solve a problem at work	For x magazine with x deadline and length requirements	People who are apathetic	Paul Revere-stance
To bring attention to a problem at work	For the editorial page of x newspaper	People who are passionately interested in the subject	Reasoned, quiet thinker to interested listener
To raise consciousness on a problem	For a speech at a political rally	People who are just unaware	Expert to novice
To give a solution from your experience	For a book on the subject	People already working in this area	More experienced to less experienced
To get recognition in your profession	For an employer	A particular group of people, occupation, profession, etc.	Concerned writer to willing reader
To contribute to the well-being of all people			Confidant to friend
To satisfy an assignment			
To sell an article			

EMPHASIS	FORM	INTENTION
On the solution	Newspaper column	To get something off writer's chest
On the problem	Letter to editor	To rally support for a solution to the problem
On the problem slightly and then on the solution	Speak-out on radio/television	To win agreement on a solution for the problem
On the problem in detail and then slightly on the solution	Magazine article	To air the problem
On what the reader can do	Speech at club, school, organization, political rally	To inform people about the intricacies/ complexities of the problem
On what the situation is	Company newsletter	To identify the problem
On what has already been done		To report on a solution that has already been put into effect
On what people won't do		

RULES FOR A PROBLEM/SOLUTION ESSAY

1. Select a problem and/or solution that you have experienced personally. Be sure that you have something to say on the subject.
2. Decide whether you want to discuss the problem, the solution, or both.
3. Know your audience and intend to give them value in the essay. Make certain that the subject is going to matter to them.
4. Use many examples and illustrations throughout the essay. Be sure these examples and illustrations will strike home to the audience.
5. Assist the readers in understanding any complex issues by breaking them down into their simpler parts.
6. End the essay by letting the readers know what to make of all you have said.

RHETORICAL PATTERNS OFTEN APPEARING IN PROBLEM/SOLUTION ESSAYS

Analysis: How to Help the Reader Understand

1. The word *analyze* means "to divide anything complex into its simple parts or pieces by separating a whole into its parts." It also means "to show the relationship among the single parts of a larger, more complex subject."
2. A good analysis actually shows the reader how to *think* about the subject.
3. To use analysis in your writing, decide what parts you can break the larger subject into. Then take these parts one at a time. Discuss or describe them, either on an individual basis or as a group, showing how they relate to each other. Finally, put the parts back together in a whole. The reader will then have been able to *understand* what may have otherwise been baffling or confusing.

Examples and Illustrations: How to Help the Reader See

1. An example or illustration is a specific instance that helps clarify a more general statement by allowing the reader to *see*. It is one single thing that shows the character of the whole.

2. Be as colorful, descriptive, detailed, and specific as you possibly can when you give examples and illustrations. Appeal to the readers' *senses*. Transport the readers to the spot and *show* what you mean.

3. Use *concrete* words. Abstract terms don't produce pictures in readers' minds. General words, too, can mean different things to different people. Concrete words appearing in examples and illustrations will let the readers know what *you* mean by the general terms. And if you've used any abstract terms, concrete words will help make them clear to the readers.

4. Choose examples and illustrations that will mean something to the particular audience for whom you are writing.

5. Be generous with examples and illustrations. A minimum ratio is one specific example or illustration to one general statement. Often, however, a higher ratio—say, two or three examples or illustrations to one general statement—will be necessary to let your reader *see* exactly what you mean. You will probably never err by having too many examples and illustrations.

The Information Essay

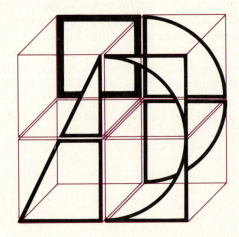

A good information essay will have these characteristics:

The information itself will be the center of attention in the essay, not the writer's perceptions, experiences, insights. The writer will almost disappear. Naturally, the writer can't *really* disappear because facts must be gathered, sorted, and arranged by a human being. But the emphasis will be clearly on the information rather than on the writer.

The writer will present this information in a way as lively and interesting as possible to avoid boring the reader with lifeless, monotonous facts. Readers do not like to be bored, even when they are reading chiefly for information. The facts will be woven together with plenty of descriptions to help readers develop mental images.

The writer will be certain that a "voice" is heard in the writing, that the reader will feel that the writer is writing for live people. The essay will sound as though a *person* wrote it, and the reader will know something about that person.

The writer will do everything possible to help the reader relate the new information to something already familiar to the reader. The essay, therefore, will be filled with specific details, colorful word pictures, familiar examples or references so that the readers are engaged by the essay and are able to relate the new information to something they already know, thereby assimilating it into their store of knowledge.

Read the information essays that follow and ask yourself these questions:

What has the writer done to keep this information from being boring to the reader?

How does the writer relate this information to something the reader already knows?

What is the possible motive(s) for the author's writing this essay?

Does the writer use personal information in the essay? If so, what keeps that from putting the attention on the writer and not on the information itself?

Are there any varieties in the forms these information essays take?

Is the audience for a particular essay considered to be the general public? Persons who have a particular kind of expertise?

How does the writer establish her or his relationship with the reader? What is that relationship?

LOREN EISELEY

This essay originally appeared as part of a book, The Immense Journey *(1957), one of the most popular books ever written about a scientific subject for the general reader. In "How Flowers Changed the World," Eiseley, a famous anthropologist and naturalist, uses cause/effect analysis to explain how flowers affected the whole cycle of nature when they appeared on earth.*

How Flowers Changed the World

1 A little while ago—about one hundred million years, as the geologist estimates time in the history of our four-billion-year-old planet—flowers were not to be found anywhere on the five continents. Wherever one might have looked, from the poles to the equator, one would have seen only the cold dark monotonous green of a world whose plant life possessed no other color.

2 Somewhere, just a short time before the close of the Age of Reptiles, there occurred a soundless, violent explosion. It lasted millions of years, but it was an explosion, nevertheless. It marked the emergence of the angiosperms—the flowering plants. Even the great evolutionist, Charles Darwin, called them "an abominable mystery," because they appeared so suddenly and spread so fast.

3 Flowers changed the face of the planet. Without them, the world we know—even man himself—would never have existed. Francis Thompson, the English poet, once wrote that one could not pluck a flower without troubling a star. Intuitively he had sensed like a naturalist the enormous interlinked complexity of life. Today we know that the appearance of the flowers contained also the equally mystifying emergence of man. . . .

4 When the first simple flower bloomed on some raw upland late in the Dinosaur Age, it was wind pollinated, just like its early pine-cone relatives. It was a very inconspicuous flower because it had not yet evolved the idea of using the surer attraction of birds and insects to achieve the transportation of pollen. It sowed its own pollen and received the pollen of other flowers by the simple vagaries of the wind. Many plants in regions where insect life is scant still follow this principle today. Nevertheless, the true flower—and the seed that it produced—was a profound innovation in the world of life.

5 In a way, this event parallels, in the plant world, what happened among animals. Consider the relative chance for survival of the exteri-

orly deposited egg of a fish in contrast with the fertilized egg of a mammal, carefully retained for months in the mother's body until the young animal (or human being) is developed to a point where it may survive. The biological wastage is less—and so it is with the flowering plants. The primitive spore, a single cell fertilized in the beginning by a swimming sperm, did not promote rapid distribution, and the young plant, moreover, had to struggle up from nothing. No one had left it any food except what it would get by its own unaided efforts.

By contrast, the true flowering plants (angiosperm itself means 6 "encased seed") grew a seed in the heart of a flower, a seed whose development was initiated by a fertilizing pollen grain independent of outside moisture. But the seed, unlike the developing spore, is already a fully equipped *embryonic plant* packed in a little enclosed box stuffed full of nutritious food. Moreover, by featherdown attachments, as in dandelion or milkweed seed, it can be wafted upward on gusts and ride the wind for miles; or with hooks it can cling to a bear's or a rabbit's hide; or like some of the berries, it can be covered with a juicy, attractive fruit to lure birds, pass undigested through their intestinal tracts and be voided miles away.

The ramifications of this biological invention were endless. Plants 7 traveled as they had never traveled before. They got into strange environments heretofore never entered by the old spore plants or stiff pine-cone-seed plants. The well-fed, carefully cherished little embryos raised their heads everywhere. Many of the older plants with more primitive reproductive mechanisms began to fade away under this unequaled contest. They contracted their range into secluded environments. Some, like the giant redwoods, lingered on as relics; many vanished entirely.

The world of the giants was a dying world. These fantastic little 8 seeds skipping and hopping and flying about the woods and valleys brought with them an amazing adaptability. If our whole lives had not been spent in the midst of it, it would astound us. The old, stiff, skyreaching wooden world had changed into something that glowed here and there with strange colors, put out queer, unheard-of fruits and little intricately carved seed cases, and, most important of all, produced concentrated foods in a way that the land had never seen before, or dreamed of back in the fish-eating, leaf-crunching days of the dinosaurs.

That food came from three sources, all produced by the reproductive system of the flowering plants. There were the tantalizing nectars and pollens intended to draw insects for pollenizing purposes, and which are responsible also for that wonderful jeweled creation, the hummingbird. There were the juicy and enticing fruits to attract larger animals, and in which tough-coated seeds were concealed, as in the tomato, for example. Then, as if this were not enough, there was the food in the actual seed itself, the food intended to nourish the embryo. All over the world, like hot corn in a popper, these incredible elaborations of the flowering plants kept exploding. In a movement that was almost instantaneous, geologically speaking, the angiosperms had taken over the world. Grass was beginning to cover the bare earth until, today, there are over six thousand species. All kinds of vines and bushes squirmed and writhed under new trees with flying seeds.

10   The explosion was having its effect on animal life also. Specialized groups of insects were arising to feed on the new sources of food and, incidentally and unknowingly, to pollinate the plant. The flowers bloomed and bloomed in ever larger and more spectacular varieties. Some were pale unearthly night flowers intended to lure moths in the evening twilight, some among the orchids even took the shape of female spiders in order to attract wandering males, some flamed redly in the light of noon or twinkled modestly in the meadow grasses. Intricate mechanisms splashed pollen on the breasts of hummingbirds, or stamped it on the bellies of black, grumbling bees droning assiduously from blossom to blossom. Honey ran, insects multiplied, and even the descendants of that toothed and ancient lizard-bird had become strangely altered. Equipped with prodding beaks instead of biting teeth they pecked the seeds and gobbled the insects that were really converted nectar.

11   Across the planet grasslands were now spreading. A slow continental upthrust which had been a part of the early Age of Flowers had cooled the world's climates. The stalking reptiles and the leather-winged black imps of the seashore cliffs had vanished. Only birds roamed the air now, hot-blooded and high-speed metabolic machines.

12   The mammals, too, had survived and were venturing into new domains, staring about perhaps a bit bewildered at their sudden eminence now that the thunder lizards were gone. Many of them, beginning as small browsers upon leaves in the forest, began to venture out upon this new sunlit world of the grass. Grass has a high silica content and demands a new type of very tough and resistant tooth enamel, but the seeds taken incidentally in the cropping of the grass are highly nutritious. A new world had opened out for the warm-blooded mammals. Great herbivores like the mammoths, horses and bisons appeared. Skulking about them had arisen savage flesh-feeding carnivores like the now extinct dire wolves and the saber-toothed tiger. . . .

13   Apes were to become men, in the inscrutable wisdom of nature, because flowers had produced seeds and fruits in such tremendous quantities that a new and totally different store of energy had become available in concentrated form. Impressive as the slow-moving, dim-brained dinosaurs had been, it is doubtful if their age had supported anything like the diversity of life that now rioted across the planet or

flashed in and out among the trees. Down on the grass by a streamside, one of those apes with inquisitive fingers turned over a stone and hefted it vaguely. The group clucked together in a throaty tongue and moved off through the tall grass foraging for seeds and insects. The one still held, sniffed, and hefted the stone he had found. He liked the feel of it in his fingers. The attack on the animal world was about to begin.

If one could run the story of that first human group like a speeded-up 14 motion picture through a million years of time, one might see the stone in the hand change to the flint ax and the torch. All that swarming grassland world with its giant bison and trumpeting mammoths would go down in ruin to feed the insatiable and growing numbers of a carnivore who, like the great cats before him, was taking his energy indirectly from the grass. Later he found fire and it altered the tough meats and drained their energy even faster into a stomach ill adapted for the ferocious turn man's habits had taken.

His limbs grew longer, he strode more purposefully over the grass. 15 The stolen energy that would take man across the continents would fail him at last. The great Ice Age herds were destined to vanish. When they did so, another hand like the hand that grasped the stone by the river long ago would pluck a handful of grass seed and hold it contemplatively.

In that moment, the golden towers of man, his swarming millions, 16 his turning wheels, the vast learning of his packed libraries, would glimmer dimly there in the ancestor of wheat, a few seeds held in a muddy hand. Without the gift of flowers and the infinite diversity of their fruits, man and bird, if they had continued to exist at all, would be today unrecognizable. Archaeopteryx, the lizard-bird, might still be snapping at beetles on a sequoia limb; man might still be a nocturnal insectivore gnawing a roach in the dark. The weight of a petal has changed the face of the world and made it ours.

FOR DISCUSSION

1. What would have happened if flowers had never existed?

2. How was the first flower pollinated?

3. This essay originally came from a book. If it had been written as an article for a popular magazine, how could Loren Eiseley have written it differently to capture the audience?

4. Eiseley used cause/effect as the rhetorical pattern in giving information on how flowers changed the world. First, find the cause that he gives. Then make a list of the ways he shows *how* that cause brought about the result.

5. What specifically is the relationship that Eiseley shows between the cause and the effect in this essay?

6. Eiseley remarks on the English poet who wrote that one could not pluck a flower without troubling a star. Why was this reference an appropriate one for Eiseley to make?

7. What does Eiseley do to make this essay accessible to a nonscientific reader?

CAROL TAVRIS AND LEONORE TIEFER

In this essay, which was originally published in Redbook *magazine, Carol Tavris and Leonore Tiefer give interesting information about the kiss down through the ages.*

The Meanings of the Kiss

1 Throughout history, people have found occasion to kiss almost every object that didn't fight back, and a few that did. We kiss icons, dice, the Bible and lottery tickets for luck; we kiss the Blarney Stone for the gift of gab; we kiss religious garments in reverence; we kiss to say hello, good-by, get well, get lost.

2 There have been so many kinds of kisses that from time to time scholars feel obliged to try to sort them into categories. The ancient rabbis divided kisses into three kinds: greeting, farewell and respect. The Romans identified *oscula* (friendly kisses), *basia* (love kisses) and *suavia* (passionate kisses)—it appears that they were somewhat bawdier than the ancient rabbis. The German language had no fewer than 30 types of kisses at the turn of the century, from *Abschiedkuss* (farewell kiss) to *Zuckerkuss* (sweet kiss). They have since lost, unfortunately, *nachküssen,* which in 1901 meant "making up for kisses that have been omitted."

3 However many types of kisses one makes up, though, they boil down into only a few basic messages:

4 *"I am your subordinate and I respect you."* The kiss as a symbol of deference and duty has a long tradition. In the Middle Ages the location of the kiss was a precise clue to the status of the participants: one kissed the mouth or cheek of an equal, the hand of a political or

religious leader, the hem of the robe of a truly great figure and—to express extreme respect—the foot or ground in front of a king, saint or revered hero. The further away one was in status from the kissee, the farther away from the face one kissed.

"I am your friend." To allow someone close enough to kiss you 5 requires a measure of trust; in its earliest form the kiss of greeting undoubtedly meant, "It's safe. I will not bite your ear or stab your back." The kiss of reconciliation preceded the handshake in many societies, and even today children—and sometimes grownups—are encouraged to "kiss and make up."

"The bargain is sealed." Originally the kiss exchanged between 6 bride and groom was a business kiss—a pagan practice that meant the couple were officially assuming their legal and economic obligations. When all the guests kissed the new wife, they were publicly recognizing the legality of the union.

"I will take care of you and ward off evil." Mothers kiss their 7 children's scraped knees, feverish foreheads and bruised arms to "make the hurt go away," just as faith healers "kiss away" the ailments of grown-up penitents. Belief in the magical powers of kisses has filtered into everyday superstition: When you kiss dice or a cross (or your crossed fingers) or any object "for luck," you are enlisting the aid of fortune, God or the fates.

"We are in and you are out." The "ins" may be family, neighbor- 8 hood, community or religious fellowship. When St. Paul instructed the faithful to "salute one another with an holy kiss," he established a ritual that came to reflect public adherence to the faith. St. Paul's kiss of peace, as it came to be known, was exchanged among Christians variously at services, baptism, confession, ordination and communion.

Because the kiss implies trust, solidarity and affection, deceptive 9 kisses are everywhere despised. Judas's betrayal of Christ in the garden of Gethsemane was, of course, the most famous Western example. The Judas kiss is practiced ritually even today. Among some Mafiosi, a man who has betrayed the organization will be kissed on the mouth by his assassin—a sign of loving farewell.

FOR DISCUSSION

1. This essay is an example of the kind of writing done because the author(s) is interested in or is an expert in a certain area and wants to give information about it. What would make a reader, for instance, want to read this particular essay? What do the authors have in their favor even before the reader begins?

2. This essay appeared in the May 1979 issue of a popular magazine, *Redbook*. What can you say about the audience, then, that the writers needed to have in mind when they sent this essay for consideration for publication?

3. The writers have used a rhetorical pattern called classification in their essay. What are the categories/classes into which they divide kisses?

4. This essay would be more complete if it had an ending that referred back to the entire essay, if it did not end with statements about the last category of kisses which is discussed. Write a concluding paragraph that would strengthen the essay.

5. What time constraints can you guess the authors were or were not under in writing this article?

6. Is there actually a definition of kissing in this essay?

7. What are the three basic messages a kiss delivers?

E. B. WHITE

In 1977 E. B. White published a collection of essays—Essays of E. B. White—*which he had written over a period of forty years. This statement, taken from the foreword to the book, presents White's view of what an essayist is.*

What Is an Essayist?

1   The essayist is a self-liberated man, sustained by the childish belief that everything he thinks about, everything that happens to him, is of general interest. He is a fellow who thoroughly enjoys his work, just as people who take bird walks enjoy theirs. Each new excursion of the essayist, each new "attempt," differs from the last and takes him into new country. This delights him. Only a person who is congenitally self-centered has the effrontery and the stamina to write essays.

2   There are as many kinds of essays as there are human attitudes or poses, as many essay flavors as there are Howard Johnson ice creams. The essayist arises in the morning and, if he has work to do, selects his garb from an unusually extensive wardrobe: he can pull on any sort of shirt, be any sort of person, according to his mood or his subject

matter—philosopher, scold, jester, raconteur, confidant, pundit, devil's advocate, enthusiast. I like the essay, have always liked it, and even as a child was at work, attempting to inflict my young thoughts and experiences on others by putting them on paper. I early broke into print in the pages of *St. Nicholas*. I tend still to fall back on the essay form (or lack of form) when an idea strikes me, but I am not fooled about the place of the essay in twentieth-century American letters—it stands a short distance down the line. The essayist, unlike the novelist, the poet, and the playwright, must be content in his self-imposed role of second-class citizen. A writer who has his sights trained on the Nobel Prize or other earthly triumphs had best write a novel, a poem, or a play, and leave the essayist to ramble about, content with living a free life and enjoying the satisfactions of a somewhat undisciplined existence. (Dr. Johnson called the essay "an irregular, undigested piece"; this happy practitioner has no wish to quarrel with the good doctor's characterization.)

There is one thing the essayist cannot do, though—he cannot indulge himself in deceit or in concealment, for he will be found out in no time. Desmond MacCarthy, in his introductory remarks to the 1928 E. P. Dutton & Company edition of Montaigne, observes that Montaigne "had the gift of natural candour. . . ." It is the basic ingredient. And even the essayist's escape from discipline is only a partial escape: the essay, although a relaxed form, imposes its own disciplines, raises its own problems, and these disciplines and problems soon become apparent and (we all hope) act as a deterrent to anyone wielding a pen merely because he entertains random thoughts or is in a happy or wandering mood. 3

I think some people find the essay the last resort of the egoist, a much too self-conscious and self-serving form for their taste; they feel that it is presumptuous of a writer to assume that his little excursions or his small observations will interest the reader. There is some justice in their complaint. I have always been aware that I am by nature self-absorbed and egoistical; to write of myself to the extent I have done indicates a too great attention to my own life, not enough to the lives of others. I have worn many shirts, and not all of them have been a good fit. But when I am discouraged or downcast I need only fling open the door of my closet, and there, hidden behind everything else, hangs the mantle of Michel de Montaigne, smelling slightly of camphor. . . . 4

FOR DISCUSSION

1. Since White wrote this piece as part of a foreword to a collection of his essays, what could he depend on, then, as far as his audience was concerned?

2. How can you tell this was written for a twentieth-century audience?

3. What fresh ideas or images does White bring to his own subject— "what is an essayist"?

4. What does White say is the lure for him of writing essays?

5. This piece uses the rhetorical form of definition; what *is* the definition White gives of an essayist? How does he develop or enlarge this definition?

6. White's analogy of the wardrobe relates to your own decision of what voice you will use when you write for class. Which of the voices mentioned by White—philosopher, scold, jester, etc.—are similar to voices you use in class assignments? List other voices you might use.

DOUGLAS COLLIGAN

In this fascinating essay from the magazine Technology Illustrated, *Douglas Colligan informs the reader about life in a space capsule: how the astronauts eat, sleep, and take care of their daily needs while they are in outer space.*

Life in Zero Gravity

1 Probably not since Christopher Columbus worried about skidding off the edge of the earth have humans had to face such an awesome unknown as surviving, let along living, in space. An almost total vacuum, an environment where temperatures of objects can routinely glide from 250 degrees Fahrenheit below zero to 250 degrees above, a world where gravity is practically nonexistent, space has hardly seemed inviting. Yet little by little scientists have learned, first, how to get air-breathing, gravity-bred earthlings out to space and back without killing them and, later on, how to get them to settle in and actually enjoy outer space.

2　　Getting a human back alive is largely a matter of packaging: wrapping an astronaut in a cocoon of simulated earth atmosphere. That problem was solved on the Mercury space flights and later refined with the Gemini and Apollo missions. Much trickier is how to cope with all the weird challenges posed by the absence of gravity. If, as some visionaries project, humans are to live and work in space, making peace with zero gravity is vital.

As a result, over the years of space flight, including the Skylab 3 missions in 1973 and 1974 and culminating with the space shuttle, there has evolved a whole zero-g technology. Earthbound engineers and designers have begun to give present and future astronauts the components of a world custombuilt for weightlessness.

Much of the attention, naturally, is on outfitting the body for weight- 4 lessness. Living in space, not just commuting through it on the way to the moon, has some strange effects on the human form, as NASA found out during the Skylab mission, when three crews of astronauts lived in zero-g for one, two, and three months. Joe Kosmo, NASA engineer and space-suit expert, recalls one curious discovery: "During flights the men had trouble getting into their space suits." They complained they were too tight. No one knew what to make of the complaint. Suits were custom-tailored, and each was meticulously checked before the launch. Once the astronauts got back to earth the mystery cleared up. The astronauts were taller than when they left earth, sometimes by as much as two inches.

In-flight growth, NASA calls it. In weightlessness the spinal column 5 becomes loose and stretches. With no gravity to compress the soft disks between the spinal bones, bodies expand and grow, at least temporarily. To compensate for this, suits now issued to space-shuttle astronauts are designed to grow with their wearers. Both the legs and sleeves of the suits have laced-in inserts to let out the suit a little when needed.

Zero-g bodies change shape as well as length. The body's fluids tend 6 to migrate away from the lower half to the torso and head. As a result astronauts find they have skinnier feet and narrower waists and slightly larger chests and shoulders. Because of this, the standard-issue uniform for shuttle occupants has a jacket with elasticized pleats built in to expand with the body.

Of course, this fluid is reversed, with a vengeance, once the weight- 7 less person returns to earth's gravity. The sudden drop of fluid to the lower part of the body is so violent that anyone not prepared for it would black out. For that reason, astronauts have been routinely wearing what are called antigravity pants when they dress for reentry. Very simply, the pants are a pair of inflatable leggings that can be pumped up to apply pressure to the lower body and minimize the fluid shock. The danger of blackout is very real, as Dr. Joseph Kerwin of the first Skylab crew found out. He had only partially inflated his suit before reentry and almost fainted. "Surprised the tar out of me," he later admitted.

8   Putting food into the weightless body has always been a special challenge for NASA. For a while no one was sure if a human could eat normally in zero-g. There were those who worried that when John Glenn made the first American around-the-world space flight he wouldn't be able to swallow his food in weightlessness and would choke to death. Once Glenn returned to earth, his stomach full, his throat clear, extraterrestrial meal planning began in earnest. Space meals have progressed from such items as gelatin-coated coconut cubes and peanut cubes to complete heat-and-serve meals on board Skylab and the space shuttle.

9   Space meals are not prepared so much as assembled. All the food is precooked and is either canned, dehydrated, or packed in aluminum-backed plastic envelopes called flex pouches. Because it's impossible to pour water in zero gravity (it congeals into silvery balls that drift around in a spacecraft), dehydrated food is revived by squirting water through a needle into the sealed plastic pouches. Each pouch has a flexible plastic top that lets the cook knead the water into the dried food. Liquids are drunk through a straw with a clamp attached to keep the straw pinched shut when not in use. All are in containers shaped to fit neatly into a compartmentalized and magnetized food tray, where they are anchored in place by Velcro tape.

10   Weightlessness affects not only how the food is packaged, but also what kind of food is inside. Even without gravity, it is possible to eat some foods off an open plate with a fork or spoon. Meals with sauces or gravies work especially well because they tend to stick to the plate and not float away. The Skylab astronauts, who tested out many space meals, found some were disasters. In one report to earth, the first crew crossed chili off their eating schedule. Every time they opened a container of it, there was an explosion of food: "Great gobbets of chili go flying all over; it's bad news."

11   Other adaptations to weightless eating include items like liquid salt and pepper. Ordinary crystals and granules are practically impossible to get out of shakers, and when something does come out, it tends not to hit the food but drift away in midair. Eating utensils are also made smaller because, in a gravity-free dining area, food sticks to the bottom as well as the top of the utensil. To keep an astronaut from spooning up more than he can chew, NASA provides utensils about three-fourths the size of what we use here on earth.

12   Even taste is affected by zero-g. "Body fluids migrate to your upper body, and you end up with engorged tissue around the nasal passages and ear," explains Gerald Carr, who was commander of the third and longest (eighty-four days) Skylab mission. "You carry with you a constant state of nasal and head congestion in a weightless environment. It feels pretty much like you have a cold all the time." As with any head cold, the senses of taste and smell are numbed. To counter

this some of the Skylab crews brought up spices and Tabasco sauce to jazz up the food, and shuttle crews will find barbecue and hot sauces in their meal packets.

And, of course, there is the matter of personal hygiene in zero-g, a great source of wonderment to earthlings. Using the toilet is much more of an adventure than here on earth. The toilet in the space shuttle has a footrest, handholds, and a seat belt to hold the user in position. The lack of gravity is solved by a suction fan. Fans are also used in water drains when astronauts wash. Getting clean is complicated by the fact that water is hard to contain in space. Using Skylab's shower, basically a collapsible cloth cylinder, was a time-consuming chore. To wash up, bathers squirted their bodies with a water gun. That turned out to be a messy design. For every astronaut scrubbing up, another would have to stand by with a vacuum cleaner to suck the escaping water globules out of the air. Designer Larry Bell, who has been working on the plans for a space village for NASA at the University of Houston's School of Architecture, says a better design would be what he calls a "human car wash" or "human dishwasher" approach, in which the bather goes inside a sealed box, is sprayed with water, and is later completely air-dried. 13

Sleeping in space, on the other hand, is a relatively simple affair. At bedtime the astronaut steps into a bag anchored vertically or horizontally to a firm surface, zips the bag up from toe to chest, and, after connecting a waist strap around the bag, tucks both arms under the strap to keep them from flailing around during sleep. Without gravity, sleepers can rest anywhere. Mattresses and pillows are unnecessary, since there's no reason for a body to sink into them; a padded board suffices. In the shuttle the sleeping area has what looks like a two-level bunk bed. One person sleeps on the top, a second on the bottom, and a third underneath the bottom bunk facing the floor. Only in zero gravity could you fit three persons this way into a two-person bed. 14

But even sleeping can have odd complications. Anyone sleeping in weightlessness is in danger of suffering from the clouds of carbon dioxide-laden air exhaled during the night. On Skylab a fan kept a steady floor-to-ceiling current of air flowing by the sleepers' mouths. One astronaut, Charles Conrad, got so annoyed by this breeze constantly blowing up his nose that he once turned his sleeping bag upside down and tried to rest that way. (It would have worked except for the fact that the air then blew into his sleeping bag, billowing it out.) 15

With little resistance to struggle against, the human body tends to lose muscle tone in weightlessness. Exercise regimens are usually prescribed for the longer space flights. Skylab astronauts kept in shape by riding a stationary bicycle exerciser and walking on an ingenious treadmill. It was nothing more than a large sheet of Teflon with some elastic bungee cords. To exercise, an astronaut would anchor himself 16 to a spot on the floor with the cords and walk on the slippery Teflon in his socks. There will be no room for a bicycle exerciser on the shuttle, but it will be carrying a Teflon treadmill.

17   One problem weightless astronauts can encounter when exercising is that, without fans blowing directly on them, the air heated by their bodies tends to hover nearby. And perspiration doesn't dry but sticks to their skin in ever-thickening layers. The Skylab crews discovered this the hard way and rigged up a fan by the bicycle to help evaporate the sweat. That, however, blew the perspiration off their bodies in sheets, which then had to be vacuumed out of the air.

18   There is hardly a part of day-to-day space living that doesn't require some zero-g forethought. Standing still is impossible, for example. Astronauts in the shuttle attach suction-cup soles to their shoes to keep them anchored. Without some means of fixing people in place, Newton's third law of motion—for every action there is an equal and opposite reaction—can conjure bizarre results from even simple actions. When trying to unscrew a bolt, astronaut William Pogue neglected to anchor himself; when he turned the screwdriver, he suddenly found his body corkscrewing through the air. Without some sort of brace, even a motion like bending over can send someone into a somersault. As a way of eliminating these problems, NASA has packed aboard the shuttle portable handholds with suction cups for use almost anywhere.

19   And because no one can truly sit down in the earthbound sense, furniture has to be redesigned to suit the zero-g stoop, a quasi-fetal slouch the human body naturally adopts when there is no gravity. The space crews on Skylab complained that many of the tables and control panels were too low and too hard to use. To remain seated at a 90-degree angle, weightless people must tense their stomach muscles constantly. Skylab astronauts finally removed a chair from one console because it was practically impossible to use. In deference to this, the shuttle has removable working and eating tables that are about a foot higher than an earth table, and its metal surface accommodates magnetic paperweights and magnetic food trays.

20   How well this kind of technology helps people adjust to a world where notions like up, down, heavy, and light take on new meaning is difficult to say. What is known is that astronauts do become totally acclimated to zero gravity. In *A House in Space,* a description of the Skylab experience, author Henry Cooper Jr. tells the story of astronaut Jack Lousma shaving one morning after his return to earth. Letting go of a can of shaving cream while it was poised in mid-air, Lousma was genuinely surprised when it fell straight to the floor.

21   Fellow Skylab veteran Gerald Carr chuckled when he heard the story. "Yeah, I had the same problem," he recalled. "It's surprisingly natural to become what I call a three-dimensional person, one who can

move in all three dimensions. It quickly gets to the point where it is no bother.'' Carr may be screening out memories of hour-long shower preparations and 3-D flotsam drifting through the cabin, but it's clear that with the proper equipment, zero-g living can be enjoyed rather than just survived.

FOR DISCUSSION

1. This article appeared in *Technology Illustrated* in 1982. Since there have been flights into space for more than a decade, the subject matter isn't new. What does the writer do to keep us interested, to make an old subject interesting?

2. This writer had to do research to know what he knows. What does he do in the article to keep it from becoming a boring summary of technical details?

3. What are the parts this essay can be divided into? Is there an apparent logic to the order in which the parts appear?

4. Identify sections of the essay which establish the writer's voice.

5. What interests you in this essay?

Aristotle

Taken from the works of Aristotle (384–322 B.C.), this selection classifies men into three categories: young men, old men, and men in their prime.

The Three Stages of Man

Let us now consider the various types of human character, in relation to the emotions and moral qualities, showing how they correspond to our various ages and fortunes. By emotions I mean anger, desire, and the like; . . . By moral qualities I mean virtues and vices; . . . as well as the various things that various types of men tend to will and to do. By ages I mean youth, the prime of life, and old age. By fortune I mean birth, wealth, power, and their opposites—in fact, good fortune and ill fortune.

2   Young men have strong passions, and tend to gratify them indis-
criminately. Of the bodily desires, it is the sexual by which they are
most swayed and in which they show absence of self-control. They are
changeable and fickle in their desires, which are violent while they last,
but quickly over: their impulses are keen but not deep-rooted, and are
like sick people's attacks of hunger and thirst. They are hot-tempered
and quick-tempered, and apt to give way to their anger; bad temper
often gets the better of them, for owing to their love of honour they
cannot bear being slighted, and are indignant if they imagine themselves unfairly treated. While they love honour, they love victory still
more; for youth is eager for superiority over others, and victory is one
form of this. They love both more than they love money, which indeed
they love very little, not having yet learnt what it means to be without
it—this is the point of Pittacus' remark about Amphiaraus. They look
at the good side rather than the bad, not having yet witnessed many
instances of wickedness. They trust others readily, because they have
not yet often been cheated. They are sanguine; nature warms their
blood as though with excess of wind; and besides that, they have as yet
met with few disappointments. Their lives are mainly spent not in
memory but in expectation; for expectation refers to the future, memory to the past, and youth has a long future before it and a short past
behind it: on the first day of one's life one has nothing at all to
remember, and can only look forward. They are easily cheated, owing
to the sanguine disposition just mentioned. Their hot tempers and
hopeful dispositions make them more courageous than older men are;
the hot temper prevents fear, and the hopeful disposition creates confidence; we cannot feel fear so long as we are feeling angry, and any
expectation of good makes us confident. They are shy, accepting the
rules of society in which they have been trained, and not yet believing
in any other standard of honour. They have exalted notions, because
they have not yet been humbled by life or learnt its necessary limitations; moreover, their hopeful disposition makes them think themselves equal to great things—and that means having exalted notions.
They would always rather do noble deeds than useful ones: their lives
are regulated more by moral feeling than by reasoning; and whereas
reasoning leads us to choose what is useful, moral goodness leads us to
choose what is noble. They are fonder of their friends, intimates, and
companions than older men are, because they like spending their days
in the company of others, and have not yet come to value either their
friends or anything else by their usefulness to themselves. All their
mistakes are in the direction of doing things excessively and vehe-
mently. They disobey Chilon's precept by overdoing everything; they
love too much and hate too much, and the same with everything else.
They think they know everything, and are always quite sure about it;
this, in fact, is why they overdo everything. If they do wrong to others,

it is because they mean to insult them, not to do them actual harm. They are ready to pity others, because they think everyone an honest man, or anyhow better than he is: they judge their neighbor by their own harmless natures, and so cannot think he deserves to be treated in that way. They are fond of fun and therefore witty, wit being well-bred insolence.

Such, then, is the character of the young. The character of Elderly Men—men who are past their prime—may be said to be formed for the most part of elements that are the contrary of all these. They have lived many years; they have often been taken in, and often made mistakes; and life on the whole is a bad business. The result is that they are sure about nothing and *under-do* everything. They 'think,' but they never 'know'; and because of their hesitation they always add a 'possibly' or a 'perhaps,' putting everything this way and nothing positively. They are cynical; that is, they tend to put the worse construction on everything. Further, their experience makes them distrustful and therefore suspicious of evil. Consequently they neither love warmly nor hate bitterly, but following the hint of Bias they love as though they will some day hate and hate as though they will some day love. They are small-minded, because they have been humbled by life; their desires are set upon nothing more exalted or unusual than what will help them to keep alive. They are not generous, because money is one of the things they must have, and at the same time their experience has taught them how hard it is to get and how easy to lose. They are cowardly, and are always anticipating danger; unlike that of the young, who are warm-blooded, their temperament is chilly; old age has paved the way for cowardice; fear is, in fact, a form of chill. They love life; and all the more when their last day has come, because the object of all desire is something we have not got, and also because we desire most strongly that which we need most urgently. They are too fond of themselves; this is one form that small-mindedness takes. Because of this, they guide their lives too much by considerations of what is useful and too little by what is noble—for the useful is what is good for oneself, and the noble what is good absolutely. They are not shy, but shameless rather; caring less for what is noble than for what is useful, they feel contempt for what people may think of them. They lack confidence in the future; partly through experience—for most things go wrong, or anyhow turn out worse than one expects; and partly because of their cowardice. They live by memory rather than by hope; for what is left to them of life is but little as compared with the long past; and hope is of the future, memory of the past. This, again, is the cause of their loquacity; they are continually talking of the past, because they enjoy remembering it. Their fits of anger are sudden but feeble. Their sensual passions have either altogether gone or have lost their vigour: consequently they do not feel their passions much, and their actions are inspired less by what they do feel than by the love of gain. Hence men at this time of life are often supposed to have a self-controlled character; the fact is that their passions have slackened, and they are slaves to the love of gain. They guide their lives by reasoning more than by moral feeling; reasoning being directed to utility and moral feeling to moral goodness. If they wrong others, they mean to injure them, not to insult them. Old men may feel pity, as well as young men, but not for the same reason. Young men feel it out of kindness; old men out of weakness, imagining that anything that befalls any one else might easily happen to them, which, as we saw it, is a thought that excites pity. Hence they are querulous, and not disposed to jesting or laughter—the love of laughter being the very opposite of querulousness. . . .

4   As for Men in their Prime, clearly we shall find that they have a character between that of the young and that of the old, free from the extremes of either. They have neither that excess of confidence which amounts to rashness, nor too much timidity, but the right amount of each. They neither trust everybody nor distrust everybody, but judge people correctly. Their lives will be guided not by the sole consideration either of what is noble or of what is useful, but by both; neither by parsimony nor by prodigality, but by what is fit and proper. So, too, in regard to anger and desire; they will be brave as well as temperate, and temperate as well as brave; these virtues are divided between the young and the old; the young are brave but intemperate, the old temperate but cowardly. To put it generally, all the valuable qualities that youth and age divide between them are united in the prime of life, while all their excesses or defects are replaced by moderation and fitness. The body is in its prime from thirty to five-and-thirty; the mind about forty-nine.

FOR DISCUSSION

1. This essay was written by a man who was born 384 years before Christ. We are still reading his essay today. What can you say, then, about Aristotle's audience?

2. Do Aristotle's classifications of human beings hold for you? Support your answer with specific examples.

3. Why do you suppose Aristotle wrote this essay?

4. Do the categories of classification which Aristotle uses overlap?

5. The men-in-their-prime section of this essay is not nearly so long as the other two parts. Discuss this difference.

6. What are the essential qualities which Aristotle provides the reader for each stage of man?

7. Why do you suppose the word *woman* does not appear in the essay?

8. After Aristotle establishes the three basic categories of man, how does he further break these categories or classes down into their component parts?

9. Look back at the definition of *to tell* in the essay that introduces this part of the text. Which of the characteristics of the definition does this essay satisfy?

RICHARD W. BULLIET

Who in the world wants to read an essay on the camel? Who in the world wants to write *an essay on the camel? Richard W. Bulliet, a professor at Columbia University, finds a way to make a subject most people would not have the time or desire to learn about almost irresistible. The article originally appeared in* GEO, *a glossy picture magazine dedicated to presenting readers with "new insights into the current world scene."*

Let's Hear It for the Camel!

Conventional wisdom holds the wheel to be one of mankind's cleverest inventions and the camel to be one of God's clumsiest. So imagine my surprise when I discovered some years ago that between about A.D. 300 and 600, wheeled transport was virtually abandoned in the vast area lying between Morocco and Afghanistan. And imagine my wonderment when I was driven to the conclusion that it was the camel that was responsible for this remarkable development. Yes indeed! God's clumsiest creation, it turned out, had proved to be a far more efficient way of moving goods and people around the ancient Middle East than man's cleverest.

Carried away by this startling insight, I proceeded to make a study of camel history and, after prolonged combat with stacks of books retrieved from dusty and richly deserved obscurity, established myself as something of a world authority on the subject. Along the arduous road to this rare expertise, I also established certain landmarks:

3   —In 1971, I taught Harvard University's first course devoted exclusively to camels. Students flocked to enroll but found it difficult to justify this action to bill-paying parents. The course did not find a place in the core curriculum.

4   —In 1974, I gave a lecture on camels to cadets at West Point, the first such exposition since the U.S. Army liquidated, for $31 a head, its camel importation experiment of 1856–66. The next year, I was again invited to lecture at West Point—but on a different subject.

5   —In 1978, I addressed executives and employees of the Exxon Corporation on camels. They listened attentively but proved unprepared for my remarkably realistic limitation of the call of a male camel in rut. Millions for camel research were not forthcoming.

6   These chastening experiences, however, did not disquiet me as much as another discovery I made in the course of my research—namely, that no one is neutral about camels. More to the point, perhaps, it is hard to find anyone who is positive about them.

7   To be sure, it is possible to find a desert-struck romantic here and there who likes camels, and there are also a number of experienced camel people who have worked extensively with the animals in veterinary or military situations. But the former tend to let their heart get the better of their good sense, and the latter are as likely to recommend violence against the fractious beast as they are to tell affectionate anecdotes. An ancient veterinary sergeant major from General Allenby's Palestine campaign of 1917–18 told me that he and his men had carried ax handles with them to help manage the thousands of camels under their care. He strongly recommended belting a difficult camel between the eyes with an ax handle or, if caught unequipped, grabbing the beast between the nostrils and giving a sharp yank. I felt there was a somewhat negative note struck by these recommendations, but they were born of great experience and could not be dismissed lightly. . . .

8   We must, I feel, find a new image for the camel that is more in tune with the contemporary world and less a captive of history. As we sail into the 1980s, perhaps there is a ready handle in the era of energy shortages. The camel is simply an ingenious biological device engineered to attain maximum energy conservation combined with greatest economic utility over the broadest geographical and climatic range. Conservation is the key to future thinking about camels.

9   The camel device comes in two models, each with a number of color options. The model with two humps and comparatively long hair is known as the Bactrian, after the parts of southern Russia and northern Afghanistan where it was traditionally used for caravan work. The one-humped model is known as a dromedary, a word of Greek origin signifying running. Some dromedaries run fast; others don't. Nonetheless, a few writers on camels confusingly use dromedary to refer only

to those one-humped camels that run fast instead of to the whole species.

Aside from the matter of humps, the two models of camel have few 10 apparent physical differences. They interbreed, and the hybrid is a large, powerful camel sporting one long mound on its back, with an indentation toward the front betraying the two-humped half of its genetic heritage. Although the hybrid was once valuable as a pack animal, it is rarely bred today and can be considered a discontinued model.

So far as conservation goes, we start with water. Camels do not 11 store water; they simply do not expend it. Instead of perspiring in hot weather to keep its blood temperature even, the camel just gets hot. Its blood temperature may rise eleven degrees Fahrenheit before reaching an upper limit, at which point the animal finally begins to sweat. By then, however, it is late in the day; with a cool night ahead to bring its blood temperature back down, the camel doesn't need to lose much water by perspiration. For added efficiency, during the heat of the day the camel sits aligned with the sun's rays to minimize exposure of surface area to radiant heat.

Water economy is further promoted by a splendid set of kidneys that 12 concentrate waste materials to minimize water loss in urine, and a remarkable bloodstream that doesn't dry up as the camel dries out. A human perspiring in a hot desert will lose moisture from his blood if the water lost through perspiration is not replenished. Eventually, the blood thickens, becomes less able to transmit heat to the surface for cooling, and produces death by explosive heat rise. A camel, by contrast, can lose a quarter of its body weight in water with little loss from the blood itself. Water is chiefly taken from other body tissues, which are then rehydrated by unknown processes in less than twenty-four hours of the animal's getting a really big drink of water.

Since water conservation enables the camel to go for seven days 13 without drinking in torrid weather, or indefinitely if the grazing is green and moist, it can forage at a much greater distance from water sources than other animals. This means it can exploit desert grazing lands that are inaccessible to other animals. But it also means that the camel has to be able to live on whatever it can find to eat in the barren land. Two special adaptations facilitate this grazing on desert vegetation.

First, the camel is able to recycle nitrogen compounds within its 14 body instead of disposing of them as waste. Consequently, while most mammals languish on a diet of low-protein plants, a camel stuck on a patch of desert poorly provided with nutritious grazing does just fine.

Second, the legs on the same side of the camel's body move together 15 when it walks—in contrast to the more common animal pattern of diagonally opposed legs moving together. For a rider, this means a swaying ride that is sometimes reported to produce seasickness. But for the camel, it means an extremely long stride, since the hind leg can step forward beyond where the front leg on the same side had been planted. This, in turn, allows the camel to cover an enormous grazing area with minimum expenditure of energy.

16   In the area of insulation, the camel also affords a sterling example for our times. The long, ultrafine wool on the two-humped camel allows it to do caravan work trekking through the bitter cold and deep snow of a central Asian winter. Yet the coat of the one-humped camel has been shown to serve as a barrier against heat in the burning desert. The temperature recorded at the surface of the skin is appreciably cooler than that of the outer layer of wool.

17   Husbanding of food is another strong point of cameline conservation technique. The camel has the ability to store up food in the good times to see him through the bad. The fat supply in the humps is the animal's food reserve, which steadily becomes depleted when the camel goes without eating. And go without eating it does. Bactrian camels may eat little or nothing for months during their winter caravan season. Moreover, male camels go without food for weeks on end during the mating season, thus demonstrating a singlemindedness that might be considered a kind of conservation of lust.

18   Finally, the camel displays a thoroughly laudable conservation of nervous energy. Although a baggage camel is prone to comment noisily and negatively whenever a heavy load is fastened to its back, it bears up with remarkably little complaint when the going really gets rough. In fact, it will normally work right up to the point of death, refusing to rise under its load only when its energy has been sapped to the limit of its ability to survive.

19   Furthermore, the camel is singularly unresponsive to many common sources of pain and excitement. In battle, it remains calm enough to be used as a barricade or as a firing platform for small cannons, and it may even suffer bullet wounds and other injuries without comment.

20   Yet as remarkable as the camel's stoicism and capacity for conservation may be, they would not commend themselves to our admiration if they could not be harnessed for useful service. Today, when the machine has taken over—at least temporarily—the functions previously performed by camels, the exceptional utility of the animal is not well known. The extent and variety of that utility are worth recording, therefore, in case we ever need to call upon camels again when the oil wells run dry.

21   Certain camel services are better known than others. Camels frequently carry loads of 500 to 600 pounds (depending upon the specific breed and species) in the deepest cold or in the most torrid heat, in mountains or in deserts, and under the most adverse conditions of deprivation. Don't try them on mud, however. The hind legs are likely to slip apart and cause a nasty injury.

Beyond these obvious services, there are the animal products pro- 22 vided by the camel. Camel meat of varying quality is eaten in a number of countries. As with other animals, age and condition determine the succulence of the cut. Also, camel's milk is still a staple for a few camel-breeding tribes. Of greater commercial importance, however, is the camel's fine wool, which is produced for the market in several countries, including China, where a good two-humped camel naturally lets fall as much as fifteen pounds of thick winter coat every spring.

So much for the common uses of the camel. The uncommon ones 23 include the following: camels are used for pulling carts in Tunisia, Pakistan, northern India, and northern China; two generations ago, they were also used in Australia, where large teams of imported camels were hitched to huge supply wagons and competed effectively with the best teams of oxen and draft horses.

Camels also pull plows. Single animals are harnessed to the plow in 24 Tunisia and northern Saharan oases, while a pair of camels or a camel and another animal harnessed together perform this service in Morocco, the Canary Islands, Egypt, and elsewhere. Related camel services include the provision of animal power for the operation of mills (as can be seen in Iran and Afghanistan), irrigation wheels (a common sight in Egypt), and wells.

Under certain circumstances, camels have entertainment value as 25 well: camel wrestling, for example, remains a spectator sport in Turkey.

The list could go on to include the fact that a camel was used, 26 according to the household accounts of the fifteenth-century English baronial family of Furnivall Lestrange, "for taking messages to the neighbors." But one can protest too much the animal's virtues, and even conservation becomes tedious if harped on too long. So in a spirit of objectivity, I will close with something negative about camels, something they are not at all good at.

Camels are simply terrible jumpers.   27

FOR DISCUSSION

1. Robert W. Bulliet is a professor at Columbia University. Since it is not likely that he teaches in the camel department or majored in camels when he was in school, what could you guess might have led him to write this essay?

2. Make a list of five things you did not know about camels before you read this article that you now know.

3. What do you suppose the editors of *GEO* magazine were counting on about their readers when they decided to publish this essay?

4. Make a list of three subjects that you could write about that
   would be about as "useful" as camels but which, because of your
   own experience or interest, you could make interesting and
   informative.

5. What angle or framework did Bulliet put this information about
   camels into? What is the value of this approach? Is it in any way
   a detriment?

6. How did the author make this odd subject for an essay interesting
   to read—and worth your while?

JOAN DIDION

Written in 1976, this selection is taken from The White Album *(1979), a
collection of Joan Didion's magazine pieces. This essay is an example
of* to tell *writing that also has the voice and sensibility of the writer very
clearly displayed. Didion begins by talking about a visit she made with
her young daughter to a museum. Notice, however, how this personal
experience adds to rather than detracts from the information about the
artist Georgia O'Keeffe.*

Georgia O'Keeffe

1 "Where I was born and where and how I have lived is unimportant,"
Georgia O'Keeffe told us in the book of paintings and words published
in her ninetieth year on earth. She seemed to be advising us to forget
the beautiful face in the Stieglitz photographs. She appeared to be
dismissing the rather condescending romance that had attached to her
by then, the romance of extreme good looks and advanced age and
deliberate isolation. "It is what I have done with where I have been
that should be of interest." I recall an August afternoon in Chicago in
1973 when I took my daughter, then seven, to see what Georgia
O'Keeffe had done with where she had been. One of the vast O'Keeffe
"Sky Above Clouds" canvases floated over the back stairs in the
Chicago Art Institute that day, dominating what seemed to be several
stories of empty light, and my daughter looked at it once, ran to the
landing, and kept on looking. "Who drew it," she whispered after a
while. I told her. "I need to talk to her," she said finally.

My daughter was making, that day in Chicago, an entirely uncon- 2
scious but quite basic assumption about people and the work they do.
She was assuming that the glory she saw in the work reflected a glory
in its maker, that the painting was the painter as the poem is the poet,
that every choice one made alone—every word chosen or rejected,
every brush stroke laid or not laid down—betrayed one's character.
Style is character. It seemed to me that afternoon that I had rarely seen
so instinctive an application of this familiar principle, and I recall being
pleased not only that my daughter responded to style as character but
that it was Georgia O'Keeffe's particular style to which she responded:
this was a hard woman who had imposed her 192 square feet of clouds
on Chicago.

"Hardness" has not been in our century a quality much admired in 3
women, nor in the past twenty years has it even been in official favor
for men. When hardness surfaces in the very old we tend to transform
it into "crustiness" or eccentricity, some tonic pepperiness to be
indulged at a distance. On the evidence of her work and what she has
said about it, Georgia O'Keeffe is neither "crusty" nor eccentric. She
is simply hard, a straight shooter, a woman clean of received wisdom
and open to what she sees. This is a woman who could early on dismiss
most of her contemporaries as "dreamy," and would later single out
one she liked as "a very poor painter." (And then add, apparently by
way of softening the judgment: "I guess he wasn't a painter at all. He
had no courage and I believe that to create one's own world in any of
the arts takes courage.") This is a woman who in 1939 could advise her
admirers that they were missing her point, that their appreciation of her
famous flowers was merely sentimental. "When I paint a red hill," she
observed coolly in the catalogue for an exhibition that year, "you say it
is too bad that I don't always paint flowers. A flower touches almost
everyone's heart. A red hill doesn't touch everyone's heart." This is a
woman who could describe the genesis of one of her most well-known
paintings—the "Cow's Skull: Red, White and Blue" owned by the
Metropolitan—as an act of quite deliberate and derisive orneriness. "I
thought of the city men I had been seeing in the East," she wrote.
"They talked so often of writing the Great American Novel—the Great
American Play—the Great American Poetry. . . . So as I was painting
my cow's head on blue I thought to myself, 'I'll make it an American
painting. They will not think it great with the red stripes down the
sides—Red, White and Blue—but they will notice it.' "

The city men. The men. They. The words crop up again and again as 4
this astonishingly aggressive woman tells us what was on her mind
when she was making her astonishingly aggressive paintings. It was
those city men who stood accused of sentimentalizing her flowers: "I
made you take time to look at what I saw and when you took time to
really notice my flower you hung all your associations with flowers on

my flower and you write about my flower as if I think and see what you think and see—and I don't.'' *And I don't.* Imagine those words spoken, and the sound you hear is *don't tread on me*. "The men" believed it impossible to paint New York, so Georgia O'Keeffe painted New York. "The men" didn't think much of her bright color, so she made it brighter. The men yearned toward Europe so she went to Texas, and then New Mexico. The men talked about Cézanne, "long involved remarks about the 'plastic quality' of his form and color," and took one another's long involved remarks, in the view of this angelic rattlesnake in their midst, altogether too seriously. "I can paint one of those dismal-colored paintings like the men," the woman who regarded herself always as an outsider remembers thinking one day in 1922, and she did: a painting of a shed "all low-toned and dreary with the tree beside the door." She called this act of rancor "The Shanty" and hung it in her next show. "The men seemed to approve of it," she reported fifty-four years later, her contempt undimmed. "They seemed to think that maybe I was beginning to paint. That was my only low-toned dismal-colored painting."

5   Some women fight and others do not. Like so many successful guerrillas in the war between the sexes, Georgia O'Keeffe seems to have been equipped early with an immutable sense of who she was and a fairly clear understanding that she would be required to prove it. On the surface her upbringing was conventional. She was a child on the Wisconsin prairie who played with china dolls and painted watercolors with cloudy skies because sunlight was too hard to paint and, with her brother and sisters, listened every night to her mother read stories of the Wild West, of Texas, of Kit Carson and Billy the Kid. She told adults that she wanted to be an artist and was embarrassed when they asked what kind of artist she wanted to be: she had no idea "what kind." She had no idea what artists did. She had never seen a picture that interested her, other than a pen-and-ink Maid of Athens in one of her mother's books, some Mother Goose illustrations printed on cloth, a tablet cover that showed a little girl with pink roses, and the painting of Arabs on horseback that hung in her grandmother's parlor. At thirteen, in a Dominican convent, she was mortified when the sister corrected her drawing. At Chatham Episcopal Institute in Virginia she painted lilacs and sneaked time alone to walk out to where she could see the line of the Blue Ridge Mountains on the horizon. At the Art Institute in Chicago she was shocked by the presence of live models and wanted to abandon anatomy lessons. At the Art Students League in New York one of her fellow students advised her that, since he would be a great painter and she would end up teaching painting in a girls' school, any work of hers was less important than modeling for him. Another painted over her work to show her how the Impression-

ists did trees. She had not before heard how the Impressionists did trees and she did not much care.

At twenty-four she left all those opinions behind and went for the first time to live in Texas, where there were no trees to paint and no one to tell her how not to paint them. In Texas there was only the horizon she craved. In Texas she had her sister Claudia with her for a while, and in the late afternoons they would walk away from town and toward the horizon and watch the evening star come out. "That evening star fascinated me," she wrote. "It was in some way very exciting to me. My sister had a gun, and as we walked she would throw bottles into the air and shoot as many as she could before they hit the ground. I had nothing but to walk into nowhere and the wide sunset space with the star. Ten watercolors were made from that star." In a way one's interest is compelled as much by the sister Claudia with the gun as by the painter Georgia with the star, but only the painter left us this shining record. Ten watercolors were made from that star.

FOR DISCUSSION

1. What keeps this from being a personal experience essay?

2. How does the information about Joan Didion's experience complement the information about Georgia O'Keeffe?

3. Didion attempts to get at the essence of O'Keeffe in this essay. In what way is the essay a *definition* of O'Keeffe? What would be the key parts of the definition?

4. How does Didion write this essay so that it is not just a narrative of O'Keeffe's life? Make a list of at least five things Didion does to add spark and significance to the details she gives about O'Keeffe.

5. How has Didion also used the rhetorical pattern of classification in this essay?

6. Think of someone whose life you know enough about to write an essay on. How would you go about selecting the details or characteristics or events that you would choose to include? In what way, by this selection, would the essay also then be about you, the writer, as well as the person about whom you were writing?

BUSINESS LETTER

Here is a business letter sent to give information. It is powerfully clear. The letter also has "heart" at the same time that it is business-like, precise, and explanatory. There is a voice behind the words, something not always true about business-letter writing.

UNITED STATES POSTAL SERVICE
SEATTLE BULK MAIL CENTER
Box 5000, 34301 - 9th Avenue South
Federal Way, Washington 98003

August 18, 1977

Dear Postal Customer:

Your mail transmitted with this letter was damaged in a vehicle accident enroute from Seattle, Washington to Dallas, Texas on August 17, 1977. The Postal Service was saddened to learn of the death of both contract drivers as a result of this accident.

We are sorry that your package was one of those involved. We have done all we can to reconstruct the package. If any item might be missing, write us immediately with a complete description, as some items were separated. We will do everything to help you.

H. J. Hays
General Manager

FOR DISCUSSION

1. This letter belies all the usual expectations about form letters: that they are impersonal, dull, and difficult to understand. What does the writer do that makes the letter "personal" even though it is addressed to "Dear Postal Customer"? What aspects of the form letter remain nonetheless?

2. What is the writer's relationship to the reader?

3. On what does the writer place emphasis?

4. What circumstances and situations existed that were the "constraints" inside which the writer had to operate?

5. How is this business letter a "found poem"?

BUSINESS REPORT

This report was prepared by a student as the first step in the preparation of the term's main project in her technical writing class. Notice how Reed manages to make a standard format, the business report, read as though a person wrote it and not a machine. Notice, also, how the form *of the report supports and structures the writing.*

DATE: June 30, 1982
TO: Professor Jane Harkins
FROM: Linda C. Reed
SUBJECT: Proposed Topic of Research for Technical Report

The topic I propose to research for my technical report is the problem people in business and science have eliminating gobbledygook from their written communications. People in any profession, however, will improve their writing by eliminating gobbledygook.

What is gobbledygook? It is bloating sentences with unnecessary words or using pompous words and phrases where a short and simple word will do. My report will outline ways to get rid of gobbledygook and ways to improve your writing style in general. Why write anything if your reader will not understand what you have written? Writing shorter and simpler letters, memos, reports, or instructions will be easier on your reader, although harder on you. But once you get the hang of it, your writing will become clearer and more concise. This will be an asset both to you and to your reader.

Sources of gobbledygook

Examples of gobbledygook are easy to find. A well-known source is the instruction manual. Most instruction manuals are so complicated that no one can understand them. For an example, look at the following sentence:

Maximum flexibility must be built into the design of curricular modules for the PBVTE system which has just been described for an organizational structure facilitating futuristic, model cooperation pedagogical curricula.

By the time you get to the end of the sentence, you have forgotten what the beginning said. You are probably familiar with the gobbledygook used in legal talk and documents, too. Real estate and insurance laws are full of jargon and repetitious phrases. Politicians and academicians are also adept at speaking and writing gobbledygook. Most people write it because they are either incompetent or wish to be vague. Sometimes, hackneyed phrases like "is of the opinion" or "comes into conflict with" seem to come to mind before "believes" or "conflicts." We just write whatever comes into our heads first. But many times, a writer who wants to avoid an issue or sound intelligent or mysterious will surround a statement with gobbledygook. Whatever the reasons for using it are, gobbledygook remains a problem. There are ways to avoid it, however, and those ways are what I will research for my technical report.

Procedure

The majority of my information will come from sources in the university library. So far I have found eleven books that have information that I may be able to use. I also have a list of five periodicals, four indexes, and a few government agencies which may have helpful publications that I could use. The books that I have already found also have bibliographies of other books that may be possible references. Some of the sources I have already looked at have copyright dates of 1978 and 1980. However, these books have used sources from the '50s and '60s as references. I assume, then, that less current books will still provide me with valuable information.

I plan to follow the following outline to carry out my project:

Task 1. *Research sources.* I have already done about half of this job. I have located several sources and have leads on a few others.

Task 2. *Gather data.* Now I need to weed through the sources I have found, writing notecards on those things that are relevant, and throwing out those that aren't.

Task 3. *Outline.* Next I will need to organize the notes I have taken according to topic and write an outline.

Task 4. *Rough Draft.* Using the outline I wrote in Task 3, I will write a rough draft,

Task 5. *Editing*. I will proofread, correct, and make any adjustments needed in the rough draft.

Task 6. *Final Report*. I will make final changes, type, and proofread my report for typing mistakes.

Task 7. *Oral Report*. I will prepare an oral presentation on my report and deliver it to the class.

Qualifications

By organizing a schedule and strictly sticking to it, I should be able to research and write my report in a short time. Because my report deals with an area of technical writing, classwork will reinforce what I learn from research. We have discussed gobbledygook (jargon) in class, and we should be conscious of it when doing assigned exercises. My interest in technical writing as a profession will make the work of writing the report more interesting. Also, I should learn from the research that I do and so improve my writing skills.

Conclusion

I propose to do research on gobbledygook and how to get rid of it. My technical report will provide information useful to me and to the rest of our technical writing class. All writers will improve their writing greatly if they work to abolish gobbledygook from their writing. I urge you to accept my proposal for the benefit of the class and, so that I may complete the report by the deadline set in my timetable, I hope that you will act quickly. I am available at any time for a conference to discuss the assets of my proposal and any revisions you may think necessary.

FOR DISCUSSION

1. If you were required to define what a *report* is after having read only this one, what could you say?

2. Specifically, how does a report differ from an essay?

3. This report is set up as a memo. In what way is it a memo, and in what way is it a report?

4. Make a list of five things in this report that add to its interest, that keep it from being boring.

5. How does this writer establish her credibility in this report? Why is it important to establish credibility in a report? Is credibility more or less critical in a report than an article? Discuss in detail.

WRITING YOUR OWN
The Information Essay

Before you begin to write your own essay, think about the configuration that comprises Loren Eiseley's essay, "How Flowers Changed the World."

Motivation (an educated guess): to educate readers about a subject.
Circumstance/Situation: a book-length manuscript.
Audience: readers with a non-specialized interest in science.
Writer's Relationship to Audience: excited expert to interested reader.
Emphasis: on details to illustrate the subject.
Form: essay (or chapter in a book).
Intention (an educated guess): to inspire readers to fathom the interrelatedness of all of life.

What are the configurations of the other essays in this chapter?

DESIGNING YOUR OWN CONFIGURATION

Here are some suggestions for writing your own information essay:

1. Write an essay about a place you have been on vacation for readers of a travel magazine.
2. Write an essay about someone you know, making that information interesting to a person who does not know her or him. Make the essay similar to those that have appeared in *Reader's Digest,* "My Most Unforgettable Character."
3. Write an essay about different kinds of car owners for a popular magazine.
4. Write an essay about something you have learned in one of your other classes—history, psychology, computer science, for example—for your classmates, and try to make a potentially boring topic interesting.

Use the suggestions in this chart to help you make your own information configuration:

Designing Your Own Configuration for an Information Essay

MOTIVE	CIRCUMSTANCE/ SITUATION	AUDIENCE	RELATIONSHIP TO AUDIENCE
To educate readers	For x magazine with x deadline and x length requirement	Classmates	Informer to not informed
To share your research		Professor	Excited researcher to interested reader
To gain recognition in your field	For any number of magazines that serve the general reader, each with its own requirements	Readers of x magazine	
To sell an article		General public	Person who has learned to person who does not yet know
To tell about something new that you have discovered	For an assignment to contribute an essay to a book	Specialized group of people	
To describe a place you love		A specific club	
To satisfy an assignment			
To give employer information			
To give customer information			

EMPHASIS	FORM	INTENTION
On facts	Essay	To give accurate facts
On organization of information	Article	To interest reader in whole area
On reader's relationship to information	Letter	To explain something that might not be known or might be confusing
On details	Report	
On examples	Speech	To educate

RULES FOR AN INFORMATION ESSAY

1. Be certain that you have *enough* information before you begin.
2. Think about how to make this information alive, stimulating, interesting for the reader.
3. Decide who your readers are going to be, and write specifically for those people.
4. Be clear.
5. Think about defining, classifying, and explaining for your readers so that they can understand the information.
6. Put the information into a frame, or give it an angle that will add interest.

RHETORICAL PATTERNS OFTEN APPEARING IN INFORMATION ESSAYS:

Cause/Effect: How to Explain the Reasons and Consequences

1. Giving the cause and effect of a situation means that you *(a)* identify the thing/person/act that brings about a particular result and *(b)* show *how* it caused that result.
2. Be sure that the causes you give are sufficient to convince the reader. Even after you have isolated the cause of a situation in your mind, ask yourself, "Are there any other causes I should include?"
3. Be sure that there actually *is* a relationship between the cause and effect. If you can't prove this relationship exists in some logical, objective way, be sure that your reader understands that you are offering a personal view of the relationship between the cause and effect. Take the time in your essay to explain to the reader the connections you see.
4. Let the purpose of your writing determine the form your essay takes.

Definition: How to Tell What Something Means

1. *To define* means *to explain the nature or essential qualities of a word, function,* etc. A definition determines or fixes the boundaries of the thing being discussed. The original meaning of the word *definition* was *to set boundaries,* and that is what a good definition does for the reader: it helps him or her stake out, limit, see the boundaries of a term.

2. A formal definition includes the term being defined, the class to which it belongs, and what differentiates it from other things in that class.

3. An informal definition takes several forms: defining by using a word that means approximately the same thing *(to gloat* means *to act superior and proud);* by using an opposite *(love* is *not using someone);* by showing the term's origin *(defining* originally meant *setting boundaries);* by using personal experience *(summer* means *time off, rest, and fun);* by giving examples *(eating well* is *having fresh vegetables and fruit, avoiding sugar, and staying off fried foods).*

4. Use definitions in your writing when there is any chance that your readers will not know the formal meaning of a word or the informal way you are using it. Being clear on the terms in a piece of writing is absolutely necessary for both the reader and the writer if communication is to occur.

Classification: How to Show Common Characteristics

1. *To classify* means *to organize into groups according to common characteristics, qualities, traits,* etc.; *to put into basic categories;* or *to break down into component parts.*

2. When you set up a classification system, be certain that the categories don't overlap. Also make very clear to the reader what the groups are and how you decide what went into each group.

3. Don't oversimplify when you classify. Sometimes in an attempt to make everything orderly, a person will push a subject, person, item, etc., into a category where it doesn't really belong just to make the classification systematic. Don't undercut your credibility with your audience by forcing an item into a group where it doesn't clearly belong.

4. Use a classification system when it will help your reader follow your thoughts or explanation point by point.

James Dickey Talks About Writing

James Dickey is regarded as one of the major poets in America in the twentieth century. Buckdancer's Choice, *a collection of his poems, won the National Book Award for poetry in 1966. In 1977 he gave the inaugural poem when Jimmy Carter became president. His novel* Deliverance *not only achieved prominence as a book but became a popular motion picture as well. Dickey's latest book of poetry,* Puella, *was published in 1982.*

In the pages that follow you will find an essay that Dickey wrote on how to enjoy poetry. Following this is an interview with James Dickey in which he discusses writing the essay. You will be able to get a clearer sense of how *writing happens after you read what Dickey has to say. You will also be able to see how the constraints of circumstance and situation in a writing configuration can actually be an asset to the writer instead of a restriction and detriment.*

The essay, "How to Enjoy Poetry," especially given its subject, has an interesting background. The International Paper Company commissioned Dickey to write the essay as part of their "Power of the Written Word" advertising program. In the note that accompanied this essay, which appeared in Newsweek *magazine, someone from International Paper wrote, "Today, the printed word is more vital than ever. Now there is more need than ever for all of us to* read *better,* write *better, and* communicate *better."*

How to Enjoy Poetry

What is poetry? And why has it been around so long? Many have suspected that it was invented as a school subject, because you have to take exams on it. But that is not what poetry is or why it is still around. That's not what it feels like, either. When you really feel it, a new part of you happens, or an old part is renewed, with surprise and delight at being what it is.

Where poetry is coming from

From the beginning, men have known that words and things, words and actions, words and feelings, go together, and that they can go together in thousands of different ways, according to who is using them. Some ways go shallow, and some go deep.

Your connection with other imaginations

The first thing to understand about poetry is that it comes to you from outside you, in books or in words, but that for it to live, something from within you must come to it and meet it and complete it. Your response with your own mind and body and memory and emotions gives the poem its ability to work its magic; if you give to it, it will give to you, and give plenty.

When you read, don't let the poet write down to you; read up to him. Reach for him from your gut out, and the heart and muscles will come into it, too.

Which sun? Whose stars?

The sun is new every day, the ancient philosopher Heraclitus said. The sun of poetry is new every day, too, because it is seen in different ways by different people who have lived under it, lived with it, responded to it. Their lives are different from yours, but by means of the special spell that poetry brings to the *fact of* the sun—everybody's sun; yours, too—you can come into possession of many suns: as many as men and women have ever been able to imagine. Poetry makes possible the deepest kind of personal possession of the world.

The most beautiful constellation in the winter sky is Orion, which ancient poets thought looked like a hunter, up there, moving across heaven with his dog Sirius. What is this hunter made out of stars hunting for? What does he mean? Who owns him, if anybody? The poet Aldous Huxley felt that he did, and so, in Aldous Huxley's universe of personal emotion, he did.

Up from among the emblems of
  the wind into its heart of power,
The Huntsman climbs, and all his
  living stars
Are bright, and all are mine.

Where to start

The beginning of your true encounter with poetry should be simple. It should bypass all classrooms, all textbooks, courses, examinations, and libraries and go straight to the things that make your own existence exist: to your body and nerves and blood and muscles. Find your own way—a secret way that just maybe you don't know yet—to open yourself as wide as you can and as deep as you can to the moment, the *now* of your own existence and the endless mystery of it, and perhaps at the same time to one other thing that is not you, but is out there: a handful of gravel is a good place to start. So is an ice cube—what more mysterious and beautiful *interior* of something has there ever been?

As for me, I like the sun, the source of all living things, and on certain days very good-feeling, too. "Start with the sun," D. H. Lawrence said, "and everything will slowly, slowly happen." Good advice. And a lot *will* happen.

What is more fascinating than a rock, if you really feel it and *look* at it, or more interesting than a leaf?

Horses,   I   mean;   butterflies,
  whales;
Mosses, and stars; and gravelly
Rivers, and fruit.

Oceans, I mean; black valleys;
  corn;
Brambles, and cliffs; rock, dirt,
  dust, ice . . .

Go back and read this list—it is quite a list, Mark Van Doren's list!—item by item. Slowly. Let each of these things call up an image out of your own life.

Think and feel. What moss do you see? Which horse? What field of corn? What brambles are *your* brambles? Which river is most yours?

The poem's way of going

Part of the spell of poetry is in the rhythm of language, used by poets who understand how powerful a factor rhythm can be, how compelling and unforgettable. Almost anything put into rhythm and rhyme is more memorable than the same thing said in prose. Why this is, no one knows completely, though the answer is surely rooted far down in the biology by means of which we exist; in the circulation of the blood that goes forth from the heart and comes back, and in the repetition of breathing. Croesus was a rich Greek king, back in the sixth century before Christ, but this tombstone was not his:

> No Croesus lies in the grave you see;
> I was a poor laborer, and this suits me.

That is plain-spoken and definitive. You believe it, and the rhyme helps you believe it and keep it.

Some things you'll find out

Writing poetry is a lot like a contest with yourself, and if you like sports and games and competitions of all kinds, you might like to try writing some. Why not?

The possibilities of rhyme are great. Some of the best fun is in making up your own limericks. There's no reason you can't invent limericks about anything that comes to your mind. No reason. Try it.

The problem is to find three words that rhyme and fit into a meaning. "There was a young man from. . ." *Where* was he from? What situation was he in? How can these things fit into the limerick form—a form everybody knows—so that the rhymes

"pay off," and give that sense of completion and inevitability that is so deliciously memorable that nothing else is like it?

How it goes with you

The more your encounter with poetry deepens, the more your experience of your own life will deepen, and you will begin to see things by means of words, and words by means of things.

You will come to understand the world as it interacts with words, as it can be re-created by words, by rhythms and by images.

You'll understand that this condition is one charged with vital possibilities. You will pick up meaning more quickly—and you will *create* meaning, too, for yourself and for others.

Connections between things will exist for you in ways that they never did before. They will shine with unexpectedness, wide-openness, and you will go toward them, on your own path. "Then. . ." as Dante says, ". . . Then will your feet be filled with good desire." You will know this is happening the first time you say, of something you never would have noticed before, "Well, would you look at *that!* Who'd 'a thunk it?" (Pause, full of new light)

"*I* thunk it!"

Interview

EC: Jim, I realize that the initial motivation for writing this essay was the request you received from International Paper Company. After you decided to write it, however, what was your *intention* in writing it? What specifically did you want to do in the essay, to accomplish?

JD: Well, I wanted to reduce my ideas about the function of poetry and the possibilities of it, and sort of get that codified by reducing it down into the basic elements: elements like what *do* I think? What do I think poetry is? What does poetry do and how should it be approached? What is the enormous value that there is in it?

EC: When you were writing the essay, did you picture a particular audience? Did you have in mind any particular group of people?

JD: No. I wanted to write to any and all *possible* audiences. I wanted it to be accessible to anybody; in Mary Ann Moore's words, "As in plain language that dogs and cats can read." [laughter]

EC: That's wonderful. What determined the length of the essay?

JD: Well, in any situation where you have a piece of writing that must fit a certain format physically—in this case double page in a magazine (and we wanted large type)—you just figure out approximately how many words will fit. And so that basically is what we did. That, actually, can be very helpful, you know, in requiring you to condense your ideas and to make the ideas flow coherently from one topic to another.

EC: Jim, how long did it take you to write this essay?

JD: I don't really know. I wrote several drafts of it until I got it. What I wanted to do was to have a sense of progression about what I was saying and lead the readers, whoever they might turn out to be, through a succession of related ideas from one poem to another.

EC: So you didn't have any kind of imposed deadline?

JD: No, not really. There was a sort of provisional one, as I remember. But that was just another limitation. Mr. Auden used to say that he welcomed that sort of restriction because it was a test and a challenge of his own creativity to be able to

satisfy artificial conditions of that sort.

EC: After you sent this essay to the company, did they ask you to revise it after they received it?

JD: No. I don't think so. No. It was slightly longer, and I think I may have taken out 50 words or something like that.

EC: Good. If this essay had the impact you wanted it to have, what would that impact be?

JD: It would change the sensibility of the human race infinitely for the better. It would make people apprehend the miracle of existence in the way it deserves to be apprehended.

EC: Did you have any false starts?

JD: No. I started with the Van Doren list of things which has always been my favorite of his poems, of that gentle and kindly fellow's poems; I started out with that list and built the essay around it. I wanted something concrete in it. Some concrete quotation that would embody what I would be talking about in the rest of the piece.

EC: So you did think about the approach before you actually started?

JD: Yes, I had an idea of what might work, and I started out with that idea. Of course, you change as you go along—you change things around a lot. That's the exciting part of it. The change. To change things for the better. You continually upgrade.

EC: So the form emerges as you write the essay?

JD: That's right. Organically.

EC: It's an organic process, then, even though often writing is *taught* as though it were a static process, as though you fit it into a box?

JD: That's true. Writing is *not* static. The worse thing you can have in any field—whether you write it or read it or apprehend it in some way—is any sort of fixed and rigid opinion. Because the whole thing is a flow.

EC: Jim, do you write—did you write this essay—in a favorite place? Where *do* you write?

JD: Well, I write anywhere. I'm a creature of the service years, and I learned to write under any and all conditions. I think the best place to learn to write is on a troop train! You learn to write on a troop train, you can write anywhere! I write anywhere I happen to be—on an airplane or in a restaurant or just walking, dawdling along.

EC: And then revision comes to you later and . . .

JD: Yes, if I have any virtue as a writer, it's in the act of revision and modification and metaphorsis of the subject from one thing to something I think is better.

EC: So, with this particular essay probably you went through three or four revisions?

JD: Many more than that. Fifty.

EC: Fifty revisions for this essay?

JD: At least. At least.

EC: I think freshmen students would be astonished to know that an essay could go through that many revisions.

JD: Yes. Well, the main thing is to get the sense of its being worked over out of it. That's what the revisions try to do—to make the writing

seem effortless and seem like the natural thing that should be said.

EC: Yes. Something new seems to emerge in every revision—each revision is a new work.

JD: Yes. I remember reading something about Dylan Thomas (I think most writers are interested in other writers' working methods—I know I am). Dylan Thomas would copy a whole poem out again if he'd changed so much as a semi-colon or a comma. If he took it out and put it back in he would copy the whole thing over again, the whole thing. Laboriously, usually in long hand. And he said that this was his way of keeping the poem together.

That is something like what I do, not because he did it, because I had been doing it for many years before I read about him—but it's nice to be in that sort of company in work methods if not in any other, if not in anything else. [laughter]

EC: How do you know, Jim, when to turn loose a piece.

JD: Well I have only one rule of thumb: if I can give the poem, or whatever the piece of writing is, the coldest and deepest scrutiny I can bring to bear on it, and I can't see that I can do anything that would not diminish it or make it less good, then it's got to be ready. Otherwise, you'd write on the same poem for your whole life and never write anything else. What the French poet Valerie says is very instructive. He says, "One never finishes a poem, one abandons it." But I don't think you should abandon it without a long and honorable fight to help it realize what its intentions seem to be.

EC: Jim, when you teach the writing

of poetry at the university, how do you teach? [James Dickey is Poet-in-Residence at the University of South Carolina in Columbia.]

JD: Well, I try to bring out whatever instruction I have to give over a period of a whole year. The first semester is dedicated to the exploration of the formal part of poetry. I don't really call the course "poetry"; poetry is difficult to achieve. Poetry is memorable and at best unforgettable rhythmical language. It's hard to get that. And a lot of it is luck.

EC: A lot of luck?

JD: Yes. But verse composition and the forms and the demands of the formal elements or what is called the received forms—the traditional forms—can be taught in the same sense that physics can be taught, or mathematics. You can teach that because that is codified.

Poetry, though, at least in the sense of formal poetry, is something that happens within the form—something miraculous that happens within the form, and to a certain extent because of the forms. That's the whole first semester—forms. One form a week. One after another, an assignment a week. And that's the whole first term. But the second semester is devoted to the working out of a single poem. Each student works the whole semester on one poem, trying it a lot of different ways and trying to find the ideal poem.

EC: A whole semester on one poem?

JD: On one poem. Right. [Pause.]

EC: Thank you, Jim. Everything you have said—about the essay and about the writing of poetry—is directly applicable to the writing classroom.

JD: It's been my pleasure.

Venita VanCaspel Talks About Writing

Venita VanCaspel is the author of a number of books on money. Her book Money Dynamics for the 1980s *has already sold over 225,000 copies. She is the president of the stock brokerage firm, VanCaspel & Company, Inc., and owner of VanCaspel Planning Services, a financial planning agency. VanCaspel is a nationally known speaker and consultant and appears on her own television program, "Money Matters," which is broadcast on 184 public television stations. National business and money magazines regularly quote VanCaspel's opinions and refer to her books.*

The following selection is taken from "You Can Become a Millionaire," a chapter in Money Dynamics for the 1980s. *In the interview with VanCaspel following the selection, she discusses the process she went through in writing the book.*

You Can Become a Millionaire

It is only fair to tell you I've never helped anyone become wealthy overnight. I've never helped someone with $10,000 turn it quickly into a million. The only people I've ever helped make a million dollars in a relatively brief period of time are those who brought me a million dollars to invest. Before you become too impressed, remember that it takes only an average return of 10 percent compounded to double your money in 7.2 years. At 12 percent it takes 6 years; and at 15 percent, 4.8 years.

I remember calling the office of Percy Foreman, the nationally known and brilliant criminal lawyer. I was calling to invite him to be my guest on my weekly television program, "Successful Texans."

When I asked to speak to him, the receptionist blurted out, "He's in jail." After chuckling over this literal response, I left word for him to call me when he "got out of jail." Later that afternoon he called, and I invited him to be my guest. He accepted my invitation; and just as I was about to say my goodbye, he said, "Aren't you that lady stock broker? Can you make me rich?" I answered, "Mr. Foreman, I understand you are already rich; but I believe I can make you richer."

Let's assume that you do not have the elusive million with which to start your high adventure. Is it still possible for you to become a millionaire? The answer is probably yes, if you have the discipline to save, the inclination to study, and a life span of sufficient length.

First, let me say that there are more desirable goals in life than becoming a millionaire. But if this is your desire, there are some very practical ways to approach your objective. To reach any goal, the first step is to divide it into its component parts so that it can be approached one step at a time.

Component parts of a million dollars

What are the component parts of a million dollars? It's $1000 multiplied by 1000, isn't it? Trying to reach a million dollars in your lifetime may not be all that difficult to do.

How do you obtain the first $1000? The most obvious beginning is to save from current income. If you save slightly under $20 per week, you should have your $1000 in a year. Or if you do not want to wait until you have saved the $1000, you can start investing as you earn on a weekly or monthly basis from your current income. Another possibility is to borrow the $1000 from the bank at the beginning and pay the bank back on a monthly basis. This could give you a head start toward your goal.

Therefore, the first requirement for reaching your goal is the ability to set aside the relatively small amount of $20 per week.

Money, yield, time

The second requirement is to obtain a high return produced by adherence to aggressive but sound investment practices. These can be readily learned if your desire is strong enough.

Third, a life span of sufficient length.

So you see, the two most important things are time and yield. If you set your sights on a million dollars, you must keep these two factors in mind. Time is something over which you have very little control. But yield is different. I personally feel that anyone of good intelligence has the potential of earning a high return on his investment, and high returns are absolute musts if you ever expect to become a millionaire. When we speak of "yield," we ordinarily think of income (dividends or interest) as an annual return on the sum invested, expressed in the form of a percentage. For instance, if you receive $5 at the end of a year on a $100 investment, your yield is 5 percent. However, we shall broaden this definition and use "yield" to describe any distribution, plus any growth in market value. For example, if $100 grows to $318 in 10 years, we would say its "yield" is 12 percent.

One thing I think you must be fully aware of is the magic that comes from compounding the rate of return. This means that you are never to treat any income, capital appreciation, or equity buildup as spendable during the period you are building toward your million-dollar goal, but only as returns that are to be reinvested to increase your accumulation. In other words, don't eat your children. Let them produce more children, and before long you'll have a whole army of dollars working for you.

For the purpose of our calculations, any taxes that you must pay on your investments are deemed as having come from another source.

One of the most important things you must remember is how important the rate of return you receive on your investment is to your compounding. For instance, if you can put to work $1000 each year and average a compound rate of 10 percent per annum, you will be able to reach your goal in 48.7 years (taxes considered as coming from another source). However, if you can increase the compound rate to 20 percent per annum, you can reach your goal in 29.2 years. So you see it does make a great deal of difference what return you obtain on your money.

Diversification—based on demand/supply

Risk in investing can be reduced by following some basic investment principles. As you have already become aware, one of the most important principles is diversification—spreading your risks.

After you've made that important

decision, what investment media do you use? You stand back and determine where the demand is greater than the supply. You learned in Basic Economics 101 something that you must never forget: the law of supply and demand. Regardless of how diligently governments and economists have tried over the years, they have never been able to repeal it for any length of time. Russia has tried it and failed, as is evidenced by the millionaires now appearing on the scene in Communist Poland; England has attempted it and brought a once proud empire of plenty to its knees, and our own Congress continues to attempt to repeal this universal law. Their action has caused shortages and disruptions in energy, beef, housing, etc.

In making your determination of where the demand is greater than the supply, be an alert reader of the daily metropolitan newspaper; also read such papers and publications as *The Wall Street Journal, Time, Business Week, U.S. News and World Report, Fortune, Forbes,* and *Money Magazine.* Also begin to study the St. Louis Federal Reserve Board reports. You'll begin to develop an awareness of demands and shortages.

Avoid the blue chip syndrome

There are those who have the mistaken idea that all one has to do to make money in the stock market is to buy "blue chips" and throw them in the drawer and forget about them. In my opinion, this can be riskier than buying more aggressive stocks and watching them like a hawk. The "blue chips" of today may become the "red chips" or "white chips" or "buffalo chips" of tomorrow. We live in a dynamic, throbbing, changing economy.

Just think back a few years. What car did the "man of distinction" drive? A Packard. I would have had difficulty convincing my father that only a few years later the manufacturers of the Packard automobile would be out of business. At the same time, what was the chief family home entertainment medium before television? It was radio, wasn't it? And who was the chief manufacturer of that half-egg-shaped wooden box in every home? Atwater-Kent. As you know, the Atwater-Kent Company no longer exists. You live in a world of constant change, and you must always be alert and ahead of this change if you want to become a millionaire through your investment know-how. You must sharpen your talents to predict trends before they happen, and move out before the trend has run its course.

If the money supply is being greatly restrained in our country, as you've already learned, you will want to develop a more conservative approach to the stock market. As the supply is even more diminished, move into money market funds so that you will have adequate liquidity to go back into the market as the money supply is accelerated and also to enjoy the higher yield that money will attract during this period of short supply.

Dollar-cost-averaging

As discussed previously, dollar-cost-averaging is another approach. Timing can be difficult. Dollar-cost-averaging in large or small amounts can be done by anyone who has a regular amount to invest over a period of years. Using this plan, you invest the same amount of money in the same security at the same interval. This will always buy you more shares at a low cost than a high cost and give you an average cost for your securities. If the market eventually goes up (so far, it always has), you should increase your capital.

The common denominator of success

During my eight years as the moderator of the television show "Successful Texans" and my eighteen years as a financial planner, I've searched for the common denominator of success. In my search, one particular characteristic seems to run through each life. That characteristic is that the successful person has formed the habit of doing the things that failures do not like to do.

Perhaps you feel that you have certain dislikes that are peculiar to you, and that successful people don't have these dislikes but like to do the very things that you don't like to do. This isn't true. They don't like to do them any more than you do. These successful people are doing these very things they don't like to do in order to accomplish the things they want to accomplish. Successful people are motivated by the desire for pleasing results. Failures search for pleasing experiences and are satisfied with results that can be obtained by doing things they like to do.

Let's assume that your purpose is to become a millionaire—that your purpose is strong enough to make you form the habit of doing things you don't like to do in order to attain this goal.

To have maximum creativity, your body needs to have pure air, wholesome food, aerobic exercise, and creative thoughts. When you get home from work, do you grab a can of beer, light up a cigar, and sit in front of the tube to watch a wrestling match or the solving of one of the three to four murders that occur on television each night? Or do you jog, ride a bicycle, exercise on a treadmill, walk a distance, eat a light nutritious dinner (sans large amounts of simple carbohydrates, sugar, salt, caffein, saturated fats, and alcohol, but high in proteins, vitamins, and minerals), and then read The *National Tax Digest,* The *Financial Planner* Magazine, *U.S. News & World Report,* The *U.S. News Washington Letter, Barron's,* The *Wall Street Journal, Newsweek,* and *Business Week*? The successful investor does these things not because he wants to, but because he must in order to accomplish his goal.

You must, too, if you desire to become knowledgeable. Then you must learn to act upon that knowledge. Failures avoid decision making. Successful people know they must act. They have no other choice if they want to reach their goal.

Time plus money plus American free enterprise may make you a millionaire. If it does, fine. If it makes you financially independent, that will be a major accomplishment of which you can be justly proud.

Interview

EC: Venita, one of the things I have heard most often about your writing is how strong the "voice" is in it. Contrasted to other money books, your books always sound as though they were written by a person.

VV: Well, evidently, I do write the way I talk. Basically, when I sit down to write, I just try to tell you, my reader, what I have been telling everybody already.

You know, I do a lot of money seminars. And probably that helps a great deal. Because during those seminars, I watch people's faces. I don't use notes. I watch people's faces and see how they react to something. If I see a cloud coming over their faces, I know I didn't communicate very well. So I just circle around, come back, and say it again in a different way. I also watch reactions to words. Some words people have a good reaction to, some bad. And so after a while I begin to know which words my audience will have a good reaction to. And, of course, all of this carries over into my writing. After you have said something a few times, it's the way you say it.

EC: When you write, do you sit down with a legal pad, a tape recorder?

VV: A yellow pad and pencil. And I write whenever I get time. I run my broker's office, and then I run back and write a little bit. And I write the books out in long hand.

EC: Do you do several drafts?

VV: [Laughing] Oh, yes. After I write a chapter in long hand, someone types it and then I redo it. I cut it all up in little pieces and then I scotch tape it back together again.

EC: Will you talk about that process in more detail?

VV: Well, it seems the easiest way for me to do my revisions. There will be an idea in the chapter that I like, but I will have it in the wrong place. So I just get out the scissors, cut it up, and then tape it back together again. In fact, I think the hardest thing about writing is knowing the best order to put ideas in.

EC: When you begin writing, do you start with a general idea of what you are going to write?

VV: No. I remember once my publisher said, "Send me an outline." I laughed. I asked him how could I send him an outline when I didn't know yet what I was going to say. I just sit down and start writing on a particular subject. I never have an outline. I just write until I have written all I know or want to say about a subject. And then I quit. And then I go on to the next subject. And then I quit. And then I go on to the next subject that I know something about. And if I don't know anything about a subject, I don't put it in my book.

EC: At this stage you don't know yet if what you are writing is actually going to end up in the book.

VV: That's right. First I write it by just keeping on writing. I worry about what to do with it later.

EC: Do you enjoy writing?

VV: I consider it almost pure hell. I don't consider it a pleasure at all. Every time I write a book I think, "Why are you doing this to yourself?" And one of the reasons I hate to start a book is that once I begin there is no peace until I have finished. I can't play. I can't do anything because every time I go to do something that is fun I have this guilty feeling that I ought to be writing the book.

EC: Is this pressure from you or from your publisher?

VV: Usually from the publisher or from somebody I have made a commitment to.

EC: Well, given that you don't really enjoy writing, how did that first book come about?

VV: I was doing a seminar, and an editor from Prentice-Hall was in the audience. He wrote me a letter later and said, ''You have the ability to make a very difficult subject simple. Have you considered writing a book?''

EC: So, did you consent then?

VV: No. I thought about it, but not much. They came back later with a contract, and I finally signed it. I had no confidence in my writing skills at all.

EC: What did you do then?

VV: Well, on that first book I had somebody go over it after I wrote it. And she destroyed it. Actually, I had to write that first book twice.

EC: What exactly did she destroy?

VV: I hadn't made a copy of the original. And she just marked through here and there, cut it up here, did this and that. There was nothing left of it.

EC: Was it your personal voice which she took out?

VV: Everything. I think she got a jug of wine and then sat down with the book. At any rate, I had to write it twice.

EC: Venita, one of the real knacks you have in writing is for finding just the right allusion or analogy that will allow your reader to understand some complicated money matter. I am thinking for instance of your use of loaves of bread to explain inflation. Or of your reference to the Robin Hood of the '80's and the story of the talents from the Bible. How do things like this evolve in your writing?

VV: Well, for the most part they are words, phrases, stories, etc., which I have used in seminars. And as I write more and more, I realize that in order to communicate I must give people something to tie on to, something that will stick in their minds and that they can repeat to you or to someone else. So that is why I try to use vivid expressions and illustrations as much as I possibly can: they give my readers something to tie on to.

EC: So when you sit down with your yellow pad, the audience from your seminars is right there in front of you as you write. And, in fact, the seminars have been a kind of oral first draft, haven't they?

VV: I have never thought about it in that way, but they probably are. And I think I do put my seminar audience in front of me when I sit down to write.

EC: Do you write in a particular place?

VV: Always at a desk. I write best at the ranch because I can look out and see the green grass. I write a while, and then I reward myself— unfortunately, it is usually food that

I use to reward myself. It is really a diversion that I am trying to get. My hand gets tired; everything gets tired!

EC: You said, Venita, earlier in the interview, that finding the best order was one of the hardest parts of writing for you. On what do you base your decisions about what should come first, second, etc.?

VV: I will give you an example. I have a chapter in my book on taking a financial inventory for oneself which in the book comes near the end. In real life I do that chapter very early in my money seminars. But when I started writing my books, I realized that if I put something in the book early that looked dull and, worse than that, looked like hard work, people probably wouldn't read it. So I put the fun things in the book in the front and then by the time the readers get all the way to the back they will find the parts that require them to do something.

EC: I know that when *Money Dynamics for the 1980s* was reviewed in *Money Magazine*, it was given very high praise, and two other books on money reviewed in the same issue were called tomes. Yet the other two were by professional writers, and you do not see yourself as a writer *per se*. What do you think makes the difference between how you write and how those professional writers put together their books?

VV: Well, I think the main difference between the other two writers' books and mine is that I *do* it: I practice financial planning. For twenty years I have sat here, the way you and I are sitting now, and I've looked at what my clients have and recommended what they should do. And every day I am on the firing line. Neither of the other two writers has ever counselled a soul, never even invested their own money. So there is a difference in collecting information and telling people things from experience that have worked. They are much better ''writers'' than I am, probably, but I have much more experience than they do in financial planning.

EC: Venita, there are probably many, many people who will read this interview who have a book they want to write or who have thought at some time, ''I ought to write a book,'' or ''I would like to publish a book on that.'' What advice would you give to people who want to write but never have?

VV: Well, the thing that held me back was that I thought I had no writing ability. I had had no training in writing whatsoever, so because I had had no training I thought I could not express myself on paper. I knew I could express myself orally, but I did not think I could do it on paper. (Actually, I now wonder if the training many people get in writing doesn't kill their creativity and interest in doing it—but I probably shouldn't be saying that, should I?)

EC: When did you decide you *could* write?

VV: It actually took me three books before I decided I knew how to write. Finally, I decided that I must be able to write, else people would not buy my books. After I sold a third of a million copies of my last book, I thought, ''Maybe you can write a book, Venita.'' But it took me that long to get past my earlier fears.

EC: How long does it take you now to write a book?

VV: I do it in such sporadic times. I think that, if I could just take off a couple of months, I could write a book. But I don't ever take off a couple of months.

EC: Thank you very much, Venita. This has been a delightful interview for me.

VV: Thank you. I have enjoyed it.

PART 2

Writing to Change

THE CATEGORY AND ITS CONFIGURATION

To Change   to make different in some way
to transform
to give a different position, course, or direction to
to reverse
to replace with another
to make a shift from one to the other
to switch
to alter
to vary
to modify
to make a transition
to interrupt

For thousands of years, human beings have been aware of the power of the written word to change people themselves, to change situations, to change what people know. Moses brought down the Ten Commandments, written in stone, to change the behavior of the Israelites in the wilderness. The founding fathers of this country wrote the *Declaration of Independence* to change their relationship with England and to change what the colonists thought of themselves. Albert Einstein made assertions that changed what we know about our universe.

So **writing to change** implies a belief and a trust on the writer's part that words have power, that words create action, that words produce change. An author's stance in **writing to tell** is that words are interesting, words convey information, words inform. But the intent of the writer is not to effect change, not to have the reader act or think a certain way as a consequence of reading the words. In **writing to change,** however, the writer intends to cause action, movement, alteration of some sort: intends you to take a position or stand that you did not have before, so that you will argue for something that you didn't argue for before, so that you will assert what you did not assert before,

so that you will judge as you have not judged before, so that you will evaluate with appropriate information, so that you will act as you have not acted before.

The emphasis in **writing to change** is on the action that results from the mix of the writer's intention and the information being communicated. The writer's emphasis is on what you, the reader, are going to say, know, do, believe when you have finished reading the writing. The writer does not always intend that you literally *do* something immediately, but rather that when you do act, it will be with the inclusion of new information, evidence, or argument that became a part of your thinking after reading what she or he wrote. The emphasis is on the dynamics of what the writer sees in the world, how the writer puts this view into words, and how the reader then acts upon this message. So, while the writer is not the center of attention, the view/assertion/position/judgment/vision held by the writer is the center of attention as it becomes a part of what a reader thinks or does.

The motivation for **writing to change** is direct experience, personal research and investigation, vision, commitment, and insights of the writer. The motivation for writing is internal and external at the same time. The external facts are perceived, filtered, and assimilated by the internal nature of the writer; and a stand, position, or viewpoint is taken. That stand or viewpoint may in some circumstances be no more "weighty" than just wanting you, the reader, to look at a situation in a different way, to see possibilities or implications you might not have seen before. In other circumstances the writer's stand or viewpoint may be requesting commitment and vision and lifelong change. Authors who **write to change** do so because they are more than casually or intellectually interested in what they are writing about.

The circumstances and situations for **writing to change** vary. If the writing is to have public presentation—in newspapers or magazines, for example—then time deadlines and manuscript restrictions apply. Often, however, what determines the deadline of the writing is the point at which an experiment is completed, an evaluation is made, or evidence is collected. There are some types of **writing to change**, however, that are called forth by the writer's vision and commitment in the world; these essays or books or letters or declarations are written from internal circumstances and situations and then presented to the outside world on the writer's own time schedule. Often a particular event may be the trigger or impetus causing the writer to begin—and complete—the writing.

The audience for **writing to change** can be the general reader, a member of a special-interest group, a segment of society that enjoys a certain event or type of entertainment, or members of a particular profession. The writer's relationship to the audience is that of one who calls for action, for the acceptance of evidence, or for the acknowledgment of an evaluation.

The forms that **writing to change** may take are essays, books, articles, reviews, critiques, research reports, evaluations, letters, memos, manifestos, tracts.

To sum up, here are the configuration points for **writing to change:**

Emphasis   the dynamic between the writer's intention, the
                        content of the writing, and the reader's response

Motivation   to state the writer's own interests, commitments,
for Writing   visions, and experience
                        to get the reader to look at a situation in a different
                        way, to see new possibilities and implications, to
                        share the writer's vision
                        to move the reader from one stance to another
                        to persuade or convince the reader
                        to get a commitment from the reader

Circumstance and Situation	deadlines and manuscript restrictions of a newspaper or magazine or the writer's personal time schedule the point at which an event happens, an experiment is completed, an evaluation is made, or evidence is collected.
Form	essays articles books reviews critiques research reports evaluations letters memos manifestos tracts
Audience	the general public the members of a group with a shared interest in something or a shared commitment to a particular cause the members of a particular profession or organization
Writer's Relationship to Reader	one whose vision, experience insight, or expertise differs from the reader's one who is calling for action from the reader, or for the acceptance of evidence, or for the acknowledgment of an evaluation
Writer's Intention	to have the reader know, accept, act upon, believe, or make decisions on the basis of the writer's words

In this part of the book you will find **writing to change** in three forms:

Essays of *assertion-with-evidence*, written to change what the reader knows, thinks, or believes about a particular thing

Essays of *evaluation*, written to change the readers' ability to judge by assisting them in being informed

Essays of *persuasion*, written to change the reader's mind and often to persuade the reader to *act*.

The Assertion-With-Evidence Essay

To Assert to state positively with great confidence
to demonstrate the existence of
to declare
to affirm
to maintain

Evidence something that furnishes proof
something that bears witness
something that is seen
something that is conspicuous
signs that point to a conclusion
something plain and clear

As you read the assertion-with-evidence essays that follow, you will discover that the most convincing and well-written ones have these characteristics:

The assertion is clearly stated early in the essay.

The evidence follows quickly and is obviously in support of the assertion.

The evidence consists of facts, examples, information that the readers can check, or of discussion so logical and convincing that the readers accept it without argument.

There is sufficient evidence cited to convince the reader.

Ask yourself these questions as you read the assertion-with-evidence essays below.

Where does the assertion appear in the essay?
What kind of evidence does the writer cite?
Is the evidence convincing?
Is enough evidence present?
What does the writer want the reader to do?

BARBARA LANG STERN

Barbara Lang Stern, in this essay which first appeared in Vogue *magazine (June 1979), supplies evidence using medical facts as her proof. By demonstrating the benefits of tears, she hopes to change the reader's attitude toward crying.*

Tears Can Be Crucial to Your Physical and Emotional Health

1   Do you let yourself go and cry from time to time? Or do you almost always hold back your tears? Chances are you've heard or read that crying is a healthy emotional release, but did you know it might help to prevent certain physical illnesses as well?

2   "All of us have two systems of tearing," says Stephen E. Bloomfield, M.D., clinical assistant professor in ophthalmology at New York Hospital-Cornell Medical Center. "There is, first of all, a constant flow of tears which is produced by tiny glands in the conjunctiva or lining inside the lids of the eye. This basic tearing creates a film that's very much like a soap bubble in the sense that it can be compressed and stretched by the eyelids without breaking or getting holes in it. The tear film does the vital job of keeping the cornea moist. If the cornea dries, it will get erosions or little abrasions that can be very painful. Eventually, if there is severe drying, vision will be impaired because the cornea will become opaque.

3   "The second back-up system involves the lachrimal gland located at the outer corner of the eye. This good-sized gland can put out a lot of tears in response to irritants such as fumes, smoke, or foreign bodies in the eye. This reflex tearing is the eye's automatic response to *any* kind of adverse stimulus. For instance, wind and heat cause faster evaporation of the cornea's normal tear film. The lachrimal gland responds by producing extra moisture, and you may have 'teary' eyes on an exceptionally windy day. The lachrimal gland also produces the tears you may cry when your feelings are touched.

4   "Most people don't realize how fascinating and complex a tear is. It's made up of three different types of products—water, mucus, and fat—in the proper proportions to keep the tear film flexible and intact. Tears also contain sugar and protein, which nourish the cornea, as well as a bacteria-destroying enzyme known as lysozyme, which effectively protects the eye against infection by a lot of organisms that we're constantly exposed to."

Clearly, tears play a crucial role in the health of our eyes; but what about their benefit to our overall well-being?

Psychologists have long known that, whenever we have strong emotions that we hold in or deny, one way or another our unexpressed feelings show up. Sometimes they appear as substitute emotions: if we aren't able to let out our anger, we may get depressed. Feelings may manifest themselves through all kinds of behavior. One of the most familiar is the way we show restlessness or impatience by tapping a foot or drumming our fingers. Often, our strong unexpressed emotions can result in physical illnesses ranging from headaches, ulcers, and digestive problems to high blood pressure, insomnia, skin rashes, and many other conditions.

Tears represent an acknowledgment and expression of many of our feelings such as grief, sorrow, frustration, fear, helplessness, and sometimes relief or joy. Some people find that crying helps them to understand their emotions by making them more conscious of how they feel.

Furthermore, there is evidence to suggest that withholding tears can cause specific problems, while releasing them can end the difficulty.

"Asthma patients often are afraid to cry," says Walter A. Stewart, M.D., psychoanalyst, teacher, and author, "yet they will frequently abort a asthmatic attack if they do begin to shed tears. It's also been widely noticed that people who don't cry often catch a great many colds; but, once they become able to weep, their susceptibility to colds disappears."

"One reason you might have more colds if you hold back tears is that, when you're under stress, your body puts out steroids which affect your immune system and reduce your resistance to disease," Dr. Bloomfield comments.

In an intriguing book, *Your Mind Can Stop the Common Cold* (Peter Wyden), Lucy Freeman attempts to explain more specifically the connection between unshed tears and catching colds. She suggests in part that, when you feel like crying, one of the changes that takes place is your nose's becoming engorged or congested with blood. If you go ahead and weep, tears drain through your nasal tear ducts, easing your nose. But, if you suppress your tears, the nose nonetheless "becomes engorged and stays engorged as it awaits tears that never flow," writes Freeman.

"This prolonged engorgement weakens the resistance of the nose, either against invading viruses or viruses that reside in the nose in moderate numbers as protective organisms but that, when the nose has to overexert itself and falls into a weakened condition, multiply and cause an infection that the whole body is then forced to fight."

For this and other reasons, Freeman concludes that "when you catch a cold, you may have a hidden wish to weep."

As children, many of us were encouraged by our parents *not* to cry.
14 Yet today, we're revising our opinion of what constitutes weakness. Acknowledging that you feel pain and weeping may take more strength or courage than pretending that the hurt doesn't exist. And revealing your emotions to someone else often means being willing to take a risk.

15 Of course, there are times when you'll decide it's inappropriate to cry. You'll want to consider the impact it will have on others as well as on you. So you may choose to suppress your tears in front of a frightened child or perhaps a rival or boss. Yet at the right time, with the right person, tears may be a sign of trust or intimacy, of readiness to share your deeper needs and feelings with another. Letting yourself cry can be a step toward greater physical and emotional well-being.

FOR DISCUSSION

1. What specific problems does withholding tears create? What evidence does the author give to prove that this is true? Are you convinced? Why, or why not?

2. Since this essay first appeared in *Vogue* magazine, what restrictions or constraints were probably part of the circumstances and situation in which the author wrote?

3. What could have been a motive for the author's writing this essay?

4. To whom does the author seem to be writing? What relationship does she establish with the audience?

5. What is emphasized most in this essay?

DANIEL YANKELOVICH

In this essay, which appeared in the popular magazine Psychology Today *(May 1982), social researcher Daniel Yankelovich asserts that the American work ethic is still very strong. With evidence appropriate for a general audience, he attempts to show that contrary to popular opinion, American people* want *to work.*

The Work Ethic Is Underemployed

Americans hold two beliefs about why the Japanese are outdoing us in 1 autos, steel, appliances, computer chips, and even subway cars. The first is that our productivity has become stagnant. The second is that this has happened because our work ethic has deteriorated badly.

The first belief is, alas, true. Since 1965, the country's productivity 2 has improved at ever smaller rates. It now shows no growth at all, and may even be falling. But despite these signs and additional evidence that people are not working as hard as they once did, it is emphatically not true that our work ethic has become weaker. If by work ethic—a very slippery term—we mean endowing work with intrinsic moral worth and believing that everyone should do his or her best possible job irrespective of financial reward, then recent survey research shows that the work ethic in the United States is surprisingly sturdy, and growing sturdier.

To understand the findings, we need to keep in mind the sharp 3 distinction between work *behavior*—what we actually do in the work place—and the work *ethic*—a set of psychological and moral beliefs.

A 1980 Gallup study for the United States Chamber of Commerce 4 shows that an overwhelming 88 percent of all working Americans feel that it is personally important to them to work hard and do their best on the job. (This should not be confused with Gallup findings that fewer Americans are enjoying their work—a separate issue). The study concludes that a faulty work ethic is *not* responsible for the decline in our productivity; quite the contrary, the study identifies "a widespread commitment among U.S. workers to improve productivity" and suggests that "there are large reservoirs of potential upon which management can draw to improve performance and increase productivity."

In a subtler examination of American attitudes toward work, a 1982 5 pilot study for the nonprofit Public Agenda Foundation explores three conceptions of what might be called the "unwritten work contract"— the assumptions that each individual makes about what he or she will give to the job and expects to get in return. The first conception is one that historians recognize as the dominant attitude toward work throughout human history: the view that people labor only because they would not otherwise have the resources to sustain themselves. A second conception regards work as a straight economic transaction in which people relate effort to financial return: The more money they get, the harder they work; the less money they receive, the less effort they give. The third conception views work as carrying a moral imperative to do one's best apart from practical necessity or financial remuneration. The Public Agenda considers the implications of its findings so important that it intends to replicate the pilot study—from which national figures can only be surmised—among a larger cross-section of the work force within the next few months.

6   The study found that nearly four out of five people in the work force (78 percent) embrace the third conception, aligning themselves with the statement: "I have an inner need to do the very best job I can regardless of pay." Fewer than one out of 10 working Americans (7 percent) embrace the idea of work as a mere "business transaction" whereby one regulates one's effort according to the size of one's paycheck, and an additional 15 percent regard work as a necessary but disagreeable chore ("Working for a living is one of life's necessities. I would not work if I did not have to").

7   Other surveys reveal similar findings. In 1977, for example, the respected Quinn and Staines Quality of Employment Survey conducted by the University of Michigan's Survey Research Center discovered that three out of four Americans (75 percent) would prefer to go on working even if they could live comfortably without working for the rest of their lives. It is revealing of the expanding commitment to the value of work that eight years earlier, significantly fewer Americans (67 percent) had expressed the same attitude.

8   Yet at the same time that the work ethic, in the sense defined above, has actually been growing stronger, most Americans also believe that people are working less. A 1981 Harris study for Sentry Insurance reveals that:

—78 percent of all working Americans feel that "people take less pride in their work than they did 10 years ago."
—73 percent believe that "the motivation to work hard is not as strong today as it was a decade ago."
—69 percent feel that our workmanship is worse than it was.
—63 percent simply believe that "most people do not work as hard today as they did 10 years ago."

9   Polls by Harris and Gallup, and my own research firm, show that business leaders hold similar views.

10   These beliefs do not prove that Americans are actually working less effectively than in the past. But it is difficult to discount such widespread impressions among both working people and business leaders. One bit of direct evidence on the declining performance of the American worker allows us to go beyond these impressions. For a number of years, the University of Michigan asked a sample of workers to keep a diary of activities on the job. Analysis of these diaries reveals that between 1965 and 1975 the amount of time workers actually worked declined by more than 10 percent. If extrapolated to all American workers, the researchers say, this one factor alone, quite apart from such considerations as insufficient investments or aging equipment, could account for the slowed tempo of productivity growth in the decade from 1965 to 1975.

How, then, are we to reconcile these two sets of seemingly incom- 11
patible facts? Why do Americans endorse the ideal of giving one's best
to the job while their actual performance reveals a slackening effort?
What forces have produced this self-defeating situation at the precise
moment when economic competition from Japan, Korea, Taiwan, Germany, and other nations threatens to outpace us and drag down our
standard of living?

The answer lies, I believe, in the deeply flawed reward system, both 12
psychological and financial, that now rules the American work place.
To grasp this argument, we need to understand just what most work is
like today. The Public Agenda study asked people the amount of
control they exercised over how hard they worked and over the quality
of the products they made or services they performed. A huge majority
(82 percent) stated that they had some degree of discretion and control
over the effort they gave to their job, and an even larger majority (88
percent) said that they had control over the quality of the work or
service they performed (72 percent, a great deal of control; 16 percent,
moderate control). This finding illuminates a little-noted but important
fact about the modern work place: most working Americans have it in
their power to decide whether they will satisfy only the minimum
requirements of the job or exert the extra effort that makes the difference between ordinariness and high quality, between adequacy and
excellence.

When the Public Agenda asked people whether they were using this 13
freedom of choice to fulfill their ''inner need to do the very best job''
they can, fewer than one out of five (16 percent) said they were. All
others acknowledged that they could improve their effectiveness—if
they really wanted to. And many claimed that they could be twice as
effective as they are now.

Why aren't they? The answer could hardly be plainer. When Gal- 14
lup's Chamber of Commerce study asked workers whom they thought
would benefit from the improvements in their productivity, only 9
percent felt that they, the workers, would. Most assumed that the
beneficiaries would be others—consumers or stockholders or management. This finding accords with the finding of Yankelovich, Skelly, and
White several years ago that a majority of college students no longer
believe that working hard pays off. Some interpreted this finding to
mean that the work ethic was eroding. It signifies, rather, the growing
doubt that hard work will bring the rewards people have come to
cherish. When Gallup's Chamber of Commerce study asked people
whether they would work harder and do a better job if they were more
involved in decisions relating to their work, an overwhelming 84 percent said they would. One need not take this finding literally to appreciate the vast sea of yearning that underlies it.

We arrive, then, at the heart of the matter. The questions of who 15
benefits from increased productivity, and how, are the critical factors,

not the work ethic. If the American work ethic has gone to seed, there is not much anyone can do about the problem of productivity. But if, as I contend, our work *ethic* is actually thriving while our work *behavior* falters, then the prognosis for action is excellent—once we grasp the reasons for the discrepancy and confront the task of remedying it.

16   In principle, most Americans are willing to work harder and turn out a higher-quality product; indeed, their self-esteem demands that they do so. That they are not doing it points directly to a serious flaw in management and in the reward system under which they perform their jobs. Why should workers make a greater effort if (a) they don't have to and (b) they believe that others will be the beneficiaries of such efforts? It is ironic that a political administration so finely tuned to encouraging the business community should pay such scant attention to stimulating the average American to work harder.

17   As our competitive posture in traditional industries such as steel and automobiles grows ever more grim, workers and trade unions are starting to pay more attention to productivity. But in many labor circles productivity is still regarded as a code term for speedups that benefit management and threaten job security. The mismatch between the national goal of improved productivity and the inadequate system of rewards now in operation could hardly be more obvious.

18   Lest anyone dismiss the idea that a more thoughtful approach to rewards can pay off, a large body of experimental data proves otherwise. Psychologist Raymond Katzell has reviewed 103 experiments designed to test whether an improved incentive system—including both money and greater control over one's work—would lead to higher individual productivity. It did in 85 of the experiments.

19   Perhaps more to the point is the Japanese experience in this country. The Japanese distinguish between the "soft" factors of production (the dedication of the work force) and such "hard" factors as technology, capital investment, and research and development. They recognize that the soft factors are just as important as the hard ones and that, indeed, the two are interdependent. It is this understanding that underlies Japan's spectacular success not only in their homeland but also in the plants they own and manage in the United States. One Japanese strategy, for example, is to bring together both workers and managers to solve the problem of how new technology can be introduced to the advantage of both. Such participation does not just assure workers of job security; it enables them to devise with management a system that also provides job satisfaction. The Japanese success in this country is evidence that the American belief in the work ethic is not just rhetoric. Without the work ethic, the Japanese would have had to rely solely on the hard factors, by themselves not enough to spur productivity.

20   Ironically, the Japanese seem to have a better grasp of how to capitalize on our work ethic than we do. In the American approach to

work, the relevant institutions—business management, labor unions, government, professional economists— do not have a firm grasp of the soft factors and how they interact with the hard ones. Unwittingly, most "experts" hold an obsolete image of the work force as a pool of "labor" responsive solely to economic imperatives, driven by the fear of unemployment, and inspired by the promise of consumer goods— the familiar carrot-and-stick psychology that worked in the past when workers and work were different. The leaders who run our institutions do not really understand today's work force: tens of millions of well-educated Americans, proud of their achievements, zealous of their freedoms, motivated by new values, with substantial control over their own production, and ready to raise their level of effort if given the proper encouragement.

FOR DISCUSSION

1. List four pieces of evidence Yankelovich gathered to prove that his assertion is true.

2. What *is* the heart of the matter, according to Yankelovich? And where in the essay does this statement appear? What strategy do you suppose could have determined the author's placing this statement where he did in the essay?

3. This essay appeared in a magazine for people with a general interest in psychology. How is the essay's subject matter related to the study of psychology?

4. Discuss the significance/importance of this particular title for the essay.

5. If readers accept the evidence, what will be changed?

KEVIN STREHLO

Kevin Strehlo, in this article discussing John Lilly's work with dolphins, makes what one might call a mild assertion *or an* assertion of a gentle kind. *He suggests to his specialized audience—the readers of* Popular Computing—*that dolphins can or will talk, and that the computer project he writes about* may *succeed.*

Talk to the Animals

1 Almost all of us are intrigued by the idea of intelligent life forms outside the human race. We search the stars, send out satellites, dream of the meeting between equal minds from different worlds. We look "out there" for our answers. But some researchers and scientists think we should keep our eyes earthbound—or rather, ocean-bound—in the quest for intelligent companionship.

2 These seekers have set their sights on the ocean's most perplexing, precocious, and bewitching of mammals—cetaceans, specifically dolphins.

3 We apparently share many traits of intelligence with our bottlenosed brethren, and there is good evidence to suggest that one of those traits is speech. Other characteristics of intelligence are not shared—toolmaking, for instance. The creation and application of tools is, to all appearances, a cornerstone of human intellectual ability and sets us clearly apart from our planetmates.

4 Dolphins don't seem to make tools—whether from a lack of intellectual ability or a lack of hands is open to question. But, somewhat paradoxically, it is our tool-making ability that may enable us to narrow the gulf between the species. Through the use of our Ultimate Tool (so far)—the computer—we may soon share with the dolphins our respective gifts of speech.

5 The Human/Dolphin Foundation, led by Dr. John C. Lilly, famed for his dolphin research in the 1960s, is attempting to make communication between humans and dolphins a reality. By means of a powerful signal-processing system, which includes several Apple microcomputers, Lilly and his group hope to demonstrate dolphins' true capacity for language and to establish the basis for an interspecies exchange of information.

6 If they are successful, the day may come when a dolphin swims to the seaside facility of the Human/Dolphin Foundation to deliver the oral history of the dolphin—a 30-million-year history that dwarfs our own tenure on earth.

Popular skepticism concerning human/dolphin communication pre- 7
vails—the field has yet to produce the kind of breakthrough that makes
front-page headlines. But John Lilly and John Kert are confident of
eventual success.

Kert, the associate director of research for Lilly's Human/Dolphin 8
Foundation, has a background in real-time computer analysis of satel-
lite-data transmissions. He has immersed himself in the work Lilly did
with dolphins back in the sixties, and in the cognitive development and
human-potential theories that guide Lilly's efforts today, in order to
develop a computer system called JANUS. JANUS consists of two
Apple microcomputers perfoming input and output functions for a
Digital Equipment Corporation PDP-11 configured for signal processing; tone and waveform generators and a frequency analyzer complete
the setup. The purpose of JANUS: to translate human communication
into underwater sound waves a dolphin can understand, and vice
versa.

"I think the JANUS project will lead to communication about the 9
things we share together," Kert says of his work with Joe and Rosalie,
two dolphins at Marineworld/Africa USA in Redwood City, California.
"As for our rate of progress, I use the development of a human child as
a minimum time scale. With a child, it takes at least two years to begin
an interchange of ideas. There's no reason to think communication
with another species will come sooner."

Time may not be the only barrier. As Lilly once said, "A nonhuman 10
language may use a logic that is totally strange, an apparent external
form that may be bizarre to humans, and a way of looking at information that may be totally unfamiliar."

Lilly believes dolphins are more intelligent than any man or woman. 11
His interest was first aroused in the 1960s by his discovery that the
bottlenose dolphin (*Tursiops truncatus*) had 40 percent more cognitive
brain capacity than man. It is this cognitive brain capacity, housed in
the silent associational cortex of the brain, that allows abstract mental
functions and separates man from the apes and—or so we once
thought—the rest of the animal kingdom.

The dolphins seemed willing, even eager, to cooperate once Lilly 12
and his colleagues began to indicate an interest in communication.
Long known to carry on underwater exchanges of high-pitched whistles and clicks among themselves, the dolphins tried talking to the
scientists in the same manner. They soon discovered, however, that
their underwater utterances went unheard. So the dolphins learned to
rise out of the water on their powerful tails and vocalize in the air; they
were encouraged by the loud, and, to them, low-pitched chatter returned by the scientists.

John Lilly first set up a computer to sift the normal conversational 13
intercourse of dolphins for meaningful patterns in 1961, but he learned

very little (his biggest discovery was that their wolf-whistle sound was a distress call). It was the dolphins, working only with their own magnificent biocomputer, who made the first real breakthrough.

14   One day, listening to a playback of a tape he had made with a dolphin named Elvar, Lilly thought he heard something remarkable. Playing it back at half speed, it was really there, if only in a squeaky, Donald Duck voice: one of the dolphins had unmistakably repeated, after Lilly, the numbers "one, two, three."

15   The scientists began trying to teach the dolphins English. Lilly set up an affectionate, long-term interchange with the dolphins to prevent their normal, adverse reaction to treatment as ordinary lab animals in an experiment. The dolphins responded by lowering the pitch of their noises and making what seemed to the scientists to be a serious effort to imitate the vocalizations of men. Lacking the lips, tongue, and vocal chords necessary for human speech, the dolphins had little success with correct pronunciation, but succeeded in picking up such verbal nuances as the southern drawl of one of Lilly's associates. Another dolphin mimicked Lilly's voice so well his wife laughed aloud: the dolphin promptly mimicked her laugh.

16   Meanwhile, the human scientists came up with proof that dolphins did indeed transmit complex information via rapid underwater clicks and whistles when a dolphin in one tank taught a dolphin in an adjacent tank a sizable part of a newly learned routine. The dolphins couldn't see each other—their only contact was an acoustic link between the tanks. Thus, the knowledge had to have been passed in "conversation."

17   The increasing evidence of the dolphin's intellectual capacity delighted Lilly, but it also bothered him: what right did he have to confine a creature that was the intellectual equal of man? Dolphins in captivity exhibit listless, repetitive swimming patterns similar to the pacing of human prisoners in solitary confinement, and have been known to commit suicide. In 1962, John Lilly made up his mind; he left the study of dolphins to others.

18   In 1978, after a 16-year absence from dolphin research, Lilly returned to the field. He had been following the work of others and he simply wasn't satisfied with their efforts, so, along with his wife Toni and actor Burgess Meredith, Lilly formed the Human/Dolphin Foundation. Its goal; to create an interspecies laboratory to which both humans and dolphins could freely come and go to study one another.

19   At the heart of the new effort is JANUS.

20   JANUS stands for "Joint-Analog-Numerical-Understanding System." More to the point, the acronym formed by the phrase captures the spirt of Lilly's studies. "Janus" is the name of the ancient god of entrances and exits, symbolized by a mask with a face on both sides. The computerized JANUS has a dolphin face and a human face; Lilly

hopes it will be the historic doorway through which the alien intelligences of man and dolphin can first meet and speak.

"In 1962," Lilly says, "we used a ponderous computer, a tube type. 21 Everything we had then on two six-foot racks, both two feet wide, now fits one single microchip."

The new system, built around a Digital Equipment Corporation PDP 22 11/04 minicomputer, has an operating speed over 80 times faster than the transistorized LINC III Lilly was using in the 1960s. The new speed, coupled with eight times the memory of the older machines, makes Lilly believe he can accomplish nearly instantaneous translation between English and a language the dolphins can understand.

Several approaches have been contemplated. One approach would 23 use the computer as a vocoder. That is, the computer would transform human speech to a higher pitch and the dolphin's vocalizations to a lower pitch, so that each species would hear the other in their optimal hearing range and medium (air or water).

Translation would be up to the two species, however, and this 24 presents a problem. Dolphin speech proceeds at what to humans seems an incredibly rapid pace: a typical dolphin vocalization contains about ten times as much information per second as human speech. To complicate matters, dolphins have two sound-emitting mechanisms in their blowhole cavity and are capable of producing a series of rapid whistles with one, while simultaneously clicking with the other. It seems unlikely that humans will be able to cope unaided with the complexity of dolphin vocalization.

The large portion of the dolphin brain devoted to audio is matched in 25 the human brain by the size of the area devoted to processing visual information. Indeed, hearing is to dolphins what vision is to humans. It has long been known that dolphins have an extraordinary ability to recognize objects underwater by sending out high-pitched sounds and listening to the echoes. Through this sounding process, similar to but much more sophisticated than the sonar used by submarines, the dolphins can tell each other apart, identify objects, and even differentiate human friends from human strangers. In effect, the dolphin "sees" as clearly with his ears as a human does with his eyes.

Lilly has theorized that "Delphinese"—his term for the dolphin 26 language—is partially derived from this ability to form clear images from incoming sound. When the dolphin wishes to name an object, or a particular dolphin, he might do it by vocalizing an abstract version of the characteristic echo associated with that object or dolphin. It is as if humans could communicate by transmitting visual images directly.

One of Lilly's eventual goals is to develop a process whereby the 27 computer transforms what the dolphin "sees" with his sonar into a video picture for humans, and vice versa. This would allow a human to see the image that Lilly theorizes is contained in some dolphin vocalizations.

28   This audio/visual transformation, however, requires more processing power than JANUS presently possesses. According to John Kert, cost estimates for a sufficiently powerful computer system and underwater microphone array exceed a million dollars.

29   Presently Kert is pursuing a more basic approach at Marineworld's Redwood City facility. The JANUS project will first develop unique code elements usable by man and dolphin; then, through a teaching program, assign mutually understood meanings to strings of these elements. To this end, Kert is attempting to teach Joe and Rosalie how to communicate by whistling tones that stand for letters of the English alphabet. The computer system translates the whistle spelling into an English printout, and keyboard entered English words into whistle spelling.

30   "In principle," says John Kert, "dolphins can spell a word as fast as we can say it. . . ."

31   The fundamentals of communication established by JANUS should provide the basis for a more intimate and longstanding partnership between human and dolphin.

32   "We'll go as far as we can with this approach," Kert says, "but I don't think we'll share things about life in the ocean. That may come in the next phase."

33   Ultimately, the Human/Dolphin Foundation plans to set up a laboratory in a house on the ocean. The house will be flooded with 18 inches of water: enough for dolphins to swim, not too much for humans to walk. The people and the dolphins involved will live together continuously in the kind of affectionate interspecies domesticity Lilly feels is important for further progress. The house will be connected by a channel to the surrounding warm-water sea so that participating dolphins can come and go at will.

34   For the present, there's a way readers of *Popular Computing* can assist in this research. John Kert says he would welcome ideas for interactive games the dolphins could play with the computers. Output to the dolphins is in whistle tones via an underwater video terminal; the dolphins accomplish input via the whistle codes. Ideas should be sent to Kert at the Human/Dolphin Foundation, POB 4172, Malibu, CA 90265.

35   But what is to come from all this? What's in it for us if man succeeds in breaking the interspecies barrier and communicates with the dolphin, a creature who has lived peacefully in the sea for many times longer than man has been on earth? The American humorist James Thurber, in a serious moment, perhaps anticipated what our hopes might be.

"I observed a school of dolphins," Thurber said, "and something 36
told me that here was a creature, all gaiety, charm, and intelligence,
that might one day come out of the boundless deep and show us how a
world can be run by creatures dedicated not to the destruction of their
species, but to its preservation."

FOR DISCUSSION

1. What is the assertion in this essay?

2. What is the most convincing evidence for you in this essay?

3. What surprised you?

4. The author establishes a slightly unusual relationship with the
   audience. Where in the article is there evidence that this is so?
   Does this relationship between writer and reader increase the
   chance that the reader will accept the assertion in the essay?

5. Considering the context of Strehlo's article, *Popular Computing*
   (June 1982), do you find the ending surprising?

6. How would this article have been different if the writer had made
   a firm or strong assertion instead of a mild, gentle, and suggestive
   one?

BOOTH FOWLER AND SAUL BRENNER

*In this essay political scientists Booth Fowler and Saul Brenner set out
to change any reader's mind who holds that America is going to the
dogs. By publishing their essay in* The Humanist *(March/April 1982),
the authors chose to address a small and specialized audience. As you
read this piece, try to decide why Fowler and Brenner chose such a
context.*

In Defense of Optimism

Prophets of doom flood us with their wares as the United States enters 1
the 1980s. The hue and cry is loud that America is in retreat all over the
world and that our government lacks the ability to do anything about it.

Critics also contend that our political leaders are unable to adopt a workable energy policy, master the problems of unemployment, or halt the decline of the big cities of the Northeast and Midwest.

2   Are these prophets of doom true prophets? There is reason to believe that they are false prophets. The truth is that never has the American civilization been so successful and, granting our faults, never have we had so much to be proud of as a nation. We will argue that the lack of confidence in the future of the United States is more widespread than many believe, that it has occurred during the time when the United States has become a great civilization, and that the interesting question is: Why do so many people fail to appreciate our progress as a civilization?

3   Evidence of lack of confidence is everywhere. That many individuals are pessimistic regarding the future of America is so self-evident that it hardly bears substantiating. The doubters from the past—the Marxists, the New Left, the cultural critics, the more militant environmentalists, and the apocalyptic right-wingers—continue in good form. Conservative religious groups, such as Moral Majority, represent the newest, widely publicized addition to the pessimists. But all these groups have been joined of late by other voices, not at all congenital pessimists, such as Daniel Bell, Samuel Huntington, Robert Heilbroner, Milton Friedman, and, of course, Henry Kissinger. All have basked in the warmth of America's intellectual enlightenment and received its rewards. Yet their mood is grim. Each presents a unique analysis, but all agree that the American experiment is uncertain in direction, lacks a sense of community, and has lost confidence in itself.

4   This mood is not only present among intellectuals but is present among the general public as well. Public opinion polls firmly substantiate this point. Since the late 1960s there has been a dramatic drop in public confidence in American political institutions. Poll after poll confirms that the American citizens, once enthusiastic about their government, satisfied with its particular institutions, and confident of its performance, no longer hold these views. In a recent study, the Survey Research Center of Ann Arbor, Michigan, found that 65 percent of the American people believed that "the government is pretty much run by the few big interests looking out for themselves," instead of being run "for the benefit of all the people." Fifteen years previously only 35 pecent of the population took that position and in 1958 only 18 percent. Fifty-one percent of the people surveyed by the Center believed that public officials "don't care much what people like me think." In 1966, on the other hand, only 35 percent of the population responded in the same way and in 1960 only 25 percent. Different surveys report different figures, but they all report the same results in broad strokes. Enthusiasm for the American political order sharply declined in the late 1960s and has remained low since then.

No doubt this phenomenon is closely tied to the public dissatisfac- 5
tion with the performances of government and politicians in numerous
areas of public policy. The evidence is clear that this kind of dissatisfaction exists across all major policy areas, foreign and domestic. To
give one example: polls show that only a small proportion of the
American people think that the United States is stronger militarily than
the Soviet Union; most believe that the U.S.S.R. is stronger and many
contend that the United States is declining as a world power. It is no
wonder that, when citizens are asked to evaluate specific institutions
such as Congress and the presidency, few give favorable responses.
Over and over the message is the same. There is little confidence in the
leaders, policies, and institutions of the American political system.

The election of Ronald Reagan did not necessarily indicate a wide- 6
spread conviction that he can do any differently from his predecessors.
In an election which attracted the fewest voters since 1948, Reagan
received only 51 percent of the vote. On the other hand, the repudia-
tion first of Gerald Ford and then far more decisively of Jimmy Carter
does reveal the mood of unhappiness with our political leadership. It
outlines the popular determination to try the only alternative in each
case, though in neither 1976 nor 1980 did we see great citizen assurance
that the alternative was the answer. Nobody seems to have that kind of
confidence any more.

Loss of confidence shows not only in the public response of the 7
American people but also in their private lives. The 1970s was a period
of self-concern and self-preoccupation, documented so devastatingly
by commentators such as Tom Wolfe and Christopher Lasch. The "Me
Decade," with its ludicrous and mindless cults, pop psychology (saying "I'm OK; You're OK" was a form of exorcism for some), and
fascination with experience for its own sake (who doesn't love hang
gliding and smoking pot?) eloquently spoke to the confusion and the
lack of confidence of the age. Everywhere there were signs of people
adrift in America with no idea of who they were, how they got there, or
where they wished to go. There was good reason to define the 1970s as
a time of narcissism and self-indulgence; there is no reason to assume a
change in the 1980s.

Of late there has also been less enthusiasm for the idea that Ameri- 8
cans could cohere into a united community. Evidence of paralysis is
abundant. There is an explosion in the number of single-issue groups
pounding the pavement and flooding the mails for their specific goal.
Few of these groups care about anything else. Each judges politicians
exclusively in terms of how much support he or she gives to their
special cause. The struggle among contending groups over abortion,
gun control, nuclear power, and a host of other issues is as endless in
duration as it is fanatical in tone. It is obvious that few of these groups
consider the common good. Mostly, they simply advance their own

objective with an occasional assurance to the country that "what is good for ——— is good for the country." The result is a political system increasingly tied up in knots by pressure groups. It cannot seem to act decisively in domestic affairs, and popular dissatisfaction grows as a consequence.

9   Though the politicians in America rarely set an inspired example of concern for the whole, recent events have been unusually disturbing. Watergate was the nadir of a politics that no longer cares about anything but self-interest. Thus we begin the 1980s with the painful legacy of politics as selfishness intact. One needs only to be reminded of the corpus of candidates who refused to endorse Carter's proposed embargo of grain to the Soviet Union when they thought Iowa votes were at stake.

10   Finally, there is little doubt that, in the past ten years or so, we have witnessed a rising sense of suspicion among Americans that others are trying to gain advantage over them. Violent crime continues to increase together with public anxiety. There is increasing discussion of the "underground economy," the Americans who cheat other Americans by neglecting to pay taxes on substantial portions of their income. Moreover, there is more and more indication that the economic pie will no longer be growing in the old way and that economic struggle is here.

11   That there has been a remarkable and dramatic fall in public confidence is a fact. That it is an unmerited fact is the point we wish to establish. To be sure, such a view puts us with the proverbial fish who would foolishly swim upstream. But if civilization means a life of a people pursued in civil peace with a generous and respectful treatment of each other and a flourishing of individual talents, then America is a remarkably successful civilization. Enlightened civilizations are rare in human history, and our achievement, however limited, is something that ought to encourage more optimism than it does.

12   First, it is clear that we are more tolerant of each other than we have been at any other time in our history—or than other diverse societies ordinarily have been. Consider the great strides we took in the 1970s toward racial harmony and compare them to the racial conflict of the 1960s and the racial oppression before that. It is a remarkable story. For every failure to convict in Greensboro, there are numerous success stories—and a great many of them in the South, where nothing but the most bleak outcomes were predicted some years ago.

13   Consider the widespread tolerance of political dissent in this country. It is rare indeed in this or in any other era in human history. Individuals, groups, and the press have a remarkable range of political freedom, both in law and in reality. Sociologist Seymour Martin Lipset noted how the Vietnam War revealed this freedom:

We have just gone through a war . . . where opponents of the war had more rights than radical and/or anti-war groups ever had in wartime in any country I have ever heard about. . . . During World War I, the government put many opponents of the war in jail, and after the war foreign-born opponents were deported. The Korean War saw the rise of McCarthyism. During the Vietnam War, college students who were anti-war, representing campus newspapers, were flown around Vietnam by the U.S. Army. 14

Consider also the rising tolerance of diverse sexual standards. Homosexuality is increasingly practiced openly in this country. There is growing, if begrudged, acceptance of this behavior. Some states and cities now provide legal protection of homosexuals in employment and in their personal lives. The contrast between these trends and historic attitudes and treatment of homosexuals is striking. 15

Consider as well the greater concern for the handicapped and the old. The enormous cost of special education today is not always welcomed, but it is accepted. So are those convenient coveted parking places at shopping centers, which are reserved for the handicapped. The record regarding the old is not yet promising, although efforts have been made. Medicare, introduced in the 1960s, was an important step. So is the law that prohibits discrimination against the old in employment, though this law is difficult to enforce. A federal statute was recently passed which outlaws mandatory retirement prior to the age of seventy in private and federal employment. The biggest change needed in regard to the old is a change in attitude. More respect and honor for old people may come as our population ages in the late 1980s. 16

Consider also the metamorphosis in the status of women in the 1970s. In 1965, they constituted only 39 percent of the civilian labor force; in 1978 an impressive 49 percent. It is true, of course, that most women are working at low-paying and low-status jobs. But there are signs that an increasing number hold and will be holding positions at higher levels. In 1970, for example, women were awarded only 5 percent of the law degrees, 8 percent of the medical degrees, and a mere 1 percent of the dental degrees. While women lawyers and doctors are not one-quarter of the total yet, they are close, and there are more than seven times as many women garnering dental degrees than in 1970. Though the ERA has not been adopted, the courts increasingly grant support for the equal treatment of the sexes. 17

Consider also the expansion of religious tolerance in the United States. Perhaps in the nineteenth century the United States was a rather insular Protestant country, but this claim can no longer be legitimately made. The animus toward Roman Catholics, still powerful when John Kennedy ran for president, has receded. Antisemitism 18 continues its post-World War II decline and interests only a lunatic fraction of our people. Even militant atheists have their day without fear. People may view other groups with uneasiness, but they tolerate them. Only religious cults, notorious for ensnaring young people and keeping them in closed communities, have not been accepted. But even these groups receive legal protection in the courts.

19   Finally, consider the widespread acceptance of bad taste in the United States. Pornography came to the nation—it has spread far, far beyond Los Angeles and New York—and life goes on. Nude dancers of both sexes joined the "adult" bookstores and "cheerleader" movies; yet life continues. Tolerance is unmistakable, and tolerance is a mark of civilization.

20   Moreover, American society has often gone beyond tolerance. It increasingly treats people on a basis of equal moral worth. Many examples suggest themselves, and, though each is a story of incomplete revolution, the steps taken so far merit recognition. The increasing provision of lawyers for the poor in criminal and civil cases in both federal and state courts is a case in point. Another is the impressive record of school desegregation which finally took place during the 1970s in the South. Despite talk of white flight and desegregation, 80 percent of all Southern white children attend public schools. There whites and blacks learn to make their peace with each other and, in some cases, go on to achieve reciprocal genuine respect. This marks an enormous change—part of a set of changes regarding the races that have affected the South in a decade and a half and that have brought us closer to the American dream of mutual respect.

21   Another controversial, but important, illustration is the growing openness of the political system in the 1960s and 1970s. It was a great triumph of expanding respect for all members of our society. The provision of voting rights to Southern blacks, completed only in the past decade, is an obvious demonstration of this fact. The reduction of residency requirements for voting and the granting of suffrage to eighteen-year-olds is a similar, if less significant, statement. Even the much bewailed expansion of the number of presidential primaries beginning in 1972 has increased the opportunity for interested citizens to participate. So has the nationalization of politics in the United States with its concurrent spread of competitiveness into many closed corners of America. The opportunities for blacks, for women, for the divorced, and, in a few places, for the homosexual to run and get elected have grown dramatically.

22   We also are generous toward people of other lands. Despite all the criticism, we continue to reach out in a singular fashion. In the past decade, we welcomed a massive flow of immigrants to our shores. From 1975 to 1978, for example, over 590,000 refugees from Indochina entered the United States. An overwhelming number of Jews who

emigrated from the Soviet Union in the 1970s went either to Israel or to the United States. Both countries not only welcomed them but also supported them during their first year as immigrants. In 1980 a large group of Cuban refugees came to our country. The attraction of the United States for illegal immigration is also well known. There are millions more here than in any other country, and the government only half-heartedly tries to expel them. We should also consider the American generosity shown through unparalleled charitable giving, which the United States has provided for Cambodian refugees. Think of the enormous efforts of the religious and nonsectarian relief agencies. The United Way campaigns and the American Red Cross raise enormous amounts of money. So does the Federation of Jewish Charities. In 1978, private contributions to charity in the United States exceeded $39 billion.

Another unmistakable mark of the American civilization is the 23 achievement of the creative mind of the United States: the march of science, the continued growth of the social services, and the expansive flowing of the literary and fine arts. Despite alarms of the 1970s about pure research, work goes on visibly and vigorously. In the 1970s Americans were awarded more Nobel Prizes both in the physiology-medicine category and in physics than all the other nations of the world combined. Americans also won almost half the Nobel Prizes in chemistry. The story of continued vitality of the social sciences, economics, political science, psychology, and sociology could be lengthy. But its essence is that America dominates every social science—a fact which few dispute in the world intellectual community. Accomplishment in theoretical economics, for example, was recognized by the Nobel Prize committee, which in the 1970s awarded seven of the fifteen prizes to Americans and two others to people who taught at American universities. In philosophy, major scholars at Harvard and Chicago rivaled and may have surpassed their counterparts at Oxford and Cambridge for dominance in the important Anglo-American analytical school. American mathematics is flourishing and is among the best in the world. Indeed, it is difficult to perceive of any academic field in which American scholars are not in the forefront of their disciplines.

The story in the arts is similar. Two Americans won the Nobel Prize for literature in the 1970s (Saul Bellow and I. B. Singer), and the fine arts enjoy a renaissance in popularity and creativity. New York continues to be one of the few world centers of music, opera, dance, painting, and theater. But it was the spread of all of these activities across America in the 1970s that was a memorable step. Culture has become increasingly decentralized, and more and more Americans benefit.

Civilization in America is hardly unqualified. The inanities of the TV 24 sit coms, quiz shows, and soap operas are undeniable. Popular music limps along at a creative level far below that of the 1960s. New Wave fails to equal the quality of music produced by the Beatles. "Serious culture" in too many places is light comedy. Crime, including violent crime, which obviously shows no respect for human beings, marches steadily upward. So does the number of impolite drivers, salespeople, and bureaucrats. Yet, overall, there is much to praise, even celebrate. We wonder: Why has there been so scant appreciation of the contributions in America and so much pessimism and lack of confidence in America?

25   We do not know the answer. We believe, however, that it is urgent to speculate about it because the false picture that the pessimists have presented discourages us all from attempting to find solutions to America's problems. Three explanations for the decline of confidence deserve mention. One view is that it constitutes a rational reaction to the events of the past two decades. The record of the 1960s, after all, is far from beautiful. Racial upheavals, ghetto riots, crime in the streets, wild political demonstrations, and the war in Vietnam marked that decade. Nor was the 1970s an era of unchecked advances. Watergate will not go away that easily. Nor will our political leadership's ineptness. No wonder our nation continues to dwell on these failures. But the 1960s and the 1970s were also periods of impressive progress. The question therefore remains: Why have the people allowed the failures instead of the successes to dominate their attitudes?

26   A second view is that the decline of confidence is a product of the increasing democratization of America. In this view, it is argued that the United States became more democratic in the 1960s and 1970s. As a result, weak leaders gained election, men who surrendered governing authority to the interest groups and the people causing national drift and lack of leadership. As a consequence, citizens considered their leaders less and less legitimate. The people, therefore, have become pessimistic concerning the ability of leaders to solve problems in the future. Political scientist Samuel Huntington speaks of this phenomenon as the "democratic distemper." We find his argument clever, but problematic. Gains in democracy, in fact, usually lead to increases in governmental legitimacy. This association is particularly strong in modern times when there is greater expectation that the people will have a voice in choosing their rulers. People reacted against Johnson in the late 1960s and Nixon in the 1970s not because they were weak or surrendered authority but because they abused their power contrary to the people's wishes. They rejected Carter not because he abandoned authority but because he seemed unable to lead.

27   A third perspective blames the intellectuals for the growth of popular pessimism. Sociologist Daniel Bell contends that many cultural and intellectual elites are hostile to America and to its governmental lead-

ers and spread this hostility at every opportunity. He also notes that other thoughtful voices, though sympathetic to America, have been confused and uncertain about how to defend it. Historian Daniel Boorstin claims that intellectuals have never appreciated the greatness of America and since the 1960s have launched a deadly assault. The antagonism to the United States is widespread among many influential academics and cultural figures. Pessimism, as we have seen, is even more widespread. Intellectuals do set a tone, one which is often pessimistic or negative. Yet Boorstin, for one, doubts that intellectuals have been as influential as Bell thinks.

Both agree on the influence of the media, which often seems to work 28 full time to undermine our confidence, to create suspicion, and to mobilize skepticism. We refer not to the small-town weeklies in Texas or Kansas but to the news departments of the three national television networks, the well-known leading newspapers, and the national news services. The negative picture of America portrayed in these sources has not been the result of a conscious conspiracy, as the paranoid in our society would have us believe. It is partly a post-Watergate mood; it is partly a reflection of the larger intellectual mood; it is partly a natural consequence of the media's, and especially television's, lust for the dramatic and controversial. The national media has shown us our many tragedies and disappointments, but rarely has it reported the kinds of progress we have mentioned here. This dominance unfortunately has resulted in an unmerited pessimism about the future of America.

What can be done about this situation? The insularity of elite aca- 29 demic opinion is hard to penetrate. Intellectual circles outside the academy give more hope, but the real issue is how to get a more balanced media. How can we get the media to reflect both the successes as well as the failures of our time? We certainly reject governmental censorship. Governmental dominance of the news or even interference with a free press is even worse than media dominance. The only hope appears to be that the media will not only recognize the problem, which they may have already, but will begin to do something about it. Perhaps journalists and editors ought to get out of the newsroom and look at the larger picture of the United States. Perhaps they should spend some time working in other jobs, including political offices. They need to question how they present the news. They need to ask themselves what the world is which they describe in their newspapers and in television programs. Is it the real world? To do this will require a kind of modesty which too few have. But it can be done. Perspective is often dearly won, but it is vital, especially for the press. They are an increasingly central window to the world.

In 1982, there is intensified need for documentation of the underly- 30 ing successes of this century. The current force of the righteous right stems in part from the failure of all types of media to call attention to our advances as well as to our failures.

FOR DISCUSSION

1. Look at the structure of this essay: what comes first, what comes second, and so on? How is it "put together"? How does this structure work to support the assertion the writers are making?

2. How do the essay's place of appearance, *The Humanist*, and its title relate to the audience for whom the essay was written?

3. The evidence for support of this assertion is not documentation. What kind of evidence do the authors give? Is it convincing to you?

4. The authors give three explanations for the decline in confidence in our country. What are they?

5. Finally, what do the authors say can be done?

EDWARD SADALLA
AND JEFFREY BURROUGHS

In this essay psychologists Edward Sadalla and Jeffrey Burroughs assert that particular types of people eat particular kinds of food— that, in fact, personality and self image are related to food choice. Writing for a popular monthly magazine, the authors present the results of their research in a manner that is accessible to a general audience. Do you find the proof they offer convincing?

Profiles in Eating: Sexy Vegetarians and Other Diet-based Social Stereotypes

1 There is plenty of casual evidence that people choose food not only for taste and nourishment but also because it bolsters their self-image and sends strong messages about them to the rest of the world.

2   Consider the prizefighter who wolfs down a bloody steak before the title fight: photographers and reporters are usually summoned to cap-

ture the ferocious spectacle of the contender rending and tearing his dinner, steer blood trickling out of the corners of his mouth.

The late Bernarr McFadden, a health-food enthusiast whose missionary zeal would be hard to surpass, went skydiving in his 80s and skinny-dipping in the dead of winter. The press was inevitably present for McFadden's incredible geriatric feats, which were fueled, as he reminded one and all, by wheat germ and blackstrap molasses.   3

Human beings are an omnivorous species, able to survive on a wide variety of foods. Nonetheless, the diets that particular individuals or groups actually choose may be quite limited. Even today, many Eskimo eat little but great hunks of meat, yet return home after a day of seal hunting in the numbing cold with enough energy left for a night of partying.   4

By contrast, George Bernard Shaw, a lifelong and militant vegetarian, continued to write and rail with energy to burn when his white beard was down to his breastbone.   5

Intrigued by the psychological implications of human eating behavior, our team at Arizona State University set out to determine whether food choices are indeed linked to self-image and to the way others regard us.   6

We divided foods into five categories: *vegetarian, gourmet, health food, fast food,* and *synthetic food*. We asked an initial group of 500 subjects to list the foods they associated with each category. From their lists, we picked 14 specific dishes to typify each category. Vegetarian dishes include broccoli quiche, avocado sandwiches with bean sprouts, and brown rice with snow peas. Typical gourmet foods were fresh oysters, lobster Newburg, Indonesian roast lamb, and caviar. The health-food list included granola with dried fruit, wheat germ, yogurt, and carob cake. The synthetic-food category included such high-tech items as Lean Strips (processed bacon), Egg Beaters (processed eggs), Carnation Instant Breakfast, and Cheez Whiz. At the top of the fast-food list were Whoppers and Big Macs, Kentucky Fried Chicken, hot dogs and submarine sandwiches.   7

We presented 150 subjects in a second group with a list of typical foods from each category and asked them to think of the traits that described people who would prefer such foods. This procedure resulted in a list of 65 descriptions such as hypochondriac, unworried about health, executive, blue collar, late, punctual, callous, sensitive, worrier, emotionally stable.   8

Using our lists of specific foods and descriptions, we performed three separate studies to examine the relationship between food preferences and personality. In our first experiment, 75 college students evaluated a hypothetical person with specific dietary preferences by rating that person on each of the 65 items on our list. We were initially surprised at the alacrity and confidence with which subjects paired food preferences with descriptions. If a person was said to like bean   9 sprouts, for example, our subjects described him without hesitation as anti-nuclear power and pro-solar energy.

10   Our subjects not only "knew" which character traits went with what foods but also were in considerable agreement when we asked them to characterize someone with a specific food preference. They saw fast-food lovers as patriotic, pronuclear, conservative, antidrug, and dressed in polyester suits. They saw vegetarians as pacifist, hypochondriacal, drug-using, weight-conscious, liberal, and likely to drive foreign cars.

11   The first experiment was designed to assess the inferences people make about others based on food preferences. If people prefer foods that communicate an "appropriate" social identity, then the social inferences of those who observe them should show some agreement. Thus observers should be able to "read" the social information present in food preferences, and their reading should show some consensus with that of other observers. The results we obtained provided strong support for that assumption. The question that follows quite naturally from that finding concerns the validity of the observers' inferences.

12   In a second experiment, we examined the extent to which inferences made about a person based on his or her eating preferences correspond to that person's self-image. In order to test that, we screened about 2,000 students at Arizona State University and found 352 whose food preferences fell clearly within one of our five categories. We then asked them to rate themselves—in terms of the identity they project—on traits we had developed in our first experiment. Then we compared their self-descriptions with the stereotypes that others had constructed about people with those food preferences.

13   The resulting data indicated substantial agreement between stereotypes and self-descriptions for people whose food preferences fell in the health-food, vegetarian, or gourmet categories, less agreement for those in the fast-food or synthetic-food categories.

14   Those two experiments indicated that a relationship exists between perceived social identity and patterns of food preference. But to what extent are food preferences related to objective measures of personality and life-style?

15   To find out, we undertook a third experiment: we gave another group of subjects a battery of well-validated personality tests: the Future Events Test, the Social Readjustment Rating Scale, items from the Rotter External Locus of Control Scale, the Work and Family Orientation Questionnaire, and the Leisure Activities Blank.

16   All of these tests are designed to assess thought patterns, behavior, or lifestyle variables related to social identity. We had 275 volunteers—students and nonstudents—complete the battery of tests; they then rated their preferences for specific dishes in each food category.

The data we obtained suggested a significant correlation both be- 17 tween food preferences and objective personality tests and between food preferences and self-ratings of personality. In other words, the foods people prefer can—to some extent—be used to predict their personalities.

The personality portraits related to the food preferences in our 18 sample were quite distinctive. For example, vegetarians emerged as relatively noncompetitive, with a taste for handicrafts and for difficult, challenging tasks of an intellectual nature. They claim to be weight-conscious, "sexy," and to use recreational drugs.

Health-food enthusiasts projected themselves as noncompetitive, 19 intellectual, and mechanically inclined; also hypochondriacal, anti-nuclear, prosolar, likely to use recreational drugs, and, by their own admission, "weird" and individualistic.

Gourmets, who admitted to an even higher "fun" drug use than the 20 veggies, tended to be atheist, liberal, and live alone; they also reported feeling that marriage is more vital to happiness than a job. They enjoy fast living (gambling, nightclubs, etc.) and engage both in glamour sports and in neighborhood athletics. They consider themselves sensual and sophisticated.

To the extent that a fast-food portrait emerged, the preference 21 seems related to a desire to work hard at one's job, a need to win, and the urge to have children. Fast-food people described themselves as religious, conservative, family-oriented, pronuclear, antidrug. The synthetic-food fans also showed themselves to be conservative and home-oriented as well as practical and competitive.

To the best of our knowledge, our project was the first systematic 22 attempt to link social symbolism and specific food categories, examining the hypothesis that food preferences are part of the complex system of attitudes and behavior that define social identity.

Many undeveloped or unverified theories about food have been 23 advanced over the years: for example, that "we are what we eat" or that familiar foods represent security; that milk and milk-based products have a tranquilizing effect thanks to nursery memories; that wine and gourmet cooking are attempts to gain some control over eating.

In his classic anthropological work, *The Golden Bough*, James 24 Frazer wrote extensively of the ritual use of food, concluding that "among primitive tribes, there is a universal belief that by eating the flesh of a man or an animal, an individual acquires the physical, moral, and intellectual qualities of that man or animal."

The Creeks and Cherokee of North America thought man who dined 25 on venison swifter and smarter than the one who fed on the meat of the clumsy bear, the slow-footed cattle, or the wallowing swine. Similarly, the Zaparo Indians of Ecuador tried to avoid meat from heavy animals such as tapirs and pigs; they preferred birds, monkeys, deer, or fish. And in Central Africa, young men seeking instant courage ate the flesh and hearts of lions, while would-be lovers desiring sexual strength dined on the testicles of goats. Before the Zulu warriors went into battle, they would often eat meat smeared with dried powder made from the flesh of leopards, lions, and elephants in hopes of acquiring the strength and aggressiveness of those creatures.

26   The magic that primitive hunters and warriors saw in their food is not so different from the symbolic messages contemporary men and women believe their eating patterns convey. Accordingly, we think that our research helps shed light on the problem of why some people choose diets that are nutritionally poor or linked with medical problems. Medical research has begun to suggest that Americans as a group tend to overeat and to eat foods too rich in animal fat and sugar. It is possible that the patterns of American food preferences stem from the symbolism inherent in certain foods—red meat symbolizing status, success, power, achievement; sugar-laden foods representing pleasure, self-reward, and playfulness.

27   Our study, confined to middle-class Americans able to choose what they eat, suggests that the symbolism of food must also be taken into account in trying to get people to change their eating habits. Madison Avenue understands that very well, of course: witness the number of ad campaigns linking this or that food with success, status, or romance. While the particular personality portraits associated with given food preferences may change with time or geographical region, we assume that some food-identity linkages will be present even if the specific relationship changes.

FOR DISCUSSION

1. Would it be possible for the basic assertion—that food is related to self-image—to be true and the specific assertions in the essay not be true? Discuss.

2. Are there any logical flaws in these experiments?

3. What were the possible motives the authors had for writing this essay?

4. This article, which first appeared in the October 1981 issue of *Psychology Today*, presents the results of several experiments. What did the authors do to turn their results into an article accessible to a general readership?

5. If you wanted to challenge the assertion the writers have made, what evidence would you use to do so?

WRITING YOUR OWN

The Assertion-With-Evidence Essay

Before you begin to write your own assertion-with-evidence essay, let's review the individual configuration in Barbara Lang Stern's "Tears Can Be Crucial to Your Physical and Emotional Health."

Motivation (an educated guess): to share a different outlook on crying; to sell an article.

Circumstance/Situation: a monthly magazine with a deadline and space requirements.

Audience: general magazine reader.

Writer's Relationship to Audience: person who has studied the subject to persons who haven't.

Emphasis: on facts that will enlighten the reader.

Form: essay/article.

Intention (an educated guess): to change reader's knowledge and attitude about crying.

Now try to describe the configurations for the other essays in this chapter.

DESIGNING YOUR OWN CONFIGURATION

Before you write your own assertion-with-evidence essay, you'll want to pick a topic—perhaps a subject that you want to change people's opinion of, or an issue that you have strong feelings about. Think of areas of special interest to you, something you'd like to change about the way things are run at school, work, or home; or deal with a larger social problem that concerns you. Be sure to have in mind a specific audience for your writing, a specific place your writing will appear, and the specific evidence you intend to use to support your assertion. The following suggestions for writing may help you to choose a topic.

1. Give reasons why your (or some) backpack, bicycle, type-writer, or camera is superior to others you've considered. If one of these objects doesn't appeal to you, pick something you're familiar with. Be sure to use lots of graphic details.
2. Write an essay with convincing evidence in which you declare that the legal age for drinking should be lowered to eighteen. (You might prefer to argue the opposite—that the legal drinking age should be raised.)
3. Take a stand on some book, poem, play, or movie you have recently read or seen. Cite reasons why it is worth/not worth recommending. Pick a newspaper or magazine that you are writing for, and style your review accordingly.
4. A friend of yours claims that having a football team at your school wastes a lot of money that could be put to better use—that in fact, football has no place in a university or college. Try to change your friend's mind by writing an essay in support of an official school team. Or, if you prefer, defend your friend's claim in the essay.
5. Some argue that civil defense preparations will significantly reduce the number of casualities in a nuclear war; others claim that such preparations offer a false sense of security and therefore make the occurrence of nuclear war more likely. Pick a side, and write an essay with evidence that illustrates or proves your point.

The following chart will help you to define the points of your configuration for your assertion-with-evidence essay:

Designing Your Own Configuration for an Assertion-With-Evidence Essay

MOTIVE	CIRCUMSTANCE/ SITUATION	AUDIENCE	RELATIONSHIP TO AUDIENCE
To sell an article	For x magazine with x deadline and x length requirement	Readers of x magazine	Person who knows to person who doesn't
To prove that you are right	For a class assignment with x deadline and x requirements	People in x group meeting on x	Person who needs to prove to person who doesn't yet believe
To change people's erroneous views	In defense of yourself in a group	General public Classmates Professor	
To support someone's work	In a public meeting		Person who sees something to person who doesn't
To spread information about some new development			
To present new evidence you have unearthed			

EMPHASIS	FORM	INTENTION
On the evidence itself	Essay	To change reader's knowledge about a thing
On the subject	Report	
On the assertion	Article	To change what reader thinks about a certain thing
On the writer's expertise and ability to know	Speech	
	Letter to editor	To add information to what the reader knows
	Editorial	

RULES FOR AN ASSERTION-WITH-EVIDENCE ESSAY

1. Make your assertion clearly the center of emphasis for the essay.
2. Give convincing, logical, orderly evidence.
3. Acknowledge any weaknesses your evidence might have, or at least be aware of them yourself.
4. Discuss the evidence in sufficient enough detail to "unwrap" it for the reader.
5. Be committed to what you say.

RHETORICAL PATTERNS OFTEN USED IN ASSERTION-WITH-EVIDENCE ESSAYS

Examples and Illustrations: How to Help the Reader See.

1. An example or illustration is a specific instance that helps clarify a more general statement by allowing the reader to *see*. It is one single thing that shows the character of the whole.
2. Be as colorful, descriptive, detailed, and specific as you possibly can when you give examples and illustrations. Appeal to the readers' *senses*. Transport the readers to the spot and *show* what you mean.
3. Use *concrete* words. Abstract terms don't produce pictures in readers' minds. General words, too, can mean different things to different people. Concrete words appearing in examples and illustrations will let the readers know what *you* mean by the general terms. And if you've used any abstract terms, concrete words will help make them clear to the readers.
4. Choose examples and illustrations that will mean something to the particular audience for whom you are writing.
5. Be generous with examples and illustrations. A minimum ratio is one specific example or illustration to one general statement. Often, however, a higher ratio—say, two or three examples or illustrations to one general statement—will be necessary to let your reader *see* exactly what you mean. You will probably never err by having too many examples and illustrations.

Analysis: How to Help the Reader Understand

1. The word *analyze* means "to divide anything complex into its simple parts or pieces by separating a whole into its parts." It also means "to show the relationship among the single parts of a larger, more complex subject."

2. A good analysis actually shows the reader how to *think* about the subject.
3. To use analysis in your writing, decide what parts you can break the larger subject into. Then take these parts one at a time. Discuss or describe them, either on an individual basis or as a group, showing how they relate to each other. Finally, put the parts back together in a whole. The reader will then have been able to *understand* what may have otherwise been baffling or confusing.

Details: How to Be Specific

1. Details are individual or minute parts of a whole. When included in a piece of writing, details give the reader a much clearer picture of what is being discussed.
2. Select details that are relevant to the point you are making. Don't try to include everything.
3. Among those relevant details, select only the most important ones to include.
4. Make the details as specific and concise as possible.

The Evaluation Essay

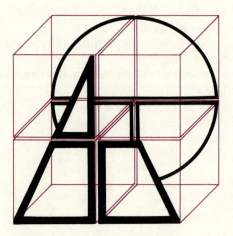

To Evaluate   to determine or set the value of
to estimate the nature, quality, or importance of
to determine the worth of

A hundred times a day we evaluate things around us, determining their value, quality, importance, or worth. The presence of some kind of standard against which the thing being measured is judged is what distinguishes evaluative writing. Sometimes these standards are *external*: this blender is better than those because *(a)* it has a stronger motor, *(b)* it is easier to wash, and *(c)* it has an unbreakable glass bowl. These features can be observed by everyone who wants to check on them and are external to the person writing the evaluation. The only thing the evaluator is taking for granted is that the reader agrees that stronger motors, easy washability, and unbreakable glass bowls are more desirable.

   In other kinds of evaluative writing, the standards the writer uses for judging are *internal*: this book isn't worth reading because *(a)* there is too much description, *(b)* the main character is unattractive, and *(c)* the plot has too many angles. In a case like this, the writer cannot assume that the reader will necessarily agree that a lot of description is bad, that a particular kind of person is unattractive, or that a complicated plot is not desirable. The evaluation is based on the internal standards of the writer, standards which may or may not be the same as the readers'. (Usually, we accept an evaluation more quickly if the writer has the same standards we do. One of the finest ways to broaden oneself, however, is to read evaluative writing done by people who think very differently.) The use of internal criteria for judging assumes that the writer has some special expertise, knowledge, experience, or the like to merit being listened to.

Whether the criteria are external and objective or internal and subjective, the value in an evaluation essay finally lies in the relationship between the person doing the evaluation and the thing being evaluated. It is this interface or friction between the one doing the judging and the thing being judged that the reader is finally left with, rather than some kind of absolute proof or truth. Even when a writer has used *external* criteria, for example, the human nature of the evaluator still intrudes on the evaluation—how many blenders were tested the day this one was proved best, for example; does the evaluator work for the company whose blender won; do other blenders have outstanding features that are more important than motor strength, washability, or the kind of glass?

There is little use, of course, even to attempt to separate an evaluation from the person doing the evaluation, and it's not even desirable. To do so would be to lose the quality—the variable—that makes evaluations interesting, real, and valuable or not valuable. Instead, when we write (and read) evaluations, we should realize that we are having the opportunity to observe both the person doing the evaluating and the thing being evaluated. We can't avoid learning about both.

A good evaluation essay will have these characteristics:

The criteria used will be clear to the reader.

The writer will explain how these criteria are appropriate to be used in the evaluation unless she or he can assume that the reader will automatically know.

The nature of the criteria—whether it is internal or external—will be established early in the essay.

The writer's qualifications for doing the evaluation will be apparent to the reader.

The writer will give ample facts, specific details, or examples to support the final judgment made in the evaluation.

The following essays are evaluations done by professional writers. Read them and think about these questions as you read:

What are the criteria the writer uses for the evaluation? Are these criteria *external* or *internal?*

Does the writer make any assumptions about what the readers will already agree with, believe, accept, or know?

What are the writer's qualifications for making this evaluation?

What kind of specific facts, details, and examples did the writer use to support the evaluation? Were you convinced?

What did you learn about the writer when you read this evaluation?

Does the place this essay appeared influence what was said?

YI-FU TUAN

Evaluative writing often takes the form of comparing and contrasting two things in order to get at the nature of each. This essay, contrasting the American's sense of space with the Chinese's sense of place, is Yi-Fu Tuan's attempt to identify the nature of two different cultures. The essay first appeared in the July 1974 issue of Harper's Magazine.

American Space, Chinese Place

Americans have a sense of space, not of place. Go to an American home in exurbia, and almost the first thing you do is drift toward the picture window. How curious that the first compliment you pay your host inside his house is to say how lovely it is outside his house! He is pleased that you should admire his vistas. The distant horizon is not merely a line separating earth from sky, it is a symbol of the future. The American is not rooted in his place, however lovely: his eyes are drawn by the expanding space to a point on the horizon, which is his future. 1

By contrast, consider the traditional Chinese home. Blank walls enclose it. Step behind the spirit wall and you are in a courtyard with perhaps a miniature garden around a corner. Once inside his private compound you are wrapped in an ambiance of calm beauty, an ordered world of buildings, pavement, rock, and decorative vegetation. But you have no distant view: nowhere does space open out before you. Raw nature in such a home is experienced only as weather, and the only open space is the sky above. The Chinese is rooted in his place. When he has to leave, it is not for the promised land on the terrestrial horizon, but for another world altogether along the vertical, religious axis of his imagination. 2

The Chinese tie to place is deeply felt. Wanderlust is an alien sentiment. The Taoist classic *Tao Te Ching* captures the ideal of rootedness in place with these words: "Though there may be another country in the neighborhood so close that they are within sight of each other and the crowing of cocks and barking of dogs in one place can be heard in the other, yet there is no traffic between them; and throughout their lives the two peoples have nothing to do with each other." In theory if not in practice, farmers have ranked high in Chinese society. The reason is not only that they are engaged in a "root" industry of producing food but that, unlike pecuniary merchants, they are tied to the land and do not abandon their country when it is in danger. 3

Nostalgia is a recurrent theme in Chinese poetry. An American reader of translated Chinese poems may well be taken aback—even 4 put off—by the frequency, as well as the sentimentality, of the lament for home. To understand the strength of this sentiment, we need to know that the Chinese desire for stability and rootedness in place is prompted by the constant threat of war, exile, and the natural disasters of flood and drought. Forcible removal makes the Chinese keenly aware of their loss. By contrast, Americans move, for the most part, voluntarily. Their nostalgia for home town is really longing for a childhood to which they cannot return: in the meantime the future beckons and the future is "out there," in open space. When we criticize American rootlessness, we tend to forget that it is a result of ideals we admire, namely, social mobility and optimism about the future. When we admire Chinese rootedness, we forget that the word "place" means both a location in space and position in society: to be tied to place is also to be bound to one's station in life, with little hope of betterment. Space symbolizes hope; place, achievement and stability.

FOR DISCUSSION

1. What makes this essay interesting to all people, not just Chinese or Americans?

2. What does the fact that the author is a professor suggest to you about a possible motivation for writing this essay? What does the fact that the author is Chinese suggest?

3. This essay is written in the second person, not the first, even though the author is Chinese. What does the second person add to the essay?

4. What do you know about the Chinese sense of place after reading this essay? What enabled you to know that clearly?

5. What is the ratio of examples of American living to Chinese living? What impact does that ratio have on the evaluation the author is making?

6. Do any of the evaluations made by the author arise from implicit, as opposed to explicit, assumptions on the author's part? Which assumptions could use further explanation?

7. What aspects of this essay do you think were determined by the fact that it first appeared in *Harper's* Magazine, a liberal, general-interest monthly, which focuses on literary and political issues?

8. Why is it appropriate that this essay appears in the section called **Writing to Change?**

E. M. Forster

E. M. Forster (1879–1970), the famous English novelist and author of
A Passage to India (1924), *wrote this tribute to Mahatma Gandhi, after
Gandhi was assassinated in 1948. Forster attempts here to estimate
the importance to the world of Gandhi, the Hindu nationalist leader
who used passive resistance and civil disobedience to lead the people
of India to independence from British rule.*

Tribute to Mahatma Gandhi

The organizers of this meeting have asked me . . . to pay a short
tribute myself. In doing so I do not desire to emphasize the note of
grief. Grief is for those who knew Mahatma Gandhi personally, or who
are close to his teaching. I have neither of these claims. Nor would it be
seemly to speak with compassion and pity of him, as though it were on
him rather than on India and the world that the blow has fallen. If I
have understood him rightly, he was always indifferent to death. His
work and the welfare of others was what mattered to him, and if the
work could have been furthered by dying rather than living, he would
have been content. He was accustomed to regard an interruption as an
instrument, and he remarks in his *Autobiography* that God seldom
intended for him what he had planned. And he would have regarded
death, the supreme interruption, as an instrument and perhaps the
supreme one—preferable to the full 125 years of life for which in his
innocence he had hoped. The murder seems so hideous and senseless
to us—as an English friend of mine put it, one would have liked that
old saint to fade away magically. But we must remember that we are
looking at it all from outside; it was not a defeat to him.

But although neither grief nor pity are in place this evening, we may
well entertain a feeling of awe and a sense of our own smallness. When
the news came to me last week, I realized intensely how small I was,
how small those around me, how impotent and circumscribed are the
lives of most of us spiritually, and how in comparison with that mature
goodness the so-called great men of our age are no more than bluster-
ing school boys. Read the newspapers tomorrow, see what they adver-
tise and whom, observe the values they imply and the actions they
emphasize. Then think anew of the career and character of Mahatma
Gandhi, and the feeling of awe will return with a salutary shock. We,
to-day—we are inventive and adaptable, we are stoical and learning to
bear things, our young men have acquired what may be termed the

"returned warrior" attitude, and that is all very well. But we are losing the sense of wonder. We are forgetting what human nature can do, and upon what a vast stage it is set. The death of this very great man may remind us, he has indicated by his existence the possibilities still to be explored.

3   His character was intricate, and this is not the place to analyze it. But all who met him, even the critical, have testified to the goodness in it, a goodness irradiated by no ordinary light. His practical teachings—the doctrine of non-violence and the doctrine of simplicity, symbolized by the spinning wheel—proceeded from that goodness, and it also inspired his willingness to suffer. He was not only good. He made good and ordinary men all over the world now look up to him in consequence. He has placed India on their spiritual map. It was always on that map for the student and scholar, but the ordinary man demands tangible evidence, spiritual proofs of moral firmness, and he has found them in the imprisonments, the fastings, the willingness to suffer, and in this death. The other day I passed a taxi-rank, and heard the drivers talking to one another about "Old Gandhi" and praising him in their own way. He would have valued it more than any tribute the scholar or the student can bring. For it sprang from simplicity.

4   "A very great man" I have called him. He is likely to be the greatest of our century. Lenin is sometimes bracketed with him, but Lenin's kingdom was of this world, and we do not know yet what the world will do with it. Gandhi's was not. Though he impinged upon events and influenced politics, he had his roots outside time, and drew strength thence. He is with the founders of religion, whether he founds a religion or not. He is with the great artists, though art was not his medium. He is with all the men and women who have sought something in life that is neither chaos nor mechanism, who have not confused happiness with possessiveness, or victory with success, and who have believed in love.

FOR DISCUSSION

1. What was Forster's experience of Gandhi's death? How is this experience important to what he is saying in the essay?

2. What contribution can the evaluation of Mahatma Gandhi's life make to the people who read this essay?

3. What do you "know" about the author after reading this essay?

4. Forster had no attachment to Gandhi either personally or through his teaching, but his best-known work, *A Passage to India* (1924),

concerns the prejudices and injustices of the British rule over colonial India. What might you guess was his motive for writing this piece?

5. How does comparing Gandhi to someone else assist Forster in the evaluation of Gandhi's life?

6. How might a reader be "changed" after reading this essay? In other words, why does this essay appear in **Writing to Change**?

WENDELL BERRY

In the following selection Wendell Berry, a Kentucky farmer, poet, novelist, essayist, and professor, compares the virtues of human-powered scythes with those of electrically-powered scythes. Berry bases his evaluation on personal experience and attempts to convince the reader of the superiority of the human-powered scythe. The essay is taken from his book, The Gift of Good Land: Further Essays Cultural and Agricultural *(1981).*

A Good Scythe

When we moved to our little farm in the Kentucky River Valley in 1965, we came with a lot of assumptions that we have abandoned or changed in response to the demands of place and time. We assumed, for example, that there would be good motor-powered solutions for all of our practical purposes. 1

One of the biggest problems from the beginning was that our place was mostly on a hillside and included a good deal of ground near the house and along the road that was too steep to mow with a lawn mower. Also, we were using some electric fence, which needed to be mowed out once or twice a year. 2

When I saw that Sears Roebuck sold a "power scythe," it seemed the ideal solution, and I bought one. I don't remember what I paid for it, but it was expensive, considering the relatively small amount of work I needed it for. It consisted of a one-cylinder gasoline engine 3

"A Good Scythe" in *The Gift of Good Land: Further Essays Cultural and Agricultural* by Wendell Berry. Copyright © 1981 by Wendell Berry. Published by North Point Press. All rights reserved. Reprinted by permission.

mounted on a frame with a handlebar, a long metal tube enclosing a flexible drive shaft, and a rotary blade. To use it, you hung it from your shoulder by a web strap, and swept the whirling blade over the ground at the desired height.

4   It did a fairly good job of mowing, cutting the grass and weeds off clean and close to the ground. An added advantage was that it readily whacked off small bushes and tree sprouts. But this solution to the mowing problem involved a whole package of new problems:

1. The power scythe was heavy.
2. It was clumsy to use, and it got clumsier as the ground got steeper and rougher. The tool that was supposed to solve the problem of steep ground worked best on level ground.
3. It was dangerous. As long as the scythe was attached to you by the shoulder strap, you weren't likely to fall onto that naked blade. But it *was* a naked blade, and it did create a constant threat of flying rock chips, pieces of glass, etc.
4. It enveloped you in noise, and in the smudge and stench of exhaust fumes.
5. In rank growth, the blade tended to choke—in which case you had to kill the engine in a hurry or it would twist the drive shaft in two.
6. Like a lot of small gas engines not regularly used, this one was temperamental and undependable. And dependence on an engine that won't run is a plague and a curse.

5   When I review my own history, I am always amazed at how slow I have been to see the obvious. I don't remember how long I used that "labor-saving" power scythe before I finally donated it to help enlighten one of my friends—but it was too long. Nor do I remember all the stages of my own enlightenment.

6   The turning point, anyhow, was the day when Harlan Hubbard showed me an old-fashioned, human-powered scythe that was clearly the best that I had ever seen. It was light, comfortable to hold and handle. The blade was very sharp, angled and curved precisely to the path of its stroke. There was an intelligence and refinement in its design that made it a pleasure to handle and look and think about. I asked where I could get one, and Harlan gave me an address: The Marugg Company, Tracy City, Tennessee 37387.

7   I wrote for a price list and promptly received a sheet exhibiting the stock in trade of the Marugg Company: grass scythes, bush scythes, snaths, sickles, hoes, stock bells, carrying yokes, whetstones, and the hammers and anvils used in beating out the "dangle" cutting edge that is an essential feature of the grass scythes.

In due time I became the owner of a grass scythe, hammer and anvil, 8 and whetstone. Learning to use the hammer and anvil properly (the Marugg Company provides a sheet of instructions) takes some effort and some considering. And so does learning to use the scythe. It is essential to hold the point so that it won't dig into the ground, for instance; and you must learn to swing so that you slice rather than hack.

Once these fundamentals are mastered, the Marugg grass scythe 9 proves itself an excellent tool. It is the most satisfying hand tool that I have ever used. In tough grass it cuts a little less uniformly than the power scythe. In all other ways, in my opinion it is a better tool:

1. It is light.
2. It handles gracefully and comfortably even on steep ground.
3. It is far less dangerous than the power scythe.
4. It is quiet and makes no fumes.
5. It is much more adaptable to conditions than the power scythe: in ranker growth, narrow the cut and shorten the stroke.
6. It always starts—provided the user will start. Aside from reasonable skill and care in use, there are no maintenance problems.
7. It requires no fuel or oil. It runs on what you ate for breakfast.
8. It is at least as fast as the power scythe. Where the cutting is either light or extra heavy, it can be appreciably faster.
9. It is far cheaper than the power scythe, both to buy and to use.

Since I bought my power scythe, a new version has come on the 10 market, using a short length of nylon string in place of the metal blade. It is undoubtedly safer. But I believe the other drawbacks remain. Though I have not used one of these, I have observed them in use, and they appear to me to be slower than the metal-bladed power scythe, and less effective on large-stemmed plants.

I have noticed two further differences between the power scythe and 11 the Marugg scythe that are not so practical as those listed above, but which I think are just as significant. The first is that I never took the least pleasure in using the power scythe, whereas in using the Marugg scythe, whatever the weather and however difficult the cutting, I always work with the pleasure that one invariably gets from using a good tool. And because it is not motor driven and is quiet and odorless, the Marugg scythe also allows the pleasure of awareness of what is going on around you as you work.

12   The other difference is between kinds of weariness. Using the Marugg scythe causes the simple bodily weariness that comes with exertion. This is a kind of weariness that, when not extreme, can in itself be one of the pleasures of work. The power scythe, on the other hand, adds to the weariness of exertion the unpleasant and destructive weariness of strain. This is partly because, in addition to carrying and handling it, your attention is necessarily clenched to it; if you are to use it effectively and safely, you *must* not look away. And partly it is because the power scythe, like all motor-driven tools, imposes patterns of endurance that are alien to the body. As long as the motor is running there is a pressure to keep going. You don't stop to consider or rest or look around. You keep on until the motor stops or the job is finished or you have some kind of trouble. (This explains why the tractor soon evolved headlights, and farmers began to do daywork at night.)

13   These differences have come to have, for me, the force of a parable. Once you have mastered the Marugg scythe, what an absurd thing it makes of the power scythe! What possible sense can there be in carrying a heavy weight on your shoulder in order to reduce by a very little the use of your arms? Or to use quite a lot of money as a substitute for a little skill?

14   The power scythe—and it is far from being an isolated or unusual example—is *not* a labor saver or a shortcut. It is a labor maker (you have to work to pay for it as well as to use it) and a long cut. Apologists for such expensive technological solutions love to say that "you can't turn back the clock." But when it makes perfect sense to do so—as when the clock is wrong—of *course* you can!

FOR DISCUSSION

1. The author begins with a personal narrative. What makes this appropriate for this evaluation essay?

2. What keeps this evaluation from being merely the writer's personal opinion?

3. There are a couple of lists in the essay. What can you say about the effectiveness of lists as a rhetorical form?

4. What do you learn about the author from reading this essay? Would you expect these kinds of insights to be common to all essays of this sort?

5. How does the author define a "good scythe"? What makes the use of definition effective in an evaluation essay? What other rhetorical devices does the author use?

6. What can you say about the relationship between the setting of the essay and the motivation for writing it?

7. Who do you imagine would be the intended audience for an essay like this?

RUSSELL BAKER

In this tongue-in-cheek comparison, columnist Russell Baker divides city dwellers into two groups: machos *and* quiche-o's. *Notice that underneath the humor, he is also making a statement about our lives. This essay first appeared in 1982, as one of Baker's regular columns in the* New York Times.

The Two Ismo's

American city life is now torn by two violently opposed doctrines of social conduct. One is machismo. Its adherents pride themselves on being "machos." The opposing dogma is quichismo (pronounced "key shizmo"), and its practitioners call themselves quiche-o's (pronounced "key shows").   1

A good study of a quichismo victory over machismo in an urban war zone can be found in Philip Lopate's "Quiche Blitz on Columbus Avenue," included in his recent book, "Bachelorhood." Curiously, however, Mr. Lopate refers to the quichismo doctrine by its French name, *quichisme*.   2

In doing so he unwittingly reveals that he is himself a quiche-o of the highest order, for no macho would dream of using a French word when discussing philosophy, and even the average quiche-o would avoid a word as difficult to pronounce as *quichisme* for fear of getting it wrong and being sneered at as unquiche-o.   3

For practitioners of quichismo there is no defense against being sneered at, and they live in dread of it. The machismo adherent, on the other hand, positively enjoys being sneered at since it entitles him to punch the sneerer in the nose, a ritual act ceremonially confirming that he is truly macho.   4

When a quiche-o is sneered at, his only recourse is to jog until he achieves a higher sense of total fulfillment. This is one reason behind the machismo slogan, "Machos have more fun."   5

Maybe so, quiche-o's say, but machos don't have French dry cleaning or white bucks. Machos prefer no dry cleaning at all though they   6 sometimes get their clothes pressed if they've slept in them all week and want to impress females during the weekend.

7   Machos impress females by taking them to bars after opening the top four buttons on their shirts to show off the hair on their chests. Quiche-o women impress males by inviting them to dinner and serving salad from the carry-out gourmet shop, followed by a kiwi fruit. There are no macho women. If there were they would serve pigs' feet and beer because machos believe that real people don't eat salad, kiwi fruit or anything else that comes from gourmet shops.

8   Quiche-o people buy Swedish toothpaste at gourmet drugstores, Italian loafers at gourmet shoe shops, newspapers at gourmet news-stands and dogs at gourmet pet centers. Afterwards they have them wormed by gourmet veterinarians. They also go to the islands for a month or two, especially Bermuda, St. Bart's, Barbados and Trinidad. Machos also go to the islands—Coney and Long—usually for a Sunday afternoon. To primp for these vacations, machos first go to the barber.

9   No quiche-o has set foot in a barber shop for the last 20 years. He goes to a gourmet hairdresser for a styling, then, before jetting off to the islands, goes to the gourmet luggage shop for suitcases covered with the initials of gourmet designers. The macho packs a change of underwear and a drip-dry shirt in a zippered plastic briefcase his uncle brought back from a 1977 convention of T-shirt salesmen.

10   Quiche-o's are always redecorating. Machos are always repainting the room that has the TV set in it. When a macho's couch and chairs are finally ruined he goes to a department store and buys "a suit of furniture." Quiche-o furniture is never ruined, but it goes out of style every two years, and when it does the quiche-o goes to an environmental systems boutique and buys a new environment.

11   No quiche-o would ever take a walk in his undershirt unless it had something amusing printed on it, like *"Ou sont les neiges d'antan?"* No macho would ever appear on the beach in a male bikini. No quiche-o would ever wear black U.S. Keds with white soles and laces. No macho would ever walk into a hardware store and ask for a wok spatula.

12   Machos don't see anything funny about New Jersey. Quiche-o's never laugh at people who drive Volvos, people who pay $5.50 for a hamburger or quiche jokes, unless they're told by another quiche-o. Quiche-o's like a lot of butcher block and stainless steel. Machos like a lot of children.

13   Machos never bake carrot cake and don't go out with women who do. Quiche-o's are proud of their cholesterol levels and never belch in public and never go out with women who do since they recognize them instantly as unquiche-o and unlikely ever to serve them a salad dinner that concludes with a kiwi fruit.

FOR DISCUSSION

1. What is the underlying message in this humorous evaluation of two stereotypes?
2. What sort of newspaper reader do you think Baker is specifically writing for? Do you think this audience would tend to identify with one of the groups Baker is evaluating more than the other? Discuss.
3. Is the author even-handed in his evaluation of *machos* and *quiche-os*, or do you sense a bias toward one of these types?
4. How is the author's style affected by the space limitation of his column? If the essay could have been twice as long, what do you think would be gained or lost in tone by further development of his comparison?
5. Analyze how this comparison differs from Wendell Berry's comparison of two kinds of scythes. Is Baker's method different from Berry's? Is his motive different? Explain.

STEPHEN KIMMEL

In this evaluation essay written for Creative Computing *magazine, (June 1982), Stephen Kimmel sings the praises of* Grammatik, *a software program for computers that checks "style, usage, punctuation, and a little bit of grammar." Kimmel's evaluation includes a personal account of his first experience with the program—when he used* Grammatik *to analyze one of his own short stories.*

I Sing the Editor Electric

Since I started reviewing software back near the dawn of time, I have seen very few programs that I thought everyone should have. I have seen many programs that were just plain bad and many programs that struggled to be adequate. I have seen several programs that were good and a few programs that I thought were extremely good. I don't get excited about many programs. The last one was *Scripsit*.

I am excited about *Grammatik*.

A short time ago (March '82) I did an article reviewing spelling checkers. I said that the proofreaders were of minimal value. After all they merely tell you which words to look up in the dictionary. Alas, spelling is only the beginning of the story. Even if all my words were spelled correctly I could still appear an idiot with my limp word choice, bad grammar, and terrible typing skills. So, while spelling is important, what I really need is something that will take care of all those other things.

4   What writer wouldn't give anything for an editor he could turn off? Who doesn't want a program that will turn out brilliant text? Or at least words the editor will buy? An electronic editor who would catch all the mistakes that make you look like an idiot would be perfect. Sigh. Such a program isn't available yet but the pieces are beginning to appear.

5   First we had the spelling checkers. Now we have *Grammatik* to check style, usage, punctuation and a little bit of grammar.

6   Bruce Wampler, the author of *Proofreader*, sits down one day and says to himself, "Self, why can't I do the same thing for grammar and style?"

7   "The answer is obvious," self says to Bruce, "spelling is a piece of cake compared to checking grammar."

8   "Yeah, but Bell Labs is doing it with the Writer's Workbench."

9   "Bell Labs has a Megalith 5000 computer and 800 computer scientists working for them."

10   Dr. Wampler, however, is undeterred, and after long hours of labor brings forth *Grammatik*, a program to check style and grammar. And, just for laughs, he decides to let it check for sexist terms as well.

11   I can hear you now. *Grammatik* can check my grammar and style? How? *Grammatik* contains a "dictionary" of 500 commonly misused phrases. . . .

12   The program scans through your ASCII or normal word processor document in search of these offenders. Whenever it finds one it stops and makes a suggestion.

13   Every time you use the word "hopefully," it will tell you that you have used a commonly misused word ("hopefully" means "in a manner that is full of hope." It doesn't mean, "it is to be hoped.") and that you should avoid it.

14   Every time it finds "I myself" the program will tell you that it is redundant and that "I" is sufficient. Unfortunately, the program won't check for endings that are misused. The endings "wise," "ize" and "ly" are horribly overused and can almost always be eliminated to the benefit of all. I think the next version will scan for things like this.

15   *Grammatik* also checks the number of sentences and words and the average length of the sentences and words. It displays the percentage of short and long sentences. Using that information, it is a simple task to calculate your "fog index." And it counts the occurrences of forms of the verb "to be" and the common prepositions.

All these are indirect measures of the readability of the document. 16
Long sentences and long words are signs that the document is hard to
understand. Too many uses of the verb "to be" indicate over-use of
the passive voice, which saps the strength from a document. A high
ratio of these and the prepositions indicate that the work can probably
be improved by rewriting.

So far, we have seen several impressive implications for *Gram-* 17
matik. Note that *Grammatik* doesn't know anything about the meaning
of words. It can't check for subject-verb agreement, dangling partici-
ples, or split infinitives.

Of course, there are cases in which *Grammatik* will call something 18
an error that is actually correct. This seems to be particularly true of
the sexist analysis of fiction. There are cases where "his" is the
correct word. Robert picked up his ball. The document must still be
checked by a regular human.

The advertisement had me drooling with desire. I had to have it. So, 19
I ordered one on Friday. Astoundingly, it arrived on Monday. I went
directly to my trusty TRS-80 and began to analyze a short story of
mine, "Snow Before the Summer Sun."

It is difficult to imagine the program being any easier to use. Typing 20
GMK starts the program. It is menu driven and most of the commands
take a single keystroke. D reads in the dictionary. I=SNOW told it
which file to check. F=> told it to ignore the Scripsit format characters. I told it to start by typing "/ /."

The story began to appear on the screen. When the program found 21
what it considered a problem, it stopped to call my attention to it and to
give its suggestion. When I hit Enter, it went on. When it was finished
with the story, it gave me its final analysis table. It only took a few
minutes.

I leaned back, sending my swivel chair to its farthest back position 22
and closed my eyes. My fingertips massaged my forehead as though
that would drive away the slowly creeping headache. Carefully, I
glanced at the screen. The program was good. Very good. Yet there
was this gnawing ache that bothered me and wouldn't go away.

Perhaps my initial expectations about *Grammatik* had brought me to 23
this: late night, tired eyes, wishing that I was a smoker so that I could
forcefully snuff out a well chewed butt. I picked up the magazine and
let it fall open to the page. The advertisement said that the program
would check capitalization, punctuation, doubled words and several
commonly misused words. The program did all that and more. If
anything, the advertisement was a classic example of undersell. I was
incredulous: here was a program that didn't claim to bring heaven on
earth and actually delivered more than it promised.

I lifted the soda can and found that it had been empty for hours. A 24 quick toss in the general direction of the waste paper basket showed why the Lakers still weren't interested in me. I settled for covering my mouth with my hand.

25   I had expected too much from the program or perhaps too little of myself. Although I like to consider myself a professional class writer I am, in my heart, still the English student who got a "C" because the teacher was merciful. I expected the program to tell me a hundred ways to improve my story. It didn't. It found six errors and I had committed all but one of those intentionally. I expected the program to turn me into Harlan Ellison. It had told me that I was a pretty good writer already.

26   Sitting down once again, I stared at the glowing white letters. I had decided that the program would be useful to a professional writer if only because it checks for doubled words. Considering the price, a mere $49 for the TRS-80 Model I, I could even recommend it on that basis. Don't tell your kids to get one though.

27   Who needs this program then? Where does it fit in the cosmology of computer software? It is such a nifty program that it has to be perfect somewhere. The connection dawned on me finally. This program is like having an English teacher available to you all the time. Running it on a regular basis would improve your writing skills.

28   Several people have reported that they receive fewer problem messages as they work with it longer. *Grammatik* would be a good choice for students and anyone who feels his writing skills could be improved. Considering the state of American literacy, that includes most of us.

29   I have a higher enthusiasm threshold than that. Like the spelling checkers, *Grammatik* can also be expanded to include phrases of particular significance to you. It can become your personal editor and English coach. I love to start sentences with "and." That's not a particularly good idea. So I loaded the *Grammatik* phrase dictionary into *Scripsit* and I added the phrase ".And" with the note to be careful not to overuse it. Now I get a reminder everytime I do it.

30   There are other words that I use too often. My copy of *Grammatik* checks for them, too, and gently tells me to watch out. I am constantly looking up "its" and "it's." Now the program stops to remind me which one is which. "Affect" and "effect" are the same way.

31   *Grammatik* has room for 300 additional phrases. That is more than enough. After three hours I added only 50 phrases. It is this utility that turned that initial evening's frustration into enthusiasm.

32   I like *Grammatik* a great deal. At $49, it is a worthy and useful addition to your word processing software. Now, if someone will write a program to detect dangling participles and split infinitives . . . Or better yet a program that will turn me into Harlan Ellison.

FOR DISCUSSION

1. The title of this essay is a play on the title of a well-known poem by Walt Whitman, "I Sing the Body Electric." What does the author's choice of this title tell you before you even begin the essay?

2. The author, writing for a computer magazine, manages to make the review of a piece of software interesting to a general audience. How does he do this?

3. The author uses a lot of personal experience and references in this essay. What, then, keeps the review from being just a personal opinion? Or is it?

4. What reservations does the author have about *Grammatik*?

5. If more and more software programs such as *Grammatik* become commonplace, what impact could this have on what we learn in school?

BOOK REVIEWS

The following three book reviews taken from the book review section of the San Francisco Chronicle *illustrate three different approaches to evaluation. Bruce Colman's review of* Down the River *by Edward Abbey places this book within the context of the writer's other works and emphasizes characteristics of the author's approach and style in general. The reader comes away from this review thinking about the man who wrote the book as much as the book itself. Henry Mayer begins the evaluation of* Martin's Hundred *by Ivor Noel Hume with enough history to let the reader know how to approach this book about the ruins of Virginia's earliest settlement. Not expecting the reader to be able to "drop into" this discussion with no background, Mayer places his evaluation inside a larger historical context. John Marlowe's review of the works of Herbert Kohl illustrates multiple evaluation: the discussion of several books by the same author. Each of these approaches to evaluation of books is appropriate to the evaluator's intention and the nature of what is to be evaluated.*

A Disagreeable Defender of the Prairie

1   In the regional sectarianism of American literature, no other contemporary writer has claimed a piece of landscape as strongly as Edward Abbey has seized the desert country of the Southwest. Starting with *Desert Solitaire*, he has made a cult for himself by writing about sagebrush, rivers, rock formations, mountains, river runners and that complex of problems popularly called "the environment," all the while using his crusty-old-bastard, wise-guy prose.

2   His profile is so high that you have to pay attention to a new book, even if it's half-baked or fully realized, a dull hash or brilliantly fresh.

3   So here we are with *Down the River*, his fourth "personal history," according to the fly-leaf. (Abbey also has a half-dozen novels and five books of natural history to his credit.) This one is a collection of essays roughly structured around a series of trips down endangered rivers . . . (all rivers are endangered), including, for the nonce, one in Alaska. The book has everything we have come to expect from Abbey: fine descriptions of landscape, a pure anger at the forces of evil, your basic wry wit, jeremiads at what "they" want to do to the untrammeled freedom Abbey enjoys in the outback.

4   Well, it's hard to be against the things Abbey is *for*, and it's hard to be for the things Abbey is *against*—"The Perpetual Power & Growth

184

Machine"—but page after page of *Down the River* exemplifies the worst of archdruidism. Abbey is a misanthrope and a racist: people he disagrees with are painted as criminals, and the people he admires come through as little more than lists of names.

Even his loved ones appear in the books as mere blips in the 5 background noise. There is almost no warmth here for people and, curiously, little warmth for things, either. Abbey admires the desert for its not being human, not yielding up secrets, not being gentle. But, again, this comes across as lists of attributes and catalogs of critters.

And then there is his prose. Abbey has never been above taking 6 another writer's best lines and giving them a different spin or rewriting a cliche and dropping it in. He thinks he is being funny, but this is wiseguyism disguised as love of language.

And yet. And yet. Those were this reviewer's thoughts while plow- 7 ing through the first section of *Down the River*: Here's a pretentious essay on Thoreau (the author of *Walden* as the author of *Down the River*, a crusty old bastard, too); there's an obnoxious introduction, which includes a list of his favorite writers ("Missing from my little list are some famous fictioneers named John . . . They uniformly lack . . . high moral purpose") to prove he's a serious *literateur*, and lines like "We . . . spend the day exploring Jasper's higher ramifications, toward the heart of the Maze. If the Maze has a heart."

But then Abbey drops in a fine piece on the MX missile. He and a companion drive across the desert where the MX was to be deployed 8 on tracks.

> Contrary to the apparent belief of the military, this region is fully inhabited. It is not empty space. Wide, free, and open, yes, but not empty. The mountains and valleys are presently (sic) occupied to the limit of their economic carrying capacity by ranchers, farmers, miners, forest rangers and inspectors of sunsets and by what remains of the original population of Indians, coyote, deer, black bear, mountain lion, eagles, hawks, buzzards, mice, lizards, snakes, antelope, and wild horses.

And after that, there is a pretty good piece on the Rocky Flats anti- 9 nuclear-weapons blockade, and a piece on wilderness and agriculture that comes up just short of the high level that Wendell Berry has set. Suddenly it is very hard not to like parts of this book very, very much.

Finally, it is impossible to dismiss a writer capable of this: 10

> Our worst fantasies have an alarming way of becoming realities; the events of the Twentieth Century may serve as illustration. Without necessarily rejecting either science or technology, it seems to me that we can keep them as servants, not masters, only by doing our best to preserve the variety and openness of life on earth. This

means, especially in America, defending the family farm against the mechanized monoculture of agribusiness; defending the family ranch against the strip-mining company; defending the selective cutting of sustained-yield forestry from the clear-cutting of quick-profit wood products corporations; defending the small town against the spreading BLOB of suburbia; protecting our surviving rivers from the dam-building mania of the politicians; saving our hills and fields, mountains and deserts, roadless areas and wild areas from the aggrandizement of the extractive industries.

11   If Abbey makes himself a sharp thistle for his allies to grab, perhaps the price isn't so high. The forces on the other side—the side that is happier with concrete than prairie, or with reservoir than mountain range, or with Gross National Product than with a clean environment—are thoroughly capable of wielding weapons far stronger, capable of inflicting damage far deeper than anything a wide-voiced, self-proclaimed river rat can muster. In the end it is good to have his weight in the balance.

—Bruce Colman

Digging into the Past; Seventeenth-Century Virginia

1 The excitement of an unexpected discovery animates this fascinating, first-hand account of how remnants of one of Virginia's earliest settlements were uncovered on the grounds of an eighteenth-century manor house called "Carter's Grove."

2   No one expected Ivor Noël Hume, the London-born director of archaeology at Colonial Williamsburg for the past 25 years, to find anything of value when his crew surveyed a two-acre tract on the Carter property. Indeed, his mission was simply to ascertain that nothing worth preserving existed on the site, so that a Williamsburg restoration project could proceed with building an information center for visitors to the plantation.

3   The digging crew, however, quickly stumbled into the seventeenth-century, first finding the graves of people who had died before 1650. Next came bits of delftware and clothing from the same period, the outlines of a dwelling, and enough fragments of impressive pottery to intrigue the National Geographic Society into subsidizing a second summer's project in search of the kiln.

4   Two summers stretched into five years of work, and while the kiln was never found, the archaeologists did discover postholes outlining a

town and fort constructed about 1620. Eventually this community
proved to be the focal point of a settlement known as Martin's Hundred (from the medieval term for a county subdivision large enough to
sustain 100 families). Since the archaeological remains of the first
Virginia settlement at Jamestown (1607) have never turned up, the discovery of Martin's Hundred provides the earliest extensive evidence of
English colonization in America.

The remnants show us a tiny village, laid out on a plan closely 5
resembling the Elizabethan settlements in Ulster. A fort and a church
were located at opposite ends of an avenue of small houses with a
communal storehouse and stable placed midway between them. This
compact arrangement did not prove effective, however, for the ruins
show clear evidence that the community was very nearly wiped out in
the colony-wide Indian uprising of 1622.

Noël Hume tells the story of this exciting find in *Martin's Hundred* 6
with great verve, a feeling for the human as well as scientific story, and
a mildly irritating tendency to stoop to conquer with lame jokes. In
giving us "the anatomy of an excavation," he successfully conveys the
thrill of the chase. He demonstrates both the painstaking way in which
disparate pieces of evidence are fitted together and the heartbreaking
moments when one twist of the spade overturns a cherished hypothesis
by laying bare an artifact that will not fit into the chain of reasoning.

Added excitement comes from the more than 150 illustrations of the 7
objects found and the processes by which they were restored and
interpreted.

Putting historical flesh on the archaeological bones found at Mar- 8
tin's Hundred involved close study of seventeenth-century genre paintings, ceramic techniques, underwater geology, visits to shipwrecks in
Bermuda and church vaults in England as well as close study of the
surviving historical documents. Noël Hume weaves the complex story
together with a sure hand, although his work lacks the breadth of vision
which makes accounts by C. W. Ceram and Geoffrey Bibby such classics of popular archaeology.

Noël Hume is more candid than these writers, however. He speaks 9
directly about the cross-pressures faced by the director of a major
project who must battle the weather, decide among competing alternatives for research, preserve the crew's morale, and maintain the scientific integrity of the excavation while providing results appealing
enough to the financial backers and the general public. The story of
Martin's Hundred demonstrates once again the extraordinary fragility
of what we know and the immense excitement that the search for
knowledge, however incomplete, can generate.

—Henry Mayer

Schools, Learning, and the Quality of Life

1   Summer *seems* like the time to pack up books and all thoughts of school, but the opposite is true. Schools are now tooling up for next year, and the year after that. The people who planned June's final tests and end of the year parties now attend meetings about September's assignments, responsibilities, budgets and curricula.

2   This is a good season to read Herbert Kohl, who is education's Sugar Ray Leonard. Both are everywhere in their fields. I mix up Sugar Ray Leonard, Sugar Ray Robinson, Smokey Robinson and Joel Grey. Likewise, I confuse my education critics who first published in the mid-sixties. Did John Holt or Herb Kohl write "The Open Classroom"? Or was it Jonathan Kozol? Confusion and ubiquity aside, their important commonality is that the writer Kohl and the boxer Leonard do what they do exceedingly well.

3   Kohl's newest books come at a time when the public needs well-reasoned but strongly felt antidotes to the budget-slashing, scape-goating uninformed critics of public, tax-supported education. We must educate all children—and make no mistake about it, American children belong to us all—if not through family, household or neighborhood, then through a sense of nation.

4   We must agree with Kohl: Teaching matters. We can create a better world, he says, by teaching our children, "to be compassionate and concerned with justice while at the same time competitive enough to survive."

5   Unfortunately, not everyone agrees that this is the purpose of the schools. The back-to-basics movement, the new academic schools, the president's effort to dismantle the Department of Education through benign neglect, all go against efforts of those educators who want to help children grow into better versions of themselves and ourselves.

6   The long fight between educators who want to free children to develop to their fullest ability and those who want them to learn specific, observable, correct basic skills continues through our national history. And Kohl's camp is clear. He is not concerned with test scores (he hates them, in fact); rather he worries about racism, which he would try to abolish by teaching children to be confident, accepting and tolerant. He gives example after example of children who, because of good teaching, learn to act fairly and to be less violent.

7   Kohl approaches the problems of a student-centered education from three different positions: the school system, the home and the classroom.

8   *Basic Skills* lays the groundwork for his ideas on education that is organized into schools and school systems. He states *his* "basics"—

goals not unlike those in most unread state department of education guidelines, committee reports and school courses of study. The words are the same, but the emotion and the historical perspective are more challenging. And the force Kohl represents, coming from outside the traditional systems as it does, is more invigorating, especially at a time when a lot of critics (like John Holt) and a lot of parents are opting for private schools or no schools.

Kohl wants children to master science and technology, use tools and 9 understand social groups. He also wants them to have strong imaginations, and he demands that schools teach to these ends rather than talk about them. If children understand language, he says, and enjoy using it, they will learn and use the rules for usage. This is a simple but tragically ignored egg-skill and chicken-attitude.

He shows us how to examine school budgets, design curricula, meet 10 with teachers and work with students. At times the advice is incomplete: While he tells us how to observe a teacher and how to ask post-observation questions, he doesn't tell us how to get past the principal who will probably discourage such observations or how to get the defensive teacher to agree to the observation. Inquisitive parents often don't get their calls returned.

Growing With Your Child—a paperback reprint of the original pub- 11 lished in 1979—chronicles Kohl's efforts to teach his own children to live decently. It is not a book on how to be a perfect parent. No list of questions; no easy answers. Though he does deal with specifics, ranging from testing and its failures to hair and personal appearance, he offers a general approach that asks us not to deal with our children out of anger or frustration. And we need to examine our motives when dealing with problems. For example, "inquisitive" parents mentioned above could be meddlers more concerned with their position in the community than with the education of their child. Kohl reminds us that in a democracy children have the right to grow into their own adults.

The immediate, emotional reaction to Kohl and his position is that 12 the youngsters will have no guidance, no rules to live by. They may not, according to Kohl, have any *easy* rules. He favors the more difficult regulations of justice, honesty, tolerance, fairness, respect and other idealistic guidelines that are much more difficult to live by when compared to scores on spelling and I. Q. tests.

Raising children is, at best, a mystery. Who knows what to do? Kohl 13 doesn't have all the answers, but he gives honest examples and opinions from which we can pick and choose.

Insights approaches the effort to teach children to live decently 14 through classroom activity. The book is a collection of essays for teachers that originally appeared in *Learning* magazine in slightly different forms. This excellent book offers specific alternatives and activities of excitement for both the teacher and the student.

15   Kohl is not a base-line researcher. He is a teacher who knows when children learn joyfully and seriously. "Insights" records these moments.

16   *Puzzlements* is fun. But not idle fun. Here are palindromes, riddles, puns, stories and other types of games that will keep families or imaginative children busy for hours: words and letter challenges as simple as spelling tic-tac-toe or as complex as the weaving of family myths. This book is for the kind of family that spends constructive time together—time that is filled with each other's intelligence, spirit and humor.

17   Finally, *Spelling For Fun,* which is available from Dept. E, 40561 Eureka Hill Road, Pt. Arena, Ca. 95468. I found these pulp paper consumable workbooks the least successful. They are designed so users will use and understand words, not just spell them correctly. The illustrations fall somewhere between Crumb's "Keep On Truckin'" and Griffith's Zippie The Pin Head and for a while they are sure to be high interest books for their audience of beginning readers. But I found them confusing and busy. They look attractive, but the fancy script, contradictory definitions, hyphenated words and use of "and" and "&" on the same page all add up to problems for struggling readers. They are more suited for older remedial students, *if* (and that's a big if) they don't see these workbooks as too childish.

—John Marlowe

FOR DISCUSSION

1. Until recently Bruce Colman was books manager for Friends of the Earth. How does this qualify him for an evaluation of *Down the River*?

2. John Marlowe is vice-principal of a high school in California and the winner of the Charles Stewart Mott award for education writing. What do these facts add to the value of his review of Kohl's works?

3. How does Henry Mayer establish his "credentials" as the reviewer for the book on the ruins in Virginia?

4. In what ways are book reviews almost as much about the reviewer as the book reviewed?

5. What kind of change will be effected in readers after they finish reading these reviews?

MUSIC REVIEWS

These three reviews of musicians and their work have been selected because they illustrate a variety of approaches a reviewer can take when evaluating music. When Gary Giddins reviews the five best recent releases in jazz for Esquire *magazine, he shows a vast knowledge of jazz even though the evaluations are short and to the point, emphasizing the albums and not the background of the performers. But when Michael Bane, who is also writing for* Esquire, *reviews the music of Charlie Daniels, he writes a full-length essay on Daniels and his band, which emphasizes the man as well as his music. In the third example—Joel Selvin's review of beach music for the* San Francisco Chronicle—*the author introduces the reader to a genre of music she or he might not know about and also evaluates current albums that represent this type of music.*

High Notes
The Five Best Recent Releases

The Great Pretender: Lester Bowie

The most sardonic jazz wit since Sonny Rollins, Lester Bowie fondles memories of the mass music that made us all brothers and sisters under the American clockwork orange of the 1950s, reclaiming deathless theme songs by the Platters, Howdy Doody, and Kate Smith. Of course, they sounded more wholesome back then. The album's magnum opus is "The Great Pretender," a song whose gospel connections were hardly explicit in the Platters' ubiquitous recording. Bowie makes the linkage clear: after a lovely rubato introduction, he states the theme as a ballad, accompanied by Donald Smith's churchy piano chords, and then initiates a triple-meter backbeat as two singers harmonize the oohing and ahing. Bowie uses "It's Howdy Doody Time" for buoyant interaction among trumpet, piano, and drums, while bassist Fred Williams sustains a steady two-beat. He concludes a bit of aggressive swagger called "Doom?" with eight bars of Kate Smith's anthem, "When the Moon Comes over the Mountain."

Side two is disappointing. Bowie's richest, purest tones are rehabilitated for "Rios Negroes," but the familiar salsa vamp petrifies into a stubborn ostinato and undoes him. The final selections are a montage of sustained pitches, console shenanigans (echoes and such), and solos

1

2

that come most alive when Phillip Wilson's hyperkinetic drums and Bowie's trumpet blasts take over. These musicians do better with melodies—even corny melodies.

Album of the Year: Art Blakey

3 If this isn't *the* album of the year, it's a definite contender; moreover, it's Blakey's best in about fifteen years, because the sextet, which is captured on this 1981 Paris session, recalls the halcyon days of hard bop. Wynton Marsalis, the twenty-year-old trumpet terror who has critics slobbering in their beer ("My God, another Clifford Brown!"), isn't as original as Clifford Brown, but he's got the taste, technique, tone, and conception to suggest unlimited promise. On other records, he recalls mid-1960s Miles, but here he's deeply in the sway of Freddie Hubbard and Lee Morgan, and his long, serpentine, evenly articulated phrases are elegantly conceived. But, hey, the rest of the front line is excellent, too. Altoist Robert Watson has a penchant for starting solos with intriguing ideas and then has to worry about living up to them; he usually does. Tenorist Bill Pierce recycles the 1960s sax hierarchy with a lustiness and tonal confidence of his own. Their consecutive performances make "In Case You Missed It" a Blakey bonanza. Blakey never lets up, pummeling, champing, goading, roaring, and press-rolling every exuberant measure. (Available from Roundup Records, Box 147, East Cambridge, Massachusetts 02141.)

Amarcord Nino Rota

4 Only benevolent obsession could produce an anomaly as altogether charming and frequently moving as this homage to Nino Rota, the Italian composer who scored Federico Fellini's films. The producer, Hal Willner, chose a broad variety of jazz-associated musicians to realize his project, and one is almost as impressed by the perspicacity of his choices as by the precision and depth of feeling they brought to their respective assignments.

5   The most enchanting orchestral arrangement is Carla Bley's "8½," which gives each of ten musicians equal footing in a gaily colored, pungently calibrated medley of themes. An irresistible combination of gentle wit and romantic longing informs Jaki Byard's exquisite piano renderings of "Amarcord" and "La Strada." Other highlights are David Amram's eerie "Satyricon," Steve Lacy's punctilious "Roma," William Fischer's Blakey-style collage of four film themes, and a "La Dolce Vita" that combines a menacing orchestration by Muhal Richard Abrams, the wordless vocalizing of Deborah Harry, and the blending of Sharon Freeman's French horn with Francis Haynes's steel drums.

Somehow, stride piano, Afro-Cuban rhythms, Orientalism, electric guitars, hard bop, and the rest find suitable accommodation in Rota's caravansary.

Vertical Form VI: George Russell

The title refers to the fact that this is the sixth major work Russell has completed during the past fifteen years to employ vertical notation. But leave phrases like "vertical tonal environment" and "disparate rhythmic modes" to theorists. Russell is an important composer because his music is eminently listenable, and *Vertical Form VI,* recorded live at a Swedish radio station in 1977 but only now available here, is a joy. Best known for his missionary work on behalf of modality, as discussed in his musicological-philosophical treatise *The Lydian Chromatic Concept of Tonal Organization,* Russell is concerned with reasserting the primacy of the composer while encouraging improvisational inventiveness. His current work is ripe with the dance rhythms, electric accoutrements, and repetitions that most of the younger composers are exploring (Anthony Davis's *Episteme* is another example), but because he allows only two improvisations, some won't consider it jazz at all. Yet the instrumentation—five reeds, nine brass, ten rhythm—and the tonalities and rhythmic momentum leave no doubt about what tradition he celebrates. He's made the orchestra sound as willful and impetuous as a lone instrumentalist in the heat of invention. (Available from Roundup Records.)

Something in Blue: Thelonious Monk

Monk's death on February 17, of complications following a stroke, brought to a close the career of an unrelenting maverick. He belonged to that rare elite of musical humorists stretching back to Haydn, and it's difficult to comprehend the anger with which he was often criticized. As Jo Jones might have said, he could swing you into bad health.

Jazz Man's reissue of *Something in Blue,* from his last studio session, in 1971, is a noteworthy occasion. It's not his most profound piano recording, but it's very likely his most entertaining. The vigorous stride of "Blue Sphere" is the very quintessence of Monk, as is the bedraggled phrasing on the fiendishly difficult "Criss Cross," the mock sobriety of "Jackie-ing," the vigorous permutations of "Hackensack," and the repeated tag line of "Something in Blue." Don't miss it this time around.

—Gary Giddins

Charlie Daniels: In Celebration of the Things We'd All Like to Believe In

1 A special joint session of the legislature of the Volunteer State of Tennessee is about to begin, and the senate chambers are totally mobbed. The galleries as well are filled to overflowing, with white-haired grandmothers jockeying for position with television crews and long-haired fourteen-year-olds chafing in suits and ties. The chambers are gaveled to order with difficulty, and when a proclamation honoring the state's newest favorite son is read, a familiar figure takes the podium. He is a huge, bearish man, peering out at the filled chambers from beneath a cowboy hat only slightly smaller than the space shuttle. He accepts a framed copy of the proclamation, starts to speak his thanks, then chokes up.

2 "Thank you, thank you," says Charlie Daniels, the long-haired country boy himself, the patron saint of southern boogie music. He pauses to push back his hat and wipe his damp eyes. "You don't know what this means to me," he begins again, only to be drowned out by a thundering ovation from legislators and spectators alike.

3 "That boy ought to run for governor," observes one of the legislators, and the crowd surges forward to engulf even the huge figure of Charlie Daniels.

4 "Governor, nothing!" snorts another. "He ought to run for king!"

> *People say I'm no good and crazy as a loon*
> *'Cause I get stoned in the morning,*
> *I get drunk in the afternoon . . .*
> *And I ain't got no money*
> *But I damn sure got it made.*

5 For Charlie Daniels, it's been a long haul from the tobacco fields and lumber mills of North Carolina to the podium at the Tennessee statehouse. He's picked tobacco and once quit a job at a creosote plant to keep a black fellow worker from being laid off. He's played sessions for Bob Dylan and cut his eyeteeth on joints so tough that, as contemporary Ronnie Hawkins said: "You had to puke twice and show your razor before they'd let you in." He brought rock 'n' roll to the White House for Jimmy Carter's inauguration and once threatened to sue the Ku Klux Klan "to hell and back" for using the lyrics to one of his songs, "The South's Gonna Do It," in a Klan radio spot. He has become a rock 'n' roll superstar singing about God, country, love of family, and the common man—the traditional fodder of country music.

He has become a country-music superstar playing the hard-edged 6
guitar-and drum fury of rock 'n' roll. The Charlie Daniels Band is, in
fact, probably the only group of musicians in the country who can walk
onstage at the biggest rock concert or the Grand Ole Opry and draw
exactly the same thundering ovation; a critic once described his songs
as "country music gone weird."

"My music is very earthy, very down to earth," he says, sprawled
across a couch in his wood-and-stone farmhouse in Mount Juliet,
Tennessee, about thirty miles from Nashville. "It's just about people,
common people. I call it blue-collar music." Almost sheepishly, he
adds that violin virtuoso Itzhak Perlman recently telephoned to say
what a fan of the CDB he was. "You could have knocked me over with
a chicken feather," Daniels says.

> *I still remember the magnolia nights*
> *And goosefeather snow in the gray morning light,*
> *Sandspurs and puppies and red autumn leaves,*
> *And the warm lights in the clear night*
> *On a cold Christmas Eve. . .*

© 1980 Hat Band Music

Born in Wilmington, North Carolina, Charlie Daniels grew up 7
around the Carolinas, following his father in the timber business. He
grew up listening to the bedrock southern music of black blues and
white country, then quickly latched on to the "new" music called
bluegrass from Bill Monroe, Lester Flatt, and Earl Scruggs. His first
band was a bluegrass group, but he quickly learned that what people
really wanted to hear was that even newer music, rock 'n' roll. When
Daniels was twenty, in 1956, he moved from North Carolina to Washington, D.C., to make his fortune playing the bars. He picked up his
band—Taz DiGregorio, Fred Edwards, Jim Marshall, Tom Crain, and
Charlie Hayward—along the way. "We played everything from 'Mal-
agueña' to 'Rock Around the Clock,' " he says. "Whatever came
down the pike, we played it. We always tried to play a little country
music on the side, too."

In 1967, at the request of record producer Bob Johnson, who had 8
heard him playing the honky-tonks, Daniels moved to Nashville to
work as a guitar player on several Dylan sessions, including the land-
mark *Nashville Skyline* album. By 1967, though, the battle lines had
already been drawn, and one of those lines ran smack through the
center of Nashville. Guys with long hair who were against the Vietnam
War were not exactly welcome in a town where President Nixon could
yo-yo on the Grand Ole Opry, and long-haired Charlie Daniels could
feel the heat.

9   He even joined the hordes of Americans protesting against the war
—until one day at a peace rally in New York City's Central Park.
There, he looked out from the stage and saw something that dismayed
him.

10   "The women's liberation was there, and gay liberation was there,
the Communist party, the Attica prison contingent, the Socialist
party—every damn body and his brown dog that had something to
bitch about was there," Daniels recently told an interviewer. "And I
said to myself, 'I'm a damn fool. I'm not a Communist. . . . Me
hating that war don't make me love the Viet Cong.' "

11   Which is, perhaps, predictable. In his music and in his life, Charlie
Daniels has refused to buy the entire package, refused to deviate from
a style and an ethos drilled into his head around the lumber camps of
the Carolinas so many years before:

> *If you don't like the way I'm living,*
> *You just leave this long-haired country boy alone.*

12   From his earliest music, including "The South's Gonna Do It,"
which replaced "Dixie" as the South's national anthem,

> *Be proud you're a Rebel*
> *'Cause the South's gonna do it again.*

to his most recent hit, "In America,"

> *This lady may have stumbled, but she ain't never fell*
> *And if the Russians don't believe it they can all go straight*
>   *to hell.*
>   © 1980 Hat Band Music

. . . Charlie Daniels's music has always glorified the common man
and the traditional values. Hard though it is to remember—after a
southern President and wave after wave of redneck chic—when Daniels recorded "The South's Gonna Do It" in 1974, the song was
nothing short of a revolutionary statement: Don't *apologize* for being
from the South; be *proud*! I recall being invited to a party along about
then; when I told the host I was from Tennessee, she replied, "I'm so
terribly sorry! How awful for you!"

13   "In America," which was savaged by the predominantly northeastern critics as jingoistic, trite, and nothing less than the latest reincarna-
tion of "Horst Wessel," he simply expanded the views of "The
South's Gonna Do It" to include the whole country: This is *your*
country; be *proud*!

And you never did think that it ever would happen again
In America, did you?
You never did think that we would ever get together again.
Well, we damn sure fooled you.
© 1980 Hat Band Music

In fact, the listener is left wondering just who the "you" in the song refers to—the Russians or the urban Northeast. There is almost the simplicity of a fairy tale—as one sympathetic critic described it—to the music of Charlie Daniels. Evil is punished, usually violently and swiftly. But Daniels shares an almost Faulknerian sense of the futility of it all: just because evil is punished doesn't necessarily mean that good triumphs. He looks across a classically southern landscape, fraught with death and evil, haunted by war and the flickering images of slavery. In his recent *Full Moon* album, for example, five out of nine songs deal with violent death—no doubt, it sets some kind of record for popular music.

14   The music itself varies wildly in style, from the ubiquitous southern-bar boogie, which is the common denominator for much of America's popular music, to more traditional blues forms to Daniels's lyrical recitations of his memories of the Carolinas. He is most at home with boogie, that shake-your-ass mixture of blues, rhythm and blues, country, and rock that virtually *demands* some sort of physical response—get up and *dance,* stupid, and if you can't dance, *fight.*

15   In many ways the Charlie Daniels Band is the last true keeper of the flame of southern rock. The great names from the mid-Seventies heyday of southern rock—the Allman Brothers' Band, Lynyrd Skynyrd, the Marshall Tucker Band, Wet Willie—have all fallen by the wayside, either through death or simply the shifting of musical styles. "We didn't all play the same kind of music," Daniels says, "but we did all have the same roots." Southern rock is like kudzu, the ubiquitous vine that is slowly covering the South; it never really goes away. Through southern rock's interplay between the root forms of rhythm and blues and of country, it mirrors the central tension of southern life, the tension between black and white. Perhaps prophetically for the South, the offspring of rhythm and blues and country is more vigorous and more adaptable than even its parent. That adaptability, in fact, is the reason the Charlie Daniels Band has survived the most recent "demise" of southern rock. When pickings look slim in the R & B boogie end of the scale, Charlie Daniels slides toward country. When the wheel comes around, there sits ol' Charlie, ready and waiting.

16   More importantly, Daniels is not afraid of being called either *too* country or *too* R & B—he knows his music and his fans. Yet more than

one southern group has committed commercial suicide trying to avoid those labels. (The Marshall Tucker Band, for example, panicked at being called country and steered toward a more jazzy and less successful direction.)

17   Still, those shared roots helped make southern rock one of the most important musical forces of the Seventies, right up there with disco and *mel*-low music from the West Coast. That it still retains its power to move people is evident from Daniels's 1979 hit "The Devil Went Down to Georgia," which describes a fiddling contest between the Devil and a good ol' boy named Johnny. That song soared to the top of both the country and the rock charts at the very height of disco fever:

> *Johnny said, "Devil, just come on back if you ever want*
> * to try again.*
> *I done told you once, you son-of-a-bitch, I'm the best*
> * that's ever been."*
> © 1972 Hat Band Music

18   Or take an even more recent example, this year's Volunteer Jam, Daniels's annual concert-cum-party in Nashville, which has featured everyone from rock wild man Ted Nugent to Grand Ole Opry icon Roy Acuff (who first came onstage at the jam a couple of years ago, unannounced, with a sheaf of sheet music. "This is the music I sing on the Opry," he told Charlie. "It's my life, and I want it to be a part of yours." It was one of the most moving moments a city full of moving moments had ever seen). At this year's jam, in the wee hours of the morning, Daniels joined former Allman Brothers Band members Richard Betts and Chuck Leavell for a rousing version of the Allmans' anthem, "Ramblin' Man." It was a strangely subdued moment, a reaffirmation of the old music and a memory of the old days.

19   Prophetically, one of the songs on Daniels's newest (and probably best) album, *Windows,* is titled "Ain't No Ramblers Anymore":

> *There ain't no ramblers anymore*
> *Least not like there used to be.*
> *Everybody's on vacation*
> *Or watching something on TV.*
> © 1982 Hat Band Music

20   That album also includes a truly exceptional song, "Still in Saigon," one of the few not written by Daniels. The song is about a returned Vietnam vet who is, after all the years, "still in Saigon in my mind":

> *Every summer when it rains*
> *I smell the jungle, I hear the planes.*
> *I can't tell no one*
> *I feel ashamed.*
> © 1981 Dreena Music/Dan Daley Music

"Still in Saigon" was written by Dan Daley of the Vietnam Veterans of 21
America, and the Charlie Daniels Band is probably the only act around
that can bring a song like this off. No other group can reach out and
appeal to all the still-warring factions:

> *The ground at home was covered with snow*
> *And I was covered with sweat.*
> *My younger brother calls me a killer*
> *And my daddy calls me a vet.*

The music of Charlie Daniels, perhaps in its simplicity, appeals not
only to those of us in the baby-boom generation but to our fathers and
younger brothers as well, and when Charlie Daniels sings songs like
"Still in Saigon," more than one generation will be listening.

—Michael Bane

Capturing the Beat of the Beach

Beach music has nothing to do with surf music. For more than 20 1
years, these sounds have provided the soundtrack to summer vacations for three generations of Southern teens flocking to beach resorts
like Myrtle Beach, South Carolina, where swimming, sunning, drinking and dancing to rhythm and blues records are the order of the day.

But it is not just regulation rhythm and blues hits that these kids 2
dance the shag to; these are obscure records, some reaching national
popularity, but most relegated to regional obscurity. Some are old and
some are new. The frothy beat is the thing.

These records all try to capture the beach beat sound—each is a 3
two-record set featuring the kind of forgotten records that still fill radio
airwaves every summer on the Southern coast. The "Ocean Drive"
sets were manufactured to be sold via TV ads, but the other two
packages are standard, retail records, heralding a new official recognition for this small slice of the American musical scene.

This is not nostalgia. These records play a vital part in the musical 4
summer diet of Southerners to this day. A playlist from WWID-FM in
Gainesville, Georgia, for a five-hour Sunday show called "Hit the
Beach" gives a detailed picture of the beach sound from just last year.
Most of the records date from the late '60s and concentrate on a kind of
bouncy, beaty soul sound perfectly summed up by records from the
Cornelius Brothers and Sister Rose, beach beat favorites, who notched
nationwide hits in the early '70s with "Treat Her Like a Lady" or
"Too Late to Turn Back Now," quintessential beach beat sides.

5   Also played heavily on "Hit the Beach" last summer were records by Chairmen of the Board, who work good money jobs each summer at clubs up and down the coastline, the Tams, Tyrone Davis, Archie Bell and the Drells, Brenton Wood, Swingin' Medallions, latter era Drifters, a sprinkling of Motown and some British soul bands.

6   The songs of summer, it would seem, last a long time. Old Clovers records like "Nip Sip" from the late '50s are played right alongside '60s soul pieces like "Girl Watcher" by the O'Kaysions and even more recent numbers like "You Ought to Be Havin' Fun" from Oakland's own Tower of Power. Furthermore, certain groups gain popularity among the beach crowd and their releases subsequent to their national hits often find favor on the beach scene, even when the follow-ups are roundly ignored by the rest of the country. The Swingin' Medallions, for instance, are only known for one record,"Double Shot of My Baby's Lovin'," but on the beach, many different Medallions records are featured. The Chairmen of the Board are best known for the early '70s rhythm and blues record, "Give Me Just a Little More Time," but this band has become such a beach beat favorite, virtually all the group's records figure popularly in the coastal sound.

7   The Epic Records "Endless Beach" focuses on beach beat hits from the past decade, while the Arista set digs up '60s numbers by James and Bobby Purify, Clifford Curry and others.

—Joel Selvin

FOR DISCUSSION

1. What circumstances and situations very likely determined the form that these three music reviews take? For instance, why did Michael Bane write an essay-length review and Gary Giddens only a list-type of review? Discuss the value and the drawbacks of such constraints and opportunities, and indicate how the form is appropriate to the subject.

2. What do you guess was the motive for each reviewer to write his evaluation?

3. How does each reviewer establish his relationship with the reader? What precisely is that relationship in each review?

4. What did you learn from each review? Was the nature of what you learned different or the same in each case? Discuss.

5. State precisely what you believe was Michael Bane's *intended* effect of his essay upon the reader. What about Selvin's? And Giddins'?

WRITING YOUR OWN
The Evaluation Essay

Before you begin to work on your own evaluation essay, let's look at the configurations of Yi-Fu Tuan's essay, "American Space, Chinese Place":

Motivation (an educated guess): to sell an article and to offer information that will help the reader define and understand one difference between American and Chinese culture.

Circumstance/Situation: Harper's Magazine—a monthly periodical with a deadline and space requirements.

Audience: general magazine reader—especially people interested in learning about other cultures in relation to their own.

Writer's Relationship to Audience: person who has studied the subject to person who hasn't.

Emphasis: on the two cultures being evaluated and their differing outlooks on a sense of space and place.

Form: essay/article.

Intention (an educated guess): to get the reader to think differently about the Chinese and American perspectives on space and place.

Now try to outline the configurations of the other evaluation essays in this chapter.

DESIGNING YOUR OWN CONFIGURATION

Here are some suggestions to get you started in picking a topic for your own evaluation essay:

1. Evaluate an aspect of life that is changing or disappearing (train travel, grand old downtown hotels, the small family-run farm, for example.) Focus on what is to be lost or gained by the change. Who is your audience? Where will the piece be presented?

2. Critics of fast food chains claim they make the American landscape dull and predictable. Write an evaluation essay in *support* of fast food chains for X magazine.

3. The city you live in plans to turn an empty school building in your neighborhood into a home for people being treated for drug addiction. Some of your neighbors have written a letter of protest to the mayor of your city. Write a letter to the mayor in *support* of the plan, evaluating the benefits of this plan.

4. Think of a historical building or an archaelogical site you are familiar with. Imagine that the building is going to be razed (or the site filled in) to accommodate a housing development. Write an essay for your local newspaper evaluating what will be lost to the community if this plan is carried out.

5. Write a comparison of two books you have read recently, or two movies, performances, or concerts you have been to lately. Or, you might try comparing the film version of a novel or play to the work on which it is based. Who is your audience? Where will your piece be presented?

Once you have decided on your own topic for an evaluation essay, use the following chart to help define all of the points of your configuration:

Designing Your Own Configuration for an Evaluation Essay

MOTIVE	CIRCUMSTANCES/ SITUATION	AUDIENCE	RELATIONSHIP TO AUDIENCE
To satisfy a request to review an album or book for a newspaper	Commission by x magazine to do evaluation by x time to fill x amount of space	General reader	Knower to person who does not know yet
Personal interest in people buying x	Offer by writer to do evaluation for magazine or newspaper by x time in x amount of space	People interested in x	Expert to novice
To read about things one really likes	Regular review column for newspaper with set deadline and set length	People writer wishes to interest in x	Experienced to inexperienced
To get clear on the pros and cons of something	Employee is about to purchase an item and requires an evaluation by x in whatever form writer wishes	People who are going to buy x	Teacher to student
To sell an article		Co-workers and/or peers	
To satisfy a classroom assignment		Professor	
To satisfy employer's request		Employer	

EMPHASIS	FORM	INTENTION
On things being evaluated	Review	To get reader to think differently after reading the evaluation
On evidence for position	Report	To get reader to buy x
On experience of writer as foundation for evaluation	Essay	To assist readers in making their own judgments
On clarity and simplicity	Lists	To have readers prefer x over y
On standards by which thing has been evaluated	Critique	To assist readers in knowing about a particular thing
	Newspaper column	
	Article	

RULES FOR AN EVALUATION ESSAY

1. Decide upon what basis you are qualified to do this evaluation and use this as the background for your essay.
2. Anticipate all the things your reader might need or want to know about the thing being evaluated, and cover all these points.
3. Place the thing being evaluated into a larger context so that the readers will know with what things it should be grouped.
4. Base your evaluation on evidence or direct experience. Discuss this evidence or experience from the place of expertise that you hold.
5. Don't let the essay reflect your personal taste or opinion only with no explanation or evidence.
6. Let the thing being evaluated hold the center of emphasis in the essay.

RHETORICAL FORMS OFTEN APPEARING IN EVALUATION ESSAYS

Comparison and Contrast: How to Show Similarities and Differences

1. *Compare* comes from a Latin word which means *equal* and means "to examine in order to observe or discover similarities or differences."
2. *Contrast* comes from an Italian word that means *to stand opposed to* and implies a comparing for the purpose of emphasizing differences.
3. When comparing two things, you will probably use one of two common patterns: discussing *A* completely and then discussing *B* or discussing a particular characteristic of *A* and *B*, then another characteristic of *A* and *B*, then another . . . until you've completed the comparison.
4. You may discover that an item is similar to another thing in an exact way—that house has the same floor plan as the one I lived in as a child—or is similar in a nonliteral way—that house is like a tomb. Both kinds of comparison are valuable to a reader who is attempting to understand your subject just the way you do.

5. Differences you spot among things may be differences of characteristics—*their car has bench seats; ours has bucket seats*—or the differences may be differences of degree—*the back seat of the Volkswagen Rabbit is bigger than the back seat of the Volkswagen Beetle.* Both kinds of contrast help the reader see the subject the way you wish to communicate it.

Classification: How to Show Common Characteristics

1. *To classify* means *to organize into groups according to common characteristics, qualities, traits,* etc.; *to put into basic categories;* or *to break down into component parts.*
2. When you set up a classification system, be certain that the categories don't overlap. Also make very clear to the reader what the groups are and how you decided what went into each group.
3. Don't oversimplify when you classify. Sometimes in an attempt to make everything orderly, a person will push a subject, person, item, etc., into a category where it doesn't really belong just to make the classification systematic. Don't undercut your credibility with your audience by forcing an item into a group where it doesn't clearly belong.
4. Use a classification system when it will help your reader follow your thoughts or explanation point by point.

Definition: How to Tell What Something Means

1. *To define* means *to explain the nature or essential qualities of a word, function,* etc. A definition determines or fixes the boundaries of the thing being discussed. The original meaning of the word *definition* was *to set boundaries,* and that is what a good definition does for the reader: it helps him or her stake out, limit, see the boundaries of a term.
2. A formal definition includes the term being defined, the class to which it belongs, and what differentiates it from other things in that class.
3. An informal definition takes several forms: defining by using a word that means approximately the same thing (*to gloat* means *to act superior and proud*); by using an opposite (*love* is *not using someone*); by showing the term's origin (*defining* originally meant *setting boundaries*); by using personal experience (*summer* means *time off, rest, and fun*); by giving examples (*eating well* is *having fresh vegetables and fruit, avoiding sugar, and staying off fried foods*).

4. Use definitions in your writing when there is any chance that your readers will not know the formal meaning of a word or the informal way you are using it. Being clear on the terms in a piece of writing is absolutely necessary for both the reader and the writer if communication is to occur.

Description: How to Present Sharp, Focused Pictures
1. Appeal to *all* the reader's senses: sight, smell, touch, hearing, taste. Be very specific.
2. *Select* the details you want to include in the description so that they give one main impression of the object, person, or scene. Don't try to describe everything at once. This means that you will choose details according to what your purpose is at the time.

Analysis by Division: How to be Clear and Orderly
1. Divide the process into distinct steps.
2. Discuss these steps in the *exact order* in which they occur when the process is done.
3. If there is a large number of steps in the process, group the steps into categories and then discuss them.
4. Define all terms and procedures that might be unfamiliar.
5. Do not omit *any* step in the procedure.

The Persuasion Essay

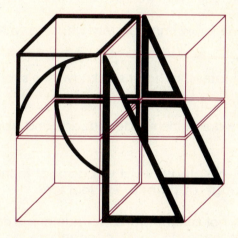

To Persuade   to move by argument, entreaty, or earnest reasoning to a course of action

All of us have ideas or beliefs that we hold valuable. Whether it's a profound idea about how people should prepare for the afterlife or simply a fervent wish that our friends would go to see a movie we just enjoyed, the usual result of strong feeling is that we want others to share that feeling and do something to show they share it. Since we usually can't force people to believe as we do, we must often persuade them; and since their response is important to us, we want to know the best ways to do that persuading.

"Will you marry me?"
"May I have the job?"
"Will you make a commitment to get this done?"
"What actions will you take now?"

If the answers to such questions would make a difference in your life, you would do well to find out how to get the right ones. To learn these skills, we will study the persuasion essays in this section of the book. The purpose of these essays is *to cause the reader to do, think, or believe something different and to act upon this change* after reading the words. In the assertion-with-evidence essays, the aim was to make a statement and back it up with evidence, but that aim did not automatically extend to causing the reader *to act upon* the information. In these persuasion essays, however, the intention is to cause the reader to act upon the words.

A good persuasion essay will have these characteristics:

The readers will know immediately what the writer wants them to do or believe.

The writer indicates that he or she knows the subject extremely well.

The writer is aware of the reader's needs and appeals to those needs.

The writer will anticipate what will appeal to the reader and choose language appropriate to that tone.

The writer will not attempt to effect numerous changes in the reader all at once, but will concentrate on one area of change.

The writer will make clear what the readers should do as a result of reading the essay.

In the selections below, pay special attention to what method the writer uses to persuade the reader to act. Have these questions in mind as you read:

What change does the writer want to happen after the reader completes the essay?

How does the writer discuss this action he or she desires?

What exactly does the writer do to persuade the reader?

Am I convinced?

How am I changed by reading this essay?

MARTIN LUTHER KING, JR.

Martin Luther King Jr. (1929–1968) wrote the following letter from the Birmingham, Alabama, jail in 1963. Addressing a group of clergymen critical of his approach, King explains and defends his use of "non-violent direct action" in the civil rights protests in Birmingham. He also asks his colleagues to support his efforts to bring fairness and justice to his people, the blacks.

Letter from Birmingham Jail

My Dear Fellow Clergymen:

1   While confined here in the Birmingham city jail, I came across your recent statement calling my present activities "unwise and untimely." Seldom do I pause to answer criticism of my work and ideas. If I sought to answer all the criticisms that cross my desk, my secretaries would have little time for anything other than such correspondence in the course of the day, and I would have no time for constructive work. But since I feel that you are men of genuine good will and that your criticisms are sincerely set forth, I want to try to answer your statement in what I hope will be patient and reasonable terms.

2   I think I should indicate why I am here in Birmingham, since you have been influenced by the view which argues against "outsiders coming in." I have the honor of serving as president of the Southern Christian Leadership Conference, an organization operating in every southern state, with headquarters in Atlanta, Georgia. We have some eighty-five affiliated organizations across the South, and one of them is the Alabama Christian Movement for Human Rights. Frequently we share staff, educational, and financial resources with our affiliates. Several months ago the affiliate here in Birmingham asked us to be on call to engage in a nonviolent direct-action program if such were deemed necessary. We readily consented, and when the hour came we lived up to our promise. So I, along with several members of my staff, am here because I was invited here. I am here because I have organizational ties here.

3   But more basically, I am in Birmingham because injustice is here. Just as the prophets of the eighth century B. C. left their villages and carried their "thus saith the Lord" far beyond the boundaries of their home towns, and just as the Apostle Paul left his village of Tarsus and carried the gospel of Jesus Christ to the far corners of the Greco-Roman world, so am I compelled to carry the gospel of freedom be-

yond my own home town. Like Paul, I must constantly respond to the Macedonian call for aid.

4   Moreover, I am cognizant of the interrelatedness of all communities and states. I cannot sit idly by in Atlanta and not be concerned about what happens in Birmingham. Injustice anywhere is a threat to justice everywhere. We are caught in an inescapable network of mutuality, tied in a single garment of destiny. Whatever affects one directly, affects all indirectly. Never again can we afford to live with the narrow, provincial, "outside agitator" idea. Anyone who lives inside the United States can never be considered an outsider anywhere within its bounds.

5   You deplore the demonstrations taking place in Birmingham. But your statement, I am sorry to say, fails to express a similar concern for the conditions that brought about the demonstrations. I am sure that none of you would want to rest content with the superficial kind of social analysis that deals merely with effects and does not grapple with underlying causes. It is unfortunate that demonstrations are taking place in Birmingham, but it is even more unfortunate that the city's white power structure left the Negro community with no alternative.

6   In any nonviolent campaign there are four basic steps: collection of the facts to determine whether injustices exist; negotiation; self-purification; and direct action. We have gone through all these steps in Birmingham. There can be no gainsaying the fact that racial injustice engulfs this community. Birmingham is probably the most thoroughly segregated city in the United States. Its ugly record of brutality is widely known. Negroes have experienced grossly unjust treatment in courts. There have been more unsolved bombings of Negro homes and churches in Birmingham than in any other city in the nation. These are the hard, brutal facts of the case. On the basis of these conditions, Negro leaders sought to negotiate with the city fathers. But the latter consistently refused to engage in good-faith negotiation.

7   Then, last September, came the opportunity to talk with leaders of Birmingham's economic community. In the course of the negotiations, certain promises were made by the merchants—for example, to remove the stores' humiliating racial signs. On the basis of these promises, the Reverend Fred Shuttlesworth and the leaders of the Alabama Christian Movement for Human Rights agreed to a moratorium on all demonstrations. As the weeks and months went by, we realized that we were the victims of a broken promise. A few signs, briefly removed, returned; the others remained.

8   As in so many past experiences, our hopes had been blasted, and the shadow of deep disappointment settled upon us. We had no alternative except to prepare for direct action, whereby we would present our very bodies as means of laying our case before the conscience of the local and the national community. Mindful of the difficulties involved, we

decided to undertake a process of self-purification. We began a series of workshops on nonviolence, and we repeatedly asked ourselves: "Are you able to accept blows without retaliating?" "Are you able to endure the ordeal of jail?" We decided to schedule our direct-action program for the Easter season, realizing that except for Christmas, this is the main shopping period of the year. Knowing that a strong economic-withdrawal program would be the by-product of direct action, we felt that this would be the best time to bring pressure to bear on the merchants for the needed change.

Then it occurred to us that Birmingham's mayoral election was 9 coming up in March, and we speedily decided to postpone action until after election day. When we discovered that the Commissioner of Public Safety, Eugene "Bull" Connor, had piled up enough votes to be in the run-off, we decided again to postpone action until the day after the run-off so that the demonstrations could not be used to cloud the issues. Like many others, we waited to see Mr. Connor defeated, and to this end we endured postponement after postponement. Having aided in this community need, we felt that our direct-action program could be delayed no longer.

You may well ask, "Why direct action? Why sit-ins, marches, and 10 so forth? Isn't negotiation a better path?" You are quite right in calling for negotiation. Indeed, this is the very purpose of direct action. Nonviolent direct action seeks to create such a crisis and foster such a tension that a community which has constantly refused to negotiate is forced to confront the issue. It seeks so to dramatize the issue that is can no longer be ignored. My citing the creation of tension as part of the work of the nonviolent-resister may sound rather shocking. But I must confess that I am not afraid of the word "tension." I have earnestly opposed violent tension, but there is a type of constructive, nonviolent tension which is necessary for growth. Just as Socrates felt that it was necessary to create a tension in the mind so that individuals could rise from the bondage of myths and half-truths to the unfettered realm of creative analysis and objective appraisal, so must we see the need for nonviolent gadflies to create the kind of tension in society that will help men rise from the dark depths of prejudice and racism to the majestic heights of understanding and brotherhood.

The purpose of our direct-action program is to create a situation so 11 crisis-packed that it will inevitably open the door to negotiation. I therefore concur with you in your call for negotiation. Too long has our beloved Southland been bogged down in a tragic effort to live in monologue rather than dialogue.

One of the basic points in your statement is that the action that I and 12 my associates have taken in Birmingham is untimely. Some have asked: "Why didn't you give the new city administration time to act?" The only answer that I can give to this query is that the new Birmingham administration must be prodded about as much as the outgoing one, before it will act. We are sadly mistaken if we feel that the election of Albert Boutwell as mayor will bring the millennium to Birmingham. While Mr. Boutwell is a much more gentle person than Mr. Connor, they are both segregationists, dedicated to maintenance of the status quo. I have hoped that Mr. Boutwell will be reasonable enough to see the futility of massive resistance to desegregation. But he will not see this without pressure from devotees of civil rights. My friends, I must say to you that we have not made a single gain in civil rights without determined legal and nonviolent pressure. Lamentably, it is an historical fact that privileged groups seldom give up their privileges voluntarily. Individuals may see the moral light and voluntarily give up their unjust posture; but, as Reinhold Niebuhr has reminded us, groups tend to be more immoral than individuals.

13   We know through painful experience that freedom is never voluntarily given by the oppressor; it must be demanded by the oppressed. Frankly, I have yet to engage in a direct-action campaign that was "well timed" in the view of those who have not suffered unduly from the disease of segregation. For years now I have heard the word "Wait!" It rings in the ear of every Negro with piercing familiarity. This "Wait" has almost always meant "Never." We must come to see, with one of our distinguished jurists, that "justice too long delayed is justice denied."

14   We have waited for more than 340 years for our constitutional and God-given rights. The nations of Asia and Africa are moving with jet-like speed toward gaining political independence, but we still creep at horse-and-buggy pace toward gaining a cup of coffee at a lunch counter. Perhaps it is easy for those who have never felt the stinging darts of segregation to say, "Wait." But when you have seen vicious mobs lynch your mothers and fathers at will and drown your sisters and brothers at whim; when you have seen hate-filled policemen curse, kick, and even kill your black brothers and sisters; when you see the vast majority of your twenty million Negro brothers smothering in an airtight cage of poverty in the midst of an affluent society; when you suddenly find your tongue twisted and your speech stammering as you seek to explain to your six-year-old daughter why she can't go to the public amusement park that has just been advertised on television, and see tears welling up in her eyes when she is told that Funtown is closed to colored children, and see ominous clouds of inferiority beginning to form in her little mental sky, and see her beginning to distort her personality by developing an unconscious bitterness toward white people; when you have to concoct an answer for a five-year-old son who is asking, "Daddy, why do white people treat colored people so mean?"; when you take a cross-country drive and find it necessary to sleep night after night in the uncomfortable corners of your automobile because no motel will accept you; when you are humiliated day

in and day out by nagging signs reading "white" and "colored"; when your first name becomes "nigger," your middle name becomes "boy" (however old you are) and your last name becomes "John," and your wife and mother are never given the respected title "Mrs."; when you are harried by day and haunted by night by the fact that you are a Negro, living constantly at tiptoe stance, never quite knowing what to expect next, and are plagued with inner fears and outer resentments; when you are forever fighting a degenerating sense of "nobodiness"— then you will understand why we find it difficult to wait. There comes a time when the cup of endurance runs over, and men are no longer willing to be plunged into the abyss of despair. I hope, sirs, you can understand our legitimate and unavoidable impatience.

You can express a great deal of anxiety over our willingness to break   15 laws. This is certainly a legitimate concern. Since we so diligently urge people to obey the Supreme Court's decision of 1954 outlawing segregation in the public schools, at first glance it may seem rather paradoxical for us consciously to break laws. One may well ask: "How can you advocate breaking some laws and obeying others?" The answer lies in the fact that there are two types of laws: just and unjust. I would be the first to advocate obeying just laws. One has not only a legal but a moral responsibility to obey just laws. Conversely, one has a moral responsibility to disobey unjust laws. I would agree with St. Augustine that "an unjust law is no law at all."

Now, what is the difference between the two? How does one deter-   16 mine whether a law is just or unjust? A just law is a man-made code that squares with the moral law or the law of God. An unjust law is a code that is out of harmony with the moral law. To put it in the terms of St. Thomas Aquinas: An unjust law is a human law that is not rooted in eternal law and natural law. Any law that uplifts human personality is just. Any law that degrades human personality is unjust. All segregation statutes are unjust because segregation distorts the soul and damages the personality. It gives the segregator a false sense of superiority and the segregated a false sense of inferiority. Segregation, to use the terminology of the Jewish philosopher Martin Buber, substitutes an "I-it" relationship for an "I-thou" relationship and ends up relegating persons to the status of things. Hence segregation is not only politically, economically, and sociologically unsound, it is morally wrong and sinful. Paul Tillich has said that sin is separation. Is not segregation an existential expression of man's tragic separation, his awful estrangement, his terrible sinfulness? Thus it is that I can urge men to obey the 1954 decision of the Supreme Court, for it is morally right; and I can urge them to disobey segregation ordinances, for they are morally wrong.

Let us consider a more concrete example of just and unjust laws. An   17 unjust law is a code that a numerical or power majority group compels a minority group to obey but does not make binding on itself. This is *difference* made legal. By the same token, a just law is a code that a majority compels a minority to follow and that it is willing to follow itself. This is *sameness* made legal.

18   Let me give another explanation. A law is unjust if it is inflicted on a minority that, as a result of being denied the right to vote, had no part in enacting or devising the law. Who can say that the legislature of Alabama which set up that state's segregation laws was democratically elected? Throughout Alabama all sorts of devious methods are used to prevent Negroes from becoming registered voters, and there are some counties in which, even though Negroes constitute a majority of the population, not a single Negro is registered. Can any law enacted under such circumstances be considered democratically structured?

19   Sometimes a law is just on its face and unjust in its application. For instance, I have been arrested on a charge of parading without a permit. Now, there is nothing wrong in having an ordinance which requires a permit for a parade. But such an ordinance becomes unjust when it is used to maintain segregation and to deny citizens the First-Amendment privilege of peaceful assembly and protest.

20   I hope you are able to see the distinction I am trying to point out. In no sense do I advocate evading or defying the law, as would the rabid segregationist. That would lead to anarchy. One who breaks an unjust law must do so openly, lovingly, and with a willingness to accept the penalty. I submit that an individual who breaks a law that conscience tells him is unjust, and who willingly accepts the penalty of imprisonment in order to arouse the conscience of the community over its injustice, is in reality expressing the highest respect for law.

21   Of course, there is nothing new about this kind of civil disobedience. It was evidenced sublimely in the refusal of Shadrach, Meshach, and Abednego to obey the laws of Nebuchadnezzar, on the ground that a higher moral law was at stake. It was practiced superbly by the early Christians, who were willing to face hungry lions and the excruciating pain of chopping blocks rather than submit to certain unjust laws of the Roman Empire. To a degree, academic freedom is a reality today because Socrates practiced civil disobedience. In our own nation, the Boston Tea Party represented a massive act of civil disobedience.

22   We should never forget that everything Adolf Hitler did in Germany was "legal" and everything the Hungarian freedom fighters did in Hungary was "illegal." It was "illegal" to aid and comfort a Jew in Hitler's Germany. Even so, I am sure that, had I lived in Germany at the time, I would have aided and comforted my Jewish brothers. If today I lived in a Communist country where certain principles dear to the Christian faith are suppressed, I would openly advocate disobeying that country's anti-religious laws.

23   I must make two honest confessions to you, my Christian and Jewish brothers. First, I must confess that over the past few years I

have been gravely disappointed with the white moderate. I have almost reached the regrettable conclusion that the Negro's great stumbling block in his stride toward freedom is not the White Citizen's Counciler or the Ku Klux Klanner, but the white moderate, who is more devoted to "order" than to justice; who prefers a negative peace which is the absence of tension to a positive peace which is the presence of justice; who constantly says, "I agree with you in the goal you seek, but I cannot agree with your methods of direct action"; who paternalistically believes he can set the timetable for another man's freedom; who lives by a mythical concept of time and who constantly advises the Negro to wait for a "more convenient season." Shallow understanding from people of good will is more frustrating than absolute misunderstanding from people of ill will. Lukewarm acceptance is much more bewildering than outright rejection.

I had hoped that the white moderate would understand that law and order exist for the purpose of establishing justice and that when they fail in this purpose they become the dangerously structured dams that block the flow of social progress. I had hoped that the white moderate would understand that the present tension in the South is a necessary phase of the transition from an obnoxious negative peace, in which the Negro passively accepted his unjust plight, to a substantive and positive peace, in which all men will respect the dignity and worth of human personality. Actually, we who engage in nonviolent direct action are not the creators of tension. We merely bring to the surface the hidden tension that is already alive. We bring it out in the open, where it can be seen and dealt with. Like a boil that can never be cured so long as it is covered up but must be opened with all its ugliness to the natural medicines of air and light, injustice must be exposed, with all the tension its exposure creates, to the light of human conscience and the air of national opinion, before it can be cured.   24

In your statement you assert that our actions, even though peaceful, must be condemned because they precipitate violence. But is this a logical assertion? Isn't this like condemning a robbed man because his possession of money precipitated the evil act of robbery? Isn't this like condemning Socrates because his unswerving commitment to truth and his philosophical inquiries precipitated the act by the misguided populace in which they made him drink hemlock? Isn't this like condemning Jesus because his unique God-consciousness and never-ceasing devotion to God's will precipitated the evil act of crucifixion? We must come to see that, as the federal courts have consistently affirmed, it is wrong to urge an individual to cease his efforts to gain his basic constitutional rights because the quest may precipitate violence. Society must protect the robbed and punish the robber.   25

I had also hoped that the white moderate would reject the myth concerning time in relation to the struggle for freedom. I have just   26 received a letter from a white brother in Texas. He writes: "All Christians know that the colored people will receive equal rights eventually, but it is possible that your are in too great a religious hurry. It has taken Christianity almost two thousand years to accomplish what it has. The teachings of Christ take time to come to earth." Such an attitude stems from a tragic misconception of time, from the strangely irrational notion that there is something in the very flow of time that will inevitably cure all ills. Actually, time itself is neutral; it can be used either destructively or constructively. More and more I feel that the people of ill will have used time much more effectively than have the people of good will. We will have to repent in this generation not merely for the hateful words and actions of the bad people, but for the appalling silence of the good people. Human progress never rolls in on wheels of inevitability; it comes through the tireless efforts of men willing to be co-workers with God, and without this hard work, time itself becomes an ally of the forces of social stagnation. We must use time creatively, in the knowledge that the time is always ripe to do right. Now is the time to make real the promise of democracy and transform our pending national elegy into a creative psalm of brotherhood. Now is the time to lift our national policy from the quicksand of racial injustice to the solid rock of human dignity.

27   You speak of our activity in Birmingham as extreme. At first I was rather disappointed that fellow clergymen would see my nonviolent efforts as those of an extremist. I began thinking about the fact that I stand in the middle of two opposing forces in the Negro community. One is a force of complacency, made up in part of Negroes who, as a result of long years of oppression, are so drained of self-respect and a sense of "somebodiness" that they have adjusted to segregation; and in part of a few middle-class Negroes who, because of a degree of academic and economic security and because in some ways they profit by segregation, have become insensitive to the problems of the masses. The other force is one of bitterness and hatred, and it comes perilously close to advocating violence. It is expressed in the various black nationalist groups that are springing up across the nation, the largest and best-known being Elijah Muhammad's Muslim movement. Nourished by the Negro's frustration over the continued existence of racial discrimination, this movement is made up of people who have lost faith in America, who have absolutely repudiated Christianity, and who have concluded that the white man is an incorrigible "devil."

28   I have tried to stand between these two forces, saying that we need emulate neither the "do-nothingism" of the complacent nor the hatred and despair of the black nationalist. For there is the more excellent way of love and nonviolent protest. I am grateful to God that, through the influence of the Negro church, the way of nonviolence became an integral part of our struggle.

If this philosophy had not emerged, by now many streets of the 29
South would, I am convinced, be flowing with blood. And I am further
convinced that if our white brothers dismiss as "rabble-rousers" and
"outside agitators" those of us who employ nonviolent direct action,
and if they refuse to support our nonviolent efforts, millions of Negroes
will, out of frustration and despair, seek solace and security in black-
nationalist ideologies—a development that would inevitably lead to a
frightening racial nightmare.

Oppressed people cannot remain oppressed forever. The yearning 30
for freedom eventually manifests itself, and that is what has happened
to the American Negro. Something within has reminded him of his
birthright of freedom, and something without has reminded him that it
can be gained. Consciously or unconsciously, he has been caught up by
the *Zeitgeist*, and with his black brothers of Africa and his brown and
yellow brothers of Asia, South America, and the Caribbean, the United
States Negro is moving with a sense of great urgency toward the
promised land of racial justice. If one recognizes this vital urge that has
engulfed the Negro community, one should readily understand why
public demonstrations are taking place. The Negro has many pent-up
resentments and latent frustrations, and he must release them. So let
him march; let him make prayer pilgrimages to the city hall; let him go
on freedom rides—and try to understand why he must do so. If his
repressed emotions are not released in nonviolent ways, they will seek
expression through violence; this is not a threat but a fact of history. So
I have not said to my people, "Get rid of your discontent." Rather, I
have tried to say that this normal and healthy discontent can be
channeled into the creative outlet of nonviolent direct action. And now
this approach is being termed extremist.

But though I was initially disappointed at being categorized as an 31
extremist, as I continued to think about the matter I gradually gained a
measure of satisfaction from the label. Was not Jesus an extremist for
love: "Love your enemies, bless them that curse you, do good to them
that hate you, and pray for them which despitefully use you, and
persecute you." Was not Amos an extremist for justice: "Let justice
roll down like waters and righteousness like an ever-flowing stream."
Was not Paul an extremist for the Christian gospel: "I bear in my body
the marks of the Lord Jesus." Was not Martin Luther an extremist:
"Here I stand; I cannot do otherwise, so help me God." And John
Bunyan: "I will stay in jail to the end of my days before I make a
butchery of my conscience." And Abraham Lincoln: "This nation
cannot survive half slave and half free." And Thomas Jefferson: "We
hold these truths to be self-evident, that all men are created
equal . . . " So the question is not whether we will be extremists, but
what kind of extremists we will be. Will we be extremists for hate or for
love? Will we be extremists for the preservation of injustice or for the

extension of justice? In that dramatic scene on Calvary's hill three men were crucified. We must never forget that all three were crucified for the same crime—the crime of extremism. Two were extremists for immorality, and thus fell below their environment. The other, Jesus Christ, was an extremist for love, truth, and goodness, and thereby rose above his environment. Perhaps the South, the nation, and the world are in dire need of creative extremists.

32   I had hoped that the white moderate would see this need. Perhaps I was too optimistic; perhaps I expected too much. I suppose I should have realized that few members of the oppressor race can understand the deep groans and passionate yearnings of the oppressed race, and still fewer have the vision to see that injustice must be rooted out by strong, persistent, and determined action. I am thankful, however, that some of our white brothers in the South have grasped the meaning of this social revolution and committed themselves to it. They are still all too few in quantity, but they are big in quality. Some—such as Ralph McGill, Lillian Smith, Harry Golden, James McBride Dabbs, Ann Braden, and Sarah Patton Boyle—have written about our struggle in eloquent and prophetic terms. Others have marched with us down nameless streets of the South. They have languished in filthy, roach-infested jails, suffering the abuse and brutality of policemen who view them as "dirty nigger-lovers." Unlike so many of their moderate brothers and sisters, they have recognized the urgency of the moment and sensed the need for powerful "action" antidotes to combat the disease of segregation.

33   Let me take note of my other major disappointment. I have been so greatly disappointed with the white church and its leadership. Of course, there are some notable exceptions. I am not unmindful of the fact that each of you has taken some significant stands on this issue. I commend you, Reverend Stallings, for your Christian stand on this past Sunday, in welcoming Negroes to your worship service on a non-segregated basis. I commend the Catholic leaders of this state for integrating Spring Hill College several years ago.

34   But despite these notable exceptions, I must honestly reiterate that I have been disappointed with the church. I do not say this as one of those negative critics who can always find something wrong with the church. I say this as a minister of the gospel, who loves the church; who was nurtured in its bosom; who has been sustained by its spiritual blessings and who will remain true to it as long as the cord of life shall lengthen.

35   When I was suddenly catapulted into the leadership of the bus protest in Montgomery, Alabama, a few years ago, I felt we would be supported by the white church. I felt that the white ministers, priests, and rabbis of the South would be among our strongest allies. Instead, some have been outright opponents, refusing to understand the free-

dom movement and misrepresenting its leaders; all too many others have been more cautious than courageous and have remained silent behind the anesthetizing security of stained-glass windows.

In spite of my shattered dreams, I came to Birmingham with the 36 hope that the white religious leadership of this community would see the justice of our cause and, with deep moral concern, would serve as the channel through which our just grievances could reach the power structure. I had hoped that each of you would understand. But again I have been disappointed.

There was a time when the church was very powerful—in the time 37 when the early Christians rejoiced at being deemed worthy to suffer for what they believed. In those days the church was not merely a thermometer that recorded the ideas and principles of popular opinion; it was a thermostat that transformed the mores of society. Whenever the early Christians entered a town, the people in power became disturbed and immediately sought to convict the Christians for being "disturbers of the peace" and "outside agitators." But the Christians pressed on, in the conviction that they were "a colony of heaven," called to obey God rather than man. Small in number, they were big in commitment. They were too God-intoxicated to be "astronomically intimidated." By their effort and example they brought an end to such ancient evils as infanticide and gladiatorial contests.

Things are different now. So often the contemporary church is a 38 weak, ineffectual voice with an uncertain sound. So often it is an arch-defender of the status quo. Far from being disturbed by the presence of the church, the power structure of the average community is consoled by the church's silent—and often even vocal—sanction of things as they are.

But the judgment of God is upon the church as never before. If 39 today's church does not recapture the sacrificial spirit of the early church, it will lose its authenticity, forfeit the loyalty of millions, and be dismissed as an irrelevant social club with no meaning for the twentieth century. Every day I meet young people whose disappointment with the church has turned into outright disgust.

Perhaps I have once again been too optimistic. Is organized religion 40 too inextricably bound to the status quo to save our nation and the world? Perhaps I must turn my faith to the inner spiritual church, the church within the church, as the true *ekklesia* and the hope of the world. But again I am thankful to God that some noble souls from the ranks of organized religion have broken loose from the paralyzing chains of conformity and joined us as active partners in the struggle for freedom. They have left their secure congregations and walked the streets of Albany, Georgia, with us. They have gone down the highways of the South on torturous rides for freedom. Yes, they have gone to jail with us. Some have been dismissed from their churches, have lost the support of their bishops and fellow ministers. But they have acted in the faith that right defeated is stronger than evil triumphant. Their witness has been the spiritual salt that has preserved the true meaning of the gospel in these troubled times. They have carved a tunnel of hope through the dark mountain of disappointment.

41   I hope the church as a whole will meet the challenge of this decisive hour. But even if the church does not come to the aid of justice, I have no despair about the future. I have no fear about the outcome of our struggle in Birmingham, even if our motives are at present misunderstood. We will reach the goal of freedom in Birmingham and all over the nation, because the goal of America is freedom. Abused and scorned though we may be, our destiny is tied up with America's destiny. Before the Pilgrims landed at Plymouth, we were here. Before the pen of Jefferson etched the majestic words of the Declaration of Independence across the pages of history, we were here. For more than two centuries our forebears labored in this country without wages; they made cotton king; they built the homes of their masters while suffering gross injustice and shameful humiliation—and yet out of a bottomless vitality they continued to thrive and develop. If the inexpressible cruelties of slavery could not stop us, the opposition we now face will surely fail. We will win our freedom because the sacred heritage of our nation and the eternal will of God are embodied in our echoing demands.

42   Before closing I feel impelled to mention one other point in your statement that has troubled me profoundly. You warmly commended the Birmingham police force for keeping "order" and "preventing violence." I doubt that you would have so warmly commended the police force if you had seen its dogs sinking their teeth into unarmed, nonviolent Negroes. I doubt that you would so quickly commend the policemen if you were to observe their ugly and inhumane treatment of Negroes here in the city jail; if you were to watch them push and curse old Negro women and young Negro girls; if you were to see them slap and kick old Negro men and young boys, if you were to observe them, as they did on two occasions, refuse to give us food because we wanted to sing our grace together. I cannot join you in your praise of the Birmingham police department.

43   It is true that the police have exercised a degree of discipline in handling the demonstrators. In this sense they have conducted themselves rather "nonviolently" in public. But for what purpose? To preserve the evil system of segregation. Over the past few years I have consistently preached that nonviolence demands that the means we use must be as pure as the ends we seek. I have tried to make clear that it is wrong to use immoral means to attain moral ends. But now I must affirm that it is just as wrong, or perhaps even more so, to use moral means to preserve immoral ends. Perhaps Mr. Connor and his policemen have been rather nonviolent in public, as was Chief Pritchett in

Albany, Georgia, but they have used the moral means of nonviolence to maintain the immoral end of racial injustice. As T. S. Eliot has said, "The last temptation is the greatest treason: To do the right deed for the wrong reason."

I wish you had commended the Negro sit-inners and demonstrators 44 of Birmingham for their sublime courage, their willingness to suffer, and their amazing discipline in the midst of great provocation. One day the South will recognize its real heroes. They will be the James Merediths, with the noble sense of purpose that enables them to face jeering and hostile mobs, and with the agonizing loneliness that characterizes the life of the pioneer. They will be old, oppressed, battered Negro women, symbolized in a seventy-two-year-old woman in Montgomery, Alabama, who rose up with a sense of dignity and with her people decided not to ride segregated buses, and who responded with ungrammatical profundity to one who inquired about her weariness: "My feets is tired, but my soul is at rest." They will be the young high school and college students, the young ministers of the gospel and a host of their elders, courageously and nonviolently sitting in at lunch counters and willingly going to jail for conscience' sake. One day the South will know that when these disinherited children of God sat down at lunch counters, they were in reality standing up for what is best in the American dream and for the most sacred values in our Judaeo-Christian heritage, thereby bringing our nation back to those great wells of democracy which were dug deep by the founding fathers in their formulation of the Constitution and the Declaration of Independence.

Never before have I written so long a letter. I'm afraid it is much too 45 long to take your precious time. I can assure you that it would have been much shorter if I had been writing from a comfortable desk, but what else can one do when he is alone in a narrow jail cell, other than write long letters, think long thoughts, and pray long prayers?

If I have said anything in this letter that overstates the truth and 46 indicates an unreasonable impatience, I beg you to forgive me. If I have said anything that understates the truth and indicates my having a patience that allows me to settle for anything less than brotherhood, I beg God to forgive me.

I hope this letter finds you strong in the faith. I also hope that 47 circumstances will soon make it possible for me to meet each of you, not as an integrationist or a civil-rights leader but as a fellow clergyman and a Christian brother. Let us all hope that the dark clouds of racial prejudice will soon pass away and the deep fog of misunderstanding will be lifted from our fear-drenched communities, and in some not too distant tomorrow the radiant stars of love and brotherhood will shine over our great nation with all their scintillating beauty.

Yours for the cause of Peace and Brotherhood,
Martin Luther King, Jr.

FOR DISCUSSION

1. This essay is written in the form of a letter. What is gained by King's use of this rhetorical form? What does this form let him do that he might not be able to do in straight essay form? What limitations does the letter form have?

2. What makes this letter worth reading twenty years after it was written? In light of your answer, what can you say about the place of the written word in the long-term contribution of a human being to society?

3. In what way are both external and internal motivations present in the writing of this essay?

4. What do you "know" about King after reading this essay?

5. How does the way King signs his letter support the point he is trying to make?

6. How does the circumstance/situation in which this essay was written relate to its effectiveness as persuasion?

PLATO

Socrates, who was a teacher of wisdom in ancient Greece, has been called by some the purest *thinker who ever lived. He was executed in 399* B.C. *after the Athenian court found him guilty of impiety and corruption of the Athenian youth. Although Socrates himself left no writings behind, the philosopher Plato c.427–c.348* B.C. *recorded Socrates' words. The following excerpt is taken from Plato's account of Socrates' attempt to persuade the court of his innocence—just before he was sentenced to death.*

Socrates' Defense (Apology)

1 I do not know what effect my accusers have had upon you, gentlemen, but for my own part I was almost carried away by them—their arguments were so convincing. On the other hand, scarcely a word of what they said was true. I was especially astonished at one of their many misrepresentations; I mean when they told you that you must be careful not to let me deceive you—the implication being that I am a

skillful speaker. I thought that it was peculiarly brazen of them to tell you this without a blush, since they must know that they will soon be effectively confuted, when it becomes obvious that I have not the slightest skill as a speaker—unless, of course, by a skillful speaker they mean one who speaks the truth. If that is what they mean, I would agree that I am an orator, though not after their pattern. . . .

Very well, then, I must begin my defense, gentlemen, and I must 2 try, in the short time that I have, to rid your minds of a false impression which is the work of many years. . . .

Let us go back to the beginning and consider what the charge is that 3 has made me so unpopular, and has encouraged Meletus to draw up this indictment. Very well, what did my critics say in attacking my character? I must read out their affidavit, so to speak, as though they were my legal accusers: Socrates is guilty of criminal meddling, in that he inquires into things below the earth and in the sky, and makes the weaker argument defeat the stronger, and teaches others to follow his example. It runs something like that. You have seen it for yourselves in the play by Aristophanes, where Socrates goes whirling round, proclaiming that he is walking on air, and uttering a great deal of other nonsense about things of which I know nothing whatsover. I mean no disrespect for such knowledge, if anyone really is versed in it—I do not want any more lawsuits brought against me by Meletus—but the fact is, gentlemen, that I take no interest in it. What is more, I call upon the greater part of you as witnesses to my statement, and I appeal to all of you who have ever listened to me talking—and there are a great many to whom this applies—to clear your neighbors' minds on this point. Tell one another whether any one of you has ever heard me discuss such questions briefly or at length, and then you will realize that the other popular reports about me are equally unreliable.

The fact is that there is nothing in any of these charges, and if you 4 have heard anyone say that I try to educate people and charge a fee, there is no truth in that either. . . .

Here perhaps one of you might interrupt me and say, But what is it 5 that you do, Socrates? How is it that you have been misrepresented like this? Surely all this talk and gossip about you would never have arisen if you had confined yourself to ordinary activities, but only if your behavior was abnormal. Tell us the explanation, if you do not want us to invent it for ourselves.

This seems to me to be a reasonable request, and I will try to explain 6 to you what it is that has given me this false notoriety. So please give me your attention. Perhaps some of you will think that I am not being serious, but I assure you that I am going to tell you the whole truth.

I have gained this reputation, gentlemen, from nothing more or less 7 than a kind of wisdom. What kind of wisdom do I mean? Human wisdom, I suppose. It seems that I really am wise in this limited sense.

Presumably the geniuses whom I mentioned just now are wise in a wisdom that is more than human. I do not know how else to account for it. I certainly have no knowledge of such wisdom, and anyone who says that I have is a liar and willful slanderer. Now, gentlemen, please do not interrupt me if I seem to make an extravagant claim, for what I am going to tell you is not my own opinion. I am going to refer you to an unimpeachable authority. I shall call as witness to my wisdom, such as it is, the god at Delphi.

8   You know Chaerephon, of course. He was a friend of mine from boyhood, and a good democrat who played his part with the rest of you in the recent expulsion and restoration. And you know what he was like, how enthusiastic he was over anything that he had once undertaken. Well, one day he actually went to Delphi and asked this question of the god—as I said before, gentlemen, please do not interrupt—he asked whether there was anyone wiser than myself. The priestess replied that there was no one. As Chaerephon is dead, the evidence for my statement will be supplied by his brother, who is here in court.

9   Please consider my object in telling you this. I want to explain to you how the attack upon my reputation first started. When I heard about the oracle's answer, I said to myself, What does the god mean? Why does he not use plain language? I am only too conscious that I have no claim to wisdom, great or small. So what can he mean by asserting that I am the wisest man in the world? He cannot be telling a lie; that would not be right for him.

10   After puzzling about it for some time, I set myself at last with considerable reluctance to check the truth of it in the following way. I went to interview a man with a high reputation for wisdom, because I felt that here if anywhere I should succeed in disproving the oracle and pointing out to my divine authority, You said that I was the wisest of men, but here is a man who is wiser than I am.

11   Well, I gave a thorough examination to this person—I need not mention his name, but it was one of our politicians that I was studying when I had this experience—and in conversation with him I formed the impression that although in many people's opinion, and especially in his own, he appeared to be wise, in fact he was not. Then when I began to try to show him that he only thought he was wise and was not really so, my efforts were resented both by him and by many of the other people present. However, I reflected as I walked away, Well, I am certainly wiser than this man. It is only too likely that neither of us has any knowledge to boast of, but he thinks that he knows something which he does not know, whereas I am quite conscious of my ignorance. At any rate it seems that I am wiser than he is to this small extent, that I do not think that I know what I do not know.

After this I went on to interview a man with an even greater reputa- 12
tion for wisdom, and I formed the same impression again, and here too
I incurred the resentment of the man himself and a number of others.

From that time on I interviewed one person after another. I realized 13
with distress and alarm that I was making myself unpopular, but I felt
compelled to put my religious duty first. Since I was trying to find out
the meaning of the oracle, I was bound to interview everyone who had
a reputation for knowledge. And by dog, gentlemen, for I must be frank
with you, my honest impression was this. It seemed to me, as I pursued
my investigation at the god's command, that the people with the
greatest reputations were almost entirely deficient, while others who
were supposed to be their inferiors were much better qualified in
practical intelligence.

I want you to think of my adventures as a sort of pilgrimage under- 14
taken to establish the truth of the oracle once for all. After I had
finished with the politicians I turned to the poets, dramatic, lyric, and
all the rest, in the belief that here I should expose myself as a comparative ignoramus. I used to pick up what I thought were some of their
most perfect works and question them closely about the meaning of
what they had written, in the hope of incidentally enlarging my own
knowledge. Well, gentlemen, I hesitate to tell you the truth, but it must
be told. It is hardly an exaggeration to say that any of the bystanders
could have explained those poems better than their actual authors. So I
soon made up my mind about the poets too. I decided that it was not
wisdom that enabled them to write their poetry, but a kind of instinct or
inspiration, such as you find in seers and prophets who deliver all their
sublime messages without knowing in the least what they mean. It
seemed clear to me that the poets were in much the same case, and I
also observed that the very fact that they were poets made them think
that they had a perfect understanding of all other subjects, of which
they were totally ignorant. So I left that line of inquiry too with the
same sense of advantage that I had felt in the case of the politicians.

Last of all I turned to the skilled craftsmen. I knew quite well that I 15
had practically no technical qualifications myself, and I was sure that I
should find them full of impressive knowledge. In this I was not
disappointed. They understood things which I did not, and to that
extent they were wiser than I was. But, gentlemen, these professional
experts seemed to share the same failing which I had noticed in the
poets. I mean that on the strength of their technical proficiency they
claimed a perfect understanding of every other subject, however
important, and I felt that this error more than outweighted their positive wisdom. So I made myself spokesman for the oracle, and asked
myself whether I would rather be as I was—neither wise with their

wisdom nor stupid with their stupidity—or possess both qualities as they did. I replied through myself to the oracle that it was best for me to be as I was.

16   The effect of these investigations of mine, gentlemen, has been to arouse against me a great deal of hostility, and hostility of a particularly bitter and persistent kind, which has resulted in various malicious suggestions, including the description of me as a professor of wisdom. This is due to the fact that whenever I succeed in disproving another person's claim to wisdom in a given subject, the bystanders assume that I know everything about that subject myself. But the truth of the matter, gentlemen, is pretty certainly this, that real wisdom is the property of God, and this oracle is his way of telling us that human wisdom has little or no value. It seems to me that he is not referring literally to Socrates, but has merely taken my name as an example, as if he would say to us, The wisest of you men is he who has realized, like Socrates, that in respect of wisdom he is really worthless.

17   That is why I still go about seeking and searching in obedience to the divine command, if I think that anyone is wise, whether citizen or stranger, and when I think that any person is not wise, I try to help the cause of God by proving that he is not. . . .

18   There, gentlemen, you have the true facts, which I present to you without any concealment or suppression, great or small. I am fairly certain that this plain speaking of mine is the cause of my unpopularity, and this really goes to prove that my statements are true, and that I have described correctly the nature and the grounds of the calumny which has been brought against me. Whether you inquire into them now or later, you will find the facts as I have just described them.

FOR DISCUSSION

1. What did Socrates say he had been accused of?

2. In list form, outline Socrates' explanation of how this accusation came about.

3. What does Socrates gain by mentioning his friend Chaerephon?

4. What is there in Socrates' assertion about wisdom that was so threatening to the men of his day?

5. What action is implicit on the listeners' part in this defense?

6. What might have been Plato's motive for writing this? How do you account for its continued usefulness as a piece of writing since Plato's day?

7. Here is a headnote written by Edith Hamilton, who edited the collection of Plato's work this excerpt is taken from. Read it and then discuss the over-all effectiveness of Socrates—and Plato—as persuaders.

In his Defense, Socrates explains himself to his fellow citizens when he is brought before an Athenian court on a most serious charge. "Socrates is guilty of corrupting the minds of the young, and of believing in deities of his own invention instead of the gods recognized by the state." In the *Apology,* as it is generally known, he gives a detailed account of the way he has lived and the convictions he has reached.

At the end, when he is condemned to death, the few words in which he accepts the sentence are in themselves a vivid picture of the man he was, unlike any other there has ever been. Great spiritual leaders and great saints adorn the pages of history, but Socrates is not like any of them. He is, indeed, the servant of the divine power, living in complete obedience to God, yet he always views the world of men with a bit of humor, a touch of irony. He spends his life in the effort to kindle into a flame the spark of good in every man, but when he fails, when he comes up against blind obstinacy or stupid conceit or the indifference of egotism, or when he draws down on himself bitter enmity, then along with his regret—because he cares for everyone—is mingled a little amusement, a feeling, as it were, of rueful sympathy, as if he said to himself, "What silly children we are." Socrates never condemned.

This significant clue to what he was is given most clearly in Socrates' Defense.

PAUL McBREARTY

In the following essay written for the Chronicle of Higher Education *in 1982, Paul McBrearty argues that the current use of anonymous student evaluations of teachers must be changed. McBrearty, who is an English professor at St. Louis Community College at Meramec, attempts to persuade us that evaluators should be responsible for their words.*

We Should Abolish Anonymous Evaluations of Teachers by Their Students

1   Anonymity in student evaluations of teachers—so we have often been told and many of us believe—encourages students to be frank. To the uncritical, frankness implies honesty, and surely it follows that what is said frankly and honestly must be true.

2   Now frankness is, of course, a virtue in certain contexts. However, it must never be mistaken for acuteness of perception, objectivity, or even accuracy, all of which may well be—and often are—missing from the "frankest" student evaluation.

3   Far more valuable for purposes of evaluation and improvement of instruction are the accuracy and reliability of the information supplied. It goes without saying that absolute accuracy and reliability in evaluations are unattainable. But we must not let that fact mislead us into imagining that if we encourage frankness by guaranteeing anonymity to evaluators we will secure more accurate observations and more reliable judgments than would otherwise be the case. Indeed, a few moments of reflection should make us realize that in many cases guaranteeing anonymity will result in just the opposite.

4   Anonymity, after all, fosters not merely frankness; more ominously (for teachers) it fosters irresponsibility, a trait of character (or a kind of behavior, if we prefer) that we ought never to encourage in the young. Formal evaluation of teachers by their students, at one time unheard of, was seen as a privilege when it was first introduced, but quite soon it came to be looked upon as a right.

5   Like all rights, however, the right to evaluate carries with it a corresponding obligation: the obligation of the evaluators to take responsibility for what they say or write. When we assure students that we will not under any circumstances reveal their identities, we in effect tell the weak, the confused, the vindictive, the morally obtuse, and the less courageous among them that they may say what they please without having to stand behind their words.

6   That is a foolish and dangerous thing to do. To give power without responsibility is to ask for abuse; to give it to students—many of whom are by definition immature, and some of whom may be enrolled in courses beyond their capacities—is unfair to us and a perversion of our duty to them.

7   We owe our students rather more than lectures on Keynesian theory, computer language, and topic sentences. We owe them the opportunity to learn to behave as mature people with full responsibility for the actions they take. Guaranteeing them anonymity in their evaluations of faculty members guarantees them precisely the avoidance of that responsibility. That is bad pedagogy, bad institutional policy, and certainly bad morality.

Anonymous testimony is discounted or ignored nearly everywhere 8 outside the peculiar world of higher education *because* it is anonymous and therefore of doubtful authenticity. Only in investigative police work is anonymous information officially acted upon, and even then never without verification. In law, it has no standing whatsoever. It is therefore intolerable that administrative and personnel decisions affecting the lives and careers of professionals are sometimes taken on the basis (to whatever extent) of unverified anonymous information. Teachers should be accorded at least the standing presently granted known lawbreakers and those accused of crimes.

Student anonymity is unfair to the faculty. As teachers, we are 9 continually called upon to defend our grading methods and standards— not only to students but also occasionally to parents and administrators—by producing verifiable support for the grades we give. At my institution, among others, administrators are required to document their negative evaluations of faculty members with specific evidence. Only students are exempt from the necessity of supporting and defending the "grades" they give, and teachers are denied the privilege of confronting their graders.

Lacking the steadying influence that would be provided by the 10 knowledge that their evaluations, too, are subject to verification, students are under no obligation even to tell the simple truth about factual matters and cannot be called to account as teachers frequently are.

Anonymity in student evaluations virtually assures lowered aca- 11 demic standards and inflated grades. The pressures on teachers to *give* good grades so as to *get* good grades are severe, pervasive, unremitting, and inescapable. Historically, the beginning of the use of student evaluations on a large scale coincides precisely with the beginning of nearly universal grade inflation. There is no doubt that other influences contributed to the upward spiral, but there is also no doubt that student evaluation of teachers has been the principal one.

There is a discouragingly widespread view—among students, ad- 12 ministrators, and the general public—that high student grades are a mark of superior teaching, despite the fact, which should be obvious to anyone of ordinary intelligence, that nothing is easier to manipulate than grades. In the face of that widely held, if unsophisticated, view, some teachers have the best possible grounds for fearing retaliation from students whose grades are lower than the students had—for whatever reason—expected. More practical-minded teachers (more cynical or more "flexible," perhaps) adjust their grading so as to reflect the "success" of their teaching. Only a fool will refuse to see what can (and does) become of academic standards and professional integrity when teachers are placed in a double-bind of this sort.

Anonymity in student evaluations obviates any meaningful research 13 into possible relationships between student behavior and student ratings. How can we justify this extraordinary refusal to procure valuable and relevant data on a matter of such importance? Incredibly, and almost uniquely, in the context of student evaluations alone, we assert—contrary to all ordinary experience and common sense—that it does not matter who says what under what conditions; in student evaluations only *what is said* matters.

14   In our courses we teach our students, as an elementary principle of discourse, that he who asserts must prove. We teach them that ignoring context is a form of falsification. Furthermore, we teach them—or we should—that when they offer the testimony of outside sources in support of a proposition, they must identify those sources fully so that their readers or hearers may judge or verify the knowledgeability of the source and the veracity of the testimony.

15   When students evaluate a teacher, however, the previous involvement of the witnesses with the subject of their testimony, and the witnesses' experience, their qualifications, their knowledge, their intelligence, their maturity, their judgment, their veracity, their *character* are suddenly of no account whatever. What more egregious instance can we find of the perverse violation of our own high principles?—and all presumably in the cause of assuring "frankness."

16   With no information as to which student is saying what, we cannot determine, for example, how the item "Informs students about how they will be graded on tests and assignments" was marked by a student who was absent on the days the tests and assignments were given or due; we cannot tell how the student who is never prepared or never able to respond in class marks the item "Explains material in response to questions." In fact, we cannot learn anything useful to help us form judgments as to the many student characteristics that may tend to correspond with particular responses.

17   Whenever student evaluations are used in any way by administrators as a basis for the denial of promotion, retention, or salary increase, or for assigning a less-than-satisfactory rating to a faculty member, the faculty member is denied the constitutional right of due process if not permitted to confront what are in effect his or her accusers.

18   It would be easy to devise safeguards that would insure that faculty members would not be given access to identifying data except in a case of clear need, as in a grievance hearing. Indeed, such a system was proposed to—and at first accepted by—the administration on my campus. In the end, however, administrators here felt that elaborate safeguards notwithstanding, even to hint to students that their identities might, under very restricted conditions, be revealed would invalidate the evaluations—since the students would not, of course, give "honest" evaluations, but only favorable ones—the two evidently being mutually exclusive. That there is an analogy between this situation and that of the instructor who gives high grades because he fears

students will retaliate if he gives low ones either does not impress those administrators or does not occur to them.

The present method of administering student evaluations must be 19 changed because:

Anonymity does not assure accuracy and reliability but more likely the opposite.

Anonymity encourages irresponsibility in students who should be learning to be responsible.

Anonymous and hence unchallengeable evaluations are inherently unfair to faculty members whose evaluations of students *are* subject to challenge.

Anonymity renders impossible most meaningful research on the reliability of student evaluations.

Anonymity in student evaluations may well result in denial of a faculty member's constitutional right to due process.

If, as administrators claim, the method itself cannot feasibly be 20 changed, then student evaluations must no longer be a component in the process of faculty evaluation.

FOR DISCUSSION

1. What change does the author call for?

2. Make a list of the points he makes to prove his case. Do you agree or disagree with these points?

3. This essay appeared in the special essay column of the *Chronicle of Higher Education* called Point of View. Who was the author's audience? What is the relationship he establishes with this audience? Although the audience for this periodical does not include students as likely readers, how do you respond when you become part of the author's audience as a result of reading the essay?

4. What can you guess might have motivated the author to write this essay?

5. What is the tone of the essay? Discuss this question with details from the essay.

6. Are you convinced by the author's words?

VIRGINIA WOOLF

In this essay, the well-known novelist, critic, and essayist, Virginia Woolf (1882–1941) uses her own experience as a point of departure in discussing professions women might have and what hinders them in achieving prominence in professions they want to have. What action is implicit in Woolf's words?

Professions for Women

1 When your secretary invited me to come here, she told me that your Society is concerned with the employment of women and she suggested that I might tell you something about my own professional experiences. It is true I am a woman; it is true I am employed, but what professional experiences have I had? It is difficult to say. My profession is literature; and in that profession there are fewer experiences for women than in any other, with the exception of the stage—fewer, I mean, that are peculiar to women. For the road was cut many years ago—by Fanny Burney, by Aphra Behn, by Harriet Martineau, by Jane Austen, by George Eliot—many famous women, and many more unknown and forgotten, have been before me, making the path smooth, and regulating my steps. Thus, when I came to write, there were very few material obstacles in my way. Writing was a reputable and harmless occupation. The family peace was not broken by the scratching of a pen. No demand was made upon the family purse. For ten and sixpence one can buy paper enough to write all the plays of Shakespeare—if one has a mind that way. Pianos and models, Paris, Vienna and Berlin, masters and mistresses, are not needed by a writer. The cheapness of writing paper is, of course, the reason why women have succeeded as writers before they have succeeded in the other professions.

2 But to tell you my story—it is a simple one. You have only got to figure to yourselves a girl in a bedroom with a pen in her hand. She had only to move that pen from left to right—from ten o'clock to one. Then it occurred to her to do what is simple and cheap enough after all—to slip a few of those pages into an envelope, fix a penny stamp in the corner, and drop the envelope into the red box at the corner. It was thus that I became a journalist; and my effort was rewarded on the first day of the following month—a very glorious day it was for me—by a letter from an editor containing a cheque for one pound ten shillings

and sixpence. But to show you how little I deserve to be called a professional woman, how little I know of the struggles and difficulties of such lives, I have to admit that instead of spending that sum upon bread and butter, rent, shoes and stockings, or butcher's bills, I went out and bought a cat—a beautiful cat, a Persian cat, which very soon involved me in bitter disputes with my neighbours.

What could be easier than to write articles and to buy Persian cats 3 with the profits? But wait a moment. Articles have to be about something. Mine, I seem to remember, was about a novel by a famous man. And while I was writing this review, I discovered that if I were going to review books I should need to do battle with a certain phantom. And the phantom was a woman, and when I came to know her better I called her after the heroine of a famous poem, The Angel in the House. It was she who used to come between me and my paper when I was writing reviews. It was she who bothered me and wasted my time and so tormented me that at last I killed her. You who come of a younger and happier generation may not have heard of her—you may not know what I mean by the Angel in the House. I will describe her as shortly as I can. She was intensely sympathetic. She was immensely charming. She was utterly unselfish. She excelled in the difficult arts of family life. She sacrificed herself daily. If there was chicken, she took the leg; if there was a draught she sat in it—in short she was so constituted that she never had a mind or a wish of her own, but preferred to sympathize always with the minds and wishes of others. Above all—I need not say it—she was pure. Her purity was supposed to be her chief beauty—her blushes, her great grace. In those days—the last of Queen Victoria— every house had its Angel. And when I came to write I encountered her with the very first words. The shadow of her wings fell on my page; I heard the rustling of her skirts in the room. Directly, that is to say, I took my pen in hand to review that novel by a famous man, she slipped behind me and whispered: "My dear, you are a young woman. You are writing about a book that has been written by a man. Be sympathetic; be tender; flatter, deceive; use all the arts and wiles of our sex. Never let anybody guess that you have a mind of your own. Above all, be pure." And she made as if to guide my pen. I now record the one act for which I take some credit to myself, though the credit rightly belongs to some excellent ancestors of mine who left me a certain sum of money—shall we say five hundred pounds a year?—so that it was not necessary for me to depend solely on charm for my living. I turned upon her and caught her by the throat. I did my best to kill her. My excuse, if I were to be had up in a court of law, would be that I acted in self-defence. Had I not killed her she would have killed me. She would have plucked the heart out of my writing. For, as I found, directly I put pen to paper, you cannot review even a novel without having a mind of your own, without expressing what you think to be the truth about human relations, morality, sex. And all these questions, according to the Angel in the House, cannot be dealt with freely and openly by women; they must charm, they must conciliate, they must—to put it bluntly—tell lies if they are to succeed. Thus, whenever I felt the shadow of her wing or the radiance of her halo upon my page, I took up the inkpot and flung it at her. She died hard. Her fictitious nature was of great assistance to her. It is far harder to kill a phantom than a reality. She was always creeping back when I thought I had dispatched her. Though I flatter myself that I killed her in the end, the struggle was severe; it took much time that had better have been spent upon learning Greek grammar; or in roaming the world in search of adventures. But it was a real experience; it was an experience that was bound to befall all women writers at that time. Killing the Angel in the House was part of the occupation of a woman writer.

4   But to continue my story. The Angel was dead; what then remained? You may say that what remained was a simple and common object—a young woman in a bedroom with an inkpot. In other words, now that she had rid herself of falsehood, that young woman had only to be herself. Ah, but what is "herself"? I mean, what is a woman? I assure you, I do not know. I do not believe that you know. I do not believe that anybody can know until she has expressed herself in all the arts and professions open to human skill. That indeed is one of the reasons why I have come here—out of respect for you, who are in process of showing us by your experiments what a woman is, who are in process of providing us, by your failures and successes, with that extremely important piece of information.

5   But to continue the story of my professional experiences. I made one pound ten and six by my first review; and I bought a Persian cat with the proceeds. Then I grew ambitious. A Persian cat is all very well, I said; but a Persian cat is not enough. I must have a motor car. And it was thus that I became a novelist—for it is a very strange thing that people will give you a motor car if you will tell them a story. It is a still stranger thing that there is nothing so delightful in the world as telling stories. It is far pleasanter than writing reviews of famous novels. And yet, if I am to obey your secretary and tell you my professional experiences as a novelist, I must tell you about a very strange experience that befell me as a novelist. And to understand it you must try first to imagine a novelist's state of mind. I hope I am not giving away professional secrets if I say that a novelist's desire is to be as unconscious as possible. He has to induce in himself a state of perpetual lethargy. He wants life to proceed with the utmost quiet and regularity. He wants to see the same faces, to read the same books, to do the same things day after day, month after month, while he is writing, so that nothing may break the illusion in which he is living—so that nothing may disturb or disquiet the mysterious nosings about, feelings round, darts, dashes and sudden discoveries of that very shy

and illusive spirit, the imagination. I suspect that this state is the same both for men and women. Be that as it may, I want you to imagine me writing a novel in a state of trance. I want you to figure to yourselves a girl sitting with a pen in her hand, which for minutes, and indeed for hours, she never dips into the inkpot. The image that comes to my mind when I think of this girl is the image of a fisherman lying sunk in dreams on the verge of a deep lake with a rod held out over the water. She was letting her imagination sweep unchecked round every rock and cranny of the world that lies submerged in the depths of our unconscious being. Now came the experience, the experience that I believe to be far commoner with women writers than with men. The line raced through the girl's fingers. Her imagination had rushed away. It had sought the pools, the depths, the dark places where the largest fish slumber. And then there was a smash. There was an explosion. There was foam and confusion. The imagination had dashed itself against something hard. The girl was roused from her dream. She was indeed in a state of the most acute and difficult distress. To speak without figure she had thought of something, something about the body, about the passions which it was unfitting for her as a woman to say. Men, her reason told her, would be shocked. The consciousness of what men will say of a woman who speaks the truth about her passions had roused her from her artist's state of unconsciousness. She could write no more. The trance was over. Her imagination could work no longer. This I believe to be a very common experience with women writers—they are impeded by the extreme conventionality of the other sex. For though men sensibly allow themselves great freedom in these respects, I doubt that they realize or can control the extreme severity with which they condemn such freedom in women.

These then were two very genuine experiences of my own. These 6 were two of the adventures of my professional life. The first—killing the Angel in the House—I think I solved. She died. But the second, telling the truth about my own experiences as a body, I do not think I solved. I doubt that any woman has solved it yet. The obstacles against her are still immensely powerful—and yet they are very difficult to define. Outwardly, what is simpler than to write books? Outwardly, what obstacles are there for a woman rather than for a man? Inwardly, I think, the case is very different; she has still many ghosts to fight, many prejudices to overcome. Indeed it will be a long time still, I think, before a woman can sit down to write a book without finding a phantom to be slain, a rock to be dashed against. And if this is so in literature, the freest of all professions for women, how is it in the new professions which you are now for the first time entering?

Those are the questions that I should like, had I time, to ask you. 7 And indeed, if I have laid stress upon these professional experiences of mine, it is because I believe that they are, though in different forms, yours also. Even when the path is nominally open—when there is nothing to prevent a woman from being a doctor, a lawyer, a civil servant—there are many phantoms and obstacles, as I believe, looming in her way. To discuss and define them is I think of great value and importance; for thus only can the labour be shared, the difficulties be solved. But besides this, it is necessary also to discuss the ends and the aims for which we are fighting, for which we are doing battle with these formidable obstacles. Those aims cannot be taken for granted; they must be perpetually questioned and examined. The whole position, as I see it—here in this hall surrounded by women practising for the first time in history I know not how many different professions—is one of extraordinary interest and importance. You have won rooms of your own in the house hitherto exclusively owned by men. You are able, though not without great labour and effort, to pay the rent. You are earning your five hundred pounds a year. But this freedom is only a beginning; the room is your own, but it is still bare. It has to be furnished; it has to be decorated; it has to be shared. How are you going to furnish it, how are you going to decorate it? With whom are you going to share it, and upon what terms? These, I think, are questions of the utmost importance and interest. For the first time in history you are able to ask them; for the first time you are able to decide for yourselves what the answers should be. Willingly would I stay and discuss those questions and answers—but not tonight. My time is up; and I must cease.

FOR DISCUSSION

1. This essay is obviously directed to women. What, however, makes it valuable to men and women alike?

2. In using her own personal experience for evidence to support the position she takes, what kind of atmosphere does the author create for the reader? What makes this approach valuable in persuasion essays?

3. What questions does the author propose as the most important? What can you say about the use of such questions in this essay in persuading the reader to the author's point of view?

4. Some essays are limited by the timeliness or immediacy of their subjects. What can you say about the value of this essay in time? How long do you think the essay will have value for readers?

5. What in the essay makes clear to the reader the position the author wishes the reader to take?

6. How does writing about women as writers translate into a discussion of professions for women in general?

THOMAS MANN

Thomas Mann (1875–1955) was exiled from Germany by Hitler's government in 1937 because of his liberal stance. Early in 1937 Mann was informed that his name had been stricken from the University of Bonn's roll of honorary doctors, and he wrote the following letter of persuasion in reply. Even though the letter is long, many young Germans—who managed to see the letter despite the Nazis' attempt to suppress it—memorized it in its entirety.

A Letter to the Dean of the Philosophical Faculty of the University of Bonn

To the Dean of the Philosophical Faculty of the University of Bonn:

1 I have received the melancholy communication which you addressed to me on the nineteenth of December. Permit me to reply to it as follows:

2 The German universities share a heavy responsibility for all the present distresses which they called down upon their heads when they tragically misunderstood their historic hour and allowed their soil to nourish the ruthless forces which have devastated Germany morally, politically, and economically.

3 This responsibility of theirs long ago destroyed my pleasure in my academic honour and prevented me from making any use of it whatever. Moreover, I hold today an honorary degree of Doctor of Letters conferred upon me more recently by Harvard University. I cannot refrain from explaining to you the grounds upon which it was conferred. My diploma contains a sentence which, translated from the Latin, runs as follows: " . . . we the President and Fellows with the approval of the honourable Board of Overseers of the University in solemn session have designated and appointed as honorary Doctor of Letters Thomas Mann, famous author, who has interpreted life to many of our fellow-citizens and together with a very few contemporaries sustains the high dignity of German culture; and we have granted to him all the rights and privileges appertaining to this degree."

4 In such terms, so curiously contradictory to the current German view, do free and enlightened men across the ocean think of me—and, I may add, not only there. It would never have occurred to me to boast of the words I have quoted; but here and today I may, nay, I must repeat them.

5   If you, Herr Dean (I am ignorant of the procedure involved), have posted a copy of your communication to me on the bulletin board of your university, it would gratify me to have this reply of mine receive the same honour. Perhaps some member of the university, some student or professor, may be visited by a sudden fear, a swiftly suppressed and dismaying presentiment, on reading a document which gives him in his disgracefully enforced isolation and ignorance a brief revealing glimpse of the free world of the intellect that still exists outside.

6   Here I might close. And yet at this moment certain further explanations seem to me desirable or at least permissible. I made no statement when my loss of civil rights was announced, though I was more than once asked to do so. But I regard the academic divestment as a suitable occasion for a brief personal declaration. I would beg you, Herr Dean (I have not even the honour of knowing your name), to regard yourself as merely the chance recipient of a communication not designed for you in a personal sense.

7   I have spent four years in an exile which it would be euphemistic to call voluntary since if I had remained in Germany or gone back there I should probably not be alive today. In these four years the odd blunder committed by fortune when she put me in this situation has never once ceased to trouble me. I could never have dreamed, it could never have been prophesied of me at my cradle, that I should spend my later years as an émigré, expropriated, outlawed, and committed to inevitable political protest.

8   From the beginning of my intellectual life I had felt myself in happiest accord with the temper of my nation and at home in its intellectual traditions. I am better suited to represent those traditions than to become a martyr for them; far more fitted to add a little to the gaiety of the world than to foster conflict and hatred in it. Something very wrong must have happened to make my life take so false and unnatural a turn. I tried to check it, this very wrong thing, so far as my weak powers were able—and in so doing I called down on myself the fate which I must now learn to reconcile with a nature essentially foreign to it.

9   Certainly I challenged the wrath of these despots by remaining away and giving evidence of my irrepressible disgust. But it is not merely in the last four years that I have done so. I felt thus long before, and was driven to it because I saw—earlier than my now desperate fellow-countrymen—who and what would emerge from all this. But when Germany had actually fallen into those hands I thought to keep silent. I believed that by the sacrifice I had made I had earned the right to silence; that it would enable me to preserve something dear to my heart—the contact with my public within Germany. My books, I said to myself, are written for Germans, for them above all; the outside

world and its sympathy have always been for me only a happy accident. They are—these books of mine—the product of a mutually nourishing bond between nation and author, and depend on conditions which I myself have helped to create in Germany. Such bonds as these are delicate and of high importance; they ought not to be rudely sundered by politics. Though there might be impatient ones at home who, muzzled themselves, would take ill the silence of a free man, I was still able to hope that the great majority of Germans would understand my reserve, perhaps even thank me for it.

These were my assumptions. They could not be carried out. I could 10 not have lived or worked, I should have suffocated, had I not been able now and again to cleanse my heart, so to speak, to give from time to time free vent to my abysmal disgust at what was happening at home— the contemptible words and still more contemptible deeds. Justly or not, my name had once and for all become connected for the world with the conception of a Germany which it loved and honoured. The disquieting challenge rang in my ears: that I and no other must in clear terms contradict the ugly falsification which this conception of Germany was now suffering. That challenge disturbed all the free-flowing creative fancies to which I would so gladly have yielded. It was a challenge hard to resist for one to whom it had always been given to express himself, to release himself through language, to whom experience had always been one with the purifying and preserving Word.

The mystery of the Word is great; the responsibility for it and its 11 purity is of a symbolic and spiritual kind; it has not only an artistic but also a general ethical significance; it is responsibility itself, human responsibility quite simply, also the responsibility for one's own people, the duty of keeping pure its image in the sight of humanity. In the Word is involved the unity of humanity, the wholeness of the human problem, which permits nobody, today less than ever, to separate the intellectual and artistic from the political and social, and to isolate himself within the ivory tower of the "cultural" proper. This true totality is equated with humanity itself, and anyone—whoever he be— is making a criminal attack upon humanity when he undertakes to "totalize" a segment of human life—by which I mean politics, I mean the State.

A German author accustomed to this responsibility of the Word—a 12 German whose patriotism, perhaps naively, expresses itself in a belief in the infinite moral significance of whatever happens in Germany— should he be silent, wholly silent, in the face of the inexpiable evil that is done daily in my country to bodies, souls, and minds, to right and truth, to men and mankind? And should he be silent in the face of the frightful danger to the whole continent presented by this soul-destroying regime, which exists in abysmal ignorance of the hour that has struck today in the world? It was not possible for me to be silent. And so, contrary to my intentions, came the utterances, the unavoidably compromising gestures which have now resulted in the absurd and deplorable business of my national excommunication. The mere knowledge of who these men are who happen to possess the pitiful outward power to deprive me of my German birthright is enough to make the act appear in all its absurdity. I, forsooth, am supposed to have dishonoured the Reich, Germany, in acknowledging that I am against *them*! They have the incredible effrontery to confuse themselves with Germany! When, after all, perhaps the moment is not far off when it will be of supreme importance to the German people not to be confused with them.

13   To what a pass, in less than four years, have they brought Germany! Ruined, sucked dry body and soul by armaments with which they threaten the whole world, holding up the whole world and hindering it in its real task of peace, loved by nobody, regarded with fear and cold aversion by all, it stands on the brink of economic disaster, while its "enemies" stretch out their hands in alarm to snatch back from the abyss so important a member of the future family of nations, to help it, if only it will come to its senses and try to understand the real needs of the world at this hour, instead of dreaming dreams about mythical "sacred necessities."

14   Yes, after all, it must be helped by those whom it hinders and menaces, in order that it may not drag down the rest of the continent with it and unleash the war upon which as the *ultima ratio* it keeps its eyes ever fixed. The mature and cultural states—by which I mean those which understand the fundamental fact that war is no longer permissible—treat this endangered and endangering country, or rather the impossible leaders into whose hands it has fallen, as doctors treat a sick man—with the utmost tact and caution, with inexhaustible if not very flattering patience. But it thinks it must play politics—the politics of power and hegemony—with the doctors. That is an unequal game. If one side plays politics when the other no longer thinks of politics but of peace, then for a time the first side reaps certain advantages. Anachronistic ignorance of the fact that war is no longer permissible results for a while of course in "successes" against those who are aware of the truth. But woe to the people which, not knowing what way to turn, at last actually seeks it way out through the abomination of war, hated of God and man! Such a people will be lost. It will be so vanquished that it will never rise again.

15   The meaning and purpose of the National Socialist state is this alone and can be only this: to put the German people in readiness for the "coming war" by ruthless repression, elimination, extirpation of every stirring of opposition; to make of them an instrument of war, infinitely compliant, without a single critical thought, driven by a blind and fanatical ignorance. Any other meaning and purpose, any other excuse

this system cannot have; all the sacrifices of freedom, justice, human happiness, including the secret and open crimes for which it has blithely been responsible, can be justified only by the end—absolute fitness for war. If the idea of war as an aim in itself disappeared, the system would mean nothing but the exploitation of the people; it would be utterly senseless and superfluous.

Truth to tell, it *is* both of these, senseless and superfluous, not only 16 because war will not be permitted it but also because its leading idea, the absolute readiness for war, will result precisely in the opposite of what it is striving for. No other people on earth is today so utterly incapable of war, so little in condition to endure one. That Germany would have no allies, not a single one in the world, is the first consideration but the smallest. Germany would be forsaken—terrible of course even in her isolation—but the really frightful thing would be the fact that she had forsaken herself. Intellectually reduced and humbled, morally gutted, inwardly torn apart by her deep mistrust of her leaders and the mischief they have done her in these years, profoundly uneasy herself, ignorant of the future, of course, but full of forebodings of evil, she would go into war not in the condition of 1914 but, even physically, of 1917 or 1918. The ten per cent of direct beneficiaries of the system—half even of them fallen away—would not be enough to win a war in which the majority of the rest would only see the opportunity of shaking off the shameful oppression that has weighed upon them so long—a war, that is, which after the first inevitable defeat would turn into a civil war.

No, this war is impossible; Germany cannot wage it; and if its 17 dictators are in their senses, then their assurances of readiness for peace are not tactical lies repeated with a wink at their partisans; they spring from a faint-hearted perception of just this impossibility.

But if war cannot and shall not be—then why these robbers and 18 murderers? Why isolation, world hostility, lawlessness, intellectual interdict, cultural darkness, and every other evil? Why not rather Germany's voluntary return to the European system, her reconciliation with Europe, with all the inward accompaniments of freedom, justice, well-being, and human decency, and a jubilant welcome from the rest of the world? Why not? Only because a regime which, in word and deed, denies the rights of man, which wants above all else to remain in power, would stultify itself and be abolished if, since it cannot make war, it actually made peace! But is that a reason?

I had forgotten, Herr Dean, that I was still addressing you. Certainly 19 I may console myself with the reflection that you long since ceased to read this letter, aghast at language which in Germany has long been unspoken, terrified because somebody dares use the German tongue with the ancient freedom. I have not spoken out of arrogant presumption, but out of a concern and a distress from which your usurpers did not release me when they decreed that I was no longer a German—a mental and spiritual distress from which for four years not an hour of my life has been free, and struggling with which I have had to accomplish my creative work day by day. The pressure was great. And as a man who out of diffidence in religious matters will seldom or never either by tongue or pen let the name of the Deity escape him, yet in moments of deep emotion cannot refrain, let me—since after all one cannot say everything—close this letter with the brief and fervent prayer: *God help our darkened and desecrated country and teach it to make its peace with the world and with itself!*

—Thomas Mann

FOR DISCUSSION:

1. Nowhere in the letter does Mann suggest a specific kind of action. Yet the entire essay is a call to action. What *kind* of action is Mann requesting?

2. What do you think may have been the *power* of this essay for young German citizens in the time of Hitler and the Second World War? Where specifically in the essay do you locate this power?

3. Discuss at least three points of persuasion Mann employs in the essay. What makes these points effective?

4. What is gained by the fact that this is a letter to a real person written about a real event? What can you say about the intertwining of external and internal motivation in this essay?

5. What makes this essay valuable almost fifty years after it was first written? What can you say, in light of this fact, about the power of **writing to change?**

DON WALL

In this essay Don Wall, writing for Omni *magazine, persuades by implication, by evoking the reader's response instead of asking directly for it. On the surface the essay looks like a reporter's story about a man and his lake. Underneath, however, the essay is an entreaty for action.*

Lake Maker

Hawk Hyde can always tell when the bald eagle is watching ducks on   1
the lake. All the ducks move close together and form a cluster, a single
mass, which confuses the eagle. But when a sick or crippled duck is
separated from the rest of the flock, the eagle flies in swiftly and
attacks it.

"He takes about a duck a day," says Hawk, whose real name is   2
Dayton O. Hyde. Hawk is a man of fifty-six, craggy-faced and
weather-beaten. "The eagle is the veterinarian of the lake. Maybe he
doesn't ever think, "Well, that's an unhealthy duck; I'd better kill it,"
but the way he works fits nature's pattern."

The setting of this natural drama suits Hawk's own pattern, too.   3
Five years ago the lake wasn't on his ranch, in southern Oregon. He
and his sons bulldozed worthless flatland into a lake bottom and
dammed off a canyon, using snow melted in the spring to supply water.
When the lake is completely filled—it's about two thirds of the way
now—it will have a shoreline of three and a half miles and a depth of 60
feet. This land once was so dry that in July and August there wasn't
enough water for a Steller's jay to drink. Now, thousands of birds and
other animals come in every day to bathe and quench their thirst.

"I created this lake out of nothing but sagebrush and snow water,"   4
Hyde recalls, sitting in a resurrected truck seat on the front porch,
wind chimes tinkling in a soft breeze. "I just looked at my worst piece
of land and wondered how I could turn it into a wildlife paradise."

Over 5,000 ducks live here, a pair of bald eagles, two pairs of   5
sandhill cranes, hawks, owls, a family of trumpeter swans, coyotes,
mountain lions, and a single loon. Hyde had expected that the osprey
who live above the lake would feed upon the rainbow trout. But the
trout are up to 12 pounds now, and that's too heavy for a bird with a
five-foot wingspan.

Hawk Hyde thinks of his wild world as the bare bones of a man's   6
dream. He lives at the lake in a small cabin he built with his own hands,
and he writes about wildlife. In 1968 he published *Sandy: The True
Story of the Sandhill Crane Who Joined Our Family*. His companions
are an old yellow dog and an Alaskan wolf, which he bought from a
trapper for the price of its pelt. Occasionally Hawk and the wolf howl
together at four in the morning.

The Hyde ranch, Yamsi—which means "home of the north wind,"   7
in Klamath Indian—spreads over 6,000 acres of a forested mountain
valley. If you look at a map of southern Oregon, you'll see that
Chiloquin is adjacent to the Fremont National Forest. It's magnificent.
Hawk owns an additional 6,000-acre tract in the vicinity and 1,500 head
of cattle. Unlike many ranchers, Hyde never thinks of wildlife as his
enemy.

8   "When our cows died in the winter, we would drag their bodies out into the woods and leave them," he says. "What we were actually adding, without knowing it, was supplementary feed for the coyotes during a time of stress. Instead of removing the coyotes we got along with them and we didn't suffer the losses that other ranchers in the area have."

9   As a rancher, Hawk understands that when a man goes out into his corral and a bunch of his sheep have been killed during the night by a coyote, it's pretty hard to turn him into a coyote lover. But Hawk objects to the view that mankind has dominion over wildlife.

10   "I hate the word *dominion* more than any other word in the English language," he says. "I've always been able to look out and see the energies of the world. I can hold my hand up to a tree and feel the energy. I can see it in the rocks—it's hard to explain. It's like seeing somebody's aura. I'm seeing the aura of the earth. I don't know. Maybe I've taken a little more trouble to communicate or to understand or to sit and look and think about these kinds of things."

11   Hawk believes that man and nature can coexist, that you can have your ranch and wildlife, too. He's putting that philosophy into practice.

12   His plan, the Wildlife Stronghold, would give the nation a natural preserve that all the federal money in the world couldn't produce. The Wildlife Stronghold calls for private agricultural land to be set aside for wildlife. So far, 1.25 million acres has been pledged by landowners nationwide. Hawk maintains that 80 percent of the wild animals already feed upon private land and, as his example shows, marginal land can be used without cutting farm production.

13   The beauty of the idea is that the landowner maintains control of his own land and, if all goes well, will receive tax breaks. Wildlife, Hawk asserts, is a resource worth cultivating, like corn, wheat, or cattle.

14   Farmers have been reluctant to make their land available to wildlife for two reasons. First, their property will attract tourists, and, instead of tending to business, they would have to patrol the area. Second, farmers fear that when land abounds with wildlife, the government buys it and takes it out of production.

15   When talking to landowners, Hawk tries to dissuade them from claiming that wildlife competes with crops and livestock. He shows them how healthy wildlife is an asset to the community: Life breeds life. What Hyde is trying to tell us is that all we have to do to reap a fuller harvest is fit in.

16   On Hawk's ranch, some 25 percent of the land has been converted back to wetland marshes, the way it used to be before his uncle drained it to make hayfields. The groundwater there is cold and the climate is harsh. In summer there is frost. In the past Yamsi and other ranches in

the area had been plagued with grasshoppers and mice. But because of Hawk's ecosystem his beef production is up 50 percent.

The standing water in his marshes, heated by the sun, acts as a 17 reservoir of heat and has actually moderated the climate. Water for irrigation is warmer. So is the air, and there is less summer frost, which helps the grass to grow. The wild animals come into the marshes to prey upon the pests.

"The coyote is as useful a tool as a shovel or a pickup," Hawk says. 18 "He's a rodent catcher. You see, our idea of coyote management is to keep them well fed. In fifty years we've never lost a calf to a coyote."

Dayton O. Hyde is on the road now, talking to ranchers, farmers, 19 sportsmen, and timber producers around the country, trying to sell them and the government the idea of the Wildlife Stronghold. But it's not a tough sale to anyone who has seen that lake and walked along its shore with Hawk, an old yellow dog, and a wolf.

"When you get out there in a canoe and the moon comes up over 20 Calimus Mountain, there is a golden path between you and the moon. Then the wolf howls and fills this whole earth with that mournful music of his, and you know why you've done all these things. When my time finally comes, I hope to have the guts to go out there in the middle of the lake in a canoe and quietly tip over. Until then I'm going to fight every day for wildlife."

FOR DISCUSSION

1. Knowing that this essay appeared in *Omni* magazine, what can you say about the audience for whom it was written?

2. How is the column in *Omni* called "Earth," in which this appeared, actually a context for what Wall has to say in this essay?

3. What is gained by talking about a real-life person and a real-life event to make the author's point?

4. What facts stand out for you in this essay? What gives them their power?

5. What change is the author asking for from the reader? Is he successful with you? How?

6. What classifies this as a good persuasion essay?

WENDELL BERRY

The following selection is taken from A Continuous Harmony *(1972), a collection of essays by Wendell Berry. Berry, a farmer, poet, novelist, and essayist, argues in this quiet yet forceful essay that the mastery of language and the knowledge of books are absolute necessities. What gives this persuasion essay power?*

In Defense of Literacy

1   In a country in which everybody goes to school, it may seem absurd to offer a defense of literacy, and yet I believe that such a defense is in order, and that the absurdity lies not in the defense, but in the necessity for it. The published illiteracies of the certified educated are on the increase. And the universities seem bent upon ratifying this state of things by declaring the acceptability, in their graduates, of adequate— that is to say, of mediocre—writing skills.

2   The schools, then, are following the general subservience to the "practical," as that term has been defined for us according to the benefit of corporations. By "practicality" most users of the term now mean whatever will most predictably and most quickly make a profit. Teachers of English and literature have either submitted, or are expected to submit, along with teachers of the more "practical" disciplines, to the doctrine that the purpose of education is the mass production of producers and consumers. This has forced our profession into a predicament that we will finally have to recognize as a perversion. As if awed by the ascendency of the "practical" in our society, many of us secretly fear, and some of us are apparently ready to say, that if a student is not going to become a teacher of his language, he has no need to master it.

3   In other words, to keep pace with the specialization—and the dignity accorded to specialization—in other disciplines, we have begun to look upon and to teach our language and literature as specialties. But whereas specialization is of the nature of the applied sciences, it is a perversion of the disciplines of language and literature. When we understand and teach these as specialties, we submit willy-nilly to the assumption of the "practical men" of business, and also apparently of education, that literacy is no more than an ornament: when one has become an efficient integer of the economy, *then* it is permissible, even desirable, to be able to talk about the latest novels. After all, the

disciples of "practicality" may someday find themselves stuck in conversation with an English teacher.

I may have oversimplified that line of thinking, but not much. There   4
are two flaws in it. One is that, among the self-styled "practical men," the practical is synonymous with the immediate. The long-term effects of their values and their acts lie outside the boundaries of their interest. For such people a strip mine ceases to exist as soon as the coal has been extracted. Short-term practicality is long-term idiocy.

The other flaw is that language and literature are always *about*   5
something else, and we have no way to predict or control what they may be about. They are about the world. We will understand the world, and preserve ourselves and our values in it, only insofar as we have a language that is alert and responsive to it, and careful of it. I mean that literally. When we give our plows such brand names as "Sod Blaster," we are imposing on their use conceptual limits which raise the likelihood that they will be used destructively. When we speak of man's "war against nature," or of a "peace offensive," we are accepting the limitations of a metaphor that suggests, and even proposes, violent solutions. When students ask for the right of "participatory input" at the meetings of a faculty organization, they are thinking of democratic process, but they are *speaking* of a convocation of robots, and are thus devaluing the very traditions that they invoke.

Ignorance of books and the lack of a critical consciousness of   6
language were safe enough in primitive societies with coherent oral traditions. In our society, which exists in an atmosphere of prepared, public language—language that is either written or being read—illiteracy is both a personal and a public danger. Think how constantly "the average American" is surrounded by premeditated language, in newspapers and magazines, on signs and billboards, on TV and radio. He is forever being asked to buy or believe somebody else's line of goods. The line of goods is being sold, moreover, by men who are trained to make him buy it or believe it, whether or not he needs it or understands it or knows its value or wants it. This sort of selling is an honored profession among us. Parents who grow hysterical at the thought that their son might not cut his hair are *glad* to have him taught, and later employed, to lie about the quality of an automobile or the ability of a candidate.

What is our defense against this sort of language—this language-as-   7
weapon? There is only one. We must know a better language. We must speak, and teach our children to speak, a language precise and articulate and lively enough to tell the truth about the world as we know it. And to do this we must know something of the roots and resources of our language; we must know its literature. The only defense against the

worst is a knowledge of the best. By their ignorance people enfranchise their exploiters.

8   But to appreciate fully the necessity for the best sort of literacy we must consider not just the environment of prepared language in which most of us now pass most of our lives, but also the utter transience of most of this language, which is meant to be merely glanced at, or heard only once, or read once and thrown away. Such language is by definition, and often calculation, not memorable; it is language meant to be replaced by what will immediately follow it, like that of shallow conversation between strangers. It cannot be pondered or effectively criticized. For those reasons an unmixed diet of it is destructive of the informed, resilient, critical intelligence that the best of our traditions have sought to create and to maintain—an intelligence that Jefferson held to be indispensable to the health and longevity of freedom. Such intelligence does not grow by bloating upon the ephemeral information and misinformation of the public media. It grows by returning again and again to the landmarks of its cultural birthright, the works that have proved worthy of devoted attention.

9   "Read not the Times. Read the Eternities," Thoreau said. Ezra Pound wrote that "literature is news that STAYS news." In his lovely poem, "The Island," Edwin Muir spoke of man's inescapable cultural boundaries and of his consequent responsibility for his own sources and renewals:

> Men are made of what is made,
> The meat, the drink, the life, the corn,
> Laid up by them, in them reborn.
> And self-begotten cycles close
> About our way; indigenous art
> And simple spells make unafraid
> The haunted labyrinths of the heart . . .

10   These men spoke of a truth that no society can afford to shirk for long: we are dependent, for understanding, and for consolation and hope, upon what we learn of ourselves from songs and stories. This has always been so, and it will not change.

11   I am saying, then, that literacy—the mastery of language and the knowledge of books—is not an ornament, but a necessity. It is impractical only by the standards of quick profit and easy power. Longer perspective will show that it alone can preserve in us the possibility of an accurate judgment of ourselves, and the possibilities of correction and renewal. Without it, we are adrift in the present, in the wreckage of yesterday, in the nightmare of tomorrow.

FOR DISCUSSION

1. What two flaws does Berry find in the current attitude about language and books in our country?

2. What does Berry mean by "language-as-weapon"?

3. What change does Berry want to effect in the reader of this essay?

4. What motive do you think Berry, who is a poet, an essayist, and a novelist, might have had for writing this essay?

5. What is gained by waiting until the last paragraph to make his point directly?

6. Does Berry offer a solution? Discuss.

THOMAS JEFFERSON

Thomas Jefferson (1743–1826) wrote the first draft of the Declaration of Independence, *which declared the independence of the 13 North American colonies from England. The Second Continental Congress revised the manifesto before adopting it on July 4, 1776, but the style and spirit of the* Declaration of Independence *is generally attributed to Jefferson. It remains one of the most powerful documents ever written.*

Declaration of Independence

When in the Course of human Events, it becomes necessary for one 1 People to dissolve the Political Bands which have connected them with another, and to assume among the Powers of the Earth, the separate and equal Station to which the Laws of Nature and of Nature's God entitle them, a decent respect to the opinions of mankind requires that they should declare the causes which impel them to the separation.

We hold these truths to be self-evident, that all men are created 2 equal, that they are endowed by their Creator with certain unalienable Rights, that among these are Life, Liberty and the pursuit of Happiness. That to secure these rights, Governments are instituted among Men, deriving their just powers from the consent of the governed, That whenever any Form of Government becomes destructive of these ends, it is the Right of the People to alter or to abolish it, and to institute new Government, laying its foundation on such principles and organizing its powers in such form, as to them shall seem most likely to effect their Safety and Happiness. Prudence, indeed, will dictate that Governments long established should not be changed for light and transient causes; and accordingly all experience hath shewn that mankind are more disposed to suffer, while evils are sufferable, than to right themselves by abolishing the forms to which they are accustomed. But when a long train of abuses and usurpations, pursuing invariably the same Object evinces a design to reduce them under absolute Despotism, it is their right, it is their duty, to throw off such Government, and to provide new Guards for their future security. Such has been the patient sufferance of these Colonies; and such is now the necessity which constrains them to alter their former Systems of Government. The history of the present King of Great Britain is a history of repeated injuries and usurpations, all having in direct object the establishment of an absolute Tyranny over these States. To prove this, let Facts be submitted to a candid world.

He has refused his Assent to Laws, the most wholesome and necessary for the public good.

He has forbidden his Governors to pass Laws of immediate and pressing importance, unless suspended in their operation till his Assent should be obtained; and when so suspended, he has utterly neglected to attend to them.

He has refused to pass other Laws for the accommodation of large districts of people, unless those people would relinquish the right of Representation in the Legislature, a right inestimable to them and formidable to tyrants only.

He has called together legislative bodies at places unusual, uncomfortable, and distant from the depository of their public Records, for the sole purpose of fatiguing them into compliance with his measures.

He has dissolved Representative Houses repeatedly, for opposing with manly firmness his invasions on the rights of the people.

He has refused for a long time, after such dissolutions, to cause others to be elected; whereby the Legislative powers, incapable of Annihilation, have returned to the People at large for their exercise; the State remaining in the mean time exposed to all the dangers of invasion from without, and convulsions within.

He has endeavored to prevent the population of these States; for that purpose obstructing the Laws for Naturalization of Foreigners; refusing to pass others to encourage their migrations hither, and raising the conditions of new Appropriations of Lands.

He has obstructed the Administration of Justice, by refusing his Assent to Laws for establishing Judiciary powers.

He has made Judges dependent on his Will alone, for the tenure of their offices, and the amount and payment of their salaries.

He has erected a multitude of New Offices, and sent hither swarms of Officers to harass our people, and eat out their substance.

He has kept among us, in times of peace, Standing Armies without the Consent of our legislatures.

He has affected to render the Military independent of and superior to the Civil power.

He has combined with others to subject us to a jurisdiction foreign to our constitution, and unacknowledged by our laws; giving his Assent to their Acts of pretended Legislation:

For quartering large bodies of armed troops among us:

For protecting them, by a mock Trial, from punishment for any Murders which they should commit on the Inhabitants of these States:

For cutting off our Trade with all parts of the world:

For imposing Taxes on us without our Consent:

For depriving us in many cases, of the benefits of Trial by Jury:

For transporting us beyond Seas to be tried for pretended offences:

For abolishing the free System of English Laws in a neighbouring Province, establishing therein an Arbitrary government, and enlarging its Boundaries so as to render it at once an example and fit instrument for introducing the same absolute rule into these Colonies:

For taking away our Charters, abolishing our most valuable Laws, and altering fundamentally the Forms of our Governments:

For suspending our own Legislatures, and declaring themselves invested with power to legislate for us in all cases whatsoever.

He has abdicated Government here, by declaring us out of his Protection and waging War against us.

He has plundered our seas, ravaged our Coasts, burnt our towns, and destroyed the lives of our people.

He is at this time transporting large Armies of foreign Mercenaries to compleat the works of death, desolation and tyranny, already begun with circumstances of Cruelty & perfidy scarcely parallelled in the most barbarous ages, and totally unworthy the Head of a civilized nation.

He has constrained our fellow Citizens taken Captive on the high Seas to bear Arms against their Country, to become the executioners of their friends and Brethren, or to fall themselves by their Hands.

He has excited domestic insurrections amongst us, and has endeavoured to bring on the inhabitants of our frontiers, the merciless Indian Savages, whose known rule of warfare is an undistinguished destruction of all ages, sexes and conditions.

In every stage of these Oppressions We have Petitioned for Redress in the most humble terms: Our repeated Petitions have been answered only by repeated injury. A Prince, whose character is thus marked by every act which may define a Tyrant, is unfit to be the ruler of a free people.

4   Nor have We been wanting in attentions to our British Brethren. We have warned them from time to time of attempts by their legislature to extend an unwarrantable jurisdiction over us. We have reminded them of the circumstances of our emigration and settlement here. We have appealed to their native justice and magnanimity, and we have conjured them by the ties of our common kindred to disavow these usurpations, which would inevitably interrupt our connections and correspondence. They too have been deaf to the voice of justice and of consanguinity. We must, therefore, acquiesce in the necessity, which denounces our Separation, and hold them, as we hold the rest of mankind. Enemies in War, in Peace Friends.

5   We, therefore, the Representatives of the United States of America, in General Congress, Assembled, appealing to the Supreme Judge of the world for the rectitude of our intentions, do, in the Name, and by authority of the good People of these Colonies, solemnly Publish and Declare, That these United Colonies are, and of Right ought to be Free and Independent States; that they are Absolved from all Allegiance to the British Crown, and that all political connection between them and the State of Great Britain, is and ought to be totally dissolved; and that as Free and Independent States, they have full Power to levy War, conclude Peace, contract Alliances, establish Commerce, and to do all other Acts and Things which Independent States may of right do. And for the support of this Declaration, with a firm reliance on the protection of divine Providence, we mutually pledge to each other our Lives, our Fortunes and our sacred Honor.

FOR DISCUSSION

1. Who was the audience for this declaration?

2. How is the declaration appropriate to this audience? What in the document shows that the writer knew his audience?

3. It is not difficult to "hear" the sound of a declaration in comparison, say, to the sound of an information essay. Find passages, phrases, and words in the *Declaration* that contribute to its sounding like a declaration. If you had to write a declaration, what would you do with words that would be different from writing a regular essay?

4. In what ways is this piece of writing an example of persuasion?

5. Where do you suppose this declaration appeared, in addition to in the hands of the King of England?

WRITING YOUR OWN
The Persuasion Essay

Before you start to write your own persuasion essay, let's review the configurations in "Letter from Birmingham Jail," by Martin Luther King, Jr.:

Motivation (an educated guess): to explain and defend nonviolent direct action and to convince others of the need for it.

Circumstance/Situation: triggered by a published statement, King initially wrote in the margin of the newspaper in which the clergymen's words appeared; later he was able to obtain scraps of paper in his cell, and finally, a pad, furnished by his lawyer; his time schedule was probably dictated by his own feeling of the urgency of the issue.

Audience: the eight clergymen from Alabama who published their statement critical of his methods, and later, when King polished his letter slightly for publication, the citizens of the United States.

Writer's Relationship to Audience: colleague to colleagues attempting, by explanation, to enlighten their perspective on civil rights protests and change their attitude.

Emphasis: on the writer's experience, as a black minister and civil rights leader, and on his vision of ending the oppression of blacks.

Form: letter

Intention (an educated guess): to get the reader to understand the writer's perspective, goal, and approach.

You may find it helpful to outline the configurations of the other essays in this chapter.

DESIGNING YOUR OWN CONFIGURATION

If you can't immediately think of a topic for a persuasion essay, the following list of suggestions may help to stir your imagination:

1. You find out that a friend of yours wants to live off campus next year. Write an essay attempting to persuade your friend of the benefits of living on campus in a dorm.

2. Imagine that you have just bought and moved into a stately old house that has fallen into a state of neglect, with the intention of rehabilitating it yourself. To help pay for the expense, you plan to rent part of it at a relatively high rate once the work is finished. Your new neighbors protest that it is people like you who are driving the rental rates up in this low-income neighborhood, and forcing them out of their homes. Invent more specifics for this situation, and then write a letter to your neighbors trying to convince them your plan is ultimately a good one. (Or, if you prefer, write a letter from their point of view.)

3. You are a member of the school entertainment committee, which is in the middle of a debate. Some members feel the committee's funds should all be spent on one large rock concert with a big-name band. Others feel that a variety of smaller, less-expensive acts booked throughout the year would be more desirable. Consider the pros and cons, pick a side, and then write an essay to your fellow members attempting to win them over.

4. In an essay, try to persuade the advocates of a volunteer army why such an army won't work for the United States. Or, you might try to argue in favor of a volunteer army.

5. Imagine that you work in an office where there is a lot of paperwork, and you have devised a plan for recycling the reams of paper thrown away each day. Think of some details on how the plan would work, and then write a letter to your boss in which you argue that your plan should be adopted.

Designing Your Own Configuration for a Persuasion Essay

MOTIVE	CIRCUMSTANCE/ SITUATION	AUDIENCE	RELATIONSHIP TO AUDIENCE
To improve the quality of human life	An event stimulates the writing	General public	Person who sees to person who hasn't seen
To startle readers into knowing x and acting x	Some emergency has occurred, and action needs to be taken	People who have x authority	Committed person to person yet to be committed
To inform readers about the larger implications of immediate events	Some historic event is occurring but change is needed	People who can take x action	Preacher to congregation
To bring about x change	Catastrophy is looming; the writer sees a way out		Visionary to those without a vision, or those with a different vision
To get reader to do x	Writer wants her/his viewpoint to win wide dissemination in magazines, newspapers, books, and writes with that in mind		
To say one's say about x			
To contribute			
To wake people up			

EMPHASIS	FORM	INTENTION
On condition discussed	Essay	To bring about change in the reader
On action/or change reader should take or bring about	Letter	To move the reader to act
On writer's vision or knowledge as it relates to change desired in reader	Book	
	Tract	
	Article	
	Manifesto	

1. Be committed to the action you wish the reader to take.
2. Think about the best and most appropriate form for your essay to take to accomplish what you intend.
3. Write a persuasion essay *only* on something you feel strongly about and have a real commitment to. Otherwise, all you can do at best is attempt to manipulate the reader.
4. Use personal experience and narrate the experience of others when that will enhance your ability to persuade.
5. Always keep your reader in mind; care about how the reader is going to respond.

RHETORICAL PATTERNS OFTEN APPEARING IN PERSUASION ESSAYS

Analysis: How to Help the Reader Understand.

1. The word *analyze* means "to divide anything complex into its simple parts or pieces by separating a whole into its parts." It also means "to show the relationship among the single parts of a larger, more complex subject."
2. A good analysis actually shows the reader how to *think* about the subject.
3. To use analysis in your writing, decide what parts you can break the larger subject into. Then take these parts one at a time. Discuss or describe them, either on an individual basis or as a group, showing how they relate to each other. Finally, put the parts back together in a whole. The reader will then have been able to *understand* what may have otherwise been baffling or confusing.

Cause/Effect: How to Explain the Reasons and Consequences

1. Giving the cause and effect of a situation means that you (*a*) identify the thing/person/act that brings about a particular result and (*b*) show *how* it caused that result.
2. Be sure that the causes you give are sufficient to convince the reader. Even after you have isolated the cause of a situation in your mind, ask yourself, "Are there any other causes I should include?"

3. Be sure that there actually *is* a relationship between the cause and effect. If you can't prove this relationship exists in some logical, objective way, be sure that your reader understands that you are offering a personal view of the relationship between the cause and effect. Take the time in your essay to explain to the reader the connections you see.
4. Let the purpose of your writing determine the form your essay takes.

Definition: How To Tell What Something Means

1. *To define* means *to explain the nature or essential qualities of a word, function,* etc. A definition determines or fixes the boundaries of the thing being discussed. The origin of the word *definition* was *to set boundaries,* and that is what a good definition does for the reader: it helps him or her stake out, limit, see the boundaries of a term.
2. A formal definition includes the term being defined, the class to which it belongs, and what differentiates it from other things in that class.
3. An informal definition takes several forms: defining by using a word that means approximately the same thing (*to gloat* means *to act superior and proud*); by using an opposite (*love* is *not using someone*); by showing the term's origin (*defining* originally meant *setting boundaries*); by using personal experience (*summer* means *time off, rest, and fun*); by giving examples (*eating well* is *having fresh vegetables and fruit, avoiding sugar, and staying off fried foods*).
4. Use definitions in your writing when there is any chance that your readers will not know the formal meaning of a word or the informal way you are using it. Being clear on the terms in a piece of writing is absolutely necessary for both the reader and the writer if communication is to occur.

Examples and Illustrations: How to Help the Reader See.

1. An example or illustration is a specific instance that helps clarify a more general statement by allowing the reader to *see*. It is one single thing that shows the character of the whole.
2. Be as colorful, descriptive, detailed, and specific as you possibly can when you give examples and illustrations. Appeal to the readers' *senses*. Transport the readers to the spot and *show* what you mean.

3. Use *concrete* words. Abstract terms don't produce pictures in readers' minds. General words, too, can mean different things to different people. Concrete words appearing in examples and illustrations will let the readers know what *you* mean by the general terms. And if you've used any abstract terms, concrete words will help make them clear to the readers.

4. Choose examples and illustrations that will mean something to the particular audience for whom you are writing.

5. Be generous with examples and illustrations. A minimum ratio is one specific example or illustration to one general statement. Often, however, a higher ratio—say, two or three examples or illustrations to one general statement—will be necessary to let your reader *see* exactly what you mean. You will probably never err by having too many examples and illustrations.

Classification: How to Show Common Characteristics.

1. *To classify* means *to organize into groups according to common characteristics, qualities, traits,* etc.; *to put into basic categories;* or *to break down into component parts.*

2. When you set up a classification system, be certain that the categories don't overlap. Also make very clear to the reader what the groups are and how you decided what went into each group.

3. Don't oversimplify when you classify. Sometimes in an attempt to make everything orderly, a person will push a subject, person, item, etc., into a category where it doesn't really belong just to make the classification systematic. Don't undercut your credibility with your audience by forcing an item into a group where it doesn't clearly belong.

4. Use a classification system when it will help your reader follow your thoughts or explanation point by point.

Peter Rosenwald lives in New York City and is dance critic for the Wall Street Journal. *He is also a business executive who has interests in many parts of the world. At present he is both a free-lance writer and vice president of an advertising firm in New York. He is highly sought after as a consultant for corporations.*

In the pages that follow you will find four of his columns from the Wall Street Journal—*three on dance and one on music. Following these essays is an interview with Rosenwald in which he discusses how he writes and, even more fascinatingly,* why *he writes.*

Classical vs. Introspective Ballet

In dance as in life, balance can have as many meanings as an onion has skins.

Some of those meanings come to mind with the appearance here of two distinctly different dance companies. The National Ballet of Canada is performing ''Sleeping Beauty'' and ''Swan Lake,'' plus a mixed bag of other ballets, at the Met. The Martha Graham Dance Company is at the Alvin Theater for its first New York season in five years. It is presenting Miss Graham's masterpiece, ''Clytemnestra,'' along with such other milestones of modern dance as ''El Penitente'' and ''Appalachian Spring,'' plus two world premieres.

These two companies provide a unique opportunity for reflection on the polarities of the classic and modern repertory. They establish a balance between the extroverted classical story ballets and introspective psychological works which characterize the modern idiom.

The National Ballet of Canada can be judged by its ''Sleeping Beauty,'' one of the greatest works of the Russian repertory and one of today's most popular classical works. The Canadian production neatly balances pageantry with Rudolph Nureyev's explosions of incredible jumps, eleva-

tions and his commanding stage presence.

In the original 1890 St. Petersburg version, French-born choreographer Marius Petipa meticulously demanded even of Tchaikovsky an adherence to a pre-planned series of set dances, pageants and star-studded variations. These created a balanced evening of dancing in a context which needed order and hierarchy as the touchstone of reality. In the ''Sleeping Beauty'' tale, it is the failure of protocol at Princess Aurora's christening which causes the wicked fairy's evil spell to be cast. Reestablishing the orderly balanced world of the court through the handsome prince marrying the beautiful princess puts things back together again.

What's left of Petipa's choreography in the Canadian production always contains a sense of this balance, especially in the famous ''Rose Adagio'' in which Aurora repeats each of her series of steps four times, one for each of the four suitors. Always on pointe, she allows each suitor to partner her for a brief moment, then lifts her hand from his supporting hand, establishing her own balance, and only then brings it down to receive the next. Physical, technical, emotional, hierarchical balance reflect the perfect and familiar fairy tale world, stated in the formal steps and movements of the classical idiom.

The romantic story ballets like "Sleeping Beauty" and "Swan Lake" present a world in order, seen from the outside looking in. In Martha Graham's "Clytemnestra," a retelling of Aeschylus' "Oresteia," the world is the world of the soul looking out, a world of the unconscious mind made into movement, an honesty so complete and original, so percussive and strident that the essential balance comes from the very opposite of the romantic fairy tale world. She strips all the conventions of classical dance away and replaces them with a discipline no less severe but with a ritualistic and mythological base, abstracted and honed to sharpness. Bare feet replace pointes, simple flowing fabrics are part of the pattern of the movement, never decoration.

Balance is established in the modern dance vocabulary by the asymmetry and angularity of bodies moving through space. Movement breaks where you expect it to continue. A body falls and writhes or holds a position on the ground as if frozen to stone. The feet move forward as on a Grecian urn but the torso turns and sometimes even seems to move in the opposite direction.

Martha Graham's handsome company is simply splendid. They dance as one, displaying a uniformly superb talent. They should not be missed by anyone eager to see how dance can say more than words.

There is so much detail in "Clytemnestra," so much beautiful and original movement, so many balancing symbols of good and evil that they cannot all be described here. But where the heart of story ballets lies in the set dances and structured formal divertissements of a "Sleeping Beauty," the core of what we know today as "dance drama" can be found in the angular tense and dramatic movement of what has come to be known as "Graham Technique."

Yet there are, surprisingly, similarities. The world of the 19th Century story ballets was balanced by the artificial disruption and equally artificial restoration of the natural hierarchy of symbolic values—the happy ending; the balanced final spinning partnered pirouettes and grand finale. The world of "Clytemnestra" is unbalanced by the violation of set rules of human conduct. Through choreography which expresses a world amiss with anguished movement and atonal music by Halim El-Dabh, and through the purging of these violations by revenge of honor and freeing the mind of guilt, balance is restored in the context of the modern idiom.

"Sleeping Beauty" and "Clytemnestra" are both acknowledged masterpieces, each in its own right. They give evidence that while conventions and idioms of expression change, the discipline of balance remains the constant measure.

A Handsome Dance Company Hits Its Stride

As Arthur Mitchell says, "Many people looked on the Dance Theater of Harlem as a novelty when it began 10 years ago. Today people realize that we are here to stay." On the evidence of the current season which continues until Jan. 27, the handsome company has finally hit its stride, and if they continue giving the superlative and exciting programs that have been packing City Center, one can only hope that they will be around forever.

A few years back critics were forced to rely on that unfortunate adjective, "promising." Here was a black dance company setting out to prove that classical ballet was not the exclusive province of whites. Arthur Mitchell had been a principal dancer with the New York City Ballet and had proven the point in his own career. But there was a substantial question whether he could take young aspiring dancers with little or no classical dance background and force-feed them into a first-rate ensemble company.

Mr. Mitchell and his co-director, Karol Shook, have turned their noble dream into a stunning reality. With just less than 40 dancers ranging in age from teens to early 20s, a school with over 1,000 students and a deep sense of commitment to excellence, the Dance Theater of Harlem is the best thing that has happened to New York dance in a long time. And not only New Yorkers benefit. The company tours widely throughout the U.S. and overseas. They are not to be missed.

Two programs presented in the current season show the diversity of their talents and the depth of their strength. In the first, the company performed the Second Act of "Swan Lake." The Petipa choreography had been lovingly taught the dancers by Frederic Franklin, and the entire cast gave a performance that was distinguished by its cleanliness and focus. As an ensemble, they were the enchanted swans and their sinuous movement was highly sensitive to the music. Lydia Abarca and Ronald Perry as the Swan Queen and the Prince both danced with an authority and a sureness which had been lacking in previous seasons.

In many ways the test of the company's technique and their ability to master a difficult idiom comes in Glen Tetley's "Greening." Originally choreographed for the Stuttgart Ballet, "Greening" is one of those Tetley ballets that are chock full of choreographic vocabulary but fail to say anything. However, the work makes major demands on the dancers. The pace is very fast, the steps complicated, the lifts articulated and precise. To perform it well takes talent. Virginia Johnson, Lewell Smith, Eddie Shellmen and again the lovely Lydia Abarca gave the best performance of the ballet this critic has seen.

A second program included George Balanchine's "Serenade," Arthur Mitchell's "Manifestations," Petipa's classic masterpiece of bravura dancing "Paquita" and Robert North's "Troy Game." It is a demanding choice of works and there is probably no other dance company in the world that could have brought to each the special qualities displayed by Dance Theater of Harlem.

"Serenade" was Mr. Balanchine's first ballet when he came to America in 1934, a seminal work that captures both the Russian Imperial Ballet style and the speed that is his particular contribution to American classical dance. The work looked as if it had been made for the Harlem dancers. They captured all its grace without missing a beat, and if the work has sometimes seemed lacking in heart, the passion finally shone through.

"Manifestations" is a wonderful Garden of Eden piece with the Snake slithering down from the leaves on a vine. Eddie Shellman, Stephanie Baxter and Mel Tomlinson gave it humor as well as superb dancing. "Paquita" was coached for the company by Alexandra Danilova. For dancers of this generation to work with this legendary Russian Imperial Ballet dancer, now in her 80s, is an extraordinary experience. Mr. Mitchell says, "If you are going to learn to do classics, go to the source." Certainly Madame Danilova is the source and she must have been immensely proud of these young dancers, executing the classical vocabulary with style and elan.

"Troy Game" is a romp for 11 boys, with a deliciously parodied approach. The jumps take your breath away; just when you think that it is all getting too serious, one of the dancers will do a wonderful comic gesture to bring back the humor. Supported by the Dance Theater of Harlem's own Percussion Ensemble, "Troy Game" is good dance and good theater.

Mr. Mitchell says that he tries to find a proper balance between quality and popularity. While he had vowed a few years ago that his company would never do "Swan Lake," he changed his mind. "I'd be cheating them as artists if I didn't let them try classic dance," he says, explaining that for any other company an act of "Swan Lake" or "Paquita" would be taken for granted, the result of two centuries of tradition. But for the Harlem dancers the problem was different. Many of the steps and shapes of the movement were unfamiliar and learning was sometimes painfully slow. The results have proven beyond a doubt that these dancers can master any technique they are given.

Swan Lake/Nixon

There could hardly have been a wider juxtaposition of art and life than this occasion at New York State Theatre: during the interval between Acts II and III of the American Ballet Theatre's "Swan Lake" the audience heard the resignation speech of Richard Nixon.

They had come to see Makarova and Nagy in the Petipa classic, particularly effective and sumptous production, concentrating on grace and line and the classic tradition instead of the dramatic rendering. Natalia Makarova's Odette is better than her Odile; she melts and rises, her body shimmers with the music, and above all her grace makes the encaptured swan princess believable. Ivan Nagy partners her delicately. He is noble above all else, clearly a romantic ideal. He is not a Sigfried of imperial mannerisms but rather a carefully measured character, falling in love, betraying that love with Odile in the Black Swan pas de deux, but on realising his betrayal, rushing back to the forest to try to make good his vow and recapture his love. This production allows him to succeed. It is one of those with the ultimate death of the evil Rothbart and a happy ending. The audience cheered and cheered the variations and the joyous quality of the dancing.

They also sat quietly to listen to the beginning of the resignation speech of the President. There were the occasional catcalls of "liar" and there was a burst of relieved applause when he finally announced that he was resign-ing. But as he went on through his speech, cataloguing his triumphs, the audience got restless, and many got up and left.

They had come to the theatre for grace and nobility and they had seen it in Makarova and Nagy, in the court ritual and in the happy ending. In the President's speech these were the elements so sadly lacking.

A Beautiful Building Enhanced by Bach

Music has an extraordinary way of giving added dimension to architecture. The environment in which one listens to music conditions both what we hear and our reactions to it.

A rock concert in a huge sports stadium has an aura of vibrant participation and often mass hysteria, the performance becoming as much a spectators' sport as an artistic endeavor. Music played on home hi-fi, however expensive and sophisticated the equipment, will never reproduce the sound (and, more importantly, the feel) of a concert hall.

At the same time, music has a magical way of catching the more profound elements of certain architectural forms and enhancing them. This phenomenon was brought home recently by two events experienced half-way around the world from one another, one in the medieval Bath Abbey in England, the other at the ultra-modern Sydney Opera House in Australia.

Bath Abbey is a church in the late Gothic "perpendicular" style. Although the Abbey was founded in 1499, its main architectural elements date from the Gothic period, particularly from the restoration of the original site by Bishop Montague in the seventeenth century. It is a church of grand columns and soaring arches, its ceilings and 52 windows articulated by intricate stonework. The church has a solidity, yet its impression is one of lightness and grace.

A recent organ recital of music by J. S. Bach, played during lunch-time by Dudley Holroyd, began with the "Fantasia in C Minor," and there was an immediate sense of unity between music and architecture. Bach's music reinforced the emotions one gets from letting one's eye follow the fluted columns and gently pointed arches which border the nave, and on to the counterpoint of the intricate ribbing of the ceilings in the side chapels. A long musical phrase seemed to run along a molding and trace its way over a column head, then go on to blend into the light splintering through the church's stained glass windows.

Bach's labyrinthian variations indeed dazzle the mind, but the variations are as firmly anchored to the thematic structure of the music as the vaultings, however intricate, are to the central pillars of Bath Abbey. Like the architecture, the music is both a grand conception and a myriad of aural diversions and adventures.

Perhaps all this sensation was stim-ply an environmental trick, caused by the interplay of the emotive force of the music and the visual splendor of the building. But there is reason to believe that the experience was more substantive than that.

The low registers of the "Toccata and Fugue in D Minor" speak eloquently, not only to the solid foundations of the architectural construct, but to profound religious faith, the creative force which built the church and created the music. Bach said that the aim and final reason for music "should be none else but the glory of God and the recreation of the mind." Bach lived, of course, in a time in which heaven and hell were not metaphors but were real.

His music, swelling, as critic Harold Schonberg has written, from "mannerist qualities: mysticism, exuberance, complexity, decoration, allegory, distortion, the exploitation of the supernatural or grandiose, all co-mingled" has in its architecture the same qualities that make the Abbey at Bath one of the last and best ecclesiastical examples of the Gothic period. Like Bach's compositions, the church, as one architectural critic pointed out, "is throughout quite exceptionally uniform in design; the system, once it had been established, was not altered in any major way." Yet, listening to Bach's music and following its parallel line in the architecture, one cannot but be struck by the infinitely varying details shared by this "uniform" architecture and the music that fills it.

If spiritual inspiration guided the hands of Bach and the craftsmen who built Bath Abbey, divine presence must have been elsewhere when the Australian Opera House was conceived. Without doubt one of the most beautiful architectural monuments of the century, it's a soaring group of spinnaker-like shapes rising from Sydney Harbor, and white-tiled canopies which reflect the hot sun during the day and catch the cool moonlight in the evening. Walking around its terraces is a treat and the building's internal perspectives are startlingly beautiful in their simplicity.

Yet the unity of the art of the architect and the musician, developed in the seventeenth century from a common purpose, were lost in the creation of this splendidly visual building.

It is not really an opera house but rather a cultural center, with a number of theaters presenting everything from opera and ballet to pop and legitimate theater. Its stages are inadequate in size for big works, and its unique architectural shape does not permit either the contemporary mechanics of stage-craft, which one would expect from such a house. Yet it is the wonder of Australia and no one visiting it can fail to be captured by its sheer architectural splendor.

Performers who work there usually quit complaining about its drawbacks during the second or third week, says Frank Barnes, the opera house's general manager. "The building has a spirit of its own," he says, claiming that it is a triumph of architecture for architecture's sake, over utilitarian usage. Even it if wasn't intended that way, that special "life of its own" has redeemed its obvious faults. Listening to performances on the hard seats of the opera theater takes perseverance, despite the generally high quality of the performances. And the eye tends to wander, not in search of the music's inner spirit as in Bath, but because Sydney Opera House is a scene-stealer.

Must the architecture of music and the music of architecture be closely related to provide maximum impact? The answer is most certainly not. However, there are times and places where by chance or intent, the interplay of these two art forms enriches both. In Bath, art and architecture joined beautifully. In Sydney, the beauty was present but the spirit was missing.

Interview

EC: Peter, to continue our conversation from yesterday, we were talking about the teaching of writing in the university classroom and how most of the time the constraints under which a piece of writing occurs in the outside world—time demands and deadlines, restrictions of column widths, policies of place of publication, and so on—are never brought into the classroom. When examples of writing by professional writers are read in the classroom, there is often no discussion at all of what motivated the piece of writing, what circumstances and situations affected how it was written—in other words the "environment" in which the writer had to live and breathe while doing the writing. Therefore, students often think that a piece of writing is all inspiration, that a professional writer gets to write a piece just the way the heart wants it.

PR: Pieces that have it all just as your heart wants appear once in a lifetime. Any writing you do—and I consider writing a craft—is related totally to what has to be produced. I write for a number of people, but regularly for the *Wall Street Journal*, which publishes the arts only on its editorial page. On Fridays— the day the arts page appears—it takes only three pieces, because that's all the space available around the advertisement. And those three pieces usually break down to one lead piece and two secondaries, and the secondaries are never more than ninety lines at seventy characters on the typewriter. You also have to write according to a special format. The *Wall Street Journal* doesn't want paragraphs running over from one page to another. You have to put the word "more" at the bottom of every page because the same typesetter doesn't always set pages one and three. They would never get it back together again if you had run-overs from one page to another. And deadlines are critical; in writing about the performing arts you obviously want to get the piece out as quickly as possible. There are a lot of technical details like that that affect your writing.

EC: Peter, how prominent is your reader in your mind as you are writing one of your essays?

PR: Totally. I have an idea in mind of the reader being somebody who really wants to know more about the subject, but who doesn't care or want to know how much I know. I picture a person who wants to know more, who is reasonably intelligent, so I don't have to explain everything, but who basically doesn't know a lot about the particular form, whether it be dance or music or drama. Therefore, I have to give them enough so that if they really don't know anything, they'll get something.

What I try to do is convey the feeling of the experience rather than the reportage. I'm not really interested in the reportage. I don't think it's significant if one marvelous ballerina happens to have tripped over her toe shoes and fallen on her nose or if a string broke on Casals' cello. These events don't all of a sudden make a dancer lousy or a cellist inept. What I try to do is get inside. The other thing I try to do is develop a theme. I'm usually thinking about a piece long before I walk into a theater. I've usually got some idea, a certain "idée fixe" of what the piece is likely to be about. This often changes, sometimes totally, when I actually write, but the idea is a place to start.

EC: Could you talk about that a bit more?

PR: Well, let me use an example. If you look at the piece I wrote on classical versus introspective ballet, which I wrote some years ago, the problem was that I had to write one review, dictated by the publication, covering two things. One was the National Ballet of Canada, which was performing *Sleeping Beauty* and *Swan Lake,* and the other was Martha Graham.

Now, what could be less alike than classical ballet and Martha Graham, who was a great revolutionary? What commonality do they have? Dance? Sure. They're both dance, and that would have been a fairly easy shot. But that is so obvious that it is not usable.

But I began to think about the subject of balance, and balance in classical ballet has certain values. For instance, in imperial Russian ballet, such as *Swan Lake,* and in *Sleeping Beauty* even more, balance is a metaphor for protocol, a metaphor for order—and this was a very ordered society. The balance of the dancer reveals a great deal about the society. Therefore, Aurora, the sleeping beauty, dances the famous "rose adagio" with her four suitors and stays on balance the entire time, moving in a circle from one to the other. Each suitor gives her a rose and then she gives the rose back. It's a whole number. That states something very important about what was going on in imperial Russian society.

In the Martha Graham modern vocabulary, balance is equally important. In *Clytemnestra,* which is the main piece that I talked about in the article, society was out of balance. Helen had been taken to Troy, the whole of the Greek legend was developing, and the fact was that society was terribly imbalanced as a result of that act, which led to the Trojan wars. The lack of balance of the dancers seemed to me to be in fascinating contrast with the balance of the nineteenth-century society which had produced *Sleeping Beauty* and *Swan Lake.* Therefore, I saw the opportunity to talk about balance in dance and in life.

EC: That's what you were thinking before you wrote your piece?

PR: Yes. For instance, I was wondering why the "rose adagio" or a similar piece of choreography appears in every one of the Russian classics. Why does it happen? Why are the cygnets in *Swan Lake*? You know, the four girls with their arms crossed in—almost Rockette, in fact, in better than Rockette-like motion? Why does that appear in virtually every Petipa ballet?

And the answer, of course, began to emerge that it has to do with order, that the court—which was paying the bills for this exercise—because it was an imperial court, wanted a reaffirmation all the time of the balance of society. Then I looked for opposites—balance and imbalance—and the piece just developed. It developed kind of fast. I tend to write pieces of about a thousand words; I don't really like to spend more than two and a half hours on the actual writing.

EC: Would you talk about your method of writing? Do you do a lot of rough drafts? Do you "write" in your head before you do the piece, and then. . . .

PR: Well, yes, I write in my head. I've read lots of books on writing which say you should do an outline, and some people definitely should. But I don't. I have a pretty good idea what's going to happen; but then it doesn't always come out that way. I'm a creature of transition. If I happen to come upon a word in the course of creating a sentence—and this is at the almost subconscious level—it triggers another idea, and that becomes the transition into the next paragraph. It may take me off into a somewhat different direction. But I know where I want to get to. I'm just not always sure *how* I'm going to get there.

And there's an awful moment, frequently, when you have to make the decision—you know you've only got, say, ninety lines, and you're not sure how to space the stuff you want to say over the ninety lines; you find you're either only at thirty lines and you've got to figure out how to do the other sixty, or you're at sixty and there's a lot more you wanted to say in the other thirty. You get caught up in it, and it makes you go back and look. But what I do is to try to get through a whole piece, more or less. I use a lot of TKM's, which means "to come." That means there's more material that will be added, so if I don't know something, I just put "TKM." I won't stop to find out the information right then. I can always go back and get that. Facts—you just don't let them get in your way; I mean that kind of facts. I continue to write and then go back and fix them up. Because of my own style, I happen always to write on the typewriter if I can, but I've written virtually upside down in airplanes if it was absolutely necessary.

The necessary part of it we were talking about yesterday—why am I writing and why are you reading? The answer is because I have something I want to say. It's an act of arrogance, there's no question about that. But I have something I want to say, and, therefore, I've got to say it in a way that you're going to want to keep reading. I can't chain you to a chair and make you read it. The piece has to capture the reader, and then keep the reader, and make the reader want to come back, which is even more important.

EC: Peter, will you discuss the relationship between the conversational forms in which you write and what you want to say?

PR: There are certain traditional forms that dictate the content. For instance, a *notice* is a form which is a review of a particular dance piece. One has to say it's a world premiere; one has to make sure that everybody knows that this is one of the world's greatest choreographers, that this is a new work, that it is plotless rather than narrative, what music it uses, where it's being performed, and who's dancing in it.

EC: What is the form of a piece like the one you did on the Dance Theatre of Harlem just recently?

PR: A good example of another form. In that essay, which was a piece of evaluation, I had freer range than with a notice because I was not reviewing a particular evening of dance. I was bringing the reader up to date on what the Dance Theatre of Harlem is doing these days.

EC: So in the traditional form, the *notice*, it's just a given that you must do X, Y, or Z; and in an evaluative essay you can do T, U, V, and Z—and all because it is a "given" of the particular form?

PR: Yes. There are givens that come with the form, givens that in a way constrain what you as the writer do—but they don't have to dictate it. And there are times when I write first with no form in mind and then draw down on that experience.

EC: Can you give an example?

PR: The piece "A Beautiful Building Enhanced by Bach" had no form. I was walking past an abbey in London on a rainy, cold day, and I had nothing to do for an hour and a half. They were having a Bach concert inside, so I paid my pound and went in. I heard this wonderful, wonderful music. I began to see the music in the context of the architecture.

So I wrote an architectural piece. I made copious notes about what I was seeing while it was going on, and then I went home, sat down, and wrote the piece.

EC: So you wrote that essay with no idea where you would get it published; you were not writing into a form or into a format with that one.

PR: Yes, that's right. The same thing happened when I wrote that short piece for *The Guardian* in England on the resignation of Richard Nixon. That was a situation in which I had no intention of writing a piece. I had gone to the ballet just for the fun of it. But the experience of being at the ballet and having someone come out on stage and announce the resignation of Richard Nixon—that juxtaposition of circumstances—made me take a reportial piece about something about which I felt very strongly and lift it to a metaphorical piece.

The piece was never planned. It happened while I was sitting there. And I went to the telephone and dictated it on the transatlantic phone to a scribe at the other end so that it would make the next morning's paper. That kind of piece really comes out of you. You want to tell everybody what you are seeing in a way to verify that you're really seeing it, and also to give it some permanence as a moment.

EC: That essay—and the Bach one, too—did come from the "heart," with the writing coming first and thoughts of publication second.

PR: Yes, that's right.

EC: What about that terrific piece you did some time ago on the songs of the Beatles?

PR: I like that piece. And there is a wonderful story about it. A kid who worked for me in London came to me and asked if he could have a couple of days off. He seemed upset and I asked him what the problem was. He said his brother had been arrested on an armed-robbery charge, which is very serious anywhere, but it's particularly serious in the UK where most people are not armed. I asked him if his brother had proper legal help, etc., to see if I could do anything.

In the course of things I hired a lawyer and did a number of other things, but I went up to a mitigation hearing in which each of the defendants' lawyers—and they can call witnesses—pleads guilty but asks for a mitigation of the sentence on one ground or another. Sitting there, listening to one mitigation plea after another, I began to hear certain recurrent themes, and those themes were basically lines from pop music that I hadn't really been listening to but I recognized. Suddenly it clicked. A mother, in fact, said on the stand, "We gave her most of our lives, sacrificed most of our lives; we gave her everything money could buy." She didn't even realize that she was quoting from the Beatles' marvelous song, "She's Leaving Home."

Then I began to ask myself whether the poetry of pop music had, in fact, infiltrated the brain, the collective consciousness—or unconsciousness—of parents who were saying, "Why do you keep playing those damned records?" Had they actually begun to hear it even though they didn't listen to it? And for the first time I started listening to it and found there was marvelous poetry there. I decided that that would make a nice piece.

Now that was, if you want, pure *inspiration*—but it wasn't inspiration; I mean inspiration is not usually the muse landing on your shoulder. It's a question of being open, listening, looking, and then finding something that has added value, that has leverage, that adds to the total understanding of something else—and if you're a writer, and you like to write—that pleads with you to write an essay.

EC: And what kind of completion, Peter, does finally doing the essay bring? You said it "pleads" to be put into an essay, so then you write it. Why does it plead to be put into an essay?

PR: Well, I think it gets it out of your system. I mean, if you like to communicate with people, it allows you to communicate with them in a form that is totally acceptable. If I go out on a street corner and start saying, "Hey, guys, come on over; I'm going to tell you about this wonderful thing . . ." I could see if I could gather some people on the street and tell them that, but I imagine they would think I was some kind of a nut.

EC: Like a sidewalk preacher, or the ancient mariner.

PR: You say that, but it's not all that . . .

EC: Far-fetched?

PR: Right. If you go today to Marrakesh, the story-tellers are there. The sad thing is now they're using electric bullhorns to tell the stories with loud speakers mounted on the tops of their cars. They've been there for hundreds and hundreds of years telling the same stories to audiences who know the stories, but they're such good story tellers that people come. And the story-tellers obviously want to express something, a perception, a vision, whatever.

That's what I do; I do care about sharing. But I'm not building that into a religion. I like seeing my by-line, too; it's also an ego trip.

EC: Will you just say another sentence or two about how writing something gets it out of your system?

PR: Well, it's wrong, in fact, my own usage, "It gets it out of my system." No, it doesn't; it gets it in.

EC: Integrated into?

PR: No, what I was thinking—I suddenly slipped into my current frame of reference, which is my micro-computer—is that it saves it for you. You know, instead of loading it, you save it. But the fact is, the act of writing it down so that someone else can understand it helps *you* to understand it, certainly. I didn't really understand about balance in any of those terms until I got into that classical/Martha Graham piece. I didn't know anything about the lyric poetry of pop music until I had a chance encounter with that sentence in the courtroom. In that sense the article got into me—I don't know if it got into other people; I hope it did because that was the purpose in the first place. But having done it, you've added a whole; you've filled a whole hunk of memory, in computer terms, and you can always recall it, it's always there. It's there in a certain order, and usually the order is something you don't know about until much later.

EC: Peter, is there anything else you would like to say?

PR: Yes, I want to end by saying that writing is fun. Words are the means by which we can communicate our most bestial instincts through agression, through yelling, through swearing. But they are also such marvelous tools for focusing your own thinking, even if you don't write for publication. The ability to communicate something without gestures, physical gestures, through the written word, is a very exciting thing. It's very satisfying.

It's as satisfying as kicking a ball perfectly or smashing a serve or skiing a deep powder descent; all your energy can go pleasurably into creating a written piece, whether it be a document, a letter, a furious note to the local utility company, an angry protest to the government, or an expression of true sympathy and bereavement over the death of a friend. To be able to express that is a joy. It's like any other physical or mental accomplishment, and it's something that can mean . . . that can mean a lot because it broadens you and it lets you be appreciated by more than the people who can hear you at any given moment.

EC: Any other final words?

PR: Yes. Good writing seems to me to come back to this question: do you have something you want to say that's worth saying, and can you say it in such a way that people, who might or might not be interested, will suddenly become interested in it? That's what it's all about.

EC: Peter, thank you very much.

Cynthia Mandelberg Talks About Writing

Cynthia Mandelberg is a screenplay writer, novelist, and dramatist who lives in Los Angeles. She was the recipient of the Samuel Goldwyn Creative Writing Award in 1973 for her novel Almost Empty Rooms. *Her play* Looking Glass, *based on the life of Lewis Carroll and co-authored with Michael Sutton, was produced in June of 1982 at the Entermedia Theatre in New York City. Among her feature-film screenplays are* Love Out of Season, *bought by MGM, and* Grand Slam. *Her television movies include* Helen and Annie, *a CBS special on the lives of Helen Keller and Annie Sullivan;* The Grace Kelly Story, *to appear on ABC-TV, starring Cheryl Ladd;* Eleanor, First Lady of the World, *starring Jean Stapleton and appearing in May of 1982 on CBS-TV;* Leave 'Em Laughing, *shown on CBS-TV and starring Mickey Rooney. Cynthia Mandelberg was also nominated for the Humanitas Award for humanizing achievement in television in 1981 for* Leave 'Em Laughing.

Mandelberg wrote the letter below to the president and Congress on December 9, 1981. It appeared as a full page advertisement in the Washington Post. *Following the letter is an interview with Cynthia Mandelberg in which she discusses the particular needs and problems of writing a screenplay.*

An Open Letter to the President and Congress

We are fortunate to live in one of the few countries in the world that was actually, consciously created for a purpose. We joined together and created the United States of America out of our commitment to make real in the world this truth which we hold to be self-evident, "that all men are created equal, that they are endowed by their creator with certain unalienable rights."

This statement is the cornerstone on which our nation was built. It is our reason for existing, our purpose—To honor and celebrate each individual being, for his or her uniqueness and special contribution to the whole.

Every human being—not just the powerful or the poor, or the Americans. We are committed to all persons and their well-being, whether a poor farmer in Peru, a starving peasant in Somalia, or a factory worker in the United States.

This nation is founded on the principle of "you and me". It is when we forget, when we slip into the pettiness of "you or me" or "them versus us" that no one wins.

Either the world will work for all of us or it won't truly work for any of us.

As a nation, when we keep our purpose in mind, choices become more clear—and by using our power as a people to further that purpose, we can truly create a world that will work for everyone, with no one left out.

Signed,

Cynthia Whitcomb Mandelberg

Cynthia Whitcomb Mandelberg

Interview

EC: Cynthia, how did you begin writing?

CM: I actually began by writing short stories and novels. I wrote several short stories and two novels and won a couple of awards for those.

EC: And what brought about the move from writing these short stories and novels to writing screenplays?

CM: I decided I didn't have the patience to be a novelist. And I had always been crazy about movies. I went to film school at UCLA. It seemed the clear thing for me to do to write screenplays.

EC: What is the process you go through from the first time you have the "urge" to write until you have a piece of writing in hand?

CM: When I get an idea that excites me, the first thing I do is some research on it: find out everything I can about that subject, those kinds of people, or that place. I get a lot of background on the idea.

EC: What next?

CM: Then I use three-by-five-inch index cards, and I write down all the ideas that I have. Then when I have jotted down everything I can think of, I lay them out in order so that I have a sort of shifting outline. I want to see them all laid out so that I can move the pieces around until I have a structure that really works. Then I can see where the holes are.

EC: Then do you begin writing?

CM: When I see that I have a solid story that will carry me all the way through, I usually go to one of the television networks and orally pitch my idea to them.

EC: What do you mean by "go to a network"?

CM: Well, for example, if I thought it was the kind of movie that CBS would likely be interested in doing, I would go to the office of one of the executives there who is in charge of buying television movies.

EC: And you would take your written manuscript?

CM: No. I would go in and *tell them* my idea. If they liked it, they would pay me to go home and write the screenplay. That's what I would do. I no longer write unless I know that it is sold in advance.

EC: Is this true for your plays, too?

CM: No, that's not true for the theatre. I still write for the theatre just for myself, on speculation, with no money attached. But I write television plays only when I am commissioned to do so.

EC: Do you regularly sell them?

CM: Yes, I do. I have sold ten television movies in the last two years.

EC: Cynthia, do you think everybody is capable of writing?

CM: Well, I think there are certain kinds of people who are observant and who are interested in other people and the world around them. And, too, some people seem to be natural writers, have a natural feel for language, have a natural affinity for writing and actually enjoy writing. But I think that anyone who really wants to and loves it could become a writer. You could train yourself in observation. You could train yourself in vocabulary.

EC: Do you still train yourself?

CM: Yes. For instance, I inundate myself with high-quality writing. I just went to London and New York and saw twenty-three plays in a month.

EC: Twenty-three in a month?

CM: Yes. I believe that you have to put good quality in—you know, feed the computer with good quality work—if you want to keep your sensibilities really heightened as to what is good. If you just sit around your office all the time, you will run out of inspiration. It is just good to keep yourself stimulated.

EC: How do you relate your own experience to the teaching of writing?

CM: I just did a one-week intensive dramatic-writing course in New York City, and it was very exciting. I start out by insisting that the writers get clear on what they want to say.

EC: How do you do that?

CM: Well, I start by getting them to tell about the things that they have loved in books or in movies or whatever, to remember what it was that inspired them and that they enjoyed so much they wanted to do writing themselves. After they talk about these things that excited them, we begin to look at what it was about those books, movies, etc., that created the excitement. What were the qualities in those? The messages behind them? My next step, then, is to get them to see that they could create that experience themselves in other readers.

EC: Cynthia, I imagine that the people in your class when you were teaching that course were people who wanted to be there, who had a strong motivation to write. But what about college freshman?

CM: Who take required writing courses?

EC: Yes, who take required freshman English.

CM: I would guess that almost all people who get as far as college have read something that turned them on, seen some movie that really excited them, or heard a song that they loved that somebody wrote. So I would do the same thing with these students: get them to remember some form of the written word that inspired them.

EC: But how to jump that chasm between remembering something they liked and knowing how to do it themselves?

CM: It is a gradual process. As soon as I get my students in touch with what they might want to say—the idea, the theme, the communication that they want to give to someone else—then they start looking around at *how* they want to tell it.

EC: What is the secret here?

CM: Not a secret really. If a writer really cares about what she or he is writing, then the writer can stay with the piece long enough to finish it. But if writers don't care about their subject, their readers won't either. And I actually get my students to tell their stories to each other, actually talk the writing out loud.

EC: Before the writing is done?

CM: Yes. Students can actually know if their writing is getting across so that other people are moved by it or amused by it or interested in it. And if the writing doesn't work when it is told out loud, we find out quickly where the structure or development falls off and actually start making it stronger before any of the formal writing is done at all. The students get feedback, and they find out if it works. [pause and a laugh] Actually, the students go through all the same steps that I go through.

EC: Cynthia, back to your taking your idea to a television network. How soon in the writing process do you know which network you are going to go to this time, and how do you decide this?

CM: Well, since this is my life, since that's my job to know, I do know the different people who are in charge of buying stories at all three networks. Hollywood is a very small town, you know, only three networks. And there are only two or three people at each network who make those decisions. I have worked with all them enough so that I know their tastes. I know the kinds of movies ABC is looking for as contrasted to the kinds CBS is looking for. I know who is not buying anything right now and who still needs three more pictures for the fall season. You know, I *know* what the market is.

EC: So when you have the idea originally, is this the point at which you begin thinking about the audience, about who might buy it?

CM: Well, actually, in that early stage the only thing I demand is that I personally be in love with the idea. If I am really excited about it, I assume there will be an audience for it. I trust my own taste. I trust myself, and I am usually right.

EC: Could we talk for a minute about how you came to write the letter that I am including in this text, the letter to the President and Congress that appeared in the *Washington Post*?

CM: Well, I was listening to a tape in my car. And the subject of the tape was the possibility of having a world that worked for all people. And as I was driving along, suddenly I thought, "The reason that the government doesn't really work is because it has lost touch with its purpose." What I decided was needed was a reminder that we started our country in the first place to celebrate and protect individual rights, to celebrate and protect each person's contribution to the community at large.

EC: Did you spend a long time writing the letter?

CM: No. I just sat down, and it wrote itself out. Very simply and straightforwardly. It happened very fast.

EC: What about its being published? How did you get it to appear as a full-page piece in the *Washington Post*?

CM: I paid for it.

EC: You paid for it yourself?

CM: Yes. I had got the chance to write a screenplay very quickly—actually to rewrite a screenplay that someone else had done—and I took the $20,000 which I made on the rewrite and paid to have the letter published.

EC: What has been the reaction to the letter?

CM: I got about a hundred letters from people all over the country—a lot of people in Washington—and several famous people, like Ralph Nader, a White House Senior Adviser, my Congressman. A White House correspondent reprinted the letter in American foreign language newspapers. The response was overwhelmingly positive, saying yes, that is right. It was even translated into Japanese and circulated in Japan where they told me, "It is not just for America but for all people."

EC: Then as far as you are concerned, the letter accomplished its purpose?

CM: Well, I will never know what the end results of the letter will be. But the way I look at it, the letter started a little ripple which will invisibly continue to move.

EC: You are talking about the *power* inherent in an act of communication?

CM: Yes. One of the most moving things about the act of communicating well is that people can somehow use the communication for themselves. When I do a television movie, 25 million people see it. To a lot of people, of course, it is just another evening's entertainment. But I always put something in my movies that if people want, they can keep for themselves; some way of looking at their lives, a new way of appreciating life, of remembering what they thought was important in life at some earlier time, something really important to them rather than just the daily, mundane repeat of it all. I write wishing always for my audience that they will, through my writing, get back in touch with their own vision of what they want their lives to be about, and that they take my communication for themselves, use it in their own lives, and then pass it on to someone else. That's really what it is all about.

EC: Thank you for taking the time to talk with me today, Cynthia.

CM: You're very welcome.

PART 3

Writing to Express

The Category and Its Configuration

To Express   say
give release to
get off one's chest
press out or squeeze out
put into words
represent by language
state
make known, reveal, show
picture, symbolize
show by a sign
give expression to one's feelings
    and imagination

    This is the most *personal* section of the book. In **writing to express** the author is stirred inside herself or himself to make a statement or share some very intimate part of life. Notice that the definition of **to express** includes to *reveal, show, state one's thoughts, give expression to one's feelings and imagination.*

    How *do* we know people? By things they say and do. In **writing to express** writers let readers know them. In this kind of writing—when done authentically—a writer says, "Here I am, without defenses. This is what I have done. This is what I have thought. This is what I have felt." And the risk is that we might not like it. We might think it is stupid. We might not even respond. There are no facts to hide behind for the writer, no external purpose for writing except to put one's self forward. Now, some people may **write to express** to show off, to be

arrogant, to dominate, to be right, to push individual ideas off on the reader. Some people do use **writing to express** actually to hide themselves and to be clever or show-offish. But you soon recognize this because you realize you are not getting a *person*; you are getting an *act*. Honest writing in this genre has a ring of truth. You are touched by it. The writing allows you to see the value, the essence, of an individual person. The writing, therefore, is a kind of "photograph" of the person inside.

How can you recognize **writing to express**? What pattern do the points of this configuration make?

You will notice that in all three chapters of **Writing to Express** which follow, the person writing is the center of the writing. Not the center of attention but the center of the writing. This kind of writing has as its emphasis the *person* writing—that person's sensibilities, experiences, thoughts, feelings, realizations. You leave **writing to express** knowing more about the person who wrote the piece.

The form that **writing to express** can take is much less predictable than the forms of **writing to tell** or **writing to change.** In **writing to express**, there is no customary way of presentation. Since the purpose of the writing is personal expression and since each person is unique, this kind of writing takes on a particular form emanating from the sensibilities of the writer; the person writes as he or she is. But one thing can be counted on: the writing will have a personal voice. You will be able to hear the person behind the writing and know that person. So, the recognizable thing will not be the form but the voice in it.

A writer cannot count on the reader's being interested in **writing to express** for external and obviously utilitarian reasons—like finding some fact in order to handle something at work. **Writing to express** doesn't have the same kind of immediacy that you find in the writing in the other two categories we have read in this book. Readers will read only if the writing "speaks" to them. Actually, however, if this kind of writing is done authentically and well, it will captivate readers because they will find *themselves* in the writing—their own lives, their own thoughts and experiences.

In summary, the points in the configuration of **Writing to Express** are these:

Emphasis	the writer's sensibilities, experience, thought
Motivation for Writing	some inner need
	some stirring of who one is
	some desire to share oneself
	some stirring of one's emotions
	some recognition that one matters in the world
	a dedication to others' quality of life
	a love for personal form
	a love for words
Circumstance and Situation	deadlines not usual
	length and time usually determined by writer and organic to the writing itself
	often not written for publication; publication may come "after the fact"

Forms	essays books articles editorials sermons diaries and journals letters forewords and prefaces announcements aphorisms travel accounts
Audience	persons like the author all human beings people who are interested in a particular subject
Writer's Relationship to Reader	friend to friend writer as a sharer, community with the reader
Writer's Intention	to reveal, show, share who the writer is and what the writer sees in the world

In this section of the book you will find PERSONAL EXPERI-ENCE essays, in which writers tell their own stories. You will find PERSONAL PERSPECTIVE essays in which authors share their personal ideas, viewpoints, stands. And, finally, you will find a miscellany of PERSONAL FORMS, the chapter in which some of the *variety* of forms a person's expression can take is illustrated.

The Personal Experience Essay

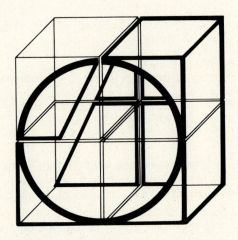

This category of **writing to express** is made up of essays people have written about their own experiences.

Writers write personal experience essays for several reasons:

They may want to get something out of their systems that is bothering them or about which they feel incomplete.

They may want to share something special that happened to them.

They may just want to tell a good story.

They may want to make sense of something that has happened to them.

They may want to share an insight they have had about something in their experience.

They may want to put words down that will last after they are gone.

They may want to use their personal experiences to suggest some truth about life itself.

Personal experience essays are written because of inner desires or needs to reveal, show, share, or tell something that has happened. These essays are still pictures of moving incidents, times that mattered to the writer, times that may have made the writer who she/he is, times when everyday experience was more than just that.

Writing a personal experience essay is valuable to the writer even if no one else ever reads the essay. As William Stafford says, "If a thing occurs to me, that makes it important enough to write down." Personal experience essays come from writers' having a sense of their own worth. These essays are enjoyable to readers in part because we human beings are a story-telling species. They are also valuable to readers because readers can gain insights from them, can recognize their own experiences in the writers' experiences, can be inspired, can be stimulated to think about their own lives, or can just enjoy good stories.

MAYA ANGELOU

Maya Angelou, a black writer, dancer, actress, and poet, tells about graduating from school in Stamps, Arkansas, in the following essay, taken from her autobiographical I Know Why the Caged Bird Sings *(1969). But the essay is about something much more far-reaching than graduation. During the ceremony something happened which, from her viewpoint years later as she writes about it, gives insight into the strength and perseverance of black people as a race. Not merely a narrative of a particular time and place, this personal experience essay reveals a recognition and celebration of the life of black people as a whole.*

Graduation in Stamps

1 The children in Stamps trembled visibly with anticipation. Some adults were excited too, but to be certain the whole young population had come down with graduation epidemic. Large classes were graduating from both the grammar school and the high school. Even those who were years removed from their own day of glorious release were anxious to help with preparations as a kind of dry run. The junior students who were moving into the vacating classes' chairs were tradition-bound to show their talents for leadership and management. They strutted through the school and around the campus exerting pressure on the lower grades. Their authority was so new that occasionally if they pressed a little too hard it had to be overlooked. After all, next term was coming, and it never hurt a sixth grader to have a play sister in the eighth grade, or a tenth-year student to be able to call a twelfth grader Bubba. So all was endured in a spirit of shared understanding. But the graduating classes themselves were the nobility. Like travelers with exotic destinations on their minds, the graduates were remarkably forgetful. They came to school without their books, or tablets or even pencils. Volunteers fell over themselves to secure replacements for the missing equipment. When accepted, the willing workers might or might not be thanked, and it was of no importance to the pre-graduation rites. Even teachers were respectful of the now quiet and aging seniors, and tended to speak to them, if not as equals, as beings only slightly lower than themselves. After tests were returned and grades given, the student body, which acted like an extended family, knew who did well, who excelled, and what piteous ones had failed.

Unlike the white high school, Lafayette County Training School 2
distinguished itself by having neither lawn, nor hedges, nor tennis
court, nor climbing ivy. Its two buildings (main classrooms, the grade
school and home economics) were set on a dirt hill with no fence to
limit either its boundaries or those of bordering farms. There was a
large expanse to the left of the school which was used alternately as a
baseball diamond or a basketball court. Rusty hoops on the swaying
poles represented the permanent recreational equipment, although bats
and balls could be borrowed from the P.E. teacher if the borrower was
qualified and if the diamond wasn't occupied.

Over this rocky area relieved by a few shady tall persimmon trees 3
the graduating class walked. The girls often held hands and no longer
bothered to speak to the lower students. There was a sadness about
them, as if this old world was not their home and they were bound for
higher ground. The boys, on the other hand, had become more
friendly, more outgoing. A decided change from the closed attitude
they projected while studying for finals. Now they seemed not ready
to give up the old school, the familiar paths and classrooms. Only a
small percentage would be continuing on to college—one of the
South's A & M (agricultural and mechanical) schools, which trained
Negro youths to be carpenters, farmers, handymen, masons, maids,
cooks and baby nurses. Their future rode heavily on their shoulders,
and blinded them to the collective joy that had pervaded the lives of the
boys and girls in the grammar school graduating class.

Parents who could afford it had ordered new shoes and ready-made 4
clothes for themselves from Sears and Roebuck or Montgomery Ward.
They also engaged the best seamstresses to make the floating graduating dresses and to cut down secondhand pants which would be pressed
to a military slickness for the important event.

Oh, it was important, all right. Whitefolks would attend the cere- 5
mony, and two or three would speak of God and home, and the Southern way of life, and Mrs. Parsons, the principal's wife, would play the
graduation march while the lower-grade graduates paraded down the
aisles and took their seats below the platform. The high school seniors
would wait in empty classrooms to make their dramatic entrance

In the Store I was the person of the moment. The birthday girl. The 6
center. Bailey had graduated the year before, although to do so he had
had to forfeit all pleasures to make up for his time lost in Baton Rouge.

My class was wearing butter-yellow piqué dresses, and Momma 7
launched out on mine. She smocked the yoke into tiny crisscrossing
puckers, then shirred the rest of the bodice. Her dark fingers ducked in
and out of the lemony cloth as she embroidered raised daisies around
the hem. Before she considered herself finished she had added a
crocheted cuff on the puff sleeves, and a pointy crocheted collar.

8   I was going to be lovely. A walking model of all the various styles of fine hand sewing and it didn't worry me that I was only twelve years old and merely graduating from the eighth grade. Besides, many teachers in Arkansas Negro schools had only that diploma and were licensed to impart wisdom.

9   The days had become longer and more noticeable. The faded beige of former times had been replaced with strong and sure colors. I began to see my classmate's clothes, their skin tones, and the dust that waved off pussy willows. Clouds that lazed across the sky were objects of great concern to me. Their shiftier shapes might have held a message that in my new happiness and with a little bit of time I'd soon decipher. During that period I looked at the arch of heaven so religiously my neck kept a steady ache. I had taken to smiling more often, and my jaws hurt from the unaccustomed activity. Between the two physical sore spots, I suppose I could have been uncomfortable, but that was not the case. As a member of the winning team (the graduating class of 1940) I had outdistanced unpleasant sensations by miles. I was headed for the freedom of open fields.

10   Youth and social approval allied themselves with me and we trammeled memories of slights and insults. The wind of our swift passage remodeled my features. Lost tears were pounded to mud and then to dust. Years of withdrawal were brushed aside and left behind, as hanging ropes of parasitic moss.

11   My work alone had awarded me a top place and I was going to be one of the first called in the graduating ceremonies. On the classroom blackboard, as well as on the bulletin board in the auditorium, there were blue stars and white stars and red stars. No absences, no tardinesses, and my academic work was among the best of the year. I could say the preamble to the Constitution even faster than Bailey. We timed ourselves often: "WethepeopleoftheUnitedStatesinordertoformamoreperfectunion . . ." I had memorized the Presidents of the United States from Washington to Roosevelt in chronological as well as alphabetical order.

12   My hair pleased me too. Gradually the black mass had lengthened and thickened, so that it kept at last to its braided pattern, and I didn't have to yank my scalp off when I tried to comb it.

13   Louise and I had rehearsed the exercises until we tired out ourselves. Henry Reed was class valedictorian. He was a small, very black boy with hooded eyes, a long, broad nose and an oddly shaped head. I had admired him for years because each term he and I vied for the best grades in our class. Most often he bested me, but instead of being disappointed, I was pleased that we shared top places between us. Like many Southern black children, he lived with his grandmother, who was a strict as Momma and as kind as she knew how to be. He was courteous, respectful and softspoken to elders, but on the playground he

chose to play the roughest games. I admired him. Anyone, I reckoned, sufficiently afraid or sufficiently dull could be polite. But to be able to operate at a top level with both adults and children was admirable.

His valedictory speech was entitled "To Be or Not to Be." The rigid 14 tenth-grade teacher had helped him write it. He'd been working on the dramatic stresses for months.

The weeks until graduation were filled with heady activities. A 15 group of small children were to be presented in a play about buttercups and daisies and bunny rabbits. They could be heard throughout the building practicing their hops and their little songs that sounded like silver bells. The older girls (non-graduates, of course) were assigned the task of making refreshments for the night's festivities. A tangy scent of ginger, cinnamon, nutmeg and chocolate wafted around the home economics building as the budding cooks made samples for themselves and their teachers.

In every corner of the workshop, axes and saws split fresh timber as 16 the woodshop boys made sets and stage scenery. Only the graduates were left out of the general bustle. We were free to sit in the library at the back of the building or look in quite detachedly, naturally, on the measures being taken for our event.

Even the minister preached on graduation the Sunday before. His 17 subject was, "Let your light so shine that men will see your good works and praise your Father, Who is in Heaven." Although the sermon was purported to be addressed to us, he used the occasion to speak to backsliders, gamblers and general ne'er-do-wells. But since he had called our names at the beginning of the service we were mollified.

Among Negroes the tradition was to give presents to children going 18 only from one grade to another. How much more important this was when the person was graduating at the top of the class. Uncle Willie and Momma had sent away for a Mickey Mouse watch like Bailey's. Louise gave me four embroidered handkerchiefs. (I gave her three crocheted doilies.) Mrs. Sneed, the minister's wife, made me an underskirt to wear for graduation, and nearly every customer gave me a nickel or maybe even a dime with the instruction "Keep on moving to higher ground," or some such encouragement.

Amazingly the great day finally dawned and I was out of bed before I 19 knew it. I threw open the back door to see it more clearly, but Momma said, "Sister, come away from that door and put your robe on."

I hoped the memory of that morning would never leave me. Sunlight 20 was itself still young, and the day had none of the insistence maturity would bring it in a few hours. In my robe and barefoot in the backyard, under cover of going to see about my new beans, I gave myself up to the gentle warmth and thanked God that no matter what evil I had done in my life He had allowed me to live to see this day. Somewhere in my fatalism I had expected to die, accidentally, and never have the chance to walk up the stairs in the auditorium and gracefully receive my hard-earned diploma. Out of God's merciful bosom I had won reprieve.

21   Bailey came out in his robe and gave me a box wrapped in Christmas paper. He said he had saved his money for months to pay for it. It felt like a box of chocolates, but I knew Bailey wouldn't save money to buy candy when we had all we could want under our noses.

22   He was as proud of the gift as I. It was a soft-leather-bound copy of a collection of poems by Edgar Allan Poe, or, as Bailey and I called him, "Eap." I turned to "Annabel Lee" and we walked up and down the garden rows, the cool dirt between our toes, reciting the beautifully sad bath.

23   Momma made a Sunday breakfast although it was only Friday. After we finished the blessing, I opened my eyes to find the watch on my plate. It was a dream of a day. Everything went smoothly and to my credit. I didn't have to be reminded or scolded for anything. Near evening I was too jittery to attend to chores, so Bailey volunteered to do all before his bath.

24   Days before, we had made a sign for the Store, and as we turned out the lights Momma hung the cardboard over the doorknob. It read clearly: CLOSED. GRADUATION.

25   My dress fitted perfectly and everyone said that I looked like a sunbeam in it. On the hill, going toward the school, Bailey walked behind with Uncle Willie, who muttered, "Go on, Ju." He wanted him to walk ahead with us because it embarrassed him to have to walk so slowly. Bailey said he'd let the ladies walk together, and the men would bring up the rear. We all laughed, nicely.

26   Little children dashed by out of the dark like fireflies. Their crepe-paper dresses and butterfly wings were not made for running and we heard more than one rip, dryly, and the regretful "uh uh" that followed.

27   The school blazed without gaiety. The windows seemed cold and unfriendly from the lower hill. A sense of ill-fated timing crept over me, and if Momma hadn't reached for my hand I would have drifted back to Bailey and Uncle Willie, and possibly beyond. She made a few slow jokes about my feet getting cold, and tugged me along to the now-strange building.

28   Around the front steps, assurance came back. There were my fellow "greats," the graduating class. Hair brushed back, legs oiled, new dresses and pressed pleats, fresh pocket handkerchiefs and little handbags, all homesewn. Oh, we were up to snuff, all right. I joined my comrades and didn't even see my family go in to find seats in the crowded auditorium.

29   The school band struck up a march and all classes filed in as had been rehearsed. We stood in front of our seats, as assigned, and on a signal from the choir director, we sat. No sooner had this been accom-

plished than the band started to play the national anthem. We rose
again and sang the song, after which we recited the pledge of allegiance. We remained standing for a brief minute before the choir
director and the principal signaled to us, rather desperately I thought,
to take our seats. The command was so unusual that our carefully
rehearsed and smooth-running machine was thrown off. For a full minute we fumbled for our chairs and bumped into each other awkwardly.
Habits change or solidify under pressure, so in our state of nervous
tension we had been ready to follow our usual assembly pattern: the
American national anthem, then the pledge of allegiance, then the song
every Black person I knew called the Negro National Anthem. All
done in the same key, with the same passion and most often standing
on the same foot.

Finding my seat at last, I was overcome with a presentiment of 30
worse things to come. Something unrehearsed, unplanned, was going
to happen, and we were going to be made to look bad. I distinctly
remember being explicit in the choice of pronoun. It was "we," the
graduating class, the unit, that concerned me then.

The principal welcomed "parents and friends" and asked the Bap- 31
tist minister to lead us in prayer. His invocation was brief and punchy,
and for a second I thought we were getting back on the high road to
right action. When the principal came back to the dais, however, his
voice had changed. Sounds always affected me profoundly and the
principal's voice was one of my favorites. During assembly it melted
and lowed weakly into the audience. It had not been in my plan to listen
to him, but my curiosity was piqued and I straightened up to give him
my attention.

He was talking about Booker T. Washington, our "late great 32
leader," who said we can be as close as the fingers on the hand,
etc. . . . Then he said a few vague things about friendship and the
friendship of kindly people to those less fortunate than themselves.
With that his voice nearly faded, thin, away. Like a river diminishing to
a stream and then to a trickle. But he cleared his throat and said, "Our
speaker tonight, who is also our friend, came from Texarkana to deliver the commencement address, but due to the irregularity of the train
schedule, he's going to, as they say, 'speak and run.' " He said that we
understood and wanted the man to know that we were most grateful for
the time he was able to give us and then something about how we were
willing always to adjust to another's program, and without more ado—
"I give you Mr. Edward Donleavy."

Not one but two white men came through the door offstage. The 33
shorter one walked to the speaker's platform, and the tall one moved
over to the center seat and sat down. But that was our principal's seat,
and already occupied. The dislodged gentleman bounced around for a
long breath or two before the Baptist minister gave him his chair, then

with more dignity than the situation deserved, the minister walked off the stage.

34   Donleavy looked at the audience once (on reflection, I'm sure that he wanted only to reassure himself that we were really there), adjusted his glasses and began to read from a sheaf of papers.

35   He was glad "to be here and to see the work going on just as it was in the other schools."

36   At the first "Amen" from the audience I willed the offender to immediate death by choking on the word. But Amens and Yes, sir's began to fall around the room like rain through a ragged umbrella.

37   He told us of the wonderful changes we children in Stamps had in store. The Central School (naturally, the white school was Central) had already been granted improvements that would be in use in the fall. A well-known artist was coming from Little Rock to teach art to them. They were going to have the newest microscopes and chemistry equipment for their laboratory. Mr. Donleavy didn't leave us long in the dark over who made these improvements available to Central High. Nor were we to be ignored in the general betterment scheme he had in mind.

38   He said that he had pointed out to people at a very high level that one of the first-line football tacklers at Arkansas Agricultural and Mechanical College had graduated from good old Lafayette County Training School. Here fewer Amen's were heard. Those few that did break through lay dully in the air with the heaviness of habit.

39   He went on to praise us. He went on to say how he had bragged that "one of the best basketball players at Fisk sank his first ball right here at Lafayette County Training School."

40   The white kids were going to have a chance to become Galileos and Madame Curies and Edisons and Gauguins, and our boys (the girls weren't even in on it) would try to be Jesse Owenses and Joe Louises.

41   Owens and the Brown Bomber were great heroes in our world, but what school official in the white-goddom of Little Rock had the right to decide that those two men must be our only heroes? Who decided that for Henry Reed to become a scientist he had to work like George Washington Carver, as a bootblack, to buy a lousy microscope? Bailey was obviously always going to be too small to be an athlete, so which concrete angel glued to what country seat had decided that if my brother wanted to become a lawyer he had to first pay penance for his skin by picking cotton and hoeing corn and studying correspondence books at night for twenty years?

42   The man's dead words fell like bricks around the auditorium and too many settled in my belly. Constrained by hard-learned manners I couldn't look behind me, but to my left and right the proud graduating class of 1940 had dropped their heads. Every girl in my row had found something new to do with her handkerchief. Some folded the tiny

squares into love knots, some into triangles, but most were wadding them, then pressing them flat on their yellow laps.

On the dais, the ancient tragedy was being replayed. Professor Par- 43 sons sat, a sculptor's reject, rigid. His large, heavy body seemed devoid of will or willingness, and his eyes said he was no longer with us. The other teachers examined the flag (which was draped stage right) or their notes, or the windows which opened on our now-famous playing diamond.

Graduation, the hush-hush magic time of frills and gifts and con- 44 gratulations and diplomas, was finished for me before my name was called. The accomplishment was nothing. The meticulous maps, drawn in three colors of ink, learning and spelling decasyllabic words, memorizing the whole of *The Rape of Lucrece*—it was for nothing. Donleavy had exposed us.

We were maids and farmers, handymen and washerwomen, and 45 anything higher that we aspired to was farcical and presumptuous.

Then I wished that Gabriel Prosser and Nat Turner had killed all 46 whitefolks in their beds and that Abraham Lincoln had been assassinated before the signing of the Emancipation Proclamation, and that Harriet Tubman had been killed by that blow on her head and Christopher Columbus had drowned in the *Santa Maria*.

It was awful to be Negro and have no control over my life. It was 47 brutal to be young and already trained to sit quietly and listen to charges brought against my color with no chance of defense. We should all be dead. I thought I should like to see us all dead, one on top of the other. A pyramid of flesh with the whitefolks on the bottom, as the broad base, then the Indians with their silly tomahawks and tepees and wigwams and treaties, the Negroes with their mops and recipes and cotton sacks and spirituals sticking out of their mouths. The Dutch children should all stumble in their wooden shoes and break their necks. The French should choke to death on the Louisiana Purchase (1803) while silkworms ate all the Chinese with their stupid pigtails. As a species, we were an abomination. All of us.

Donleavy was running for election, and assured our parents that if 48 he won we could count on having the only colored paved playing field in that part of Arkansas. Also—he never looked up to acknowledge the grunts of acceptance—also, we were bound to get some new equipment for the home economics building and the workshop.

He finished, and since there was no need to give any more than the 49 most perfunctory thank-you's, he nodded to the men on the stage, and the tall white man who was never introduced joined him at the door. They left with the attitude that now they were off to something really important. (The graduation ceremonies at Lafayette County Training School had been a mere preliminary.)

The ugliness they left was palpable. An uninvited guest who 50 wouldn't leave. The choir was summoned and sang a modern arrangement of "Onward, Christian Soldiers," with new words pertaining to graduates seeking their place in the world. But it didn't work. Elouise, the daughter of the Baptist minister, recited "Invictus," and I could have cried at the impertinence of "I am the master of my fate, I am the captain of my soul."

51   My name had lost its ring of familiarity and I had to be nudged to go and receive my diploma. All my preparations had fled. I neither marched up to the stage like a conquering Amazon, nor did I look in the audience for Bailey's nod of approval. Marguerite Johnson, I heard the name again, my honors were read, there were noises in the audience of appreciation, and I took my place on the stage as rehearsed.

52   I thought about colors I hated: ecru, puce, lavender, beige and black.

53   There was shuffling and rustling around me, then Henry Reed was giving his valedictory address, "To Be or Not to Be." Hadn't he heard the whitefolks? We couldn't *be*, so the question was a waste of time. Henry's voice came clear and strong. I feared to look at him. Hadn't he got the message? There was no "nobler in the mind" for Negroes because the world didn't think we had minds, and they let us know it. "Outrageous fortune"? Now, that was a joke. When the ceremony was over I had to tell Henry Reed some things. That is, if I still cared. Not "rub," Henry, "erase." "Ah, there's the erase." Us.

54   Henry had been a good student in elocution. His voice rose on tides of promise and fell on waves of warnings. The English teacher had helped him to create a sermon winging through Hamlet's soliloquy. To be a man, a doer, a builder, a leader, or to be a tool, an unfunny joke, a crusher of funky toadstools. I marveled that Henry could go through the speech as if we had a choice.

55   I had been listening and silently rebutting each sentence with my eyes closed; then there was a hush, which in an audience warns that something unplanned is happening. I looked up and saw Henry Reed, the conservative, the proper, the A student, turn his back to the audience and turn to us (the proud graduating class of 1940) and sing, nearly speaking,

> "Lift ev'ry voice and sing
> Till earth and heaven ring
> Ring with the harmonies of Liberty . . ."[1]

It was the poem written by James Weldon Johnson. It was the music composed by J. Rosamond Johnson. It was the Negro national anthem. Out of habit we were singing it.

---

[1] "Lift Ev'ry Voice and Sing"—words by James Weldon Johnson and music by J. Rosamond Johnson. Copyright by Edward B. Marks Music Corporation. Used by permission.

Our mothers and fathers stood in the dark hall and joined the hymn 56
of encouragement. A kindergarten teacher led the small children onto
the stage and the buttercups and daisies and bunny rabbits marked time
and tried to follow:

> "Stony the road we trod
> Bitter the chastening rod
> Felt in the days when hope, unborn, had died.
> Yet with a steady beat
> Have not our weary feet
> Come to the place for which our fathers sighed?"

Every child I knew had learned that song with his ABC's and along 57
with "Jesus Loves Me This I Know." But I personally had never heard
it before. Never heard the words, despite the thousands of times I had
sung them. Never thought they had anything to do with me.

On the other hand, the words of Patrick Henry had made such an 58
impression on me that I had been able to stretch myself tall and trem-
bling and say, "I know now what course others may take, but as for
me, give me liberty or give me death."

And now I heard, really for the first time: 59

> "We have come over a way that with tears has been watered,
> We have come, treading our path through the blood of
> the slaughtered."

While echoes of the song shivered in the air, Henry Reed bowed his 60
head, said "Thank you," and returned to his place in the line. The tears
that slipped down many faces were not wiped away in shame.

We were on top again. As always, again. We survived. The depths 61
had been icy and dark, but now a bright sun spoke to our souls. I was
no longer simply a member of the proud graduating class of 1940; I was
a proud member of the wonderful beautiful Negro race.

FOR DISCUSSION

1. Where does this essay take place and under what circumstances?
   At what point in the essay do you know this specifically? Why do
   you suppose the specifics are not revealed until then?

2. The incident that occurs in this essay could have produced only
   anger and bitterness in Maya Angelou. What did the incident
   contribute to her? What does she realize because this incident
   happened?

3. Who is honored through this essay?

4. What makes the audience for this essay *all* people, no matter what race, color, or creed?

5. What is the point of this essay? What makes it worth reading or even worth writing about?

6. Since graduation is an occurrence in many people's lives, how does Angelou create interest in such a common subject?

RUSTY CAWLEY

In the following selection newspaper reporter Rusty Cawley gives an intimate personal account of the meaning of John Lennon's death for him. Cawley wrote this essay for the Bryan-College Station Eagle *newspaper in Texas, on the first anniversary of Lennon's death.*

Mentor and Friend: Memory of John Lennon

1 I remember today a year ago so well.

2 Too well.

3 My brand-new wife and I sat in front of the television watching some meaningless game on ABC's *Monday Night Football*.

4 Howard Cosell told me that John Lennon was dead.

5 I remember going to a Houston department store with my grandmother. I was 10. The year was 1967.

6 Whether it was my birthday or something else, I can't recall. All I can remember is that my grandmother had promised to buy me a record.

7 I went wanting a copy of *The Unicorn*, a tepid little tune by a band of hairy singers who called themselves "The Irish Rovers." I ended up with something quite different.

8 While thumbing through the racks, I found an album with a picture of a funeral on the cover. Among the many mourners were Johnny Weismuller, W. C. Fields, Jayne Mansfield, Bob Dylan, Karl Marx, Marlon Brando, Diana Dors and Aleister Crowley. And four tidy young men in matching black suits.

9 They were the Beatles, the guests of honor.

The same four young men also stood in the center of the crowd. 10
They wore hot-colored marching band uniforms. Each sported a mus-
tache and carried a horn. This was Sergeant Pepper's Lonely Hearts
Club Band.

The new Beatles were burying the old Beatles.   11

I stopped looking for the Irish Rovers that second. I handed 12
Sergeant Pepper to my grandmother. "I want this one," I said.

She looked at it, turned several colors, and said, "No, you don't."   13
She bought it.   14

I still have that album. It was the first I ever owned. To play it on my 15
stereo these days, I have to give the needle a nudge. Otherwise the
record will simply turn and turn without producing a note.

Those first few grooves wore away a long, long time ago.   16

I remember sitting on the floor of my room, night after night, listen- 17
ing to my monophonic record player. I had two albums. One was *Sgt.
Pepper*. The other was the Beatles' next album, *Magical Mystery Tour*.

Sometime later, a school chum introduced me to stereo. He owned 18
every album the Beatles had issued to that time, which was about 1969.

He soon became my best friend.   19

Whenever a new Beatle record came out, my friend would always 20
seem to be the first to get a copy. We'd close ourselves in his bedroom
and just play the disc over and over again. We's argue about the lyrics.
We'd try to copy the harmonies with our adolescent voices and our
pathetically dull ears.

We like each of the Beatles, but we both loved John Lennon.   21

While we enjoyed Paul McCartney's voice, we found his music too 22
saccharin. George Harrison never seemed to have anything to say.
Ringo Starr was . . . well, he was just Ringo. He always had that look
of a puppy in the dog pound.

But Lennon appealed to the intellectual renegades we fancied our- 23
selves to be. He was brash and tough and eccentric. He wrote about
strawberry fields and glass onions and plasticine porters with looking-
glass ties. We spent most of our afterschool hours mining what we
could from his lyrics.

We began writing our own songs long before either of us learned 24
how to play a musical instrument. It just seemed like the next step.

Frustrated by our lack of talent, my friend soon gave up. When the 25
Beatles split in 1970, he put away their records.

We drifted apart.   26

I remember hating Yoko Ono.   27

I considered her an enemy, a threat.   28

Who is she to turn John's own strangeness against himself? I won- 29
dered. And when he started mailing acorns to world leaders in the
name of peace, I began to doubt his sanity.

30   Still I bought each and every record as it came out. Not every John Lennon album was a great album, or even a good one. But each presented me with a new challenge, a new standard.

31   I outgrew Kurt Vonnegut and Phillip Roth and Eldridge Cleaver. I never outgrew John Lennon.

32   He always stood ahead of everyone else, a position as dangerous as running point in a guerrilla raid. He marched against Vietnam and railed against Tricky Dicky and became pop music's first muckraker.

33   The President of the United States tried to deport him. It didn't work. By the mid-70's, Richard Nixon was out of office and John Lennon was a United States citizen.

34   But the personal cost was terrible. Yoko suffered two miscarriages during those years. She and John came close to divorce. When the court battles ended, they headed for Japan.

35   That was 1975.

36   I remember a party during the spring of 1980. "Do you realize," someone asked me, "that it's been five years since John Lennon last made a record?"

37   Not a week later, I read Lennon planned to release another album. He called it *Double Fantasy*.

38   I wanted it badly. But for one reason or another, most of it having to do with my approaching wedding, I never got around to buying it.

39   I did, however, hear the single cuts on the radio. John sounded so well, so bright, so full of fun again. I remember how happy I was for him.

40   I remember those first few moments after Howard Cosell had told me that John Lennon was dead.

41   I remember flipping the channel over and over to see if anyone had more news.

42   I remember my wife asking me what was wrong and my saying "John Lennon's dead." And, when that didn't get the proper response, screaming, "Don't you understand? John Lennon's dead!"

43   But most of all, I remember the next day.

44   I had classes to attend; I did not go.

45   I sat in our chilly mobile home with the lights out, listening to the radio as some clown played the least-significant Beatles songs he could find and asked people what Lennon's death meant to them. They all seemed to say the same thing, how it was the end of a era, how the Beatles would never get back together again, and so on.

46   How superficial. How pathetic.

47   For a year now, I've tried to explain this to others. I've found it useless. Yet, I find I must try.

48   I never met John Lennon. Never came close. Yet, through his recordings, his scribblings, and his interviews, I came to know him better than I know most people who enter and exit my life.

He was my mentor, a major influence on what I am and how I think. 49
Without knowing me, he managed to get me through those strange and
turbulent years we call adolescence. There is a word for a person such
as this: Friend.

John Lennon was my friend.   50

Yes.   51

FOR DISCUSSION

1. Why would this essay be of interest to someone who had not
   even cared or known much about the Beatles?

2. What makes this essay not a tear-jerker, not a self-indulgent
   lament? What gives it dignity?

3. Why do you think it was important to Rusty Cawley to write this
   essay? (He certainly was not assigned to write it as part of his job
   as reporter.)

4. What makes the essay even more powerful for having been
   written a year *after* John Lennon's death instead of at the time he
   was killed?

5. How does a personal experience essay like this contribute to you,
   the reader?

6. There are many short, even one-sentence, paragraphs in this
   essay. How is this style related to the place the essay appeared—
   the *Bryan-College Station Eagle* newspaper—and how is the
   style related to the power and impact of the essay itself?

7. Even though you don't know Cawley, in some way after reading
   this essay, you do. What kind of man does he seem like to you?

MARK TWAIN

---

*No one has told a funnier story than the American humorist Mark
Twain (1835–1910). The following selection, taken from his* Autobiography, *is a description of his uncle's farm and the pranks he used to
play on his aunt and mother.*

Uncle's Farm

1 My uncle, John A. Quarles, was a farmer and his place was in the country four miles from Florida. He had eight children . . . and was also fortunate in other ways, particularly in his character. I have not come across a better man than he was. I was his guest for two or three months every year, from the fourth year after we removed to Hannibal till I was eleven or twelve years old. . . .

2   It was a heavenly place for a boy, that farm of my uncle John's. The house was a double log one with a spacious floor (roofed in) connecting it with the kitchen. In the summer the table was set in the middle of that shady and breezy floor, and the sumptuous meals—well, it makes me cry to think of them. Fried chicken, roast pig, wild and tame turkeys, ducks and geese, venison just killed, squirrels, rabbits, pheasants, partridges, prairie-chickens, biscuits, hot batter-cakes, hot buckwheat cakes, hot "wheat bread," hot rolls, hot corn pone; fresh corn boiled on the ear, succotash, butterbeans, string-beans, tomatoes, peas, Irish potatoes, sweet potatoes; buttermilk, sweet milk; "clabber"; watermelons, muskmelons, cantaloupes—all fresh from the garden—apple pie, peach pie, pumpkin pie, apple dumplings, peach cobbler—I can't remember the rest. . . .

3   I can see the farm yet with perfect clearness. I can see all its belongings, all its details: the family room of the house with a "trundle" bed in one corner and a spinning-wheel in another, a wheel whose rising and falling wail, heard from a distance, was the mournfulest of all sounds to me and made me homesick and low-spirited and filled my atmosphere with the wandering spirits of the dead; the vast fireplace, piled high on winter nights with flaming hickory logs from whose ends a sugary sap bubbled out but did not go to waste, for we scraped it off and ate it; the lazy cat spread out on the rough hearth-stones; the drowsy dogs braced against the jambs and blinking; my aunt in one chimney corner, knitting; my uncle in the other, smoking his corn-cob pipe; the slick and carpetless oak floor faintly mirroring the dancing flame-tongues and freckled with black indentations where fire-coals had popped out and died a leisurely death; half a dozen children romping in the background twilight; split-bottomed chairs here and there, some with rockers; a cradle, out of service but waiting with confidence; in the early cold mornings a snuggle of children in shirts and chemises occupying the hearth-stone and procrastinating—they could not bear to leave that comfortable place and go out on the wind-swept floorspace between the house and kitchen where the general tin basin stood, and wash.

4   Along outside of the front fence ran the country road, dusty in the summertime and a good place for snakes—they liked to lie in it and sun themselves; when they were rattlesnakes or puff adders, we killed them; when they were black snakes or racers or belonged to the fabled

"hoop" breed, we fled, without shame; when they were "house-snakes" or "garters" we carried them home and put them in Aunt Patsy's workbasket for a surprise; for she was prejudiced against snakes and always when she took the basket in her lap and they began to climb out of it, it disordered her mind. She never could seem to get used to them, her opportunities went for nothing. And she was always cold toward bats, too, and could not bear them; and yet I think a bat is as friendly a bird as there is. My mother was Aunt Patsy's sister and had the same wild superstitions. A bat is beautifully soft and silky; I do not know any creature that is pleasanter to the touch or is more grateful for caressings, if offered in the right spirit. I know all about these coleoptera because our great cave, three miles below Hannibal, was multitudinously stocked with them and often I brought them home to amuse my mother with. It was easy to manage if it was a school-day, because then I had ostensibly been to school and hadn't any bats. She was not a suspicious person but full of trust and confidence, and when I said, "There's something in my coat-pocket for you," she would put her hand in. But she always took it out again, herself; I didn't have to tell her. It was remarkable, the way she couldn't learn to like private bats. The more experience she had, the more she could not change her views. . . .

As I have said, I spent some part of every year at the farm until I was ₅ twelve or thirteen years old. The life which I led there with my cousins was full of charm and so is the memory of it yet. . . .

FOR DISCUSSION

1. Mark Twain describes a personal experience that took place more than 125 years ago. What do you gain from reading about this experience today, even if you have never been on a farm?

2. You might say about a person who writes about going to his uncle's farm, "Well, who cares?" Why do you care? What keeps Twain from being guilty of arrogance in writing this personal experience?

3. This personal experience is a very happy one. What makes writing about pleasurable experiences as valuable and important to a writer as writing about tragic or serious experiences?

4. This is *good* writing. Why?

5. What do you know about the author from reading this essay?

6. Mark Twain was famous for introducing colloquial speech into American fiction, but do you notice much use of colloquial language in this selection? How is his tone—as he narrates his autobiography—different from the tone used by Huckleberry Finn to narrate an incident? What purpose does this difference serve?

EDWARD IWATA

Edward Iwata, a Japanese-American reporter, writes a personal experience essay about his family during the Second World War. The essay, which first appeared int he San Francisco Chronicle, *is about his family's experience, but it is also very much about Iwata himself today.*

Barbed-Wire Memories

1 My parents rarely spoke about it, and I rarely asked them to.

2   Manzanar has emerged in recent years as a symbol of racial oppression for many Asian Americans, but it remained a painful subject in my family home.

3   For my parents, the very word "Manzanar" calls up shameful memories of a four-year period of their lives when their citizenship and patriotism, their simple belief in the unalienable goodness of America, meant nothing amid the flood of wartime racism.

4   I never asked them about it in any detail because a fearful part of me had refused to believe that my parents had been imprisoned by their own country. Their only crime was their color of skin and slant of eye.

5   It was as if too long a glimpse into their tragic past would shatter the rules of our relationship, a relationship peculiar to Japanese people that relies heavily on unspoken but deeply understood values, emotions, and expectations.

6   My knowledge of their stay in Manzanar was scant, a hazy mix of childhood tales and harmless anecdotes they told with a smile whenever their curious kids asked about "that camp in the desert."

7   Until recently, I did not know that my mother and father had met and fallen in love while behind barbed wires at Manzanar. I did not know that my grandmother cried daily the first two weeks in camp, hoping somehow that the tears would wash away the injustice of it all. I

did not know that my mother's youngest brother, who later died in the Korean war, dreamed of fighting for the United States while he grew up as a little boy in Manzanar.

I learned all of this in what seems the most absurd, impersonal 8 manner: while interviewing my parents for a newspaper story. In my role as a reporter, I was able for the first time to ask them about their concentration camp experience. In their roles as interview subjects, they spoke about Manzanar for the first time in an unashamed manner to their son.

Japanese Americans learn the stark facts early: On February 19, 9 1942, President Roosevelt issued Executive Order 9066, sanctioning the evacuation of our people. One hundred ten thousand, most of them citizens, were evacuated to ten camps throughout the United States, where they would remain for four years. Most of the evacuees were given two to seven days to sell a lifetime of belongings, although some ministers and language instructors were arrested immediately with not even that much notice.

The sudden evacuation order shocked the Issei, the industrious first 10 generation in this country, and the Nisei, their children. One Pismo Beach man shot himself in the head to spare his family from his shame. He was found clasping an honorary citizenship certificate from Monterey Country, which thanked him for his "loyal and splendid service to the country in the Great World War."

In my own family, my uncle, a minister, was not given the custom- 11 ary notice to evacuate. He was visited at his San Fernando home by two FBI agents at nine o'clock one evening. Within the hour, he was carted off, without his wife, for an undisclosed location.

Ironically, the evacuations came despite the fact that the only pre- 12 war government study found a high degree of loyalty among Japanese Americans and concluded, "There is no Japanese 'problem' on the (West) Coast."

But the government ignored the study's findings. As historians later 13 pointed out, U.S. wartime morale was sinking. West Coast farmers were accusing "treacherous" Japanese American farmers of stealing their land and monopolizing agriculture. Japanese Americans became easy, visible scapegoats. They looked like the enemy. They spoke and read Japanese. Their fishermen owned shortwave radios.

More important, they probably wouldn't fight back. The govern- 14 ment was right; the Japanese Americans acquiesced without a struggle and filed silently into their prisons. . . .

As her sketchy recollections continue, my mother's long-buried 15 thoughts grow fuller, more vivid.

The family was housed, she says, in wooden, tar-papered barracks 16 that offered little protection against the furious desert winds. Seven people were crammed into a bare 12-foot by 20-foot room, with a hung sheet providing privacy for one of my aunts and her husband.

17   My mother worked for $19 a month as a secretary for the camp administrators; white secretaries there made $40. One of her sisters, Sue Kunitomi Embrey, edited the camp newspaper, The Manzanar Free Press.

18   During that same year, my father's parents lost their fruit and vegetable farm in the San Fernando Valley. The sudden evacuation to a prison camp, my father told me, "was hard to believe. It was kind of scary. I guess the older people, the parents, took it the worst.

19   "We went to Manzanar on red buses from Burbank. I thought, where are we going to, all out in the desert with no trees . . ."

20   My parents do not dwell on the bad parts. But they had to endure a riot, armed guards and fierce political factions—pro- and anti-American—among the residents. My mother recalls one night when her brother, a member of the camp's unarmed Japanese internal police, ripped off his uniform and dashed into their barrack, shouting, "I quit, I quit!"

21   A large mob of camp residents, fueled by rumors that the camp administrators were withholding sugar from them, had rioted. Two Japanese were shot and killed by white camp guards.

22   In one of those oppressive chapters of history that often give birth to monumental hope, the residents of Manzanar created a small, thriving, all-American town.

23   My parents prefer to talk about the high school, the social clubs and dances, the sports leagues they and their friends plunged into with enthusiasm.

24   They shined their shoes and fixed their hair so they could jitterbug to Glenn Miller and Tommy Dorsey records in the Manzanar gymnasium. They trudged through dust storms to see scratchy, black-and-white Laurel and Hardy movies. They watched boisterous baseball and basketball games that often erupted into bloody fights.

25   "You had fun there," my father says. "It was not a place to be, but you make the best of it."

26   Still versed in the old ways, the grandparents would sew, arrange flowers, write haiku. They did not always understand that their children, prisoners of a crime not of their own making, were reacting to the camp in the only way they knew—as children of American culture.

27   As our family history unfolds, I see that every future move, every development, hinges on the war and evacuation in some way.

28   I find that the Japanese Americans, ghettoized in "Little Tokyos" before the war, embarked after their release on a lightning drive for middle-class respectibility unprecedented in U.S. immigration history. It was the surest way they could prove their worth again in the eyes of white America.

I learn that Manzanar, while a devastating psychological experience 29 for my parents and their family, also gave them a mental resolve and emotional stamina that would surface again and again over the years.

The camp also spawned a curious brand of conservatism among 30 Nisei that blends traditional Japanese values such as *enryo* (a quiet reserve) and *on* (loyalty and obligation) with America's aggressive, individualistic work ethic and love of material and cultural status.

The Sansei—my generation—are the children of that wartime 31 tragedy. The spirit and gallantry, the shame and disillusionment of my parents and the Nisei are not lost upon us. Forty years later, that legacy strengthens us, and it also is our burden.

FOR DISCUSSION

1. What keeps this essay from being a diatribe—a bitter and angry complaint—against the United States government?

2. What personal need of Edward Swata's do you guess was met by writing this essay?

3. What makes the essay valuable to you, the reader, even if you are not Japanese-American? How does Swata make the essay interesting and valuable to all readers, not just people who have had the experience related in the essay?

4. In what way was the writing of this essay comparable to the actual pilgrimage Swata took to the site?

5. What did you learn from the essay?

6. What writing techniques make the essay come alive for you, the reader?

CAPTAIN JOSHUA SLOCUM

On April 24, 1895, Joshua Slocum, the builder, owner, captain, and one-man crew of the Spray, *set sail on a voyage around the world. In the early morning of June 27, 1898, he sailed back into the Newport, Rhode Island harbor having sailed 46,000 miles, clear around the world. Shortly after his return, Captain Slocum wrote the story of his voyage, which was first published in 1899–1900 in the* Century Illustrated *magazine. This excerpt is from Joshua Slocum's account of his personal experiences,* Sailing Alone Around the World.

Sailing Alone Around the World

1 I now stowed all my goods securely, for the boisterous Atlantic was before me, and I sent the topmast down, knowing that the *Spray* would be the wholesomer with it on deck. Then I gave the lanyards a pull and hitched them afresh, and saw that the gammon was secure, also that the boat was lashed, for even in summer one may meet with bad weather in the crossing.

2 In fact, many weeks of bad weather had prevailed. On July 1, however, after a rude gale, the wind came out nor'west and clear, propitious for a good run. On the following day, the head sea having gone down, I sailed from Yarmouth, and let go my last hold on America. The log of my first day on the Atlantic in the *Spray* reads briefly: "9:30 A.M. sailed from Yarmouth. 4:30 P.M. passed Cape Sable; distance, three cables from the land. The sloop making eight knots. Fresh breeze N.W." Before the sun went down I was taking my supper of strawberries and tea in smooth water under the lee of the east-coast land, along which the *Spray* was now leisurely skirting.

3 At noon on July 3 Ironbound Island was abeam. The *Spray* was again at her best. A large schooner came out of Liverpool, Nova Scotia, this morning, steering eastward. The *Spray* put her hull down astern in five hours. At 6:45 P.M. I was in close under Chebucto Head light, near Halifax harbor. I set my flag and squared away, taking my departure from George's Island before dark to sail east of Sable Island. There are many beacon lights along the coast. Sambro, the Rock of Lamentations, carries a noble light, which, however, the liner *Atlantic*, on the night of her terrible disaster, did not see. I watched light after light sink astern as I sailed into the unbounded sea, till Sambro, the last of them all, was below the horizon. The *Spray* was then alone, and

sailing on, she held her course. July 4, at 6 A.M., I put in double reefs, and at 8:30 A.M. turned out all reefs. At 9:40 P.M. I raised the sheen only of the light on the west end of Sable Island, which may also be called the Island of Tragedies. The fog, which till this moment had held off, now lowered over the sea like a pall. I was in a world of fog, shut off from the universe. I did not see any more of the light. By the lead, which I cast often, I found that a little after midnight I was passing the east point of the island, and should soon be clear of dangers of land and shoals. The wind was holding free, though it was from the foggy point, south-southwest. It is said that within a few years Sable Island has been reduced from forty miles in length to twenty, and that of three lighthouses built on it since 1880, two have been washed away and the third will soon be engulfed.

On the evening of July 5 the *Spray*, after having steered all day over 4 a lumpy sea, took it into her head to go without the helmsman's aid. I had been steering southeast by south, but the wind hauling forward a bit, she dropped into a smooth lane, heading southeast, and making about eight knots, her very best work. I crowded on sail to cross the track of the liners without loss of time, and to reach as soon as possible the friendly Gulf Stream. The fog lifting before night, I was afforded a look at the sun just as it was touching the sea. I watched it go down and out of sight. Then I turned my face eastward, and there, apparently at the very end of the bowsprit, was the smiling full moon rising out of the sea. Neptune himself coming over the bows could not have startled me more. "Good evening, sir," I cried; "I'm glad to see you." Many a long talk since then I have had with the man in the moon; he had my confidence on the voyage.

About midnight the fog shut down again denser than ever before. 5 One could almost "stand on it." It continued so for a number of days, the wind increasing to a gale. The waves rose high, but I had a good ship. Still, in the dismal fog I felt myself drifting into loneliness, an insect on a straw in the midst of the elements. I lashed the helm, and my vessel held her course, and while she sailed I slept.

During these days a feeling of awe crept over me. My memory 6 worked with startling power. The ominous, the insignificant, the great, the small, the wonderful, the commonplace—all appeared before my mental vision in magical succession. Pages of my history were recalled which had been so long forgotten that they seemed to belong to a previous existence. I heard all the voices of the past laughing, crying, telling what I had heard them tell in many corners of the earth.

The loneliness of my state wore off when the gale was high and I 7 found much work to do. When fine weather returned, then came the sense of solitude, which I could not shake off. I used my voice often, at first giving some order about the affairs of a ship, for I had been told that from disuse I should lose my speech. At the meridian altitude of the sun I called aloud, "Eight bells," after the custom on a ship at sea. Again from my cabin I cried to an imaginary man at the helm, "How does she head, there?" and again, "Is she on her course?" But getting no reply, I was reminded the more palpably of my condition. My voice sounded hollow on the empty air, and I dropped the practice. However, it was not long before the thought came to me that when I was a lad I used to sing; why not try that now, where it would disturb no one? My musical talent had never bred envy in others, but out on the Atlantic, to realize what it meant, you should have heard me sing. You should have seen the porpoises leap when I pitched my voice for the waves and the sea and all that was in it. Old turtles, with large eyes, poked their heads up out of the sea as I sang "Johnny Boker," and "We'll Pay Darby Doyl for his Boots," and the like. But the porpoises were, on the whole, vastly more appreciative than the turtles; they jumped a deal higher. One day when I was humming a favorite chant, I think it was "Babylon's a-Fallin'," a porpoise jumped higher than the bowsprit. Had the *Spray* been going a little faster she would have scooped him in. The sea-birds sailed around rather shy.

8   July 10, eight days at sea, the *Spray* was twelve hundred miles east of Cape Sable. One hundred and fifty miles a day for so small a vessel must be considered good sailing. It was the greatest run the *Spray* ever made before or since in so few days. On the evening of July 14, in better humor than ever before, all hands cried, "Sail ho!" The sail was a barkantine, three points on the weather bow, hull down. Then came the night. My ship was sailing along now without attention to the helm. The wind was south; she was heading east. Her sails were trimmed like the sails of the nautilus. They drew steadily all night. I went frequently on deck, but found all well. A merry breeze kept on from the south. Early in the morning of the 15th the *Spray* was close aboard the stranger, which proved to be *La Vaguisa* of Vigo, twenty-three days from Philadelphia, bound for Vigo. A lookout from his masthead had spied the *Spray* the evening before. The captain, when I came near enough, threw a line to me and sent a bottle of wine across slung by the neck, and very good wine it was. He also sent his card, which bore the name of Juan Gantes. I think he was a good man, as Spaniards go. But when I asked him to report me "all well" (the *Spray* passing him in a lively manner), he hauled his shoulders much above his head; and when his mate, who knew of my expedition, told him that I was alone, he crossed himself and made for his cabin. I did not see him again. By sundown he was as far astern as he had been ahead the evening before.

9   There was now less and less monotony. On July 16 the wind was northwest and clear, the sea smooth, and a large bark, hull down, came in sight on the lee bow, and at 2:30 P.M. I spoke the stranger. She was

the bark *Java* of Glasgow, from Peru for Queenstown for orders. Her
old captain was bearish, but I met a bear once in Alaska that looked
pleasanter. At least, the bear seemed pleased to meet me, but this
grizzly old man! Well, I suppose my hail disturbed his siesta, and my
little sloop passing his great ship had somewhat the effect on him that a
red rag has upon a bull. I had the advantage over heavy ships, by long
odds, in the light winds of this and the two previous days. The wind
was light; his ship was heavy and foul, making poor headway, while the
Spray, with a great mainsail bellying even to light winds, was just
skipping along as nimbly as one could wish. "How long has it been
calm about here?" roared the captain of the *Java,* as I came within hail
of him. "Dunno, cap'n," I shouted back as loud as I could bawl. "I
haven't been here long." At this the mate on the forecastle wore a
broad grin. "I left Cape Sable fourteen days ago," I added. (I was now
well across toward the Azores.) "Mate," he roared to his chief officer—"mate, come here and listen to the Yankee's yarn. Haul down
the flag, mate, haul down the flag!" In the best of humor, after all, the
Java surrendered to the *Spray.*

The acute pain of solitude experienced at first never returned. I had 10
penetrated a mystery, and, by the way, I had sailed through a fog. I had
met Neptune in his wrath, but he found that I had not treated him with
contempt, and so he suffered me to go on and explore.

In the log for July 18 there is this entry: "Fine weather, wind south- 11
southwest. Porpoises gamboling all about. The S. S. *Olympia* passed at
11:30 A.M., long. W. 34° 50'."

"It lacks now three minutes of the half-hour," shouted the captain, 12
as he gave me the longitude and the time. I admired the businesslike air
of the *Olympia;* but I have the feeling still that the captain was just a
little too precise in his reckoning. That may be all well enough, however, where there is plenty of sea-room. But over-confidence, I believe, was the cause of the disaster to the liner *Atlantic,* and many more
like her. The captain knew too well where he was. There were no
porpoises at all skipping along with the *Olympia!* Porpoises always
prefer sailing-ships. The captain was a young man, I observed, and had
before him, I hope, a good record.

Land ho! On the morning of July 19 a mystic dome like a mountain 13
of silver stood alone in the sea ahead. Although the land was completely hidden by the white, glistening haze that shone in the sun like
polished silver, I felt quite sure that it was Flores Island. At half-past
four P.M. it was abeam. The haze in the meantime had disappeared.
Flores is one hundred and seventy-four miles from Fayal, and although
it is a high island, it remained many years undiscovered after the
principal group of the islands had been colonized.

Early on the morning of July 20 I saw Pico looming above the clouds 14 on the starboard bow. Lower lands burst forth as the sun burned away the morning fog, and island after island came into view. As I approached nearer, cultivated fields appeared, "and oh, how green the corn!" Only those who have seen the Azores from the deck of a vessel realize the beauty of the mid-ocean picture.

15   At 4:30 P.M. I cast anchor at Fayal, exactly eighteen days from Cape Sable. The American consul, in a smart boat, came alongside before the *Spray* reached the breakwater, and a young naval officer, who feared for the safety of my vessel, boarded, and offered his services as pilot. The youngster, I have no good reason to doubt, could have handled a man-of-war, but the *Spray* was too small for the amount of uniform he wore. However, after fouling all the craft in port and sinking a lighter, she was moored without much damage to herself. This wonderful pilot expected a "gratification," I understood, but whether for the reason that his government, and not I, would have to pay the cost of raising the lighter, or because he did not sink the *Spray*, I could never make out. But I forgive him.

16   It was the season for fruit when I arrived at the Azores, and there was soon more of all kinds of it put on board than I knew what to do with. Islanders are always the kindest people in the world, and I met none anywhere kinder than the good hearts of this place. The people of the Azores are not a very rich community. The burden of taxes is heavy, with scant privileges in return, the air they breathe being about the only thing that is not taxed. The mother-country does not even allow them a port of entry for a foreign mail service. A packet passing never so close with mails for Horta must deliver them first in Lisbon, ostensibly to be fumigated, but really for the tariff from the packet. My own letters posted at Horta reached the United States six days behind my letter from Gibraltar, mailed thirteen days later.

17   The day after my arrival at Horta was the feast of a great saint. Boats loaded with people came from other islands to celebrate at Horta, the capital, or Jerusalem, of the Azores. The deck of the *Spray* was crowded from morning till night with men, women, and children. On the day after the feast a kind-hearted native harnessed a team and drove me a day over the beautiful roads all about Fayal, "because," said he, in broken English, "when I was in America and couldn't speak a word of English, I found it hard till I met some one who seemed to have time to listen to my story, and I promised my good saint then that if ever a stranger came to my country I would try to make him happy." Unfortunately, this gentleman brought along an interpreter, that I might "learn more of the country." The fellow was nearly the death of me, talking of ships and voyages, and of the boats he had steered, the last thing in the world I wished to hear. He had sailed out of New Bedford, so he said, for "that Joe Wing they call 'John.'" My friend

and host found hardly a chance to edge in a word. Before we parted my host dined me with a cheer that would have gladdened the heart of a prince, but he was quite alone in his house. "My wife and children all rest there," said he, pointing to the churchyard across the way. "I moved to this house from far off," he added, "to be near the spot, where I pray every morning."

I remained four days at Fayal, and that was two days more than I 18 had intended to stay. It was the kindness of the islanders and their touching simplicity which detained me. A damsel, as innocent as an angel, came alongside one day, and said she would embark on the *Spray* if I would land her at Lisbon. She could cook flying-fish, she thought, but her forte was dressing *bacalhao*. Her brother Antonio, who served as interpreter, hinted that, anyhow, he would like to make the trip. Antonio's heart went out to one John Wilson, and he was ready to sail for America by way of the two capes to meet his friend. "Do you know John Wilson of Boston?" he cried. "I knew a John Wilson," I said, "but not of Boston." "He had one daughter and one son," said Antonio, by way of identifying his friend. If this reaches the right John Wilson, I am told to say that "Antonio of Pico remembers him."

FOR DISCUSSION

1. At one point Captain Slocum's book, *Sailing Alone Around the World,* was required reading in the public schools. Can you surmise why?

2. This account is an example of a masterpiece of vivid story telling. Locate examples from this excerpt that illustrate vividness and expert narrative writing.

3. Even though the *Spray* was the first craft that circumnavigated the globe with a one-man crew, the tone of *Sailing Alone Around the World* is not one of boasting or bragging. Discuss Slocum's tone, especially *how* he establishes it in the essay and *why* this tone is appropriate.

4. Who was the audience for this writing? What specifically does Slocum do to reach this audience? How does he do this?

5. Discuss the value of personal experience writing, in light of the fact that this excerpt was written over 80 years ago and you are reading it now. (Captain Slocum left in 1909 on another voyage in the *Spray*, but he and the boat were "never heard from again.

Somewhere on the high seas the captain's luck ran out.'') What about the value for Captain Slocum? Remembering what Peter Rosenwald said about reasons for writing, discuss Captain Slocum's book as a keeping permanent of memory, etc.

CHUCK ANDERSON

Chuck Anderson, a student at the University of Iowa, wrote this personal essay for his baby on her second birthday. Read the essay in light of its universal appeal.

For You, Julie, February 27, 1982

> A time it was,
> And what a time it was.
> It was
> A time of innocence,
> A time of confidences.
> Long ago it must be,
> I have a photograph.
> Preserve your memories;
> They're all that's left you.

> —Paul Simon

1   One of my very favorite pictures of you, Julie, shows you looking up from the bottom of your crib. You are just awakening from your nap. The afternoon sun lights your room perfectly for natural light pictures. I look and am there with you again.

2   At first you move slowly, sleepily. Then your uncertain baby head begins to bob and weave. You rediscover your small world, finding your sheets, your bear, and your plastic bumpers, as usual, fascinating. Suddenly you see me above you, sitting and recording this moment, ignoring the urge to pick you up as best I can. Sleepy, tentative questions in perfect blue eyes become definitive statements. "Here I am!" they say. You add a smile, a laugh, and a shy little foray into your blanket.

No soap. I don't respond. I am only an observer observing. 3

So you show me your five months old tricks. You roll over this way. 4
You roll over that way, looking up at your dad, expecting action. You
laugh out loud, enticingly. A single squint-eyed glance accuses me of
neglect, the only unpardonable sin in your world.

I laugh, put down my camera, and swing my beautiful, tricky daugh- 5
ter out of her bed and onto my lap.

You win. 6

And you know it. . . . 7

In our family we have two sets of photo albums. One for us, your 8
mom and I, and our friends. And one for you, Julie, and your friends.
Our albums are patchy, sporadic, a picture here, a picture there,
months and years between. Yours are exhaustive, containing pictures
from every month of your life with gaps no bigger than a week or two, a
chronicle of your days, your firsts.

I spent hours this past weekend sorting a hundred and some odd 9
pictures into ours and yours, labeling yours, and putting them in your
new album. Ours I relegated to a pile in my desk drawer, unlabeled and
unorganized.

Sorting through all those pictures made me remember that I'd heard 10
once that pictures are instants of the past captured forever, little bits of
life preserved in Kodacolor, Kodachrome, or black or white. I felt your
life sliding in and out of my hands as I organized your moments into
smaller and smaller, more and more precisely accurate piles, until they
became a succession of points along a perfectly straight line, one picture per point, chronological, from beginning to end.

But all the while, a part of me resisted the imposition. A part of me 11
wanted to respond, to remember, to enter into your past, not as chroni-
cler, but as participant. That part of me sought to understand the implications of the task at hand, of the pictures, and of their ordering.

Not long ago you started doing what I call free-form narratives, 12
monologs in which you incorporate everything you see into one long,
fantastic piece of language, often with recurring themes and questions
just to be sure we are listening. A very recent picture shows you sitting
in the living room, just as you are this morning, with your Puppy, your
catalogs, my shoes, and your blanket, talking.

"I had six dollars. K-Mart. My parents go to school. I had much 13
bigger rocking chair go K-Mart. My boots much bigger. I had much
bigger. We had boots. I said whatsa matter little boy? I said whatsa
matter? He said whatsa matter. He swing it puppy dog. You know
that? I hold puppy dog right away. Some people at de door. Some
people they come in. My boots. They had six dollars. And I had that
much bigger. Why? Why, Daddy? I had that much bigger than my toes.
I taste it. It was good. Wheeeeeeee! Socky, socky, socky, socky.
Plants. I won't touch plants no more. You spank me, Daddy. See? I put

it in de hole. You lika read books now, Puppy? Don't read paper. Play me, please. I had boot. It's bigger. Step on it. I had much bigger. Tie my boots all bigger. Kleenex, please Daddy. I need Kleenex. Insey winsey spider. Rocking chair open. Time to go. Da, da, da, da, da, da. That your watch? Pat me, Daddy. Tickle my back. Don't read no more. Take your watch. I take your watch now. Daddy? That your paper? I want some juice, please (pronounced jupees). Thanks. You made it? OOOOOOOOOO! Six dollars at K-Mart. We go K-Mart today? Brennan coming today? Genivive comin'? Laura my friend? Where Jerome? I make him dance. Jerome dancin'. See, Daddy? You dance him, Daddy? Please, Daddy? My boot so big. One, two, three, four, five, six. A big fat hen. Where Mommy? Asleep? Sleepin', Daddy? My boot so big. Oh my gosh! Look, Daddy! Oh my gosh! Mud in it! Fix it, Daddy. Have some more jupees? Kleenex, please Daddy. Tuna fish. Don't go up here. Work is done. OK. Read book to Puppy. OK. You sit by me. You want somepin' from Santa Claus? OK. Whatsa matter? You have to go to school, Puppy? Uh-oh! We have to clean it up. Wanta see? OK. You sit here. You see. That's it. Whatsa you doin'? Old MacDonald had a farm. We go McDonalds? Puppy, too? Blanket, too? David isn't born yet. He in Germany. Nancy. Randy. Grumpy comin'? Dat's what I need. Grapes. Some milk. I have that s'mornin'. S'good. S'good. I want this one. That's one I need. I need one of those. That. You want one, Puppy? Puppy? I have big boots. Six dollars. We go K-Mart, Daddy?''

14   Not exactly a monolog, not exactly a narrative, certainly a languaging of your world, strangely picturesque, wonderfully a-chronological, inviting me at every pause.

15   In one picture you are making for the coffee table, your arms outstretched, your face intense, a hint of a smile in the corners of your mouth. I'm behind you, a headless figure with arms about to encircle you completely, perhaps to drag you away, perhaps to encourage you forward. Impossible to tell which.

16   That was the day you took your first step. My arms encircle to protect. Then you took eighteen more.

17   "We couldn't believe she took that many steps," your Grammy wrote. "Where are there eighteen steps in a row in your apartment?"

18   When most people look at your albums, they find them visually delightful, but incomplete. They want to know more. "Who's this?" "Where are you here?" "What's that?" "Why is she so dressed up?" "What happened?" "Where was this one taken?" "What's she looking at?" "How old . . .?" Questions that sound like essay exams, but aren't. Questions we answer with words and phrases, mostly names of things, places, and people, explaining without really explaining. Most people accept, no, expect this. They nod their heads yes, taking the

pieces for the whole, and close the books, satisfied, seduced by shapes on cardboard and chronology, believing they know your story.

For Halloween this past year you dressed up as an angel in a white 19 robe, silver wings and halo, and a gold chain belt. Your friend, Cathy, from across the way, dressed as a Cardinal, complete with collar, cross, and floppy red hat. Her father, a Lutheran Seminary graduate, explained,

"Actually, a Cardinal is higher than an angel in God's hierarchy. 20 That's because a Cardinal can hear Confession and grant Absolution, which an angel can't do. All angels are good for is flying around and singing eternal praises. So you see, Cathy is a little higher on the totem pole than Julie."

In the pictures, you both look about equally devilish to me, smiling 21 up at the camera over identical green suckers, wickedly.

There is one picture near the front of your first album that almost 22 captures more than a moment. It is of you and your mother the day after you were born. You are cradled in her right arm; on her left arm is an ID bracelet and an IV needle almost covered with surgical tape. You have that skrunched-up newborn baby look. She wears a strangely wistful look, an ambiguous blending of joy and sorrow. It is a look I remember well, will not ever forget.

Scattered, through your albums are your friends. Charley, Katie, 23 Erin G., Kevin, Shorey, Big Katie, Kristi, Angela, Becky, Gary, Clay, Erin A., Nathan, Kathi, Ken, Cathy, Lori, Laura, Paula, Bob, Jennifer, Bobby, Deanna, Michelle, Brandon, Cindy, Dave, Danny, Stephanie, Tom, Ricky, Monty, Katie L, and a host of others.

And your animals and babies. Puppy, Time Out, Baby, Rabbit, 24 Rabbit, Bear, Bear, Bear, Reggie, Anabel, Jerome, Becky, Monkey, Snoopy, Dexter, Snake, Myrtle, Sea Serpent, Woodstock, Zeph, Rudolph, and K-Mart Baby.

I can't remember all their names, but you can. And you know where 25 they fit into your life, how they contribute to your history, miraculous for 23 months old, complete, un-photolike. . . .

There's a sequence of pictures from May of 1980 that were taken on 26 a trip that Grammy and Grumpy gave us so we could come to Texas and show you off for the first time. It begins with a picture of you in your stroller holding a plane ticket and ends with one of Grampa playing Trac-Ball in Great Granny Albers' backyard in Austin, Texas. In between are cousins and friends and aunts and uncles and grandparents and great grandparents, all arranged around a central theme, Julie. Everyone looks happy. Smiles and laughter light up every face.

But something is missing. Something important. The stress and 27 strain of traveling with a six-week old baby, the long nights walking the floor when your schedule got completely confused, the anger of not having tickets to get back on, and the total, wonderful release of getting home.

28   The last picture in your album, for now, is another one of you in your bed. You have all your babies and animals piled around you. A huge smile lights up your whole face. A perfect picture of childlike happiness and innocence.

29   But your mother and I remember it as "one of those days." You had cried and whined all morning long with snotty nose and incessant demands for attention. Your mother had made you sit in your room, and I had spanked you twice. Then you had hugged us both before your nap and told us that you loved us. You woke up happy as that picture, told us again that you loved us, and dirtied your pants three times in a row.

30   And that is why I write to you. Because your pictures tell only part of your story. They are keys to the past, not the past; not moments, hints. They are only colors and shapes on cardboard, 1/250th of a second projected against the fullness and complexity of your whole self. Individually, they are invitations to participate in your life, to live and relive the trips, the ambiguity, the smiles, the anger, the I love you's. Collectively, they impose an illusion of completeness, a thesis of absolute fixity argued chronologically through the pages of your albums, beginning to end. But they are not complete. They lack the associations that tie all the hints together, not always chornologically, but certainly, to bring you to life before me, here, now, in memory.

FOR DISCUSSION

Chuck Anderson said this about the writing of this essay:

> I wrote the essay in its original form as an act of memory, so that I would not forget the things that surrounded Julie's first two years. Secondarily, I wrote it as a piece to submit to a writing class I was in, not really for discussion, but to show off a little (you know how I am).
>
> I had as long as I needed to write it. It took me almost two years to work the stuff out enough to be able to begin, and about five very intense days to get a draft ready for the typewriter—not a final one. After that I felt completely finished with it. I still see some very minor things I'd like to fine tune, but not too much.
>
> As I said, my real intention was to remember it all. Actually, the piece was to be a bit for the place in Julie's baby book that says, "A few words from Daddy." By the time I got it to final draft, I wanted to create something I could hand her someday to tell her things I

might not ever be able to say. I wanted to give her something I think most of us wish our fathers had given us.

I can't even begin to explain the revision process. I began with eighteen pages and cut it down to sharpen and focus the emotional impact of what I had to say.

The question of audience is an interesting one. Originally, I wrote the essay in third person so that it would speak to a wider audience, specifically, my writing class. But as I typed it, I was struck by the possibility that I might do it for Julie. I think this shift in audience created some tension. Some members of my class hated the essay because they didn't want to get that close to anybody. I think the final audience is one that includes only people who will care about the piece, my close friends, and my family. The rest don't really matter. Though I still toy with the possibilities of the third person.

1. Do you think Chuck is right—that the final audience will be his family, close friends, and people who will care about the piece? Is there anything in the phrase "People who will care about the piece" that automatically and swiftly enlarges the audience from family and close friends? Who *will* care about the piece?

2. This essay took two years and five days to write. Discuss this process.

3. In what way is the fact that this essay is to Julie herself an important part of its impact on the reader?

4. What value was the writing of this essay to Chuck himself? What value is there to you, the reader?

5. What keeps this essay from being a piece of self-indulgence? What keeps it from being only a family keepsake?

6. How is this essay organized? Into what parts does it fall? What is the "logic" of these parts?

7. What will you remember from the essay?

SCOTT MOZISEK

Often things happen to people that are so emotional—happy, sad, shocking, moving—that the experience needs to be written down so that the writer can get it off his or her mind. This kind of writing can be very powerful to read, because often the writer is able to recapture the experience so vividly that the readers feel they were there. Here a college freshman, Scott Mozisek, writes about the sudden death of his friend. This is a very personal essay.

Death

Wade died today; coming home from school.
We were walking by the highway.
That car was coming so fast; we could hear the engine racing behind us.

Those two kids ran past us on the sidewalk.
They didn't stop at the corner; just kept running, right into the street.
They didn't see the car; didn't even look.

Wade started running.

A foot locked the brakes, and the car began singing.

The kids, they finally saw it.
But one kid froze.

Wade was at the corner.

The other kid made the side of the street.

Wade was in the street.

I was running, too.

The car was getting near(er).

Wade's long, lean strides ruffled the back of his shirt.

The car was beside me, sliding.

Miles in front of us, Wade was reaching out toward the kid.

The car was close. So close. Too close.

Wade was at the kid, grasping him under the arms, lifting, pushing him through the air.

The car was there. Time stopped; Wade had run out.

Wade twisted as the hood pushed in his hip, his knees molded like a bumper. He was the front of the car until his feet jerked out and up from under it, flipping him onto his back on the hood.

With his legs high above his body, he hit the windshield with his face and cracked it, his shoulder breaking it out. His chest caught the roof at the end of the window with such force that it hurled him up and over the back of the car toward the roadside.

The back of Wade's neck touched ground first, his legs coming down behind his head. He rolled and scraped in the gravel as he slid off the road into the grass.

When Wade finally came to rest he was flat on his back. Just lying there, with no contorted expression or twisted muscles. Just lying there, simply and quietly in the grass by the road.

The car stopped.

I was standing in the road, staring.

I walked across to Wade thinking about how long we had been friends. Always.

The things we did: swimming, traveling, running, fighting. How we were going out with Jill and Susan tonight.

Always "Wade and I."

So much we were going to do: college, business. How much we had planned.

Always "Wade and I."

Always together.

Standing over him, watching his living pour itself out of his body, I knew our friendship had been—postponed.

Wade's Dead.

FOR DISCUSSION

1. How does the *form* of this essay convey the experience of the essay?

2. This essay was written for a college freshman English class. What time restrictions might you guess were imposed on the author as a requirement for the assignment?

3. How is the sentence "Wade had run out" connected to the title of the essay? What other examples such as this can you find in the essay?

4. What can you say about the audience for this essay?

5. What keeps this essay from being valuable only to the writer?

6. What makes the description in this essay so effective?

7. What impact does the essay have on you? To what can you attribute that impact?

WRITING YOUR OWN
The Personal Experience Essay

Let's take a look now at the configuration for Maya Angelou's personal experience essay, "Graduation in Stamps."

Motivation (an educated guess): to tell the story of her graduation from eighth grade.
to share her insights about growing up as a black girl in a rural American town in the '30s.
to share a revelation she had during graduation about the black experience and her heritage.

Circumstance/Situation: autobiography—she is telling *her* story.

Audience: all human beings.

Writer's Relationship to Audience: storyteller to listener.
person who has experienced a serious discrimination to both those who have and have not shared this experience.

Emphasis: on the narrative itself—the *experience* of graduation.
on her *feelings* and how they changed during the story.
on the transformation of her outlook—her renewed sense of self-esteem and pride at being black, at being a survivor.

Form: book.

Intention (an educated guess): to share a meaningful memory, and perhaps—in the process of telling it—to come to a better understanding of her experience.

Before you begin to plan your own personal experience essay, you might try to determine the configurations of the other essays in this chapter.

DESIGNING YOUR OWN CONFIGURATION

Here are some suggestions for possible topics to use in creating your own personal experience essay:

1. Look at each essay in this section. Think about an incident in your own life which would correspond to the subject of each essay. Choose one of these to write your own personal experience essay.

2. For a writing contest in *Redbook* magazine write a personal experience essay which is called "A Day After Which I Was Never the Same."

3. Pretend that you are being interviewed for a job. The interviewer has just asked you to tell a story about your childhood. Write an essay based on this request, an essay which would give the interviewer an inside view of your life as a child.

4. Your family is putting together a history in which each member is writing something about her or his life. Write the personal experience essay which you would like to be a part of this scrap book, an essay based on some incident which you would like the family to know about or remember you by.

Use this chart to select an audience, place of presentation, motivation, etc., for your own essay.

Designing Your Own Configuration for a Personal Experience Essay

MOTIVATION	CIRCUMSTANCE/ SITUATION	AUDIENCE	RELATIONSHIP TO AUDIENCE
To tell a story you have been wanting to tell	For a Most Memorable Moment column of x magazine	Readers of x magazine	Friend to friend
To sell a story		Classmates	Story teller to listener
To win a contest		Professor	Person who has done or lived it to person who has not
To honor someone with your story	For a speech at a toastmaster's club	General public	
To meet a classroom assignment	For your own pleasure or use	A specific club	Person who can tell a good story about x experience to person who has had the same experience
To get something off your mind	For a letter you are writing after a trip		
To give an insight	For x magazine as a feature article		

EMPHASIS	FORM	INTENTION
On the experience	Essay	To have reader remember x
On the story	Article	To complete x for the writer
On the details	Story	To provide an insight about x
On the writer's life, sensibilities, and experiences		To entertain
		To delight
		To instruct
		To enjoy telling a story
		To enjoy remembering x for her/himself

RULES FOR A PERSONAL EXPERIENCE ESSAY

1. Think of a personal experience essay as an opportunity for your readers to know more about you.
2. Choose an incident, occasion, event, or situation which you remember vividly and which will be interesting to other people and make it the focus of your essay.

3. Think always of your audience: what do they need to know to understand what happened, what will make them feel they are *there*?

4. Use vivid language. ("Vivid" here means forming clear or striking mental images; clearly perceived by the mind; bringing strikingly realistic or lifelike images to the mind)

5. Tell a good story.

RHETORICAL PATTERNS OFTEN USED IN PERSONAL EXPERIENCE ESSAYS

Description: How to Present Sharp, Focused Pictures

1. Appeal to *all* the reader's senses: sight, smell, touch, hearing, taste. Be very specific.

2. *Select* the details you want to include in the description so that they give one main impression of the object, person, or scene. Don't try to describe everything at once. This means that you will choose details according to what your purpose is at the time.

Narration: How to Tell a Good Story

1. Be sure to give the reader a clear time order. Provide a clear sequence of events. Often this sequence will be *chronological*— first this happened, then this, then that. . . . You may, however, use a *flashback* technique in which you show an earlier scene and then relate that scene to the main story you are telling at the moment.

2. Let your readers feel the *action* of your story. Don't just tell them *about* what happened. Let them *live* through what happened. Make a movie of the sequence of actions. The more *immediate* the details and the more *descriptive* the scenes, the more your readers will feel a part of what is going on in the story.

3. Be very *selective* in the details you choose. Don't give the readers a lot of information they don't need to understand to see your story. Stick to details that are directly related to your purpose in telling the story.

4. Decide on a *point of view*. Very likely the *first person point of view* (when the author/narrator is a character in the story) will be the easiest way to tell a story that has happened to you. Later, however, when you are using narration as part of other pieces of writing, you may want to adopt the *omniscient point of view*, in which the writer knows everything and gives an objective, outside account of the sequence of events.

Writing to Express

The Personal Perspective Essay

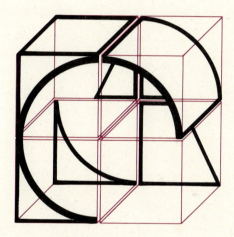

There are occasions when a writer gives a personal opinion or a personal view that does not have to be supported, documented, or even explained. The writer of a personal perspective essay is saying, "This is how I see the world; this is what I think." And although the reader may or may not agree, agreement is not what the writing is about. The writing exists because the writer wanted to say something about her or his view of the world. It's as if the writer were standing on top of a mountain and calling down, "This is what I am seeing from here."

Reading personal perspective essays can be enlightening, amusing, angering, thought-provoking, enjoyable, or boring. Sometimes we learn to see things a new way. Sometimes we realize that we still see something our way in spite of reading what a writer has said. Sometimes we take what a writer thinks and incorporate it into our own view of the world where it both changes and stays the same.

One of the most enjoyable aspects of reading personal perspective essays is just the opportunity to look at the world through other people's eyes—to see, for a moment, what they see. Since each of us can never live long enough to see all places or have ideas on all things, reading what other people see in their own worlds is broadening and enlarging and, ultimately, a lot of fun.

As you read the following essays, ask yourself these questions:

What can I learn about the writer from this essay?
Is this a perspective I have never thought of before?
How did the writer gain this perspective?
What is my own reaction to reading this writer's view?

MAY SARTON

In this personal statement May Sarton, the novelist and poet, argues that living alone brings many rewards. Her essay first appeared on the editorial page of the New York Times *in 1975.*

Rewards of Living a Solitary Life

The other day an acquaintance of mine, a gregarious and charming man, told me he had found himself unexpectedly alone in New York for an hour or two between appointments. He went to the Whitney and spent the "empty" time looking at things in solitary bliss. For him it proved to be a shock nearly as great as falling in love to discover that he could enjoy himself so much alone. 1

What had he been afraid of, I asked myself? That, suddenly alone, he would discover that he bored himself, or that there was, quite simply, no self there to meet? But having taken the plunge, he is now on the brink of adventure; he is about to be launched into his own inner space, space as immense, unexplored and sometimes frightening as outer space to the astronaut. 2

His every perception will come to him with a new freshness and, for a time, seem startlingly original. For anyone who can see things for himself with a naked eye becomes, for a moment or two, something of a genius. 3

With another human being present vision becomes double vision, inevitably. We are busy wondering, what does my companion see or think of this, and what do I think of it? The original impact gets lost, or diffused. 4

"Music I heard with you was more than music." Exactly. And therefore music *itself* can only be heard alone. Solitude is the salt of personhood. It brings out the authentic flavor of every experience. 5

"Alone one is never lonely: the spirit adventures, walking/In a quiet garden, in a cool house, abiding single there." 6

Loneliness is most acutely felt with other people, for with others, even with a lover sometimes, we suffer from our differences, differences of taste, temperament, mood. Human intercourse often demands that we soften the edge of perception, or withdraw at the very instant of personal truth for fear of hurting, or of being inappropriately present, which is to say naked, in a social situation. Alone we can afford to be wholly whatever we are, and to feel whatever we feel absolutely. That is a great luxury! 7

8   For me the most interesting thing about a solitary life, and mine has been that for the last twenty years, is that it becomes increasingly rewarding. When I can wake up and watch the sun rise over the ocean, as I do most days, and know that I have an entire day ahead, uninterrupted, in which to write a few pages, take a walk with my dog, lie down in the afternoon for a long think (why does one think better in a horizontal position?), read and listen to music, I am flooded with happiness.

9   I am lonely only when I am overtired, when I have worked too long without a break, when for the time being I feel empty and need filling up. And I am lonely sometimes when I come back home after a lecture trip, when I have seen a lot of people and talked a lot, and am full to the brim with experience that needs to be sorted out.

10   Then for a little while the house feels huge and empty, and I wonder where my self is hiding. It has to be recaptured slowly by watering the plants, perhaps, and looking again at each one as though it were a person, by feeding the two cats, by cooking a meal.

11   It takes a while, as I watch the surf blowing up in fountains at the end of the field, but the moment comes when the world falls away, and the self emerges again from the deep unconscious, bringing back all I have recently experienced to be explored and slowly understood, when I can converse again with my own hidden powers, and so grow, and so be renewed, till death do us part.

FOR DISCUSSION

1. Make a list of the rewards the author describes in living alone. Where are these placed in the essay in relation to the less positive aspects of living alone? What can you say about this positioning and the effect it has on the reader?

2. What is the proportion of pros to cons in this essay?

3. Considering that this essay first appeared on the editorial page of the *New York Times,* what audience do you think it was written for?

4. Imagine that you are to rewrite this piece as an assertion-with-evidence essay. What would you change about it?

5. What comes through to you in this essay about the personality of the author? How well do you feel you know her?

RICHARD RODRIGUEZ

In this excerpt from his autobiography, published in 1981, Richard Rodriguez asserts that bilingual education is a detriment to school-children who speak a native language which is not English. A Mexican-American who grew up in California, Rodriguez uses his own personal experience as a point of departure for his writing.

from Hunger of Memory

Supporters of bilingual education today imply that students like me 1
miss a great deal by not being taught in their family's language. What
they seem not to recognize is that, as a socially disadvantaged child, I
considered Spanish to be a private language. What I needed to learn in
school was that I had the right—and the obligation—to speak the
public language of *los gringos*. The odd truth is that my first-grade
classmates could have become bilingual, in the conventional sense of
that word, more easily than I. Had they been taught (as upper-middle-
class children are often taught early) a second language like Spanish or
French, they could have regarded it simply as that: another public
language. In my case such bilingualism could not have been so quickly
achieved. What I did not believe was that I could speak a single public
language.

Without question, it would have pleased me to hear my teachers 2
address me in Spanish when I entered the classroom. I would have felt
much less afraid. I would have trusted them and responded with ease.
But I would have delayed—for how long postponed?—having to learn
the language of public society. I would have evaded—and for how long
could I have afforded to delay?—learning the great lesson of school,
that I had a public identity.

Fortunately, my teachers were unsentimental about their responsi- 3
bility. What they understood was that I needed to speak a public
language. So their voices would search me out, asking me questions.
Each time I'd hear them, I'd look up in surprise to see a nun's face
frowning at me. I'd mumble, not really meaning to answer. The nun
would persist, 'Richard, stand up. Don't look at the floor. Speak up.
Speak to the entire class, not just to me!' But I couldn't believe that the
English language was mine to use. (In part, I did not want to believe it.)
I continued to mumble. I resisted the teacher's demands. (Did I somehow suspect that once I learned public language my pleasing family life

would be changed?) Silent, waiting for the bell to sound, I remained dazed, diffident, afraid.

4   Because I wrongly imagined that English was intrinsically a public language and Spanish an intrinsically private one, I easily noted the difference between classroom language and the language of home. At school, words were directed to a general audience of listeners. ('Boys and girls.') Words were meaningfully ordered. And the point was not self-expression alone but to make oneself understood by many others. The teacher quizzed: 'Boys and girls, why do we use that word in this sentence? Could we think of a better word to use there? Would the sentence change its meaning if the words were differently arranged? And wasn't there a better way of saying much the same thing?' (I couldn't say. I wouldn't try to say.)

5   Three months. Five. Half a year passed. Unsmiling, ever watchful, my teachers noted my silence. They began to connect my behavior with the difficult progress my older sister and brother were making. Until one Saturday morning three nuns arrived at the house to talk to our parents. Stiffly, they sat on the blue living room sofa. From the doorway of another room, spying the visitors, I noted the incongruity—the clash of two worlds, the faces and voices of school intruding upon the familiar setting of home. I overheard one voice gently wondering, 'Do your children speak only Spanish at home, Mrs. Rodriguez?' While another voice added, 'That Richard especially seems so timid and shy.'

6   *That Rich-heard!*

7   With great tact the visitors continued, 'Is it possible for you and your husband to encourage your children to practice their English when they are home?' Of course, my parents complied. What would they not do for their children's well-being? And how could they have questioned the Church's authority which those women represented? In an instant, they agreed to give up the language (the sounds) that had revealed and accentuated our family's closeness. The moment after the visitors left, the change was observed. '*Ahora,* speak to us *en inglés,*' my father and mother united to tell us.

8   At first, it seemed a kind of game. After dinner each night, the family gathered to practice 'our' English. (It was still then *inglés,* a language foreign to us, so we felt drawn as strangers to it.) Laughing, we would try to define words we could not pronounce. We played with strange English sounds, often overanglicizing our pronunciations. And we filled the smiling gaps of our sentences with familiar Spanish sounds. But that was cheating, somebody shouted. Everyone laughed. In school, meanwhile, like my brother and sister, I was required to attend a daily tutoring session. I needed a full year of special attention. I also needed my teachers to keep my attention from straying in class by calling out, *Rich-heard*—their English voices slowly prying loose my

ties to my other name, its three notes, *Ri-car-do*. Most of all I needed to hear my mother and father speak to me in a moment of seriousness in broken—suddenly heartbreaking—English. The scene was inevitable: One Saturday morning I entered the kitchen where my parents were talking in Spanish. I did not realize that they were talking in Spanish however until, at the moment they saw me, I heard their voices change to speak English. Those *gringo* sounds they uttered startled me. Pushed me away. In that moment of trivial misunderstanding and profound insight, I felt my throat twisted by unsounded grief. I turned quickly and left the room. But I had no place to escape to with Spanish. (The spell was broken.) My brother and sisters were speaking English in another part of the house.

Again and again in the days following, increasingly angry, I was 9 obliged to hear my mother and father: 'Speak to us *en inglés*.' (*Speak*.) Only then did I determine to learn classroom English. Weeks after, it happened: One day in school I raised my hand to volunteer an answer. I spoke out in a loud voice. And I did not think it remarkable when the entire class understood. That day, I moved very far from the disadvantaged child I had been only days earlier. The belief, the calming assurance that I belonged in public, had at last taken hold.

Shortly after, I stopped hearing the high and loud sounds of *los* 10 *gringos*. A more and more confident speaker of English, I didn't trouble to listen to *how* strangers sounded, speaking to me. And there simply were too many English-speaking people in my day for me to hear American accents anymore. Conversations quickened. Listening to persons who sounded eccentrically pitched voices, I usually noted their sounds for an initial few seconds before I concentrated on *what* they were saying. Conversations became content-full. Transparent. Hearing someone's *tone* of voice—angry or questioning or sarcastic or happy or sad—I didn't distinguish it from the words it expressed. Sound and word were thus tightly wedded. At the end of a day, I was often bemused, always relieved, to realize how 'silent,' though crowded with words, my day in public had been. (This public silence measured and quickened the change in my life.)

At last, seven years old, I came to believe what had been technically 11 true since my birth: I was an American citizen.

But the special feeling of closeness at home was diminished by then. 12 Gone was the desperate, urgent, intense feeling of being at home; rare was the experience of feeling myself individualized by family intimates. We remained a loving family, but one greatly changed. No longer so close; no longer bound tight by the pleasing and troubling knowledge of our public separateness. Neither my older brother nor sister rushed home after school anymore. Nor did I. When I arrived home there would often be neighborhood kids in the house. Or the house would be empty of sounds.

13   Following the dramatic Americanization of their children, even my parents grew more publicly confident. Especially my mother. She learned the names of all the people on our block. And she decided we needed to have a telephone installed in the house. My father continued to use the word *gringo*. But it was no longer charged with the old bitterness or distrust. (Stripped of any emotional content, the word simply became a name for those Americans not of Hispanic descent.) Hearing him, sometimes, I wasn't sure if he was pronouncing the Spanish word *gringo* or saying gringo in English.

14   Matching the silence I started hearing in public was a new quiet at home. The family's quiet was partly due to the fact that, as we children learned more and more English, we shared fewer and fewer words with our parents. Sentences needed to be spoken slowly when a child addressed his mother or father. (Often the parent wouldn't understand.) The child would need to repeat himself. (Still the parent misunderstood.) The young voice, frustrated, would end up saying, 'Never mind'—the subject was closed. Dinners would be noisy with the clinking of knives and forks against dishes. My mother would smile softly between her remarks; my father at the other end of the table would chew and chew at his food, while he stared over the heads of his children.

15   My *mother!* My *father!* After English became my primary language, I no longer knew what words to use in addressing my parents. The old Spanish words (those tender accents of sound) I had used earlier— *mamá* and *papá*—I couldn't use anymore. They would have been too painful reminders of how much had changed in my life. On the other hand, the words I heard neighborhood kids call *their* parents seemed equally unsatisfactory. *Mother* and *Father; Ma, Papa, Pa, Dad, Pop* (how I hated the all-American sound of that last word especially)—all these terms I felt were unsuitable, not really terms of address for *my* parents. As a result, I never used them at home. Whenever I'd speak to my parents, I would try to get their attention with eye contact alone. In public conversations, I'd refer to 'my parents' or 'my mother and father.'

16   My mother and father, for their part, responded differently, as their children spoke to them less. She grew restless, seemed troubled and anxious at the scarcity of words exchanged in the house. It was she who would question me about my day when I came home from school. She smiled at small talk. She pried at the edges of my sentences to get me to say something more. (What?) She'd join conversations she overhead, but her intrusions often stopped her children's talking. By contrast, my father seemed reconciled to the new quiet. Though his English improved somewhat, he retired into silence. At dinner he spoke very little. One night his children and even his wife helplessly giggled at his garbled English pronunciation of the Catholic Grace

before Meals. Thereafter he made his wife recite the prayer at the start of each meal, even on formal occasions, when there were guests in the house. Hers became the public voice of the family. On official business, it was she, not my father, one would usually hear on the phone or in stores, talking to strangers. His children grew so accustomed to his silence that, years later, they would speak routinely of his shyness. (My mother would often try to explain: Both his parents died when he was eight. He was raised by an uncle who treated him like little more than a menial servant. He was never encouraged to speak. He grew up alone. A man of few words.) But my father was not shy, I realized, when I'd watch him speaking Spanish with relatives. Using Spanish, he was quickly effusive. Especially when talking with other men, his voice would spark, flicker, flare alive with sounds. In Spanish, he expressed ideas and feelings he rarely revealed in English. With firm Spanish sounds, he conveyed confidence and authority English would never allow him.

The silence at home, however, was finally more than a literal silence. Fewer words passed between parent and child, but more profound was the silence that resulted from my inattention to sounds. At about the time I no longer bothered to listen with care to the sounds of English in public, I grew careless about listening to the sounds family members made when they spoke. Most of the time I heard someone speaking at home and didn't distinguish his sounds from the words people uttered in public. I didn't even pay much attention to my parents' accented and ungrammatical speech. At least not at home. Only when I was with them in public would I grow alert to their accents. Though, even then, their sounds caused me less and less concern. For I was increasingly confident of my own public identity. 17

I would have been happier about my public success had I not 18 sometimes recalled what it had been like earlier, when my family had conveyed its intimacy through a set of conveniently private sounds. Sometimes in public, hearing a stranger, I'd hark back to my past. A Mexican farmworker approached me downtown to ask directions to somewhere. '*¿Hijito* . . . ?' he said. And his voice summoned deep longing. Another time, standing beside my mother in the visiting room of a Carmelite convent, before the dense screen which rendered the nuns shadowy figures, I heard several Spanish-speaking nuns—their busy, singsong overlapping voices—assure us that yes, yes, we were remembered, all our family was remembered in their prayers. (Their voices echoed faraway family sounds.) Another day, a dark-faced old woman—her hand light on my shoulder—steadied herself against me as she boarded a bus. She murmured something I couldn't quite comprehend. Her Spanish voice came near, like the face of a never-before-seen relative in the instant before I was kissed. Her voice, like so many of the Spanish voices I'd hear in public, recalled the golden age of my youth. Hearing Spanish then, I continued to be a careful, if sad, listener to sounds. Hearing a Spanish-speaking family walking behind me, I turned to look. I smiled for an instant, before my glance found the Hispanic-looking faces of strangers in the crowd going by.

19   Today I hear bilingual educators say that children lose a degree of 'individuality' by becoming assimilated into public society. (Bilingual schooling was popularized in the seventies, that decade when middle-class ethnics began to resist the process of assimilation—the American melting pot.) But the bilingualists simplistically scorn the value and necessity of assimilation. They do not seem to realize that there are *two* ways a person is individualized. So they do not realize that while one suffers a diminished sense of *private* individuality by becoming assimilated into public society, such assimilation makes possible the achievement of *public* individuality.

20   The bilingualists insist that a student should be reminded of his difference from others in mass society, his heritage. But they equate mere separateness with individuality. The fact is that only in private— with intimates—is separateness from the crowd a prerequisite for individuality. (An intimate draws me apart, tells me that I am unique, unlike all others.) In public, by contrast, full individuality is achieved, paradoxically, by those who are able to consider themselves members of the crowd. Thus it happened for me: Only when I was able to think of myself as an American, no longer an alien in *gringo* society, could I seek the rights and opportunities necessary for full public individuality. The social and political advantages I enjoy as a man result from the day that I came to believe that my name, indeed, is *Rich-heard Road-ree-guess*. It is true that my public society today is often impersonal. (My public society is usually mass society.) Yet despite the anonymity of the crowd and despite the fact that the individuality I achieve in public is often tenuous—because it depends on my being one in a crowd—I celebrate the day I acquired my new name. Those middle-class ethnics who scorn assimilation seem to me filled with decadent self-pity, obsessed by the burden of public life. Dangerously, they romanticize public separateness and they trivialize the dilemma of the socially disadvantaged.

21   My awkward childhood does not prove the necessity of bilingual education. My story discloses instead an essential myth of childhood— inevitable pain. If I rehearse here the changes in my private life after my Americanization, it is finally to emphasize the public gain. The loss implies the gain: The house I returned to each afternoon was quiet. Intimate sounds no longer rushed to the door to greet me. There were other noises inside. The telephone rang. Neighborhood kids ran past the door of the bedroom where I was reading my schoolbooks— covered with shopping-bag paper. Once I learned public language, it would never again be easy for me to hear intimate family voices. More

and more of my day was spent hearing words. But that may only be a way of saying that the day I raised my hand in class and spoke loudly to an entire roomful of faces, my childhood started to end.

FOR DISCUSSION

1. What did you learn from this essay?
2. What response do you have to Richard Rodriguez' viewpoint?
3. From what "authority" does Rodriguez speak? What does this add to the essay?
4. How does the author keep his writing from *demanding* agreement?
5. What makes this a personal perspective essay and not, say, an information essay?

HELEN KELLER

Helen Keller (1880–1968), who lost her sight and hearing when she was nineteen months old, writes about what she would do if she could see for only three days.

Three Days to See

If I were the president of a university I should establish a compulsory 1 course in "How To Use Your Eyes." The professor would try to show his pupils how they could add joy to their lives by really seeing what passes unnoticed before them. He would try to awake their dormant and sluggish faculties.

Perhaps I can best illustrate my imagining what I should most like to 2 see if I were given the use of my eyes, say, for just three days. And while I am imagining, suppose you, too, set your mind to work on the problem of how you would use your own eyes if you had only three more days to see. If with the oncoming darkness of the third night you knew that the sun would never rise for you again, how would you spend those three precious intervening days? What would you most want to let your gaze rest upon?

3   I, naturally, should want most to see the things which have become dear to me through my years of darkness. You, too, would want to let your eyes rest long on the things that have become dear to you so that you could take the memory of them with you into the night that loomed before you.

4   If, by some miracle, I were granted three seeing days, to be followed by a relapse into darkness, I should divide the period into three parts.

5   On the first day, I should want to see the people whose kindness and gentleness and companionship have made my life worth living. First I should like to gaze long upon the face of my dear teacher, Mrs. Anne Sullivan Macy, who came to me when I was a child and opened the outer world to me. I should want not merely to see the outline of her face, so that I could cherish it in my memory, but to study that face and find in it the living evidence of the sympathetic tenderness and patience with which she accomplished the difficult task of my education. I should like to see in her eyes that strength of character which has enabled her to stand firm in the face of difficulties, and that compassion for all humanity which she has revealed to me so often.

6   I do not know what it is to see into the heart of a friend through that "window of the soul," the eye. I can only "see" through my fingertips the outline of a face. I can detect laughter, sorrow, and many other obvious emotions. I know my friends from the feel of their faces. But I cannot really picture their personalities by touch. I know their personalities, of course, through other means, through the thoughts they express to me, through whatever of their actions are revealed to me. But I am denied that deeper understanding of them which I am sure would come through sight of them, through watching their reactions to various expressed thoughts and circumstances, through noting the immediate and fleeting reactions of their eyes and countenance.

7   Friends who are near to me I know well, because through the months and years they reveal themselves to me in all their phases; but of casual friends I have only an incomplete impression, an impression gained from a handclasp, from spoken words which I take from their lips with my fingertips, or which they tap into the palm of my hand.

8   How much easier, how much more satisfying it is for you who can see to grasp quickly the essential qualities of another person by watching the subtleties of expression, the quiver of a muscle, the flutter of a hand. But does it ever occur to you to use your sight to see into the inner nature of a friend or acquaintance? Do not most of you seeing people grasp casually the outward features of a face and let it go at that?

9   For instance, can you describe accurately the faces of five good friends? Some of you can, but many cannot. As an experiment, I have questioned husbands of long standing about the color of their wives' eyes, and often they express embarrassed confusion and admit that

they do not know. And, incidentally, it is a chronic complaint of wives that their husbands do not notice new dresses, new hats, and changes in household arrangements.

The eyes of seeing persons soon become accustomed to the routine 10 of their surroundings, and they actually see only the startling and spectacular. But even in viewing the most spectacular sights the eyes are lazy. Court records reveal every day how inaccurately "eyewitnesses" see. A given event will be "seen" in several different ways by as many witnesses. Some see more than others, but few see everything that is within the range of their vision.

Oh, the things that I should see if I had the power of sight for just 11 three days!

The first day would be a busy one. I should call to me all my dear 12 friends and look long into their faces, imprinting upon my mind the outward evidences of the beauty that is within them. I should let my eyes rest, too, on the face of a baby, so that I could catch a vision of the eager, innocent beauty which precedes the individual's consciousness of the conflicts which life develops.

And I should like to look into the loyal, trusting eyes of my dogs— 13 the grave, canny little Scottie, Darkie, and the stalwart, understanding Great Dane, Helga, whose warm, tender, and playful friendships are so comforting to me.

On that busy first day I should also view the small simple things of 14 my home. I want to see the warm colors in the rugs under my feet, the pictures on the walls, the intimate trifles that transform a house into home. My eyes would rest respectfully on the books in raised type which I have read, but they would be more eagerly interested in the printed books which seeing people can read, for during the long night of my life the books I have read and those which have been read to me have built themselves into a great shining lighthouse, revealing to me the deepest channels of human life and the human spirit.

In the afternoon of that first seeing day, I should take a long walk in 15 the woods and intoxicate my eyes on the beauties of the world of Nature, trying desperately to absorb in a few hours the vast splendor which is constantly unfolding itself to those who can see. On the way home from my woodland jaunt my path would lie near a farm so that I might see the patient horses plowing in the field (perhaps I should see only a tractor!) and the serene content of men living close to the soil. And I should pray for the glory of a colorful sunset.

When dusk had fallen, I should experience the double delight of 16 being able to see by artificial light, which the genius of man has created to extend the power of his sight when Nature decrees darkness.

In the night of that first day of sight, I should not be able to sleep, so 17 full would be my mind of the memories of the day.

The next day—the second day of sight—I should arise with the 18 dawn and see the thrilling miracle by which night is transformed into day. I should behold with awe the magnificent panorama of light with which the sun awakens the sleeping earth.

19   This day I should devote to a hasty glimpse of the world, past and present. I should want to see the pageant of man's progress, the kaleidoscope of the ages. How can so much be compressed into one day? Through the museums, of course. Often I have visited the New York Museum of Natural History to touch with my hands many of the objects there exhibited, but I have longed to see with my eyes the condensed history of the earth and its inhabitants displayed there— animals and the races of men pictured in their native environment; gigantic carcasses of dinosaurs and mastodons which roamed the earth long before man appeared, with his tiny stature and powerful brain, to conquer the animal kingdom; realistic presentations of the processes of evolution in animals, in man, and in the implements which man has used to fashion for himself a secure home on this planet; and a thousand and one other aspects of natural history.

20   I wonder how many readers of this article have viewed this panorama of the face of living things as pictured in that inspiring museum. Many, of course, have not had the opportunity, but I am sure that many who *have* had the opportunity have not made use of it. There, indeed, is a place to use your eyes. You who see can spend many fruitful days there, but I, with my imaginary three days of sight, could only take a hasty glimpse, and pass on.

21   My next stop would be the Metropolitan Museum of Art, for just as the Museum of Natural History reveals the material aspects of the world, so does the Metropolitan show the myriad facets of the human spirit. Throughout the history of humanity the urge to artistic expression has been almost as powerful as the urge for food, shelter, and procreation. And here, in the vast chambers of the Metropolitan Museum, is unfolded before me the spirit of Egypt, Greece, and Rome, as expressed in their art. I know well through my hands the sculptured gods and goddesses of the ancient Nile-land. I have felt copies of Parthenon friezes, and I have sensed the rhythmic beauty of charging Athenian warriors. Apollos and Venuses and the Winged Victory of Samothrace are friends of my fingertips. The gnarled, bearded features of Homer are dear to me, for he, too, knew blindness.

22   My hands have lingered upon the living marble of Roman sculpture as well as that of later generations. I have passed my hands over a plaster cast of Michelangelo's inspiring and heroic Moses; I have sensed the power of Rodin; I have been awed by the devoted spirit of Gothic wood carving. These arts which can be touched have meaning for me, but even they were meant to be seen rather than felt, and I can only guess at the beauty which remains hidden from me. I can admire

the simple lines of a Greek vase, but its figured decorations are lost to me.

So on this, my second day of sight, I should try to probe into the soul 23 of man through his art. The things I knew through touch I should now see. More splendid still, the whole magnificent world of painting would be opened to me, from the Italian Primitives, with their serene religious devotion, to the Moderns, with their feverish visions. I should look deep into the canvases of Raphael, Leonardo da Vinci, Titian, Rembrandt. I should want to feast my eyes upon the warm colors of Veronese, study the mysteries of El Greco, catch a new vision of Nature from Corot. Oh, there is so much rich meaning and beauty in the art of the ages for you who have eyes to see!

Upon my short visit to this temple of art I should not be able to 24 review a fraction of that great world of art which is open to you. I should be able to get only a superficial impression. Artists tell me that for a deep and true appreciation of art one must educate the eye. One must learn through experience to weigh the merits of line, of composition, of form and color. If I had eyes, how happily would I embark upon so fascinating a study! Yet I am told that, to many of you who have eyes to see, the world of art is a dark night, unexplored and unilluminated.

It would be with extreme reluctance that I should leave the Metro- 25 politan Museum, which contains the key to beauty—a beauty so neglected. Seeing persons, however, do not need a Metropolitan to find this key to beauty. The same key lies waiting in smaller museums, and in books on the shelves of even small libraries. But naturally, in my limited time of imaginary sight, I should choose the place where the key unlocks the greatest treasures in the shortest time.

The evening of my second day of sight I should spend at a theater or 26 at the movies. Even now I often attend theatrical performances of all sorts, but the action of the play must be spelled into my hand by a companion. But how I should like to see with my own eyes the fascinating figure of Hamlet, or the gusty Falstaff amid colorful Elizabethan trappings! How I should like to follow each movement of the graceful Hamlet, each strut of the hearty Falstaff! And since I could see only one play, I should be confronted by the many-horned dilemma, for there are scores of plays I should want to see. You who have eyes can see any you like. How many of you, I wonder, when you gaze at a play, a movie, or any spectacle, realize and give thanks for the miracle of sight which enables you to enjoy its color, grace, and movement?

I cannot enjoy the beauty of rhythmic movement except in a sphere 27 restricted to the touch of my hands. I can vision only dimly the grace of a Pavlova, although I know something of the delight of rhythm, for often I can sense the beat of music as it vibrates through the floor. I can well imagine that cadenced motion must be one of the most pleasing sights in the world. I have been able to gather something of this by tracing with my fingers the lines in sculptured marble; if this static grace can be so lovely, how much more acute must be the thrill of seeing grace in motion.

28   One of my dearest memories is of the time when Joseph Jefferson allowed me to touch his face and hands as he went through some of the gestures and speeches of his beloved Rip Van Winkle. I was able to catch thus a meager glimpse of the world of drama, and I shall never forget the delight of that moment. But, oh, how much I must miss, and how much pleasure you seeing ones can derive from watching and hearing the interplay of speech and movement in the unfolding of a dramatic performance! If I could see only one play, I should know how to picture in my mind the action of a hundred plays which I have read or had transferred to me through the medium of the manual alphabet.

29   So, through the evening of my second imaginary day of sight, the great figures of dramatic literature would crowd sleep from my eyes.

30   The following morning, I should again greet the dawn, anxious to discover new delights, for I am sure that, for those who have eyes which really see, the dawn of each day must be a perpetually new revelation of beauty.

31   This, according to the terms of my imagined miracle, is to be my third and last day of sight. I shall have no time to waste in regrets or longings; there is too much to see. The first day I devoted to my friends, animate and inanimate. The second revealed to me the history of man and Nature. Today I shall spend in the workaday world of the present, amid the haunts of men going about the business of life. And where one can find so many activities and conditions of men as in New York? So the city becomes my destination.

32   I start from my home in the quite little suburb of Forest Hills, Long Island. Here, surrounded by green lawns, trees, and flowers, are neat little houses, happy with the voices and movements of wives and children, havens of peaceful rest for men who toil in the city. I drive across the lacy structure of steel which spans the East River, and I get a new and startling vision of the power and ingenuity of the mind of man. Busy boats chug and scurry about the river—racy speedboats, stolid, snorting tugs. If I had long days of sight ahead, I should spend many of them watching the delightful activity upon the river.

33   I look ahead, and before me rise the fantastic towers of New York, a city that seems to have stepped from the pages of a fairy story. What an awe-inspiring sight, these glittering spires, these vast banks of stone and steel—structures such as the gods might build for themselves! This animated picture is a part of the lives of millions of people every day. How many, I wonder, give it so much as a second glance? Very few, I

fear. Their eyes are blind to this magnificent sight because it is so familiar to them.

I hurry to the top of one of those gigantic structures, the Empire State Building, for there, a short time ago, I "saw" the city below through the eyes of my secretary. I am anxious to compare my fancy with reality. I am sure I should not be disappointed in the panorama spread out before me, for to me it would be a vision of another world. 34

Now I begin my rounds of the city. First, I stand at a busy corner, merely looking at people, trying by sight of them to understand something of their lives. I see smiles, and I am happy. I see determination, and I am proud. I see suffering, and I am compassionate. 35

I stroll down Fifth Avenue. I throw my eyes out of focus so that I see no particular object but only a seething kaleidoscope of color. I am certain that the colors of women's dresses moving in a throng must be a gorgeous spectacle of which I should never tire. But perhaps if I had sight I should be like most other women—too interested in styles and the cut of individual dresses to give much attention to the splendor of color in the mass. And I am convinced, too, that I should become an inveterate window shopper, for it must be a delight to the eye to view the myriad articles of beauty on display. 36

From Fifth Avenue I make a tour of the city—to Park Avenue, to the slums, to factories, to parks where children play. I take a stay-at-home trip abroad by visiting the foreign quarters. Always my eyes are open wide to all the sights of both happiness and misery so that I may probe deep and add to my understanding of how people work and live. My heart is full of the images of people and things. My eye passes lightly over no single trifle; it strives to touch and hold closely each thing its gaze rests upon. Some sights are pleasant, filling the heart with happiness; but some are miserably pathetic. To these latter I do not shut my eyes, for they, too, are part of life. To close the eyes on them is to close the heart and mind. 37

My third day of sight is drawing to an end. Perhaps there are many serious pursuits to which I should devote the few remaining hours, but I am afraid that on the evening of that last day I should again run away to the theater, to a hilariously funny play, so that I might appreciate the overtones of comedy in the human spirit. 38

At midnight my temporary respite from blindness would cease, and permanent night would close in on me again. Naturally in those three short days I should not have seen all I wanted to see. Only when darkness had again descended upon me should I realize how much I had left unseen. But my mind would be so crowded with glorious memories that I should have little time for regrets. Thereafter the touch of every object would bring a glowing memory of how that object looked. 39

Perhaps this short outline of how I should spend three days of sight 40 does not agree with the program you would set for yourself if you knew that you were about to be stricken blind. I am, however, sure that if you actually faced that fate your eyes would open to things you had never seen before, storing up memories for the long night ahead. You would use your eyes as never before. Everything you saw would become dear to you. Your eyes would touch and embrace every object that came within your range of vision. Then, at last, you would really see, and a new world of beauty would open itself before you.

41   I who am blind can give one hint to those who see—one admonition to those who would make full use of the gift of sight: Use your eyes as if tomorrow you would be stricken blind. And the same method can be applied to the other senses. Hear the music of voices, the song of a bird, the mighty strains of an orchestra, as if you would be stricken deaf tomorrow. Touch each object you want to touch as if tomorrow your tactile sense would fail. Smell the perfume of flowers, taste with relish each morsel, as if tomorrow you could never smell and taste again. Make the most of every sense; glory in all the facets of pleasure and beauty which the world reveals to you through the several means of contact which Nature provides. But of all the senses, I am sure that sight must be the most delightful.

FOR DISCUSSION

1. At the beginning of the essay, Helen Keller lets you know that she isn't writing this personal essay for her own benefit, and thus engages you in a partnership right away. What does she want you, the reader, to do?

2. What would the author do on each of the three days she had sight? What insight might the readers have about themselves after reading about what Keller would do?

3. What keeps this essay from sounding preachy—like a sermon—or bossy?

4. What is gained in the essay by the author's writing many paragraphs about each day; she could have, of course, written one paragraph about friends, one paragraph about the world, and one paragraph about business. She takes pains, however, to develop each point. What is added by this development?

5. What keeps this essay from being pitiful? Sorrowful? Sad?

ANAÏS NIN

Anaïs Nin, (1903–1977), one of the most famous diary writers of the twentieth century, gives her personal viewpoint on sensitive men in this essay. Nin discusses the effects that living in the age of liberation has had on women and, consequently, on the type of men they prefer. This essay is part of Nin's collection of essays In Favor of The Sensitive Man *(1976), but first appeared in* Playgirl *magazine in 1974.*

In Favor of the Sensitive Man

This last year I spent most of my time with young women in colleges, young women doing their Ph.D.'s on my work. The talk about the diaries always led to private and intimate talks about their lives. I became aware that the ideals, fantasies, and desires of these women were going through a transition. Intelligent, gifted, participating in the creativity and activities of their time in history, they seem to have transcended the attraction for the conventional definition of a man. 1

They had learned to expose the purely macho type, his false masculinity, physical force, dexterity in games, arrogance, but more dangerous still, his lack of sensitivity. The hero of *Last Tango in Paris* repulsed them. The sadist, the man who humiliates woman, whose show of power is a facade. The so-called heroes, the stance of a Hemingway or a Mailer in writing, the false strength. All this was exposed, disposed of by these new women, too intelligent to be deceived, too wise and too proud to be subjected to this display of power which did not protect them (as former generations of women believed) but endangered their existence as individuals. 2

The attraction shifted to the poet, the musician, the singer, the sensitive man they had studied with, to the natural, sincere man without stance or display, nonassertive, the one concerned with true values, not ambition, the one who hates war and greed, commercialism and political expediencies. A new type of man to match the new type of woman. They helped each other through college, they answered each other's poems, they wrote confessional and self-examining letters, they prized their relationship, they gave care to it, time, attention. They did not like impersonal sensuality. Both wanted to work at something they loved. 3

I met many couples who fitted this description. Neither one dominated. Each one worked at what he did best, shared labors, unobtrusively, without need to establish roles or boundaries. The 4 characteristic trait was gentleness. There was no head of the house. There was no need to assert which one was the supplier of income. They had learned the subtle art of oscillation, which is human. Neither strength nor weakness is a fixed quality. We all have our days of strength and our days of weakness. They had learned rhythm, suppleness, relativity. Each had knowledge and special intuitions to contribute. There is no war of the sexes between these couples. There is no need to draw up contracts on the rules of marriage. Most of them do not feel the need to marry. Some want children and some do not. They are both aware of the function of dreams—not as symptoms of neurosis, but as guidance to our secret nature. They know that each is endowed with both masculine and feminine qualities.

5   A few of these young women displayed a new anxiety. It was as though having lived so long under the direct or indirect domination of man (setting the style of their life, the pattern, the duties) they had become accustomed to it, and now that it was gone, now that they were free to make decisions, to be mobile, to speak their wishes, to direct their own lives, they felt like ships without rudders. I saw questions in their eyes. Was sensitivity felt as overgentle? Permissiveness as weakness? They missed authority, the very thing they had struggled to overcome. The old groove had functioned for so long. Women as dependents. A few women independent, but few in proportion to the dependent ones. The offer of total love was unusual. A love without egocentricity, without exigencies, without moral strictures. A love which did not define the duties of women (you must do this and that, you must help me with my work, you must entertain and further my career).

6   A love which was almost a twinship. No potentates, no dictators. Strange. It was new. It was a new country. You cannot have independence and dependence. You can alternate them equally, and then both can grow, unhampered, without obstacles. This sensitive man is aware of woman's needs. He seeks to let her be. But sometimes women do not recognize that the elements they are missing are those which thwarted woman's expansion, her testing of her gifts, her mobility, her development. They mistake sensitivity for weakness. Perhaps because the sensitive man lacks the aggressiveness of the macho man (which sends him hurtling through business and politics at tragic cost to family and personal relationships).

7   I met a young man, who although the head of a business by inheritance, did not expect his wife to serve the company, to entertain people not attractive to her, to assist in his contacts. She was free to pursue her own interests, which lay in psychology and training welfare workers. She became anxious that the two different sets of friends, his business associates and her psychologists, would create totally sepa-

rate lives and estrange them. It took her a while to observe that her psychological experiences were serving his interests in another way. He was learning to handle those who worked for him in a more humanistic way. When an employee was found cheating while pumping the company's gas to the other employees, he called him in and obtained his life history. He discovered the reason for the cheating (high hospital bills for a child) and remedied it instead of firing him, thus winning a loyal employee from then on. The couple's interests, which seemed at first divergent, became interdependent.

Another couple decided that, both being writers, one would teach 8 one year and leave the other free to write, and the other would take on teaching the next year. The husband was already a fairly well known writer. The wife had only published poems in magazines but was preparing a book of criticism. It was her turn to teach. He found himself considered a faculty member's husband and was asked at parties, "Do you also write?" The situation could have caused friction. The wife remedied it by having reprinted in the school paper a review of her husband's last novel, which established his standing.

Young women are engaging in political action when young men are 9 withdrawing because of disillusionment. And the new woman is winning new battles. The fact that certain laws were changed renewed the faith of the new man. Women in politics are still at the stage of David and Goliath. They believe in the effect of a single stone! Their faith is invigorating when they and their husbands have sympathetic vibes, as they call it.

The old situation of the man obsessed with business, whose life was 10 shortened by stress, and whose life ended at retirement, was reversed by a young wife who encouraged his hobby, painting, so that he retired early to enjoy art and travel.

In these situations the art of coordination manifests itself rather than 11 the immature emphasis on irreconcilable differences. With maturity comes the sense that activities are interrelated and nourish one another.

Another source of bewilderment for the new woman is that many of 12 the new men do not have the old ambitions. They do not want to spend their lives in the pursuit of a fortune. They want to travel while they are young, live in the present. I met them hitchhiking in Greece, Spain, Italy, France. They were living entirely in the present and accepting the hardships for the sake of the present adventures. One young woman felt physically unfit for the difficulties and carried a lot of vitamins in her one and only pack. She told me: "At first he made fun of me, but then he understood I was not sure I could take the trip physically, and he became as protective as possible. If I had married a conventional man, his concept of protection would have been to keep me home. I would not have enjoyed all these marvels I have discovered with David, who challenged my strength and made me stronger for it.'' Neither one thought of surrendering the dream of travel while young.

13   One of the most frequent questions young women ask me is: How can a woman create a life of her own, an atmosphere of her own when her husband's profession dictates their lifestyle? If he is a doctor, a lawyer, a psychologist, a teacher, the place they live in, the demands of the neighbors, all set the patterns of life.

14   Judy Chicago, the well-known painter and teacher, made a study of women painters and found that, whereas the men painters all had studios separate from the house, the women did not, and painted either in the kitchen or some spare room. But many young women have taken literally Virginia Woolf's *A Room of One's Own* and rented studios away from the family. One couple who lived in a one-room house set up a tent on the terrace for the wife's writing activities. The very feeling of ''going to work,'' the physical act of detachment, the sense of value given to the work by isolating it, became a stimulant and a help. To create another life, they found, was not a breaking away or separating. It is striking that for woman any break or separation carries with it an aura of loss, as if the symbolic umbilical cord still affected all her emotional life and each act were a threat to unity and ties.

15   This fear is in women, not in men, but it was learned from men. Men, led by their ambitions, did separate from their families, were less present for the children, were absorbed, submerged by their professions. But this happened to men and does not necessarily have to happen to women. The unbroken tie lies in the feelings. It is not the hours spent with husband or children, but the quality and completeness of the presence. Man is often physically present and mentally preoccupied. Woman is more capable of turning away from her work to give full attention to a weary husband or a child's scratched finger.

16   If women have witnessed the father ''going away'' because of his work, they will retain anxiety about their own ''going away'' to meetings, conferences, lectures, or other professional commitments.

17   For the new woman and the new man, the art of connecting and relating separate interests will be a challenge. If women today do not want a nonexistent husband married to Big Business, they will accept a simpler form of life to have the enjoyment of a husband whose life blood has not been sucked by big companies. I see the new woman shedding many luxuries. I love to see them, simply dressed, relaxed, natural, playing no roles. For the transitional stage was woman's delicate problem: how to pass from being submerged and losing her identity in a relationship, how to learn to merge without loss of self. The new man is helping by his willingness to change too, from rigidities to suppleness, from tightness to openness, from uncomfortable roles to the relaxation of no roles.

One young woman was offered a temporary teaching job away from 18 home. The couple had no children. The young husband said: ''Go ahead if that is what you want to do.'' If he had opposed the plan, which added to her teaching credits, she would have resented it. But because he let her go, she felt he did not love her deeply enough to hold on to her. She left with a feeling of being deserted, while he felt her leaving also as a desertion. These feelings lay below the conscious acceptance. The four months' separation might have caused a break. But the difference is that they were willing to discuss these feelings, to laugh at their ambivalence and contradictions.

If in the unconscious there still lie reactions we cannot control, at 19 least we can prevent them from doing harm to the present situation. If both were unconsciously susceptible to the fear of being deserted, they had to find a way to grow independent from a childhood pattern. Otherwise, enslaved by childhood fears, neither one could move from the house. In exposing them they were able to laugh at the inconsistency of wanting freedom and yet wanting the other to hold on.

Very often in the emerging new woman, the assertion of differences 20 carries too heavy an indication of dissonances, disharmony, but it is a matter of finding the relationships, as we are finding the relationship between art and science, science and psychology, religion and science. It is not similarities that create harmony, but the art of fusing various elements that enrich life. Professional activities tend to demand almost too much concentration; this becomes a narrowing of experience for each one. The infusion of new currents of thoughts, stretching the range of interests, is beneficial to both men and women.

Perhaps some new women and new men fear adventure and change. 21 The life of Margaret Mead indicates that she sought a man with the same passionate devotion to anthropology, but the result was that her husband studied the legends, the myths of the tribe, and she was left to study childbirth and the raising of children. So a common interest does not necessarily mean equality.

All of us carry seeds of anxieties left from childhood, but the 22 determination to live with others in close and loving harmony can overcome all the obstacles, provided we have learned to *integrate the differences*.

Watching these young couples and how they resolve the problems of 23 new attitudes, new consciousness, I feel we might be approaching a humanistic era in which differences and inequalities may be resolved without war.

Yoko Ono proposed the ''feminization of society. The use of femi- 24 nine tendencies as a positive force to change the world . . . We can evolve rather than revolt.''

The empathy these new men show woman is born of their ac- 25 ceptance of their own emotional, intuitive, sensory, and humanistic approach to relationships. They allow themselves to weep (men never wept), to show vulnerability, to expose their fantasies, share their inmost selves. Some women are baffled by the new regime. They have not yet recognized that to have empathy one must to some extent feel what the other feels. That means that if woman is to assert her creativity or her gifts, man has to assert his own crucial dislike of what was expected of him in the past.

26   The new type of young man I have met is exceptionally fitted for the new woman, but she is not yet totally appreciative of his tenderness, his growing proximity to woman, his attitude of twinship rather than differentiation. People who once lived under a dictatorship often are at a loss to govern themselves. This loss is a transitional one: It may mean the beginning of a totally new life and freedom. The man is there. He is an equal. He treats you like an equal. In moments of uncertainty you can still discuss problems with him you could not have talked about twenty years ago. Do not, I say to today's women, please do not mistake sensitivity for weakness. This was the mistake which almost doomed our culture. Violence was mistaken for power, the misuse of power for strength. The subjection is still true in films, in the theater, in the media. I wanted the hero of *Last Tango in Paris* to die immediately. He was only destroyed at the end! The time span of a film. Will it take women as long to recognize sadism, arrogance, tyranny, reflected so painfully in the world outside, in war and political corruption? Let us start the new regime of honesty, of trust, abolishment of false roles in our personal relationships, and it will eventually affect the world's history as well as women's development.

FOR DISCUSSION

1. Since this article first appeared in *Playgirl*, it might, therefore, seem to be written for women only. However, upon reading the essay, one sees that it is valuable for men as well as women. What did Anaïs Nin do in the essay that makes this possible?

2. The title of the article appears to say that the essay will be about sensitive men. Actually the essay is as much about the transformation of women. Therefore, what can you say about the author's selection of title in relation to her probable intention?

3. What comparisons does Nin make between the modern woman and the modern man? How does she fit this comparison into the overall focus of the article?

4. What is your response to this personal perspective?

H. W. FOWLER

H. W. Fowler (1858–1933), the well-known lexicographer and usage expert, gives his personal viewpoint on whether one should or should not split an infinitive. Taking a potentially very boring subject, Fowler manages to infuse it with his personal wit and style. This selection is taken from his Dictionary of Modern English Usage.

Split Infinitive

The English-speaking world may be divided into (1) those who neither know nor care what a split infinitive is; (2) those who do not know, but care very much; (3) those who know and condemn; (4) those who know and approve; and (5) those who know and distinguish. [1]

1. Those who neither know nor care are the vast majority, and are a happy folk, to be envied by most of the minority classes. 'To really understand' comes readier to their lips and pens than 'really to understand'; they see no reason why they should not say it (small blame to them, seeing that reasons are not their critics' strong point), and they do say it, to the discomfort of some among us, but not to their own. [2]

2. To the second class, those who do not know but do care, who would as soon be caught putting their knives in their mouths as splitting an infinitive but have only hazy notions of what constitutes that deplorable breach of etiquette, this article is chiefly addressed. These people betray by their practice that their aversion to the split infinitive springs not from instinctive good taste, but from tame acceptance of the misinterpreted opinion of others; for they will subject their sentences to the queerest distortions, all to escape imaginary split infinitives. 'To really understand' is a s. i.; 'to really be understood' is a s. i.; 'to be really understood' is not one; the havoc that is played with much well-intentioned writing by failure to grasp that distinction is incredible. Those upon whom the fear of infinitive-splitting sits heavy should remember that to give conclusive evidence, by distortions, of misconceiving the nature of the s. i. is far more damaging to their literary pretentions than an actual lapse could be; for it exhibits them as deaf to the normal rhythm of English sentences. No sensitive ear can fail to be shocked, if the following examples are read aloud, by the strangeness of the indicated adverbs. Why on earth, the reader wonders, is that word out of its place? He will find, on looking through again, that each has been turned out of a similar position, viz. between the word *be* and a passive participle. Reflection will assure him that the cause of dis- [3]

location is always the same—all these writers have sacrificed the run of their sentences to the delusion that 'to be really understood' is a split infinitive. It is not; and the straitest non-splitter of us all can with a clear conscience restore each of the adverbs to its rightful place: He was proposed at the last moment as a candidate likely *generally* to be accepted. / When the record of this campaign comes *dispassionately* to be written, and in just perspective, it will be found that . . . / New principles will have *boldly* to be adopted if the Scottish case is to be met. / This is a very serious matter, which clearly ought *further* to be inquired into. / The Headmaster of a public school possesses very great powers, which ought *most carefully and considerately* to be exercised. / The time to get this revaluation put through is when the amount paid by the State to the localities is *very largely* to be increased.

4   3. The above writers are bogy-haunted creatures who for fear of splitting an infinitive abstain from doing something quite different, i.e., dividing *be* from its complement by an adverb; see further under POSITION OF ADVERBS. Those who presumably do know what split infinitives are, and condemn them, are not so easily identified, since they include all who neither commit the sin nor flounder about it saving themselves from it—all who combine a reasonable dexterity with acceptance of conventional rules. But when the dexterity is lacking, disaster follows. It does not add to a writer's readableness if readers are pulled up now and again to wonder—Why this distortion? Ah, to be sure, a non-split-die-hard! That is the mental dialogue occasioned by each of the adverbs in the examples below. It is of no avail merely to fling oneself desperately out of temptation; one must so do it that no traces of the struggle remain. Sentences must if necessary be thoroughly remodelled instead of having a word lifted from its original place and dumped elsewhere: What alternative can be found which the Pope has not condemned, and which will make it possible *to organize legally* public worship? / It will, when better understood, tend *firmly to establish* relations between Capital and Labour. / Both Germany and England have done ill in not combining *to forbid flatly* hostilities. / Every effort must be made *to increase adequately* professional knowledge and attainments. / We have had *to shorten somewhat* Lord D_____'s letter. / The kind of sincerity which enables an author *to move powerfully* the heart would . . . / Safeguards should be provided *to prevent effectually* cosmopolitan financiers from manipulating these reserves.

5   4. Just as those who know and condemn the s. i. include many who are not recognizable, since only the clumsier performers give positive proof of resistance to temptation, so too those who know and approve are not distinguishable with certainty. When a man splits an infinitive, he may be doing it unconsciously as a member of our class I, or he may

be deliberately rejecting the trammels of convention and announcing that he means to do as he will with his own infinitives. But, as the following examples are from newspapers of high repute, and high newspaper tradition is strong against splitting, it is perhaps fair to assume that each specimen is a manifesto of independence: It will be found possible *to considerably improve* the present wages of the miners without jeopardizing the interests of capital. / Always providing that the Imperialists do not feel strong enough *to decisively assert* their power in the revolted provinces. / But even so, he seems *to still be allowed* to speak at Unionist demonstrations. / It is the intention of the Minister of Transport *to substantially increase* all present rates by means of a general percentage. / The men in many of the largest districts are declared *to strongly favour* a strike if the minimum wage is not conceded.

It should be noticed that in these the separating adverb could have been placed outside the infinitive with little or in most cases no damage to the sentence-rhythm (*considerably* after *miners, decisively* after *power, still* with clear gain after *be, substantially* after *rates,* and *strongly* at some loss after *strike*), so that protest seems a safe diagnosis.

5. The attitude of those who know and distinguish is something like this: We admit that separation of *to* from its infinitive is not in itself desirable, and we shall not gratuitously say either 'to mortally wound' or 'to mortally be wounded'; but we are not foolish enough to confuse the latter with 'to be mortally wounded', which is blameless English, nor 'to just have heard' with 'to have just heard', which is also blameless. We maintain, however, that a real s. i., though not desirable in itself, is preferable to either of two things, to real ambiguity, and to patent artificiality. For the first, we will rather write 'Our object is to further cement trade relations' than, by correcting into 'Our object is further to cement . . .', leave it doubtful whether an additional object or additional cementing is the point. And for the second, we take it that such reminders of a tyrannous convention as 'in not combining to forbid flatly hostilities' are far more abnormal than the abnormality they evade. We will split infinitives sooner than be ambiguous or artificial; more than that, we will freely admit that sufficient recasting will get rid of any s. i. without involving either of those faults, and yet reserve to ourselves the right of deciding in each case whether recasting is worth while. Let us take an example: 'In these circumstances, the Commission, judging from the evidence taken in London, has been feeling its way to modifications intended to better equip successful candidates for careers in India and at the same time to meet reasonable Indian demands.' To better equip? We refuse 'better to equip' as a shouted reminder of the tryanny; we refuse 'to equip better' as ambiguous (*better* an adjective?), we regard 'to equip successful candidates

better' as lacking compactness, as possibly tolerable from an anti-splitter, but not good enough for us. What then of recasting? 'intended to make successful candidates fitter for' is the best we can do if the exact sense is to be kept; it takes some thought to arrive at the correction; was the game worth the candle?

8   After this inconclusive discussion, in which, however, the author's opinion has perhaps been allowed to appear with indecent plainness, readers may like to settle the following question for themselves. 'The greatest difficulty about assessing the economic achievements of the Soviet Union is that its spokesmen try absurdly to exaggerate them; in consequence the visitor may tend badly to underrate them.' Has dread of the s. i. led the writer to attach his adverbs to the wrong verbs, and would he not have done better to boldly split both infinitives, since he cannot put the adverbs after them without spoiling his rhythm? Or are we to give him the benefit of the doubt, and suppose that he really meant *absurdly* to qualify *try* and *badly* to qualify *tend*?

9   It is perhaps hardly fair that this article should have quoted no split infinitives except such as, being reasonably supposed (as in 4) to be deliberate, are likely to be favourable specimens. Let it therefore conclude with one borrowed from a reviewer, to whose description of it no exception need be taken: 'A book . . . of which the purpose is thus—with a deafening split infinitive—stated by its author: "Its main idea is *to* historically, even while events are maturing, and divinely—from the Divine point of view—*impeach* the European system of Church and States".'

FOR DISCUSSION

1. This is a long essay on a short subject. What is added to Fowler's statement of his own "personal perspective" by the audacity of this length?

2. How does the author make this essay interesting?

3. How do you react to Fowler's viewpoint?

4. The book from which this comes, *Modern English Usage,* is a standard reference book on many shelves. Knowing this fact, how would you describe the audience Fowler is writing for?

MAX LERNER

In his personal column in Newsweek *Magazine (October 8, 1979), journalist Max Lerner discusses our future as a society.*

On Being a Possibilist

In a time such as ours, when man acts like a wolf to man, it may seem 1 more than a little absurd to question the prevailing gloom. Yet I want to break a lance in defense of the possible.

In my teaching, lecturing and column writing, I get a question thrust 2 at me constantly: "Are you an optimist or a pessimist?" At times I get impatient. Do they think this is Wall Street, where you are bullish or bearish about stocks you can't control? Our destiny as a people rests not in our stars but in ourselves. I am neither optimist nor pessimist. I am a possibilist.

To believe either that everything is bound to work out or that 3 nothing will ever work out is equally an exercise in mindlessness. There are no blank-check guarantees that we will survive and prosper, and no inevitability that we won't. I believe in the possible. More options are open for us than we dare admit. Everything depends on our collective intelligence in making choices, and our will to carry them out.

The prevailing view is that all our options have narrowed. I don't 4 believe it. There is a sense of being trapped—the feeling that nothing we do makes much difference. Which leads to frantic group pressures and single-issue politics, or to the cynical rejection of all forms of public life and to a wallowing in our egos.

Let's face it. We used up our resources, polluted our environment 5 and laid staggering burdens on our government. Which means we must now place limits on our desires, needs, greeds. The historians call it the Age of Limits.

But it is equally an Age of Breakthroughs which compensate for the 6 narrowed options. It is hard to see this because the limits are concrete and urgent while the breakthroughs are less visible.

But they are nonetheless real. I ask the black students in my semi- 7 nars: would you rather have come of age in the years before the civil-rights movement—or now? I ask the women of every age: would you rather be living in the days of male power and swagger, with slim options for jobs and careers and meager life chances—or now?

8   I ask the professionals—the athletes, film and TV performers, photographers, playwrights, musicians, architects, writers, artists of every kind: would you rather have plied your craft before the large audiences were opened up to you—or now?

9   I ask the young scientists, the doctors and researchers, teachers, law and medical students, staff workers, young business executives: would you rather have lived and worked before the great breakthroughs of the knowledge revolution—or now?

10   I ask the code breakers who deviate from the narrow social norms of the past, and who have found new life-styles: would you rather have lived before society accepted your lifeways, and before the breakthroughs that gave you a new identity—or now?

11   I say to the chronologically aging who still feel young in spirit: would you rather have lived out your years at a time when elderly Americans were shunted aside and were held to have lost their capacity to function creatively—or now?

12   I hold with Freud that civilizations are caught between the twin gods, Eros and Thanatos—love and death, the life-affirming and life-denying principles. I find the conventional terms like ''liberal'' and ''conservative'' less and less useful. What counts is whether we are on the side of life affirmations or life denials. If I have to belong to a party, I am of the party of Eros, not of Thanatos.

13   I am no believer in automatic progress. I have experienced too much to wear blinders readily. But I can point to the real revolutions in process—in research, in access to life chances, in sexual attitudes, in awareness of the phases of the life cycle, in values and life-styles. The '60s were the most revolutionary decade in American history. The revolutions of the '70s—and those to come—were and will be less dramatic and visible but they may prove deeper.

14   We have too long allowed ourselves to be blinkered by the naysayers of our time. An Age of Limits can also be an Age of Trade-offs. As a possibilist I believe there are practical ways to resolve conflicts by contriving trade-offs in which you swap something marginal or formal to achieve what neither camp can do without. We see it done every day in the Supreme Court decisions, which give trade-offs the authority of law. I have to add, however, that you can't trade off the essential life principle for a death principle.

15   I am aware of the uprootings and unravelings which threaten the cultural health of America. Every society has them, but ours seem to be piling up—the fragmenting of life, the battering of the family, the erosion of work, the breaking of connections, the intensity of pressure-group and single-issue politics, the imperial ego, the conspiracy hunt-

ing, the cult of the image, the moral relativism, the ethics of "anything goes," the refusal to see anything in life as sacred.

Yet, to counter this, America for me, even today, is the world's most revolutionary culture. It is in a phase of rapid change which belies the familiar charge of decay. In every area of thought and action, those who know most testify to the stunning, almost unimaginable transformations they are witnessing in their fields. How then can the civilization as a whole be stagnant or dying? 16

The great event of the twentieth century—greater than the Russian or Chinese revolutions—has been America's defining of itself as a complex civilization, growing and enduring amidst the wrack of change. People around the world recognize it. They want to come here—by boat, by plane, by swimming, by cutting the barbed wire at the frontiers, by sneaking in. Their instinct is sounder than the self-hating doubts of some intellectuals. 17

The violences and excesses, the uprootings and unravelings of our culture are best seen as the agonizing inner changes of a social organism as it moves toward a higher degree of complexity. They are evidences not of a senile but of a still-adolescent society, not of a dying civilization but of one that has not wholly found itself. If America dies, it will not be a running down of energies but of an explosion of energies. 18

Call this the manifesto of a possibilist. When I am asked whether America has come to the end of its tether, my answer is that of the lyric in "Porgy and Bess": "It ain't necessarily so." I believe, as yeasayers have insisted from Walt Whitman to Thomas Wolfe to our own day, that the true discovery of America still lies ahead. 19

FOR DISCUSSION

1. Compare Max Lerner's essay to "In Defense of Optimism" by Booth Fowler and Saul Brenner, which is similar in subject. What are the differences in tone and development between these two essays? What does the place of publication for each of these pieces (the *Humanist* for "In Defense of Optimism" and *Newsweek* for "On Being a Possibilist") have to do with their differences?

2. What is the proportion of pros to cons mentioned in Lerner's essay? Pinpoint where in the essay he focuses on the negative aspects of our society and try to explain why he chose that spot. Do you think he deals with these negative points effectively?

3. Try to define the audience for this essay.

4. Do you think that very many of Lerner's readers would tend to agree with him even before they read the essay? Would they tend to agree with him after reading it? Do you?

5. Why do you think this essay as categorized as *writing to express* rather than *writing to change?*

WRITING YOUR OWN

The Personal Perspective Essay

Before you begin to write your own essay, let's examine the configurations of the first essay in this chapter, May Sarton's "Rewards of Living a Solitary Life."

Motivation (an educated guess): to express her opinion on the subject of living alone and to give a distinctly different view of it.

Circumstance/Situation: time deadline and manuscript requirements of the *New York Times*.

Audience: Readers of the *New York Times* editorial page.

Relationship to Audience: person who has thought a lot about the advantages of living alone to person who may not have.

Emphasis: on the writer's thoughts and views about solitary living— and on vivid examples of what it's like.

Form: editorial.

Intention (an educated guess): to entice the reader to see living alone in the same positive light she does by explaining and by giving provocative examples.

DESIGNING YOUR OWN CONFIGURATION

If you're having trouble thinking of a topic for your personal perspective essay, use the following list of suggestions to stimulate your imagination.

1. Look at a copy of *Newsweek* magazine and examine the weekly Personal Viewpoint column. Write an essay for this column.

2. Write an editorial for your local or school newspaper.
3. Write an essay for x magazine on your views on raising children, going on vacations, or establishing relationships.
4. Pretend you have been invited to speak at a local civics club. Write an essay in which you give your personal perspective on some issue which would be of interest to the club members.

Once you have decided on a topic, use the columns of the following chart to help design the configurations for your personal perspective essay.

Designing Your Own Configuration for a Personal Perspective Essay

MOTIVE	CIRCUMSTANCE/ SITUATION	AUDIENCE	RELATIONSHIP TO AUDIENCE
For your own column in x magazine or newspaper	Time deadline and manuscript requirements of x magazine or newspaper	Readers of x magazine or newspaper	Friend to friend
To sound off on your local television station	A chapter of a book being edited by a friend	Viewers of x television station	Person who has thought a lot about this to person who probably hasn't
To sell an article	A class assignment with a deadline and essay requirements	Readers of your column	Person who has studied x to person who hasn't
To meet a classroom assignment	For your autobiography	Classmates	Person who has done x to person who hasn't
To write your autobiography		Professor	

EMPHASIS	FORM	INTENTION
The writer's opinion, thoughts, ideas, or views	Editorial	To give one's opinions, thoughts, ideas, or views
The details or examples of the above	Essay	Perhaps to entice others to think this way too, by the examples or provocative thoughts or ideas being presented
The development of these opinions, thoughts, ideas, or views.	Article	
	Speech	

RULES FOR A PERSONAL PERSPECTIVE ESSAY

1. Write about something which has engaged your interest previously, something to which you have given thought.
2. Take your own perspective on this subject; do not use other people's opinions, views, or positions.
3. Develop your perspective fully.
4. Write with your readers in mind at all times, anticipating what they might want or need to know.
5. Be audacious.

RHETORICAL PATTERNS OFTEN APPEARING IN PERSONAL PERSPECTIVE ESSAYS

Examples and Illustrations: How to Help the Reader See

1. An example or illustration is a specific instance that helps clarify a more general statement by allowing the reader to *see*. It is one single thing that shows the character of the whole.
2. Be as colorful, descriptive, detailed, and specific as you possibly can when you give examples and illustrations. Appeal to the readers' *senses*. Transport the readers to the spot and *show* what you mean.
3. Use *concrete* words. Abstract terms don't produce pictures in readers' minds. General words, too, can mean different things to different people. Concrete words appearing in examples and illustrations will let the readers know what *you* mean by the general terms. And if you've used any abstract terms, concrete words will help make them clear to the readers.
4. Choose examples and illustrations that will mean something to the particular audience for whom you are writing.
5. Be generous with examples and illustrations. A minimum ratio is one specific example or illustration to one general statement. Often, however, a higher ratio—say, two or three examples or illustrations to one general statement—will be necessary to let your reader *see* exactly what you mean. You will probably never err by having too many examples and illustrations.

Description: How to Present Sharp, Focused Pictures.

1. Appeal to *all* the reader's senses: sight, smell, touch, hearing, taste. Be very specific.

2. *Select* the details you want to include in the description so that they give one main impression of the object, person, or scene. Don't try to describe everything at once. This means that you will choose details according to what your purpose is at the time.

Definition: How to Tell What Something Means.

1. *To define* means *to explain the nature or essential qualities of a word, function,* etc. A definition determines or fixes the boundaries of the thing being discussed. The original of the word *definition* was *to set boundaries,* and that is what a good definition does for the reader: it helps him or her stake out, limit, see the boundaries of a term.

2. A formal definition includes the term being defined, the class to which it belongs, and what differentiates it from other things in that class.

3. An informal definition takes several forms: defining by using a word that means approximately the same thing (*to gloat* means to act superior and proud); by using an opposite (*love* is *not using someone*); by showing the term's origin (*defining* originally meant *setting boundaries*); by using personal experience (*summer* means *time off, rest, and fun*); by giving examples (*eating well* is *having fresh vegetables and fruit, avoiding sugar, and staying off fried foods*).

4. Use definitions in your writing when there is any chance that your readers will not know the formal meaning of a word or the informal way you are using it. Being clear on the terms in a piece of writing is absolutely necessary for both the reader and the writer if communication is to occur.

Cause/Effect: How to Explain the Reasons and Consequences.

1. Giving the cause and effect of a situation means that you *(a)* identify the thing/person/act that brings about a particular result and *(b)* show *how* it caused that result.

2. Be sure that the causes you give are sufficient to convince the reader. Even after you have isolated the cause of a situation in your mind, ask yourself, "Are there any other causes I should include?"

3. Be sure that there actually *is* a relationship between the cause and effect. If you can't prove this relationship exists in some logical, objective way, be sure that your reader understands that you are offering a personal view of the relationship between the cause and effect. Take the time in your essay to explain to the reader the connections you see.

4. Let the purpose of your writing determine the form your essay takes.

Analysis: How to Help the Reader Understand.

1. The word *analyze* means "to divide anything complex into its simple parts or pieces by separating a whole into its parts." It also means "to show the relationship among the single parts of a larger, more complex subject."

2. A good analysis actually shows the reader how to *think* about the subject.

3. To use analysis in your writing, decide what parts you can break the larger subject into. Then take these parts one at a time. Discuss or describe them, either on an individual basis or as a group, showing how they relate to each other. Finally, put the parts back together in a whole. The reader will then have been able to *understand* what may have otherwise been baffling or confusing.

Analysis by Division: How to Be Clear and Orderly.

1. Divide the process into distinct steps.

2. Discuss these steps in the *exact order* in which they occur when the process is done.

3. If there is a large number of steps in the process, group the steps into categories and then discuss them.

4. Define all terms and procedures that might be unfamiliar.

5. Do not omit *any* step in the procedure.

Details: How to Be Specific.

1. Details are individual or minute parts of a whole. When included in a piece of writing, details give the reader a much clearer picture of what is being discussed.

2. Select details that are relevant to the point you are making. Don't try to include everything.

3. Among those relevant details, select only the most important ones to include.

4. Make the details as specific and concise as possible.

Personal Forms:
A Miscellany

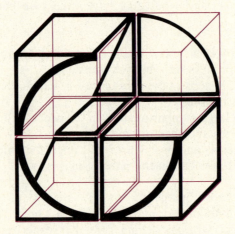

This chapter contains speeches, letters, a list, a journal, a diary, a travel account, an obituary, a will, advertisements, a song, spiritual writings, and poems.

An obituary . . . a will . . . advertisements . . . spiritual writings . . . poetry? What makes these *personal forms*?

It is often true that these forms preclude the writers' revealing who they are or how they see the world. The forms themselves can invite anonymity; the writers could go on forever *not* expressing themselves, merely "filling out" the forms.

The selections in this chapter, however, illustrate how writers— even when their identities may never be known (as in the obituary, the advertisements, some of the spiritual writings, for example)—express their own feelings, visions, views, and philosophies through and in a great variety of traditional forms.

So the forms become personal because the writers *make* them personal; the writers, using standard, conventional forms—like songs, letters, meditations, lists, wills, speeches—express *themselves*.

The selections in this section of the book, although perhaps original and novel inclusions in a college reader, could actually prove to be the most useful to you later in life. In the writing you will do after you leave college you may well have more opportunities, occasions, or need to write in the forms included in this section than to write essays, articles, and reports. If that should turn out to be the case, you will know from having studied these selections that even forms like advertisements, lists, letters, wills, speeches, and the others included here *can* be used by writers to put into words who they are, how they see life, what they think is important. The forms included here are ordinary, regular, always-available forms in which to write. And they can be—as is shown here—as personal as the people who write them.

SPEECHES

Each of the following three speeches, although prepared to be spoken to an audience, conveys a highly personal statement. And each was written for a different purpose. The first is a prophecy and a vision in which Justice Oliver Wendell Holmes (1841–1935) speaks both realistically and optimistically in the dark days before World War I. The second is the response of William Faulkner (1897–1962) upon being awarded the Nobel Prize for Literature in 1949. He speaks of the role of the writer in helping mankind to prevail. And the last is Chief Seattle's answer to the offer of the government of the United States in 1854 to buy two million acres of Indian land. Chief Seattle (1786–1866), leader of the Dwamish, Suquamish, and Allied Native American Tribes in Washington state, gently but powerfully, speaks of the relationship of the Indian and the white man—and the order of nature.

Excerpt from a Speech at a Dinner of the Harvard Law School Association of New York

If I am right it will be a slow business for our people to reach rational views, assuming that we are allowed to work peaceably to that end. But as I grow older I grow calm. If I feel what are perhaps an old man's apprehensions, that competition from new races will cut deeper than working men's disputes and will test whether we can hang together and can fight: if I fear that we are running through the world's resources at a pace that we cannot keep; I do not lose my hopes. I do not pin my dreams for the future to my country or even to my race. I think it probable that civilization somehow will last as long as I care to look ahead—perhaps with smaller numbers, but perhaps also bred to greatness and splendor by science. I think it not improbable that man, like the grub that prepares a chamber for the winged thing it never has seen but is to be—that man may have cosmic destinies that he does not understand. And so beyond the vision of battling races and an impoverished earth I catch a dreaming glimpse of peace.

The other day my dream was pictured to my mind. It was evening. I was walking homeward on Pennsylvania Avenue near the Treasury, and as I looked beyond Sherman's Statue to the west the sky was aflame with scarlet and crimson from the setting sun. But, like the note of downfall in Wagner's opera, below the sky line there came from little globes the pallid discord of the electric lights. And I thought to myself the *Götterdämmerung* will end, and from those globes clustered like evil eggs will come the new masters of the sky. It is like the time in which we live. But then I remembered the faith that I partly have expressed, faith in a universe not measured by our fears, a universe that has thought and more than thought inside of it, and as I gazed, after the sunset and above the electric lights, there shone the stars.

—Oliver Wendell Holmes

On Receiving the Nobel Prize

I feel that this award was not made to me as a man but to my work—a life's work in the agony and sweat of the human spirit, not for glory and least of all for profit, but to create out of the materials of the human spirit something which did not exist there before. So this award is only mine in trust. It will not be difficult to find a dedication for the money part of it commensurate with the purpose and significance of its origin. But I would like to do the same with the acclaim, too, by using this moment as a pinnacle from which I might be listened to by the young men and women already dedicated to the same anguish and travail, among whom is already that one who will some day stand here where I am standing.

Our tragedy today is a general and a universal physical fear so long sustained by now that we can even bear it. There are no longer problems of the spirit. There is only the question: When will I be blown up? Because of this, the young man or woman writing today has forgotten the problems of the human heart in conflict with itself which alone can make good writing because only that is worth writing about, worth the agony and the sweat.

He must learn them again. He must teach himself that the basest of all things is to be afraid; and, teaching himself that, forget it forever, leaving no room in his workshop for anything but the old verities and truths of the heart, the old universal truths lacking which any story is ephemeral and doomed—love and honor and pity and pride and compassion and sacrifice. Until he does so he labors under a curse. He writes not of love, but of lust, of defeats in which nobody loses anything of value, of victories without hope and worst of all without pity or compassion. His griefs grieve on no universal bones, leaving no scars. He writes not of the heart but of the glands.

Until he relearns these things he will write as though he stood among and watched the end of man. I decline to accept the end of man. It is easy enough to say that man is immortal simply because he will endure; that when the last ding-dong of doom has clanged and faded from the last worthless rock hanging tideless in the last red and dying evening, that even then there will still be one more sound: that of his puny inexhaustible voice still talking. I refuse to accept this. I believe that man will not merely endure: he will prevail. He is immortal, not because he alone among creatures has an inexhaustible voice, but because he has a soul, a spirit capable of compassion and sacrifice and endurance. The poet's, the writer's, duty is to write about these things. It is his privilege to help man endure by lifting his heart, by reminding him of the courage and honor and hope and pride and compassion and pity and sacrifice which have been the glory of his past. The poet's voice need not merely be the record of man, it can be one of the props, the pillars to help him endure and prevail.

—William Faulkner

Reply to the U.S. Government

1 Yonder sky that has wept tears of compassion upon my people for centuries untold, and which to us appears changeless and eternal, may change. Today is fair. Tomorrow may be overcast with clouds. My words are like the stars that never change. Whatever Seattle says the great chief at Washington can rely upon with as much certainty as he can upon the return of the sun or the seasons. The White Chief says that Big Chief at Washington sends us greetings of friendship and goodwill. That is kind of him for we know he has little need of our friendship in return. His people are many. They are like the grass that covers vast prairies. My people are few. They resemble the scattering trees of a storm-swept plain. The great, and—I presume—good, White Chief sends us word that he wishes to buy our lands but is willing to allow us enough to live comfortably. This indeed appears just, even generous, for the Red Man no longer has rights that he need respect, and the offer may be wise also, as we are no longer in need of an extensive country. . . . I will not dwell on, nor mourn over, our un-timely decay, nor reproach our paleface brothers with hastening it, as we too may have been somewhat to blame.

2   Youth is impulsive. When our young men grow angry at some real or imaginary wrong, and disfigure their faces with black paint, it denotes that their hearts are black, and then they are often cruel and relentless, and our old men and old women are unable to restrain them. Thus it has ever been. Thus it was when the white men first began to push our forefathers further westward. But let us hope that the hostilities be-tween us may never return. We would have everything to lose and nothing to gain. Revenge by young men is considered gain, even at the cost of their own lives, but old men who stay at home in times of war, and mothers who have sons to lose, know better.

Our good father at Washington—for I presume he is now our father ₃
as well as yours, since King George has moved his boundaries further
north—our great good father, I say, sends us word that if we do as he
desires he will protect us. His brave warriors will be to us a bristling
wall of strength, and his wonderful ships of war will fill our harbors so
that our ancient enemies far to the northward—the Hydas and Tsimp-
sians—will cease to frighten our women, children, and old men. Then
in reality will he be our father and we his children. But can that ever
be? Your God is not our God! Your God loves your people and hates
mine. He folds his strong and protecting arms lovingly about the
paleface and leads him by the hand as a father leads his infant son—but
He has forsaken His red children—if they really are his. Our God, the
Great Spirit, seems also to have forsaken us. Your God makes your
people wax strong every day. Soon they will fill the land. Our people
are ebbing away like a rapidly receding tide that will never return. The
white man's God cannot love our people or He would protect them.
They seem to be orphans who can look nowhere for help. How then
can we be brothers? How can your God become our God and renew
our prosperity and awaken in us dreams of returning greatness? If we
have a common heavenly father He must be partial—for He came to
his paleface children. We never saw Him. He gave you laws but He
had no word for His red children whose teeming multitudes once filled
this vast continent as stars fill the firmament. No; we are two distinct
races with separate origins and separate destinies. There is little in
common between us.

To us the ashes of our ancestors are sacred and their resting place is ₄
hallowed ground. You wander far from the graves of your ancestors
and seemingly without regret. Your religion was written upon tables of
stone by the iron finger of your God so that you could not forget. The
Red Man could never comprehend nor remember it. Our religion is the
traditions of our ancestors—the dreams of our old men, given them in
solemn hours of night by the Great Spirit; and the visions of our
sachems; and it is written in the hearts of our people.

Your dead cease to love you and the land of their nativity as soon as ₅
they pass the portals of the tomb and wander way beyond the stars.
They are soon forgotten and never return. Our dead never forget the
beautiful world that gave them being.

Day and night cannot dwell together. The Red man has ever fled the ₆
approach of the White Man, as the morning mist flees before the
morning sun. However, your proposition seems fair and I think that my
people will accept it and will retire to the reservation you offer them.
Then we will dwell apart in peace, for the words of the Great White
Chief seem to be the words of nature speaking to my people out of
dense darkness.

7   It matters little where we pass the remnant of our days. They will not be many. A few more moons; a few more winters—and not one of the descendants of the mighty hosts that once moved over this broad land or lived in happy homes, protected by the Great Spirit, will remain to mourn over the graves of a people once more powerful and hopeful than yours. But why should I mourn at the untimely fate of my people? Tribe follows tribe, and nation follows nation, like the waves of the sea. It is the order of nature, and regret is useless. Your time of decay may be distant, but it will surely come, for even the White Man whose God walked and talked with him as friend with friend, cannot be exempt from the common destiny. We may be brothers after all. We will see.

8   We will ponder your proposition, and when we decide we will let you know. But should we accept it, I here and now make this condition that we will not be denied the privilege without molestation of visiting at any time the tombs of our ancestors, friends and children. Every part of this soil is sacred in the estimation of my people. Every hillside, every valley, every plain and grove, has been hallowed by some sad or happy event in days long vanished. . . . The very dust upon which you now stand responds more lovingly to their footsteps than to yours, because it is rich with the blood of our ancestors and our bare feet are conscious of the sympathetic touch. . . . Even the little children who lived here and rejoiced here for a brief season will love these somber solitudes and at eventide they greet shadowy returning spirits. And when the last Red Man shall have perished, and the memory of my tribe shall have become a myth among the White Men, these stores will swarm with the invisible dead of my tribe, and when your children's children think themselves alone in the field, the store, the shop, upon the highway, or in the silence of the pathless woods, they will not be alone. . . . At night when the streets of your cities and villages are silent and you think them deserted, they will throng with the returning hosts that once filled and still love this beautiful land. The White Man will never be alone.

9   Let him be just and deal kindly with my people, for the dead are not powerless. Dead, did I say? There is no death, only a change of worlds.

—Chief Seattle

FOR DISCUSSION

1. Sum up Oliver Wendell Holmes' philosophy about life in one sentence.

2. What makes Holmes' speech useful to readers even now?

3. Discuss William Faulkner's use of a traditional circumstance—receiving a prize in public—as an opportunity to make a personal statement to young people around the world.

4. What is Faulkner's main point?

5. What was Chief Seattle's actual answer about the selling of the land?

6. Discuss how Chief Seattle accomplishes two aims simultaneously: answering an offer and making a personal statement.

7. How has each of these writers made this conventional form—a speech—personal?

8. Locate passages, phrases, words in the three speeches that make them vivid, clear, and memorable. Compare the uses of language in the speeches.

9. What makes these speeches powerful to read even though they were given orally first?

10. What value are these speeches to you?

LETTERS

The personal letter is one of the most common forms used for expressive writing. The three letters that follow illustrate this use of the form, each for a different kind of purpose. In the first—written before the Civil War, well over a century ago—a father writes to his son who is away at college. The second is taken from a letter written on shipboard by Carl Jung (1875-1961) to his wife. In the last, E. B. White writes Stanley Hart White, his brother, a unique message of thanks.

Reverend C. C. Jones to His Son

Maybank Plantation, Liberty County, Georgia
Monday Morning, May 22nd, 1854

Dear Charles,

I do not think my dear son, that anyone wrote you last week. I did not, it having been a busy week. Mother is always busy, you know, and has had company. She is remarkably well, and was never so fleshy. I must give you a sketch of her daily life.

2   She rises about six in the morning, or now half-past five; takes her bath, reads, and is ready for family worship about seven; then breakfasts with a moderate appetite and enjoys a cup of good tea. Breakfast concluded and the cups, etc., washed up and dinner ordered, Little Jack gathers up his *"weepons,"* as he calls them—the flower trowel, the trimming saw, the nippers and pruning shears and two garden hoes—and follows his mistress, with her sunbonnet on and her large India-rubber-cloth working gloves, into the flower and vegetable gardens. In these places she spends sometimes near two hours hoeing, planting, pruning, etc., Little Jack and frequently Beck and several other little fellows and Gilbert in the bargain all kept as busy as bees about her—one sweeping, another watering, another weeding, another planting and trimming, and another carrying off the limbs and trash. Then she dismisses the forces, and they go off in separate detachments to their respective duties about the house and premises, and she takes a walk of observation and superintendence about the kitchen yard and through the orchard and lawn, accompanied by any friends she may have with her and who may be disposed to take a walk of a quiet domestic nature.

3   About ten her outdoor exercise is over, and she comes in, sets aside her bonnet, draws off her gloves, and refreshes herself with a basin of cool water, after which she disposes of her seamstresses and looks that the house has been well put to rights and in point and in perfect order—flowerpots dressed, etc. She now devotes herself to cutting out, planning, fitting, or sewing, giving attention to the clothing department and to the condition of the furniture of chambers, curtains, towels, linens, etc. The wants of the servants' wardrobe are inquired into, and all the thousand and one cares of the family attended to.

4   Meanwhile the yards have been swept, the walk sanded, and Patience has her culinary world all in neat order. The two milk-white cats have had their breakfast, and are lying in each other's paws in the shade on the green grass in the flower garden; and the young dog *Rex,* having enjoyed his repast, has stretched himself at full length in the sun, and ever and anon rolls over and wallows and kicks his feet into the air. The old turkey hen has spread her young ones like scouts around her, and is slowly picking along the green, and the gobbler is strutting with two or three idle dames in another direction. The fowls have scattered themselves everywhere in the lot, crowing and cackling and scratching; the sheep have finished their early browse, and are lying down beneath the great hickory tree; and overhead and all around is one general concert of birds.

5   The glorious sunlight, and soft south wind, and the green earth and the blue heavens—Mother sees and enjoys it all; but she is too busy now to come out and take a view. If she has visitors, she is sitting at work and in conversation with them, or for an hour or two before

dinner takes her book or pen in hand. But sometimes she indulges in a quiet little doze, and gets up refreshed just before we are called to dinner. This meal she usually enjoys, but is never much of an eater; enjoys her food, but in much moderation.

For an hour or two after dinner she retires, and about the middle of 6 the afternoon makes her appearance dressed for the evening. Then she is full of her uniform cheerfulness, and attracts everybody to her— husband, children, servants, visitors, old and young. The sea breeze is blowing sweetly. Our friends have driven over; the horses have been taken from the carriage, and the drivers have gone to pay their calls in the servants' quarters. The chairs are set out in the piazza, and here we spend a social hour and take tea. Our friends take leave, and then we have family worship. Sometimes they unite with us before they go. We all retire now to our study or rooms, and when the business of the day is over, then Mother enjoys the quiet, and loves to sit up reading and writing and conversing. She says this is the pleasantest part of *the day* to her.

You will recognize all this as very natural—what you have seen 7 many times. Surely our hearts should be full of gratitude to God for all His unnumbered and undeserved favors to us as a family. May we all through riches of grace be saved in a brighter, better, and more enduring world than this! . . . All in the house—Mother, Brother, Sister, Aunt Susan, and Cousin Laura—send much love. I hear Mary Sharpe and Laura singing at the piano, and your brother talking to Mother. He is all the time quite busy. The Lord be with and bless you, my dear son!

Your ever affectionate father,
C. C. Jones.

Carl Jung to His Wife, Emma

Steamer Kaiser Wilhelm der Grosse
North German Lloyd
Bremen
September 25, 1909

. . . . Yesterday there was a storm that lasted all day until nearly 1 midnight. Most of the day I stood up front, under the bridge, on a protected and elevated spot, and admired the magnificent spectacle as the mountainous waves rolled up and poured a whirling cloud of foam over the ship. The ship began to roll fearfully, and several times we were soaked by a salty shower. It turned cold, and we went in for a cup of tea. Inside, however, the brain flowed down the spinal canal and tried to come out again from under the stomach. Consequently I retired to my bed, where I soon felt fine again and later was able to consume a pleasant supper. Outside from time to time a wave thundered against the ship. The objects in my cabin had all come to life: the sofa cushion crawled about on the floor in the semi-darkness; a recumbent shoe sat up, looked around in astonishment, and then shuffled quietly off under the sofa; a standing shoe turned wearily on its side and followed its mate. Now the scene changed. I realized that the shoes had gone under the sofa to fetch my bag and brief case. The whole company paraded over to join the big trunk under the bed. One sleeve of my shirt on the sofa waved longingly after them, and from inside the chests and drawers came rumbles and rattles. Suddenly there was a terrible crash under my floor, a rattling, clattering, and tinkling. One of the kitchens is underneath me. There, at one blow, five hundred plates had been awakened from their deathlike torpor and with a single bold leap had put a sudden end to their dreary existence as slaves. In all the cabins round about, unspeakable groans betrayed the secrets of the menu. I slept like a top, and this morning the wind is beginning to blow from another side. . . .

E. B. White to His Brother

25 West 43
[January 1947]
Friday

Dear Bun:

1   I'm glad to report that even now, at this late day, a blank sheet of paper holds the greatest excitement there is for me—more promising than a silver cloud, prettier than a little red wagon. It holds all the hope there is, all fears. I can remember, really quite distinctly, looking a sheet of paper square in the eyes when I was seven or eight years old and thinking "This is where I belong, this is it." Having dirtied up probably a quarter of a million of them and sent them down drains and through presses, I am exhausted but not done, faithful in my fashion, and fearful only that I will die before one comes out right—as though I had deflowered a quarter of a million virgins and was still expecting the perfect child. What *is* this terrible infatuation, anyway? Some mild nervous disorder, probably, that compels a man to leave a fiery tail in his wake, like a ten-cent comet, or smell up a pissing post so that the next dog will know who's been along. I have moments when I wish that

I could either take a sheet of paper or leave it alone, and sometimes, in despair and vengeance, I just fold them into airplanes and sail them out of high windows, hoping to get rid of them that way, only to have an updraft (or a change of temper) bring them back in again. As for your gift of so many sheets of white bond, with rag content, I accept them in the spirit with which they were sent and shall write you a book. It will be the Greatest Book that has Ever Been Written. They all are, in the early wonderful stage before the first word gets slid into place.

Happy New Year!
En

FOR DISCUSSION

1. Each of the three letters included here "reveals" something about the writers' values—what they consider important or unimportant in life—or reveals something about how the writers respond to life. In one sentence for each letter, summarize the writers' unspoken yet revealed expression of their values or response to life.

2. Imagine that each of these writers is at a meeting. How do you think each would be dressed? What suggests this dress to you in the letters, since there is certainly nothing there specifically about how the writers might look?

3. What do these three letters have in common?

4. Look back at the letter included in **Writing to Tell:** *The Information Essay.* How could it also have appeared in this section with these letters, as well as where it actually appears in this book?

5. What makes these letters good writing?

6. In spite of the fact that these letters carry the writers' personal expression, how are they also letters communicating to the people to whom they are addressed? For instance, how would Stanley White, E. B. White's brother, know that he had received a personal letter even though there is nothing said to him directly about his relationship with his brother? Look at the other letters in this light also.

LIST

Here is a list; *an unusual personal form of writing. Psychologist Stephen Kopp uses this list to close his fascinating book called* If You Meet the Buddha on the Road, Kill Him!

An Eschatological Laundry List: A Partial Register of the 927 (or was it 928?) Eternal Truths

1. This is it!
2. There are no hidden meanings.
3. You can't get there from here, and besides there's no place else to go.
4. We are all already dying, and we will be dead for a long time.
5. Nothing lasts.
6. There is no way of getting all you want.
7. You can't have anything unless you let go of it.
8. You only get to keep what you give away.
9. There is no particular reason why you lost out on some things.
10. The world is not necessarily just. Being good often does not pay off and there is no compensation for misfortune.
11. You have a responsibility to do your best nonetheless.
12. It is a random universe to which we bring meaning.
13. You don't really control anything.
14. You can't make anyone love you.
15. No one is any stronger or any weaker than anyone else.
16. Everyone is, in his own way, vulnerable.
17. There are no great men.
18. If you have a hero, look again: you have diminished yourself in some way.
19. Everyone lies, cheats, pretends (yes, you too, and most certainly I myself).
20. All evil is potential vitality in need of transformation.
21. All of you is worth something, if you will only own it.
22. Progress is an illusion.
23. Evil can be displaced but never eradicated, as all solutions breed new problems.
24. Yet it is necessary to keep on struggling toward solution.
25. Childhood is a nightmare.
26. But it is so very hard to be an on-your-own, take-care-of-yourself-cause-there-is-no-one-else-to-do-it-for-you grown up.

27. Each of us is ultimately alone.
28. The most important things, each man must do for himself.
29. Love is not enough, but it sure helps.
30. We have only ourselves, and one another. That may not be much, but that's all there is.
31. How strange, that so often, it all seems worth it.
32. We must live within the ambiguity of partial freedom, partial power, and partial knowledge.
33. All important decisions must be made on the basis of insufficient data.
34. Yet we are responsible for everything we do.
35. No excuses will be accepted.
36. You can run, but you can't hide.
37. It is most important to run out of scapegoats.
38. We must learn the power of living with our helplessness.
39. The only victory lies in surrender to oneself.
40. All of the significant battles are waged within the self.
41. You are free to do whatever you like. You need only face the consequences.
42. What do you know . . . for sure . . . anyway?
43. Learn to forgive yourself, again and again and again and again. . . .

FOR DISCUSSION

1. What do you "know" about the author after reading this list?

2. Speculate on why the author put this information in a list instead of in an essay.

3. What personal statement does the author make, using the conventional list form?

4. What value is the list to you?

JOURNAL

In 1805 Meriwether Lewis (1774–1809) and William Clark (1770–1838) and their party began the long trek over what is now known as the Oregon Trail. But as you will soon see, these men made the trail. The journals served as a means to make their personal observations; these excerpts document the long and arduous trip.

from the Journals of Lewis and Clark

April 7, 1805

1 Our vessels consisted of six small canoes and two large pirogues. This little fleet, although not quite so respectable as that of Columbus or Captain Cook, was still viewed by us with as much pleasure as those deservedly famed adventurers ever beheld theirs, and, I daresay, with quite as much anxiety for their safety and preservation. We were now about to penetrate a country at least two thousand miles in width, on which the foot of civilized man had never trod. The good or evil it had in store for us was for experiment yet to determine, and these little vessels contained every article by which we were to expect to subsist or defend ourselves. However, as the state of mind in which we are, generally gives the coloring to events, when the imagination is suffered to wander into futurity, the picture which now presented itself to me was a most pleasing one.

2 Entertaining as I do the most confident hope of succeeding in a voyage which had formed a darling project of mine for the last ten years, I could but esteem this moment of my departure as among the most happy of my life. The party are in excellent health and spirits, zealously attached to the enterprise, and anxious to proceed. Not a whisper or murmur of discontent to be heard among them, but all act in unison and with the most perfect harmony.

May 14th, 1805

3 In the evening, the men in two of the rear canoes discovered a large brown bear lying in the open grounds about 300 paces from the river, and six of them went out to attack him—all good hunters. They took the advantage of a small eminence which concealed them, and got within 40 paces of him, unperceived. Two of them reserved their fires as had been previously concerted; the four others fired nearly at the same time, and put each his bullet through him. Two of the balls passed

through the bulk of both lobes of his lungs. In an instant, this monster ran at them with open mouth. The two who had reserved their fires discharged their pieces at him as he came toward them. Both of them struck him—one only slightly, and the other, fortunately, broke his shoulder. This, however, only retarded his motion for a moment.

The men, unable to reload their guns, took to flight. The bear 4 pursued, and had very nearly overtaken them before they reached the river. Two of the party betook themselves to a canoe, and the others separated and concealed themselves among the willows, [*and*] reloaded their pieces; each discharged his piece at him as they had an opportunity. They struck him several times again, but the guns served only to direct the bear to them. In this manner he pursued two of them, separately, so close that they were obliged to throw away their guns and pouches, and throw themselves into the river, although the bank was nearly twenty feet perpendicular. So enraged was this animal that he plunged into the river only a few feet behind the second man he had compelled to take refuge in the water.

When one of those who still remained on shore shot him through the 5 head and finally killed him, they then took him on shore and butchered him, when they found eight balls had passed through him in different directions. The bear being old, the flesh was indifferent. They therefore only took the skin and fleece; the latter made us several gallons of oil. It was after the sun had set before these men came up with us, where we had been halted by an occurrence which I have now to recapitulate, and which, although happily passed without ruinous injury, I cannot recollect but with the utmost trepidation and horror. This is the upsetting and narrow escape of the white pirogue.

It happened, unfortunately for us this evening, that Charbonneau 6 was at the helm of this pirogue instead of Drouilliard, who had previously steered her. Charbonneau cannot swim, and is perhaps the most timid waterman in the world. Perhaps it was equally unlucky that Captain Clark and myself were both on shore at that moment, a circumstance which rarely happened, and though we were on the shore opposite to the pirogue, were too far distant to be heard, or to do more than remain spectators of her fate. In this pirogue were embarked our papers, instruments, books, medicine, a great part of our merchandise—and, in short, almost every article indispensably necessary to further the view or ensure the success of the enterprise in which we are now launched to the distance of 2,200 miles.

Suffice it to say that the pirogue was under sail when a sudden squall 7 of wind struck her obliquely and turned her considerably. The steersman, alarmed, instead of putting her before the wind, luffed her up into it. The wind was so violent that it drew the brace of the squaresail out of the hand of the man who was attending it, and instantly upset the pirogue, and would have turned her completely topsy-turvy had it not have been for the resistance made by the awning against the water.

8   In this situation, Captain Clark and myself both fired our guns to attract the attention, if possible, of the crew, and ordered the halyards to be cut and the sail hauled in, but they did not hear us. Such was their confusion and consternation at this moment that they suffered the pirogue to lie on her side for half a minute before they took the sail in. The pirogue then righted but had filled within an inch of the gunwales.

9   Charbonneau, still crying to his God for mercy, had not yet recollected the rudder, nor could the repeated orders of the bowsman, Cruzat, bring him to his recollection until he threatened to shoot him instantly if he did not take hold of the rudder and do his duty.

10   The waves by this time were running very high, but the fortitude, resolution, and good conduct of Cruzat saved her. He ordered 2 of the men to throw out the water with some kettles that fortunately were convenient, while himself and two others rowed her ashore, where she arrived scarcely above the water. We now took every article out of her and laid them to drain as well as we could for the evening, bailed out the canoe, and secured her.

11   There were two other men besides Charbonneau on board who could not swim and who, of course, must also have perished had the pirogue gone to the bottom.

12   While the pirogue lay on her side, finding I could not be heard, I, for a moment, forgot my situation, and involuntarily dropped my gun, threw aside my shot pouch, and was in the act of unbuttoning my coat, before I recollected the folly of the attempt I was about to make, which was to throw myself into the river and endeavor to swim to the pirogue. The pirogue was three hundred yards distant, the waves so high that a person could scarcely live in any situation, the water excessively cold, and the stream rapid. Had I undertaken this project, therefore, there was a hundred to one but what I should have paid the forfeit of my life for the madness of my project, but this—had the pirogue been lost—I should have valued but little.

13   After having all matters arranged for the evening as well as the nature of circumstances would permit, we thought it a proper occasion to console ourselves and cheer the spirits of our men, and accordingly took a drink of grog, and gave each man a gill of spirits.

June 13th, 1805

14   This morning we set out about sunrise after taking breakfast off our venison and fish. We again ascended the hills of the river and gained the level country. Fearing that the river bore to the south, and that I might pass the Falls if they existed between this and the snowy mountains, I altered my course nearly to the south and proceeded through the plain. I sent Fields on my right and Drouilliard and Gibson on my left, with orders to kill some meat and join me at the river, where I should halt for dinner.

I had proceeded on this course about two miles with Goodrich at 15 some distance behind me, when my ears were saluted with the agreeable sound of a fall of water, and advancing a little further, I saw the spray rise above the plain like a column of smoke, which would frequently disappear again in an instant, caused, I presume, by the wind which blew pretty hard from the S.W. I did not, however, lose my direction to this point, which soon began to make a roaring too tremendous to be mistaken for any cause short of the Great Falls of the Missouri. Here I arrived about 12 o'clock, having traveled, by estimate, about 15 miles. I hurried down the hill, which was about 200 feet high and difficult of access, to gaze on this sublimely grand spectacle.

I took my position on the top of some rocks about 20 feet high 16 opposite the center of the Falls. This chain of rocks appears once to have formed a part of those over which the waters tumbled, but in the course of time has been separated from it to the distance of 150 yards, lying parallel to it, and an abutment against which the water, after falling over the precipice, beats with great fury. This barrier extends on the right to the perpendicular cliff which forms that border of the river, but to the distance of 120 yards next to the cliff it is but a few feet above the level of the water, and here the water in very high tides appears to pass in a channel of 40 yards next to the higher part of the ledge of rocks. On the left, it extends within 80 or 90 yards of the larboard cliff, which is also perpendicular. Between this abrupt extremity of the ledge of rocks and the perpendicular bluff, the whole body of water passes with incredible swiftness.

Immediately at the cascade, the river is about 300 yards wide. About 17 90 or 100 yards of this, next the larboard bluff, is a smooth even sheet of waterfalling over a precipice of at least 80 feet; the remaining part, about 200 yards wide, on my right, forms the grandest sight I ever beheld. The height of the fall is the same as the other, but the irregular and somewhat projecting rocks below receive the water in its passage down, and break it into a perfect white foam which assumes a thousand forms in a moment, sometimes flying up in jets of sparkling foam to the height of fifteen or twenty feet, which are scarcely formed before large rolling bodies of the same beaten and foaming water are thrown over and conceal them. In short, the rocks seem to be most happily fixed to present a sheet of the whitest beaten froth for 200 yards in length and about 80 feet perpendicular.

The water, after descending, strikes against the abutment before 18 mentioned, or that on which I stand, and seems to reverberate, and being met by the more impetuous current, they roll and swell into half-formed billows of great height which rise and again disappear in an instant. The abutment of rock defends a handsome little bottom of about three acres which is diversified and agreeably shaded with some cottonwood trees.

19   In the lower extremity of the bottom there is a very thick grove of the same kind of trees which are small. In this wood, there are several Indian lodges formed of sticks. A few small cedar grow near the ledge of rocks where I rest. Below the point of these rocks, at a small distance, the river is divided by a large rock which rises several feet above the water, and extends downward with the stream for about 20 yards. About a mile before the water arrives at the pitch, it descends very rapidly, and is confined on the larboard side by a perpendicular cliff of about 100 feet. On the starboard side it is also perpendicular for about three hundred yards above the pitch, where it is then broken by the discharge of a small ravine, down which the buffalo have a large beaten road to the water, for it is but in very few places that these animals can obtain water near this place, owing to the steep and inaccessible banks. I see several skeletons of the buffalo lying in the edge of the water near the starboard bluff which I presume have been swept down by the current and precipitated over this tremendous fall.

20   About 300 yards below me, there is another abutment of solid rock with a perpendicular face and about 60 feet high, which projects from the starboard side at right angles to the distance of 134 yards, and terminates the lower part nearly of the bottom before mentioned, there being a passage around the end of this abutment, between it and the river, of about 20 yards. Here the river again assumes its usual width, soon spreading to near 300 yards but still continuing its rapidity. From the reflection of the sun on the spray or mist which arises from these Falls, there is a beautiful rainbow produced which adds not a little to the beauty of this majestically grand scenery.

21   After writing this imperfect description, I again viewed the Falls, and was so much disgusted with the imperfect idea which it conveyed of the scene, that I determined to draw my pen across it and begin again; but then reflected that I could not perhaps succeed better than penning the first impressions of the mind. I wished for the pencil of Salvator Rosa, a Titian, or the pen of [*James*] Thomson, that I might be enabled to give to the enlightened world some just idea of this truly magnificent and sublimely grand object which has, from the commencement of time, been concealed from the view of civilized man. But this was fruitless and vain. I most sincerely regretted that I had not brought a camera obscura with me, by the assistance of which even I could have hoped to have done better, but alas, this was also out of my reach.

22   I therefore, with the assistance of my pen only, endeavored to trace some of the stronger features of this scene by the assistance of which, and my recollection aided by some able pencil, I hope still to give to the world some faint idea of an object which at this moment fills me with such pleasure and astonishment; and which of its kind, I will venture to assert, is second to but one in the known world.

FOR DISCUSSION

1. What underlying philosophies of life do Lewis and Clark "reveal" through their journals?

2. Of what value and interest are these journals to you?

3. Find several passages in the journals that make a strong impression on you, and discuss what there is in the writing that makes the impact.

4. What have Lewis and Clark added to their journals that make this form personal?

DIARY

The diary is the most obviously personal form that writers use. Edith Holden in 1906 kept one of the most beautiful hand-written and hand-painted diaries ever found. This excerpt—which loses much in being typed on a page instead of appearing in Holden's own penmanship—is from March of 1906.

from The Country Diary of an Edwardian Lady

March 1 March has come in like a lamb with a warm wind and rain from the South-West.

4 Glorious sunshine. First warm day of Spring. All the sky-larks up and singing in the blue. Went for a long walk. Found the colt's-foot and Procumbent Field Speedwell in flower and down at the edge of a copse, where a little stream ran, on a sunny bank I found a great many Primrose roots with quite large buds in the midst of their crowns of green leaves; the Celandine buds too were very large, another week or two of warm weather will bring them quite out. Everywhere the birds were very active, and such a chorus of voices from every hedge and tree!

6 Tonight a toad was discovered jumping about in the hall; it must have come in through the garden door which has been standing open all day. Another day of bright sunshine. . . . In the morning I visited the field where the

daffodils grow; the buds are all standing up above the grass, standing up straight like little green lance-heads among their spears of blue green leaves.

10 Cycled to the withy-beds within half a mile of Bushwood. It was a dull day with frequent showers of rain, so the country looked rather cold and grey. There was no sunshine to light up the ruddy blossom on the elm and alder trees. As I cycled between the hedges, I saw numbers of birds carrying on their house-building operations. I went a little out of my way down the lane to Kingswood to visit the steep banks where the blue periwinkle grows. There were numbers of flowers just opening; I only found one blossom fully expanded. The beds of white violets and the bank where the white periwinkle used to grow, that I had come to see, were some way off the road, and I had to carry my cycle nearly a quarter of a mile down a steep, muddy fordrough, set thick with thorns, with high banks on each side. On these sheltered banks, I found numbers of the small celandine blossom, and the first flowers of the little strawberry-leaved cinquefoil.

FOR DISCUSSION

1. What makes a reader interested in reading Edith Holden's diary?
2. What does Holden reveal about herself through the diary? How do you know this since the diary is not *about* herself?
3. What makes this diary good writing?
4. In what way was Holden a "modern woman"?

TRAVEL ACCOUNT

Isabella Bird, an English horsewoman, world traveler, founder of hospitals and a college for medical missionaries, and humanitarian, made a trip through the Rocky Mountains in 1873, alone. This excerpt is from her travel account. As you read the account notice its similarity to and difference from the journals of Lewis and Clark.

---

from A Lady's Life in the Rocky Mountains

Canyon, *September 12.*

I was actually so dull and tired that I deliberately slept away the afternoon in order to forget the heat and flies. Thirty men in working clothes, silent and sad looking, came in to supper. The beef was tough and greasy, the butter had turned to oil, and beef and butter were black with living, drowned, and half-drowned flies. The greasy table-cloth was black also with flies, and I did not wonder that the guests looked melancholy and quickly escaped. I failed to get a horse, but was strongly recommended to come here and board with a settler, who, they said, had a saw-mill and took boarders. The person who recommended it so strongly gave me a note of introduction, and told me that it was in a grand part of the mountains, where many people had been camping out all the summer for the benefit of their health. The idea of a boardinghouse, as I know them in America, was rather formidable in the present state of my wardrobe, and I decided on bringing my carpet-bag, as well as my pack, lest I should be rejected for my bad clothes.

Early the next morning I left in a buggy drawn by light *broncos* and driven by a profoundly melancholy young man. He had never been to the canyon; there was no road. We met nobody, saw nothing except antelope in the distance, and he became more melancholy and lost his way, driving hither and thither for about twenty miles till we came upon an old trail which eventually brought us to a fertile "bottom," where hay and barley were being harvested, and five or six frame houses looked cheerful. I had been recommended of two of these, which professed to take in strangers, but one was full of reapers, and in the other a child was dead. So I took the buggy on, glad to leave the glaring, prosaic settlement behind. There was a most curious loneliness about the journey up to that time. Except for the huge barrier to the right, the boundless prairies were everywhere, and it was like being at sea without a compass. The wheels made neither sound nor indentation as we drove over the short, dry grass, and there was no cheerful clatter of horses' hoofs. The sky was cloudy and the air hot and still. In one place we passed the carcass of a mule, and a number of vultures soared up from it, to descend again immediately. Skeletons and bones of animals were often to be seen. A range of low, grassy hills, called the Foot Hills, rose from the plain, featureless and monotonous, except where streams, fed by the snows of the higher regions, had cut their way through them. Confessedly bewildered, and more melancholy than ever, the driver turned up one of the wildest of these entrances, and in another hour the Foot Hills lay between us and the prairie sea, and a higher and broken range, with pitch pines of average size, was revealed behind them. These Foot Hills, which swell up uninterestingly from the plains on their eastern side, on their western have the appearance of having broken off from the next range, and the break is abrupt, and takes the form of walls and terraces of rock of the most brilliant color, weathered and stained by ores, and, even under the grey sky, dazzling to the eyes. The driver thought he had understood the directions given, but he was stupid, and once we lost some miles by arriving at a river too rough and deep to be forded, and again we were brought up by an impassable canyon. He grew frightened about his horses, and said no money would ever tempt him into the mountains again; but average intelligence would have made it all easy.

3   The solitude was becoming somber, when, after driving for nine hours, and traveling at the least forty-five miles, without any sign of fatigue on the part of the *broncos,* we came to a stream, by the side of which we drove along a definite track, till we came to a sort of tripartite valley, with a majestic crooked canyon 2,000 feet deep opening upon it. A rushing stream roared through it, and the Rocky Mountains, with pines scattered over them, came down upon it. A little farther, and the canyon became utterly inaccessible. This was exciting; here was an inner world. A rough and shaky bridge, made of the outsides of pines laid upon some unsecured logs, crossed the river. The *broncos* stopped and smelt it, not liking it, but some encouraging speech induced them to go over. On the other side was a log cabin, partially ruinous, and the very rudest I ever saw, its roof of plastered mud being broken into large holes. It stood close to the water among some cotton-wood trees. A little higher there was a very primitive saw-mill, also out of repair, with some logs lying about. An emigrant wagon and a forlorn tent, with a camp-fire and a pot, were in the foreground, but there was no trace of the boarding-house, of which I stood a little in dread. The driver went for further directions to the log cabin, and returned with a grim smile deepening the melancholy of his face to say it was Mr. Chalmers', but there was no accommodation for such as him, much less for me! This was truly "a sell." I got down and found a single room of the rudest kind, with the wall at one end partially broken down, holes in the roof, holes for windows, and no furniture but two chairs and two unplaned wooden shelves, with some sacks of straw upon them for beds. There was an adjacent cabin room, with a stove, benches, and table, where they cooked and ate, but this was all. A hard, sad-looking woman looked at me measuringly. She said that they sold milk and butter to parties who camped in the canyon, that they had never had any boarders but two asthmatic old ladies, but they would take me for five dollars per week if I "would make myself agreeable." The horses had to be fed, and I sat down on a box, had some dried beef and milk, and considered the matter. If I went back to Fort Collins, I thought I was farther from a mountain life, and had no choice but Denver, a place from which I shrank, or to take the cars for New York. Here the life

was rough, rougher than any I had ever seen, and the people repelled me by their faces and manners; but if I could rough it for a few days, I might, I thought, get over canyons and all other difficulties into Estes Park, which has become the goal of my journey and hopes. So I decided to remain.

September 16.

Five days here, and I am no nearer Estes Park. How the days pass I know not; I am weary of the limitations of this existence. This is "a life in which nothing happens." When the buggy disappeared, I felt as if I had cut the bridge behind me. I sat down and knitted for some time— my usual resource under discouraging circumstances. I really did not know how I should get on. There was no table, no bed, no basin, no towel, no glass, no window, no fastening on the door. The roof was in holes, the logs were unchinked, and one end of the cabin was partially removed! Life was reduced to its simplest elements. I went out; the family all had something to do, and took no notice of me. I went back, and then an awkward girl of sixteen, with uncombed hair, and a painful repulsiveness of face and air, sat on a log for half an hour and stared at me. I tried to draw her into talk, but she twirled her fingers and replied snappishly in monosyllables. Could I by any effort "make myself agreeable"? I wondered. The day went on. I put on my Hawaiian dress, rolling up the sleeves to the elbows in an "agreeable" fashion. Towards evening the family returned to feed, and pushed some dried beef and milk in at the door. They all slept under the trees, and before dark carried the sacks of straw out for their bedding. I followed their example that night, or rather watched Charles's Wain while they slept, but since then have slept on blankets on the floor under the roof. They have neither lamp nor candle, so if I want to do anything after dark I have to do it by the unsteady light of pine knots. As the nights are cold, and free from bugs, and I do a good deal of manual labor, I sleep well. At dusk I make my bed on the floor, and draw a bucket of ice-cold water from the river; the family go to sleep under the trees, and I pile logs on the fire sufficient to burn half the night, for I assure you the solitude is *eerie* enough. There are unaccountable noises, (wolves), rummagings under the floor, queer cries, and stealthy sounds of I know not what. One night a beast (fox or skunk) rushed in at the open end of the cabin, and fled through the window, almost brushing my face, and on another, the head and three or four inches of the body of a snake were protruded through a chink of the floor close to me, to my extreme disgust. My mirror is the polished inside of my watchcase. At sunrise Mrs. Chalmers comes in—if coming into a nearly open shed can be called *in*—and makes a fire, because she thinks me too stupid to do it, and mine is the family room; and by seven I am dressed, have folded the blankets, and swept the floor, and then she puts some milk and bread or stirabout on a box by the door. After breakfast I draw more water, and wash one or two garments daily, taking care that there are no witnesses of my inexperience. Yesterday a calf sucked one into hopeless rags. The rest of the day I spend in mending, knitting, writing to you, and the various odds and ends which arise when one has to do all for oneself. At twelve and six some food is put on the box by the door, and at dusk we make up our beds. A distressed emigrant woman has just given birth to a child in a temporary shanty by the river, and I go to help her each day.

5   I have made the acquaintance of all the careworn, struggling settlers within a walk. All have come for health, and most have found or are finding it, even if they have not better shelter than a wagon tilt or a blanket on sticks laid across four poles. The climate of Colorado is considered the finest in North America, and consumptives, asthmatics, dyspeptics, and sufferers from nervous diseases, are here in hundreds and thousands, either trying the "camp cure" for three or four months, or settling here permanently. People can safely sleep out of doors for six months of the year. The plains are from 4,000 to 6,000 feet high, and some of the settled "parks," or mountain valleys, are from 8,000 to 10,000. The air, besides being much rarefied, is very dry. The rainfall is far below the average, dews are rare, and fogs nearly unknown. The sunshine is bright and almost constant, and three-fourths of the days are cloudless. The milk, beef, and bread are good. The climate is neither so hot in summer nor so cold in winter as that of the States, and when the days are hot the nights are cool. Snow rarely lies on the lower ranges, and horses and cattle don't require to be either fed or housed during the winter. Of course the rarefied air quickens respiration. All this is from hearsay.[1] I am not under favorable circumstances, either for mind or body, and at present I feel a singular lassitude and difficulty in taking exercise, but this is said to be the milder form of the affection known on higher altitudes as *soroche,* or "mountain sickness," and is only temporary. I am forming a plan for getting farther into the mountains, and hope that my next letter will be more lively. I killed a rattlesnake this morning close to the cabin, and have taken its rattle, which has eleven joints. My life is embittered by the abundance of these reptiles rattlesnakes and moccasin snakes, both deadly, carpet snakes and "green races," reputed dangerous, water snakes, tree snakes, and mouse snakes, harmless but abominable. Seven rat-

---

[1] The curative effect of the climate of Colorado can hardly be exaggerated. In traveling extensively through the Territory afterwards I found that nine out of every ten settlers were cured invalids. Statistics and medical works on the climate of the State (as it now is) represent Colorado as the most remarkable sanatorium in the world.

tlesnakes have been killed just outside the cabin since I came. A snake, three feet long was coiled under the pillow of the sick woman. I see snakes in all withered twigs, and am ready to flee at "the sound of a shaken leaf." And besides snakes, the earth and air are alive and noisy with forms of insect life, large and small, stinging, humming, buzzing, striking, rasping, devouring!

FOR DISCUSSION

1. What is revealed about Isabella Bird by this travel account?
2. Often Bird wrote her travel accounts to send to her sister Henrietta in England. What keeps this travel account from being only for Henrietta?
3. What gives this travel account its power to make an impact?
4. This travel account was written in 1873. What value is it to readers in the 1980s?
5. What are Bird's qualities as a writer?

OBITUARY

Even if you do not ordinarily read the obituary column, you probably know that most obituaries follow a strict form, that they bear a strong resemblance to one another. The following obituary, which appeared on May 6, 1982 in the New York Times, *is, therefore, striking for being different—and very personal—from the usual notice written in this form.*

High-Society Glamour Girl of the '30s, Brenda Frazier

Brenda Frazier Kelly Chatfield-Taylor, whose name was once synonymous with glittering debutante balls and the social whirl, died of cancer Monday at the age of sixty.

Chatfield-Taylor, as Brenda Frazier, was in the headlines in the 1930s and '40s. Her photograph appeared in New York newspapers almost daily, as she lunched at the Stork Club, or danced with such eligible bachelors as Howard Hughes, John F. Kennedy and Douglas Fairbanks Jr. For the last twenty years, however, she had lived quietly at her homes on Beacon Hill and at East Harwich on Cape Cod.

3   Chatfield-Taylor had no fond memories of the period around 1938 when she was grouped with Hedy Lamarr, Bette Davis, Anthony Eden and the Duke of Windsor as the epitome of glamour. In a bitter memoir published in Life magazine in 1963, she spoke of the confining and meaningless life that had frozen the smile on her face.

4   "Though it hurts me, I must admit it: I have never known the true meaning of love," she wrote. "I thought at the time that I loved everyone—all my beaux, all my relatives, everyone I met. But I loved them only because I wanted them to love me, because the faintest sign of rejection by another person, even a nightclub doorman whom I might never see again, brought back all my old childhood feelings of being unwanted and depressed."

5   She said that with the help of psychoanalysis she had come to terms with herself, and vowed that her daughter would not become a debutante.

6   "I am free now to give her both love and the guidance that teenagers require and desperately want," she wrote.

7   She was born Brenda Diana Duff Frazier, and to the end her friends called her Diana. Her father, Frank Duff Frazier, who died in 1932, was from a family that had grown rich by cornering the Western wheat market. Her mother, Brenda Taylor of England, was the daughter of Sir Frederick Williams-Taylor, a banker and friend of royalty.

8   Her family left her a fortune in trust, and at the age of twelve she was called one of the richest children in the world. She said much later that her fortune was largely a myth, and that she had difficulty meeting expenses.

9   Her debut in 1938 at the Ritz-Carlton Hotel in New York was the social event of the season, attracting 1,000 people. Her picture was on the cover of the leading magazines, and in interviews she spoke of her happiness. Much later, she quoted a poem she had written at the time:

> *I given the impression of savoir-faire;*
> *Everyone I meet gives me an inward scare.*
> *They think I'm fast and they think I'm bad.*
> *For my favorite man is an invariable cad.*
> *I grit my teeth and smile at my enemies;*
> *I sit at the Stork Club and talk to non-entities.*

10   In 1941, at the age of twenty-one, she married John Sims (Shipwreck) Kelly, a stockbroker and former professional football player. They were divorced in 1956 and the next year she married Robert F.

Chatfield-Taylor, a New York sales executive. They separated a few years later, and he died in 1980.

Prior to their marriage, he had lived in San Francisco and had been 11 married to Elinor Chatfield-Taylor for seventeen years.

Chatfield-Taylor is survived by her daughter, Brenda Victoria Kelly 12 of Florida; a grandson, Jeremy Gates, and a step-brother, well-known sportsman and horse breeder Jimmy Watriss of Baltimore.

—New York Times

FOR DISCUSSION

1. Although the writer of this obituary is not identified, we "know" something about him or her after reading the piece—specifically we know something about what the writer thinks is important in life. Discuss what we can know about this unnamed writer from reading this obituary.

2. Discuss all the ways you can identify that this obituary differs from the customary obituary that appears in the newspaper.

3. What risk did the writer take in doing the obituary this way?

4. What does it say about the publishing policies of the *New York Times* that this obituary did appear in that newspaper? Does it surprise you that the obituary was printed there? Why?

WILL

Although most of us have read few—if any—wills, the will as a form is very common in many societies. Most wills follow a strict format and even contain identical sentences and paragraphs. The will of Leonardo da Vinci (1452–1519), however, is exceptional, just as da Vinci himself was. During his lifetime he painted, invented, sculpted, studied science, and accomplished engineering and architectural feats. When he died, the register of the church where he was buried recorded, "Leonard de Vincy, once Milanese, first painter, engineer, and architect of the King."

Will of Leonardo da Vinci

1 Be it known to all persons, present and to come, that at the court of our Lord the King at Amboise before ourselves in person, Messer Leonardo da Vinci, painter to the King, at present staying at the place known as Cloux near Amboise, duly considering the certainty of death and the uncertainty of its time, has acknowledged and declared in the said court and before us that he has made, according to the tenor of these presents, his testament and the declaration of his last will, as follows. And first he commends his soul to our Lord, Almighty God, and to the Glorious Virgin Mary, and to our lord Saint Michael, to all the blessed Angels and Saints male and female in Paradise.

2   Item. The said Testator desires to be buried within the church of Saint Florentin at Amboise, and that his body shall be borne thither by the chaplains of the church.

3   Item. That his body may be followed from the said place to the said church of Saint Florentin by the *collegium* of the said church, that is to say by the rector and the prior, or by their vicars and chaplains of the church of Saint Denis of Amboise, also the lesser friars of the place, and before his body shall be carried to the said church this Testator desires that in the said church of Saint Florentin three grand Masses shall be celebrated by the deacon and subdeacon and that on the day when these three high Masses are celebrated, thirty low Masses shall also be performed at Saint Grégoire.

4   Item. That in the said church of Saint Denis similar services shall be performed, as above.

5   Item. That the same shall be done in the church of the said friars and lesser brethren.

6   Item. The aforesaid Testator gives and bequeaths to Messer Francesco da Melzo, nobleman, of Milan, in remuneration for services and favors done to him in the past, each and all of the books the Testator is at present possessed of, and the instruments and portraits appertaining to his art and calling as a painter.

7   Item. The same Testator gives and bequeaths henceforth forever to Battista de Vilanis his servant one half, that is, the moiety, of his garden which is outside the walls of Milan, and the other half of the same garden to Salai his servant; in which garden aforesaid Salai has built and constructed a house which shall be and remain henceforth in all perpetuity the property of the said Salai, his heirs and successors; and this is in remuneration for the good and kind services which the said de Vilanis and Salai, his servants, have done him in past times until now.

8   Item. The said Testator gives to Maturina his waiting woman a cloak of good black cloth lined with fur, a . . . of cloth and two ducats paid

once only; and this likewise is in remuneration for good service rendered to him in past times by the said Maturina.

Item. He desires that at his funeral sixty tapers shall be carried 9 which shall be borne by sixty poor men, to whom shall be given money for carrying them, at the discretion of the said Melzo, and these tapers shall be distributed among the four above-mentioned churches.

Item. The said Testator gives to each of the said churches ten lb. of 10 wax in thick tapers, which shall be placed in the said churches to be used on the day when those said services are celebrated.

Item. That alms shall be given to the poor of the Hôtel-Dieu, to the 11 poor of Saint Lazare d'Amboise and, to that end, there shall be given and paid to the treasurers of that same fraternity the sum and amount of seventy soldi of Tours.

Item. The said Testator gives and bequeaths to the said Messer 12 Franceso da Melzo, being present and agreeing, the remainder of his pension and the sums of money which are owing to him from the past time till the day of his death by the receiver or treasurer-general M. Johan Sapin, and each and every sum of money that he has already received from the aforesaid Sapin of his said pension, and in case he should die before the said Melzo and not otherwise; which moneys are at present in the possession of the said Testator in the said place called Cloux, as he says. And he likewise gives and bequeaths to the said Melzo all and each of his clothes which he at present possesses at the said place of Cloux, and all in remuneration for the good and kind services done by him in past times till now, as well as in payment for the trouble and annoyance he may incur with regard to the execution of this present testament, which, however, shall all be at the expense of the said Testator.

And he orders and desires that the sum of four hundred *scudi del* 13 *sole,* which he has deposited in the hands of the treasurer of Santa Maria Nuova in the city of Florence, may be given to his brothers now living in Florence with all the interest and usufruct that may have accrued up to the present time, and be due from the aforesaid treasurer to the aforesaid Testator on account of the said four hundred crowns, since they were given and consigned by the Testator to the said treasurers.

Item. He desires and orders that the said Messer Francesco da 14 Melzo shall be and remain the sole and only executor of the said will of the said Testator; and that the said testament shall be executed in its full and complete meaning and according to that which is here narrated and said, to have, hold, keep, and observe, the said Messer Leonardo da Vinci, constituted Testator, has obliged and obliges by these presents the said his heirs and successors with all his goods movable and immovable present and to come, and has renounced and expressly renounces by these presents all and each of the things which to that are contrary. Given at the said place of Cloux in the presence of Magister Spirito Fleri, vicar, of the church of Saint Denis at Amboise, of M. Guglielmo Croysant, priest and chaplain, of Magister Cipriane Fulchin, Brother Francesco de Corton, and of Francesco da Milano, a brother of the Convent of the Minorites at Amboise, witnesses summoned and required to that end by the indictment of the said court in the presence of the aforesaid M. Francesco da Melzo, who accepting and agreeing to the same has promised by his faith and his oath which he has administered to us personally and has sworn to us never to do or say or act in any way to the contrary. And it is sealed by his request with the royal seal apposed to legal contracts at Amboise, and in token of good faith.

15   Given on the XXIIIrd day of April MDXVIII, before Easter.

16   And on the XXIIIrd day of this month of April MDXVIII, in the presence of M. Guglielmo Borian, Royal notary in the court of the bailiwick of Amboise, the aforesaid M. Leonardo da Vinci gave and bequeathed, by his last will and testament, as aforesaid, to the said M. Baptista de Vilanis, being present and agreeing, the right of water which the King Louis XII or pious memory, lately deceased, gave to this same da Vinci, the stream of the canal of Santo Cristoforo in the duchy of Milan, to belong to the said Vilanis forever in such wise and manner that the said gentleman made him this gift in the presence of M. Francesco da Melzo, gentleman, of Milan, and in mine.

17   And on the aforesaid day in the said month of April in the said year MDXVIII the same M. Leonardo da Vinci by his last will and testament gave to the aforesaid M. Baptista de Vilanis, being present and agreeing, each and all of the articles of furniture and utensils of his house at present at the said place of Cloux, in the event of the said de Vilanis surviving the aforesaid M. Leonardo da Vinci, in the presence of the said M. Francesco da Melzo and of me, Notary, etc., Borean.

FOR DISCUSSION

1. What makes this will interesting to read?

2. Where does Leonardo da Vinci express his individuality in the will?

3. What do you know about da Vinci—his values and philosophy of life, for instance—from reading this will?

4. Where do you find vivid writing in this will? What keeps this vivid writing from being incompatible with the form of a will?

ADVERTISEMENTS

Advertisements might be one of the last places in the world that you would look to for personal expression of the writer. Yet the advertisements reprinted here do tell you something about the values and philosophies of somebody in these companies—perhaps the chief executive, perhaps the public relations officer, perhaps the executive in charge of advertising. The first advertisement is an essay from the Mobil Oil Company which appeared in Time *magazine. The next four each appeared in full-page form in the* Wall Street Journal, *all paid for by United Technologies Corporation, Hartford, Connecticut.*

World Without End

1 The world did not come to an end March of this year as some people had feared. True, the planets were aligned in syzygy on that day— meaning that they were all on the same side of the sun. (We didn't know the meaning of the word syzygy, either. So we looked if up and also found it's pronounced *sizz*-a-jee.) In the minds of some psuedo-astronomers, this rare configuration augured that celestial forces would prevent the earth from spinning and propel us all into the blackness of outer space.

2 Well, it didn't happen, but for some pessimists it might as well have. After all, an apocalyptic syzygy would be no worse than sudden thermonuclear war. Those with a lower threshold of pain might find it more bearable even than a downward slide of the stock market. For starving or oppressed millions around the globe, life is little more than a heart-rending journey toward an elusive apocalypse which refuses to arrive in time to end their suffering. And for the fortunate among us, the end of the world is akin to the stroke of midnight which dispatches Cinderella home from the ball.

3 But let's be serious. To contemplate the end of the world in realistic terms is to come face-to-face with the treasures life holds in even the worst of circumstances. Not only one's own life. Witness Lenny Skutnik, who thought enough of life to leap into the freezing Potomac to rescue a crash victim he never knew. Or the dedication of medical researchers who cling to mere threads of clinical evidence with only a minuscule chance that they will save a life many years hence.

4 If life is precious, then so are the ingredients which sustain it. Some of these ingredients are quite pedestrian. Agricultural products for food, hydrocarbons for warmth and mobility, chemicals for health and creature comforts are all within the grasp of human ingenuity. When

they become scarce—by dint of nature's whims or man-made dislocations—their shortage reflects itself in economic suffering, sometimes of cataclysmic proportions.

5   But this need not spell the end of the world, literally or figuratively. Humanity has the power and determination to overcome such adversity. What is sometimes lacking is the good will or the resourcefulness. If inflation gnaws away at ready access to the necessities of life, there are ways of stemming it, but sometimes with the side effect of unemployment—equally undesirable. If political squabbling interferes with the delivery of life's requisites, there are often non-political solutions—but some of them place unfair burdens on one group or another.

6   If any one human had the solution to all of the world's problems without creating new ones, we should be grateful—but also fearful that the millennium would spell the end of human challenge.

7   Serious scientists postulate that the solar system may, indeed, disintegrate in another few billion years—not necessarily during syzygy and not necessarily on any day. In any event, this gives us all a little time.

8   It gives us time to do some cogent thinking about the efficacy of war as a way of settling things, notably as a way to allocate the world's resources among nations and peoples.

9   It gives us time to devise means by which the world's economies can eliminate poverty.

10   It gives us time to find answers to the medical mysteries which annually doom millions to pain and untimely deaths.

11   It gives us time to cultivate a bumper crop of good will which can often heal the conflicts for which we arm ourselves constantly, usually at the expense of the better things of life.

12   It gives us time for research to learn more about life itself, particularly about our environment—how we can serve it while it serves us.

13   After all, if the world isn't coming to an end in the foreseeable future, why not make it a better place in which to live?

This Will Make You Feel Better

If you sometimes
get discouraged,
consider this fellow:
He dropped out
of grade school.
Ran a country store.
Went broke.
Took 15 years
to pay off
his bills.
Took a wife.
Unhappy marriage.
Ran for House.
Lost twice.
Ran for Senate.
Lost twice.
Delivered speech
that became
a classic.
Audience indifferent.
Attacked daily
by the press
and despised
by half the country.
Despite all this,
imagine
how many people
all over the world
have been
inspired
by this awkward,
rumpled,
brooding man
who signed his name
simply,
A. Lincoln.

Keep It Simple

Strike three.
Get your hand off my knee.
You're overdrawn.
Your horse won.
Yes.
No.
You have the account.
Walk.
Don't walk.
Mother's dead.
Basic events
require simple language.
Idiosyncratically euphuistic
eccentricities are the
promulgators of
triturable obfuscation.
What did you do last night?
Enter into a meaningful
romantic involvement
or
fall in love?
What did you have for
breakfast this morning?
The upper part of a hog's
hind leg with two oval
bodies encased in a shell
laid by a female bird
or
ham and eggs?
David Belasco, the great
American theatrical producer,
once said, "If you can't
write your idea on the
back of my calling
card,
you don't have a clear idea."

FOR DISCUSSION

1. What values and philosophies are "revealed" by these advertisements?

2. Discuss how these advertisements differ from most advertisements.

3. Since the person or persons responsible for these advertisements are not identified, speculate on what kind of satisfaction they could get from seeing the advertisements in print even though they are not credited with the writing.

4. Can you see any relationship between the content of the Mobil Oil advertisement and the services/business that the company does? What about United Technologies in relation to their ads?

SPIRITUAL WRITING

Spiritual writing takes many forms. Three broad categories are represented here: the sermon, meditations and philosophical writing, and prayers. Through these forms individuals or a whole people can find expression.

The sermon is another form intended for oral delivery. The one reprinted here is by Meister Eckhart, a mystic and preacher who lived in Germany in the 1200's. Writers attempting to describe Eckhart's work have said that he had one intent—and that intent was God.

The meditations and philosophical writings as well as the prayers here come from many cultures. The formats of these pieces do not reveal which fall into one category and which into the other. But you can easily distinguish the prayers from the other writings by determining the "audience"; prayers are addressed to a higher power or a deity, while meditations and philosophical writings are addressed to the self or to other people.

SERMON

God Laughs and Plays

I have read two texts in Latin. One is in the lection for today and is 1 quoted from the prophet Isaiah: "Sing, O heavens; and be joyful, O earth; for the Lord hath comforted his people and will have mercy on his afflicted." The other is from the Gospel and quotes our Lord: "I am the light of the world: he that followeth me shall not walk in darkness, but shall have the light of life."

Now, notice the first text in which the prophet is quoted: "Rejoice, 2 O heavens and earth." Truly! Truly! By God! By God! Be as sure of it as you are that God lives: at the least good deed, the least bit of good will, or the least of good desires, all the saints in heaven and on earth rejoice, and together with the angels, their joy is such that all the joy in this world cannot be compared to it. The more exalted a saint is, the greater his joy; but the joy of them all put together amounts to as little as a bean when compared to the joy of God over good deeds. For truly, God plays and laughs in good deeds, whereas all other deeds, which do not make for the glory of God, are like ashes before him. Thus he says: "Rejoice, O heavens! For the Lord hath comforted his people!"

3   Notice that he says: "God hath comforted his people and will have mercy on his afflicted—his poor ones." The poor are left to God alone, for no one bothers with them. If one has a friend who is poor, he does not open his heart to him; but if he is good and wise, he says: "You belong to my crowd!"—and quickly opens his heart to him. But to the poor, they say: "God take care of you!"—and are ashamed of them. The poor are left to God and wherever they go they find him, and everwhere he is theirs. God takes charge of them because they are given to him. That is why the gospel says: "Blessed are the poor."

4   Now let us look at the text in which he says: "I am the light of the world." "I am" has to do with essence. The authorities say that any creature at all could say "I," for that word is general property, but the word "*sum*—am" belongs to God alone, and none may use it but he. *Sum* expresses the thought of one thing containing all good. To creatures this is denied, so that none of them may have what is exclusively assigned to persons for their comfort. If I had all I could wish for, and yet hurt my finger, I should not have this *all,* for my finger would be hurt and complete comfort would not be mine as long as that was the case. Bread is comfortable to people who are hungry, but if they are thirsty they get as little comfort out of bread as they would out of a stone. It is the same with clothing when one is cold, but when one is hot he gets little comfort out of clothing. So it is with all kinds of creatures: they all have a certain bitterness in them and as surely they contain a certain comfort, like the sweetness of honey, to be skimmed off the surface. But among other things, all that is good in creatures, all their honey-sweetness is from God. Thus it is written in the Book of Wisdom: "All the good of my soul comes from thee."

5   Creature comfort is never perfect. It is faulty and never comes unmixed. God's comfort is pure and without any admixture. It is full and complete and he needs so much to give it that he can do nothing else until he has. So prodigal is God with his love for us that it might seem as if he had forgotten about the Kingdoms of Heaven and earth, all the blessing of his Godhead, and could have nothing to do with anything else than me alone, so that he might be free to give me all my comfort requires. And to me he gives it—constantly—completely and perfectly—in its purest form—and so he gives it to every creature.

6   He says: "He that followeth me shall not walk in darkness." Notice that "he that followeth me." The authorities say that the soul has three agents. The first is always seeking what is sweetest. The second is always seeking the highest. The third always seeks the best, for the soul is too aristocratic ever to rest except at its own point of origin, from which there drops what makes for goodness. See, so sweet is God's comfort that every creature is looking for it, hunting it. I shall go even further and say that their very existence and life depend on their search for it, their hunting it.

But you may ask: "Where is this God, after whom all creatures seek 7 and from whom they have their life and being?" (I prefer to speak of the Godhead, from whence all our blessings flow.) The Father says: "My Son, I have begotten thee today in the light reflected from the saints." Where is this God? "I am caught in the perfection of the saints." Where is this God? In the Father. Where is this God? In eternity. Just as a man who is hiding clears his throat and thus reveals his whereabouts, so it is with God. Nobody could ever find God. He has to discover himself.

A saint says: "Sometimes I feel such a sweetness in my soul that I 8 forget everything else—and myself too—and dissolve in thee. But when I try to catch it perfectly, O Lord, thou takest it away. Lord, what do you mean by that? You entice me. Then why do you withdraw? If you love me, why do you run away? Ah, Lord, you do this because you want me to have a lot of experience with you!"

The prophet says: "My God!"   9

"Who told you that I am your God?"   10

"Lord, I cannot rest except in you and nothing goes well with me 11 except in you."

That we may ever seek God like this, and even find him, may God 12 the Father, the Son, and the Holy Ghost help us! Amen.

—Meister Eckhart
(trans. Raymond B. Blakney)

MEDITATIONS AND PHILOSOPHICAL WRITINGS

St. Teresa's Bookmark

Let nothing trouble thee,	Nada te turbe,	1
Let nothing affright thee,	Nada te espante,	
All things are passing,	Todo se pasa.	
God never changes;	Dios no se muda.	
Patience obtains everything,	La paciencia todo lo alcanza,	5
Nothing is wanting to him who possesses God,	Quien a Dios tiene nada le falta.	
God alone suffices.	Solo Dios basta.	

—St. Teresa   —Santa Teresa de Avila

Ninth Meditation

1   The infinite creative power of Universal Subconscious Mind lies within me. I attune myself, remove all barriers from my thought, become receptive to the purposes of God. I know that my life is great and good when I perform service with love. The right ideas are deliv-
5 ered to me, I accept them, and Subconscious Mind provides me with the means of bringing them into my world. I know that all things spring from Universal Mind, which is infinitely abundant. Lack and limitation are errors of thinking, and I banish them from my consciousness. There can be no lack. I need only let Universal Mind express itself
10 through me, and my world is filled with creativeness and achievement and prosperity; my goals will be delivered to me, for they will be the goals of God, who never fails. Whatever my task I perform it with love, for I know that when I serve another I serve the purposes of a greater design. All about me I see the law of mutual exchange; therefore I give
15 as I would receive. I know that abundance and prosperity are mental conditions; I create them on the plane of mind with complete trust and confidence that they will manifest in my life. I refuse to accept undesirable circumstance as having final reality. First cause is mental and is never found in the world about me. A mighty truth is at the center of
20 my consciousness, where no work is difficult, where peace always reigns, where all things are possible. I know that life is a journey which must be traveled step by step, and I am patient, enjoying the wonder of the way, with unshakeable faith in my destination. I submit my will, knowing that success will come when I fulfill the indwelling Self.

—U.S. Anderson

from the Tao Te Ching

47

1   There is no need to run outside
For better seeing,
Nor to peer from a window. Rather abide
At the center of your being;
5 For the more you leave it, the less you learn.
Search your heart and see
If he is wise who takes each turn:
The way to do is to be.

—Lao Tzu
6th Century B.C.
(Taoist)

from **the Metta Sutra**

May all living things be happy and at their ease! May they be joyous 1
and live in safety! All beings, whether weak or strong—omitting
none—in high, middle, or low realms of existence, small or great,
visible or invisible, near or far away, born or to be born—may all
beings be happy and at their ease! Let none deceive another, or despise 5
any being in any state; let none by anger or ill will wish harm to
another! Even as a mother watches over and protects her only child, so
with a boundless mind should one cherish all living beings, radiating
friendliness over the entire world, above, below and all around without
limit; so let him cultivate a boundless good will toward the entire 10
world, uncramped, free from ill will or enmity.

(Buddhist)

from **the Hsin-hsin-ming**

The Perfect Way knows no difficulties   1
Except that it refuses to make preference;
Only when freed from hate and love,
It reveals itself fully and without disguise,
A tenth of an inch's difference,   5
And heaven and earth are set apart:
If you want to see it manifest,
Take no thought either for or against it.
To set up what you like against what you dislike—
This is the disease of the mind: 10
When the deep meaning [of the Way] is not understood
Peace of mind is disturbed and nothing is gained.
[The Way] is perfect like unto vast space,
With nothing wanting, nothing superfluous:
It is indeed due to making choices   15
That its suchness is lost sight of.

.   .   .   .

When the mind rests serene in the oneness of things
. . . dualism vanishes by itself.

—Seng-ts'an
trans. D. T. Suzuki
(Zen)

from the Rig Veda

1 Not one of you, gods, is small, not one a little child; all of you are
truly great.
Therefore you are worthy of praise and of sacrifice, you thirty-three
gods of Manu, arrogant and powerful.
Protect us, help us and speak for us; do not lead us into the distance
far away from the path of our father Manu.
You gods who are all here and who belong to all men, give far-
reaching shelter to us and to our cows and horses.

(Hindu)

from the Bible

Though I speak with the tongues of men and of angels, and have not
charity, I am become *as* sounding brass, or a tinkling cymbal.
  And though I have *the gift of* prophecy, and understand all mysteries, and all knowledge; and though I have all faith, so that I could
remove mountains, and have not charity, I am nothing.
  And though I bestow all my goods to feed *the poor,* and though I give
my body to be burned, and have not charity, it profiteth me nothing.

—1 Corinthians, 13
King James version
(Christian)

The Golden Rule

1 Do unto others as you would they should do unto you.

(*Christian*)

Do nothing unto others which you would not have done unto yourself.

(*Buddhist*)

May we take the word of reciprocity to serve as our rule of life—what
we do not wish others to do to us, may we not do unto them.

(*Confucian*)

5 Do unto all men as you would wish to have done unto you.

(*Muslim*)

O God!   1
May I treat others
As I would be treated
What I like not for myself
May I dispense not to others.   5

(Sufi)

Do not approve for another what you do not like for yourself.

(Zoroastrian)

Do not do unto others that which you would not have them do
unto you.

(Jewish)

PRAYERS

A Jewish Prayer

Hear, O Israel: the Lord our God, the Lord is One.   1

Blessed be the name of His glorious kingdom for ever and ever.

And thou shalt love the Lord thy God with all thy heart, with all thy
soul, and with all thy might. And these words which I command thee
this day shall be in thy heart. Thou shalt teach them diligently unto thy 5
children, speaking of them when thou sittest in thy house, when thou
walkest by the way, when thou liest down and when thou risest up.
And thou shalt bind them for a sign upon thy hand, and they shall be for
frontlets between thine eyes. And thou shalt write them upon the door
posts of thy house and upon thy gates.   10

—Deuteronomy 6:4–9

A Navaho Prayer

Tségihi.   1
House made of dawn.
House made of evening light.
House made of the dark cloud.
House made of male rain.   5
House made of dark mist.

House made of female rain.
House made of pollen.
House made of grasshoppers.
10 Dark cloud is at the door.
The trail out of it is dark cloud.
The zigzag lightning stands high upon it.
Male deity!
Your offering I make.
15 I have prepared a smoke for you.
Restore my feet for me.
Restore my legs for me.
Restore my body for me.
Restore my mind for me. . .
20 Impervious to pain, may I walk.
With lively feelings may I walk.
As it used to be long ago, may I walk.
Happily may I walk.
Happily, with abundant dark clouds, may I walk.
25 Happily, with abundant showers, may I walk.
Happily, with abundant plants, may I walk.
Happily, on a trail of pollen, may I walk.
Happily may I walk.
Being as it used to be long ago, may I walk.
30 May it be beautiful before me.
May it be beautiful behind me.
May it be beautiful below me.
May it be beautiful above me.
May it be beautiful all around me.
35 In beauty it is finished.

—trans. Washington Matthews

A Muslim Prayer

1 All thy creatures, O God, form Thy family, and he is the best loved of
Thee who loveth best Thy creatures. O Lord, Lord of my life and of
everything in the universe, I affirm that all human beings are brothers
unto one another, so may we respect Thy ways and be affectionate to
5 the Family of God.

A Sikh Prayer

Lord, Thou mighty River, all-knowing, all-seeing,   1
And I like a little fish in Thy great waters,
How shall I sound Thy depths?
How shall I reach Thy shores?
Wherever I go, I see Thee only,   5
And snatched out of Thy waters, I die of separation.
I know not the fisher, I see not the net,
But flapping in my agony, I call upon Thee for help.
O Lord who pervades all things,
In my folly I thought Thee far,   10
But no deed I do can ever be out of Thy sight.

—Guru Nanak

A Christian Prayer

Merciful God, to Thee we commend ourselves and all those who need 1
Thy help and correction. Where there is hatred, give love; where there
is injury, pardon; where there is doubt, faith; where there is despair,
hope; where there is sadness, joy; where there is darkness, light. Grant
that we may not seek so much to be consoled, as to console; to be 5
understood, as to understand; to be loved, as to love; for in giving we
receive, in pardoning we are pardoned, and dying we are born into
eternal life.

—St. Francis

FOR DISCUSSION

1. Discuss the ways these traditional forms—sermons, prayers,
   meditations, and spiritual writings—allow for personal expression
   also.

2. In the prayers the personal expression may be of a people rather
   than a person. Discuss this, with the Navaho prayer in mind.

3. What do you "know" about St. Teresa from reading her
   philosophical writing?

4. How is Meister Eckhart as a person expressed through his
   sermon?

5. What can you guess about the writer of the ninth meditation?

6. Contrast at least three of the spiritual writing selections. Is there any difference of spiritual philosophies reflected here? What is unique about each one?

POEMS

The poem is one of the most familiar forms of expressive writing. Despite the constraints of the form—even the loosest, most modern versions of the form are constraining—writers have used this means to communicate expressively for centuries.

Poems do not always appear labelled as poems. The first poem here, for example, is from the Bible. Another, by Robert Schumann, is called a "song," but is a poem nonetheless. Even prose can be so poetic that readers sense that it is poetry; the excerpt here from Woody Guthrie's memories is such a "found" poem.

You will see—and you may already know—that personal expression through poetry can be very striking and vivid. As you read these poems, try to imagine any more powerful way the writers might have used to express themselves.

from Ecclesiastes

1   To everything there is a season,
And a time to every purpose under the heaven:
A time to be born, and a time to die;
A time to plant, and a time to pluck up that which is planted;
5   A time to kill, and a time to heal;
A time to break down, and a time to build up;
A time to weep, and a time to laugh;
A time to mourn, and a time to dance . . .

3:1–4 King James version, Bible

Spring Scene

On the temple bell
    Has settled, and is fast asleep
    A butterfly.

                    —Anonymous

Sonnet 116

Let me not to the marriage of true minds   1
Admit impediments. Love is not love
Which alters when it alteration finds,
Or bends with the remover to remove.
O, no, it is an ever-fixed mark   5
That looks on tempests and is never shaken;
It is the star to every wand'ring bark,
Whose worth's unknown, although his height be taken.
Love's not Time's fool, though rosy lips and cheeks
Within his bending sickle's compass come;   10
Love alters not with his brief hours and weeks,
But bears it out even to the edge of doom.

If this be error and upon me proved,
I never writ, nor no man ever loved.

                    —Shakespeare

Widmung	Dedication
Du meine Seele, du mein Herz,	You are my soul, you are my heart, 1
du meine Wonn', o du mein Schmerz,	You my delight, and you my pain;
du meine Welt, in der ich leber,	You are my world in which I live,
mein Himmel du, darein ich schwebe.	And you my heaven in which I soar;
o du mein Grab, in das hinab	You are my grave wherein I ever 5
ich ewig meinen Kummer gab!	Buried all my grief!

Du bist die Ruh', du bist der
  frieden;
du bist vom Himmel mir
  beschieden.
Dass du mich liebst, macht
  mich mir wert,
dein Blick hat mich vor mir
  verklärt,
du hebst mich liebend über
  mich,
mein guter Geist, mein bess'res
  Ich!

Du meine Seele, du mein
  Herz,
du meine Wonn', o du mein
  Schmerz,
du meine Welt, in der ich lebe,
mein Himmel du, darein ich
  schwebe,
mein guter Geist, mein bess'res
  Ich!

You are my rest, you are my
  peace,
You were allotted me by
  heaven;
That you love me gives me my
  worth;
Your glance transfigures me in
  my own eyes;   10
You, loving, raise me up above
  myself,
My good spirit, my better I.

You are my soul, you are my
  heart,
You my delight, and you my
  pain;
You are my world in which I
  live,   15
And you my heaven in which I
  soar;
My good spirit, my better I.
              —Robert Schumann

I Wandered Lonely as a Cloud

1   I wandered lonely as a cloud
That floats on high o'er vales and hills,
When all at once I saw a crowd,
A host, of golden daffodils,
5   Beside the lake, beneath the trees,
Fluttering and dancing in the breeze.

Continuous as the stars that shine
And twinkle on the milky way,
They stretched in never-ending line
10   Along the margin of a bay;
Ten thousand saw I at a glance,
Tossing their heads in sprightly dance.

The waves beside them danced, but they
Outdid the sparkling waves in glee;
A poet could not but be gay,   15
In such a jocund company;
I gazed—and gazed—but little thought
What wealth the show to me had brought:

For oft, when on my couch I lie
In vacant or in pensive mood,   20
They flash upon that inward eye
Which is the bliss of solitude;
And then my heart with pleasure fills,
And dances with the daffodils.

                                       —William Wordsworth

Poem 318

I'll tell you how the Sun rose—   1
A Ribbon at a time—
The Steeples swam in Amethyst—
The news, like Squirrels, ran—
The Hills untied their Bonnets—   5
The Bobolinks—begun—
Then I said softly to myself—
"That must have been the Sun"!
But how he set—I know not—
There seemed a purple stile   10
That little Yellow boys and girls
Were climbing all the while—
Till when they reached the other side,
A Dominie in Gray—
Put gently up the evening Bars—   15
And led the flock away—

                                       —Emily Dickinson

The Poet

1   You start with just a match—a wet match
and you explore the darkness inside you;
you finger, you fondle your ideas and dreams
about the round gray world and you find
5   what you think is the truth and you wind up
saying the old verities, the old saws and maxims
in a fine new voice
and the voice is your own
and this is educative for
10   you have learned that hard way
to discover, to create
your own beliefs. And any other approach
to the heart's art is sham and trickery
—at best, parlor gymnastics and rubbish,
15   and it is not that you will often succeed
or often come close but you will have had
the experience which a poet has,
no matter how frail, how faulty your execution,
It is your exploration down and under
20   and you start with just a match—a wet match.

—Edgar Simmons

from Seeds of Man

1   "I'll always remember Grandmaw Tanner's good cornbread. Wonder what th' secret was about it."

2   "Well, Mammy Ollie could dish it up just as good as your grandma Tanner could, any old time. Main secret was that she didn't put any sugar in her batter. Maybe an egg or so, which sometimes she did have and sometimes she didn't have, but anyway, she put in lots of salt and left out the sugar. Said that the sugar made cornbread taste too much like oatmeal cookies. She greased her pan with good hot lard, bacon grease, hog lard, whatever kind of grease she had, and she heated her pan in the oven, or up on the stove before she would pour her dough-batter into the pan. She used a good bit of buttermilk."

3   "Likkum my slikkum. Starvin' me t' death. Keep on."

4   "Mainest secret, I suppose, was lots of hot lard. And she shoved it into the oven when the oven was scorching hot. And she threw the wood to the fire till she nearly burnt the whole place up, summer,

winter, all of the time. She always did say that she had to chase her whole family out from the house before she could bake up good cornbread. But they always came a-running back after a bit when they got the smells of it cooking up their nose holes.''

"I 'mem'er. Yeahhhm."   5

"Always did bake it a long time. Most of us liked it good and curly   6
brown all around the edges. Most of us would fight to get the corner piece, or at least an outside chunk.''

"I remember. Me, too.''   7

"I guess this was where I learned how to be such a good fighting   8
hand in the first place. Fighting to get the best piece of Mammy Ollie's cornbread. Browny. Crispish. Real hot.''

"Big glass o'buttermilk. Yeahhhmmmannn.''   9

"Big slice of green onion—I mean, dry onion. No wonder that   10
Pawpaw Jerry swung onto Mammy Ollie the way that he did. He always did say that it was her cracklin' bread that brought them together and it was this same bread that kept them together. This same cornbread that kept the whole family fighting and growing all of the time. I can just feel it sticking out of my belly button, here, right this minute. Mmmmm. Mmmm. Mmmm.'' Papa's face lit up with thoughts he was seeing walk acrost the places of his memory.

"Ymmm.''   11

—Woody Guthrie

Warning

When I am an old woman I shall wear purple   1
With a red hat which doesn't go, and doesn't suit me,
And I shall spend my pension on brandy and summer gloves
And satin sandals, and say we've no money for butter.
I shall sit down on the pavement when I'm tired   5
And gobble up samples in shops, and press alarm bells
And run my stick along the public railings
And make up for the sobriety of youth.
I shall go out in my slippers in the rain
And pick the flowers in other people's gardens   10
And learn to spit.

You can wear terrible shirts, and grow more fat
And eat three pounds of sausages at a go
Or only bread and pickle for a week
And hoard pens and pencils and beermats and things in boxes.   15

But now we must have clothes that keep us dry
And pay the rent and not swear in the street
And set a good example for the children.
We must have friends to dinner and read the papers.

20   But maybe I ought to practice a little now?
So people who know me are not too shocked and surprised
When suddenly I am old and start to wear purple.

—Jenny Joseph

I would not be here

1 I would not be here
If I hadn't been there
I wouldn't been there
if I hadn't just turned
5 on Wednesday the third
in the late afternoon
got to talking with George
who works out in the back
and only because
10 he was getting off early
to go see a man
at a Baker Street bookstore
with a rare first edition
of steamboats and cotton
15 a book he would never
have sought in the first place
had he not been inspired
by a fifth grade replacement
school teacher in Kirkwood
20 who was picked just at random
by some man on a school board
who couldn't care less
and she wouldn't been working
if not for her husband
25 who moved two months prior
to work in the office
of a man he had met
while he served in the army
and only because
30 they were in the same barracks
an accident caused
by a poorly made roster

mixed up on the desk
of a sergeant from Denver
who wouldn't be in   35
but for being in back
in a car he was riding
before he enlisted
that hit a cement truck
and killed both his buddies   40
but a back seat flew up there
and spared him from dying
and only because
of the fault of a workman
who forgot to turn screws   45
on a line up in Detroit
'cause he hollered at Sam
who was hateful that morning
hung over from drinking
alone at a tavern   50
because of a woman
he wished he'd not married
he met long ago
at a Jewish bar mitzvah
for the son of a man   55
who had moved there from Jersey
who managed the drugstore
that sold the prescription
that cured up the illness
he caught way last summer   60
he wouldn't have caught
except . . .

—John Hartford

Sea Sculpture

I've whittled   1
a peninsula
out of myself
with bays
and inlets   5
to anchor in
during storms.
I've carved
with care.
I've harbors   10
to cruise to
on vacation.
With consideration,
I've chiseled seabreezes
to cool my coastlines   15
during heatwaves
I've fashioned my dunes
so they won't wash away.
The ocean keeps me guessing.
The final structure is   20
still under construction.

—Roland Pease

FOR DISCUSSION

1. What can you say about the persons who wrote each of these poems and the song in this section, even though you know little more about them than what is revealed in these selections?

2. How could you summarize the philosophy of the poet who wrote "Sea Sculpture"? Of the poet who wrote "Warning"?

3. What do you know about Woody Guthrie after reading the piece by him?

4. Discuss how songs and poems can be vehicles for writers to express their personal views and philosophies of life.

5. Discuss how the passage from Ecclesiastes is a poem.

WRITING YOUR OWN
The Personal Form

DESIGNING YOUR OWN CONFIGURATION

A chart is not appropriate for this section of the text; listed below however, are many possibilities you might consider in writing your own personal form. Read over these, and decide which you would like to do:

1. Write an advertisement for a company for which you work which is also an expression of your own philosophy or viewpoint.
2. Write an obituary for someone you know who has died in which you make a statement of personal expression in addition to giving the customary information included in obituaries.
3. Write a will which is also personal expression.
4. Write a poem or song that reveals something about how you see the world.
5. Write a sermon which has all the features of a typical sermon at the same time that it is an expression of you.
6. Write a prayer that reflects your beliefs.

7. Write an account of a trip you have taken that also reveals something about your philosophy of life or your experience in life.
8. Keep a diary for a few days, with an eye to using it to make yourself known to a reader.
9. Write a business letter that is about you at the same time that it is about business.
10. Write a speech for a particular occasion that fits that occasion *and* expresses you at the same time.
11. Write a memo that has your voice and person in it.
12. Experiment with a traditional form—letter, advertisement, will, sermon, poem, for instance—and, without violating any of the conventions of the form, make your writing also an expression of you.

RULES FOR THE PERSONAL FORM

1. Consider every form, no matter how traditional or conventional, as a possibility for personal expression.
2. Do not confuse personal expression with personal narrative.
3. Be willing to be engaged by what you are writing so that personal expression can emerge.
4. Be courageous.

William Stafford is a poet whose work has been highly acclaimed. Traveling through the Dark, *a collection of his poetry, won the National Book Award for Poetry in 1962, and he has won many other honorary degrees and awards. The judges of the National Book Award remarked that his poems are "both tough and gentle. Their music knows the value of silence." Stafford has also served as Consultant on Poetry for the Library of Congress.*

In the pages that follow you will find an essay by Stafford about writing, several of his poems, and the interview. The essay, "The Way of Writing," written for Field *magazine, is an account of what happens when a person writes. Stafford sees the writing process as an adventure, unpredictable, exciting, and always full of surprises and possibilities. The first poem, "Shadows," is shown in three stages of development—from rough notes to final form. The next six poems are taken from Stafford's* Stories That Could Be True: New and Collected Poems *(1977) and are among his most popular. In the interview Stafford talks about writing "The Way of Writing," and his partnership with the living qualities of words and syllables when he writes.*

A Way of Writing

A writer is not so much someone who has something to say as he is someone who has found a process that will bring about new things he would not have thought of if he had not started to say them. That is, he does not draw on a reservoir; instead, he engages in an activity that brings to him a whole succession of unforeseen stories, poems, essays, plays, laws, philosophies, religions, or—but wait!

Back in school, from the first when I began to try to write things, I felt this richness. One thing would lead to another; the world would give and give. Now, after twenty years or so of trying, I live by that certain richness, an idea hard to pin, difficult to say, and perhaps offensive to some. For there are strange implications in it.

One implication is the importance of just plain receptivity. When I write, I like to have an interval before me when I am not likely to be interrupted. For me, this means usually the early morning, before others are awake. I get pen and paper, take a glance out the window (often it is dark out there), and wait. It is like fishing. But I do not wait very long, for there is always a nibble—and this is where receptivity comes in. To get started I will accept anything that occurs to me. Something always occurs, of course, to any of us. We can't keep from thinking. Maybe I have to settle for an immediate impression: it's cold, or hot, or dark, or bright, or in between! Or—well, the possibilities are endless. If I put down something, that thing will help the next thing come, and I'm off. If I let the process go on, things will occur to me that were not at all in my mind when I started. These things, odd or trivial as they may be, are somehow connected. And if I let them string out, surprising things will happen.

If I let them string out. . . . Along with initial receptivity, then, there is another readiness: I must be willing to fail. If I am to keep on writing, I cannot bother to insist on high standards. I must get into action and not let anything stop me, or even slow me much. By "standards" I do not mean "correctness"—spelling, punctuation, and so on. These details become mechanical for anyone who writes for a while. I am thinking about what many people would consider "important" standards, such matters as social significance, positive values, consistency, etc. I resolutely disregard these. Something better, greater, is happening! I am following a process that leads so wildly and originally into new territory that no judgment can at the moment be made about values, significance, and so on. I am making something new, something that has not been judged before. Later others—and maybe I myself—will make judgments. Now, I am headlong to discover. Any distraction may harm the creating.

So, receptive, careless of failure, I spin out things on the page. And a wonderful freedom comes. If something occurs to me, it is all right to accept it. It has one justification: it occurs to me. No one else can guide me. I must follow my own weak, wandering, diffident impulses.

A strange bonus happens. At times, without my insisting on it, my writings become coherent; the successive elements that occur to me are clearly related. They lead by themselves to new connections. Sometimes the language, even the syllables that happen along, may start a trend. Sometimes the materials alert me to something waiting in my mind, ready for sustained attention. At such times, I al-

low myself to be eloquent, or intentional, or for great swoops (treacherous! not to be trusted!) reasonable. But I do not insist on any of that; for I know that back of my activity there will be the coherence of my self, and that indulgence of my impulses will bring recurrent patterns and meanings again.

This attitude toward the process of writing creatively suggests a problem for me, in terms of what others say. They talk about "skills" in writing. Without denying that I do have experience, wide reading, automatic orthodoxies and maneuvers of various kinds, I still must insist that I am often baffled about what "skill" has to do with the precious little area of confusion when I do not know what I am going to say and then I find out what I am going to say. That precious interval I am unable to bridge by skill. What can I witness about it? It remains mysterious, just as all of us must feel puzzled about how we are so inventive as to be able to talk along through complexities with our friends, not needing to plan what we are going to say, but never stalled for long in our confident forward progress. Skill? If so, it is the skill we all have, something we must have learned before the age of three or four.

A writer is one who has become accustomed to trusting that grace, or luck, or—skill.

Yet another attitude I find necessary: most of what I write, like most of what I say in casual conversation, will not amount to much. Even I will realize, and even at the time, that it is not negotiable. It will be like practice. In conversation I allow myself random remarks—in fact, as I recall, that is the way I learned to talk—, so in writing I launch many expendable efforts. A result of this free way of writing is that I am not writing for others, mostly; they will not see the product at all unless the activity eventuates in something that later appears to be worthy. My guide is the self, and its adventuring in the language brings about communication.

This process-rather-than-substance view of writing invites a final, dual reflection:

1) Writers may not be special—sensitive or talented in any usual sense. They are simply engaged in sustained use of a language skill we all have. Their "creations" come about through confident reliance on stray impulses that will, with trust, find occasional patterns that are satisfying.

2) But writing itself is one of the great, free human activities. There is scope for individuality, and elation, and discovery, in writing. For the person who follows with trust and forgiveness what occurs to him, the world remains always ready and deep, an inexhaustible environment, with the combined vividness of an actuality and flexibility of a dream. Working back and forth between experience and thought, writers have more than space and time can offer. They have the whole unexplored realm of human vision.

A sample daily-writing sheet and the poem as revised.

A sample daily-writing sheet and the poem as revised.

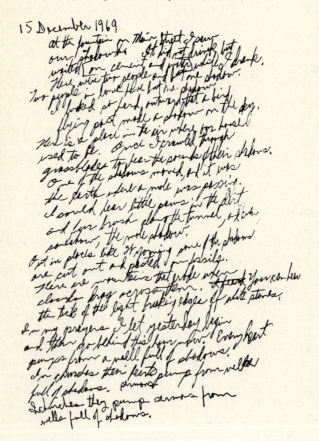

Shadows

I

Out in places like Wyoming some of the shadows

are cut out and pasted on fossils.

There are mountains that erode when
clouds drag across them. You can hear *the tick*

~~the tick~~ of the light breaking edges off white stones.

At *a* ~~the~~ fountain on Main Street I saw

our shadow. It did not drink but

waited on cement and water while I drank.

There were two people and but one shadow.

I looked up so hard outward that a bird

flying past made a shadow on the sky. **X**

There is a place in the air where/our house

used to be.

Once I crawled through grassblades to hear

the sounds of their shadows. One of the shadows

moved, and it was the earth where a mole

was passing. I could hear little

paws in the dirt, and fur brush along

the tunnel, and even, somehow, the mole shadow.

In churches *where* ~~their~~ hearts pump sermons

from wells full of shadows.

In my prayers I let yesterday begin

and then ~~go behind this hour now,~~

Shadows

1 Out in places like Wyoming some of the shadows
are cut out and pasted on fossils.
There are mountains that erode when
clouds drag across them. You hear the tick
5 of sunlight breaking edge off white stones.

At a fountain on Main Street I saw
our shadow. It did not drink but
waited on cement and water while I drank.
There were two people and but one shadow.
10 I looked up so hard outward that a bird
flying past made a shadow on the sky.

There is a place in the air where
our old house used to be.

Once I crawled through grassblades to hear
15 the sounds of their shadows. One shadow
moved, and it was the earth where a mole
was passing. I could hear little
paws in the dirt, and fur brush along
the tunnel, and even, somehow, the mole shadow.

20 In my prayers I let yesterday begin
and then go behind this hour now,
in churches where hearts pump sermons
from wells full of shadows.

An Introduction to Some Poems

1 Look: no one ever promised for sure
that we would sing. We have decided
to moan. In a strange dance that
we don't understand till we do it, we
5 have to carry on.

Just as in sleep you have to dream
the exact dream to round out your life,
so we have to live that dream into stories
and hold them close at you, close at the
10 edge we share, to be right.

We find it an awful thing to meet people,
serious or not, who have turned into vacant
effective people, so far lost that they
won't believe their own feelings
15 enough to follow them out.

The authentic is a line from one thing
along to the next; it interests us.
Strangely, it relates to what works,
but is not quite the same. It never
swerves for revenge,   20

Or profit, or fame; it holds
together something more than the world,
this line. And we are your wavery
efforts at following it. Are you coming?
Good: now it is time.   25

Vocation

This dream the world is having about itself   1
includes a trace on the plains of the Oregon trail,
a groove in the grass my father showed us all
one day while meadowlarks were trying to tell
something better about to happen.   5

I dreamed the trace to the mountains, over the hills,
and there a girl who belonged wherever she was.
But then my mother called us back to the car:
she was afraid; she always blamed the place,
the time, anything my father planned.   10

Now both of my parents, the long line through the plain,
the meadowlarks, the sky, the world's whole dream
remain, and I hear him say while I stand between the two,
helpless, both of them part of me:
"Your job is to find what the world is trying to be."   15

B.C.

The seed that met water spoke a little name.   1

(Great sunflowers were lording the air that day;
this was before Jesus, before Rome; that other air
was readying our hundreds of years to say things
that rain has beat down on over broken stones   5
and heaped behind us in many slag lands.)

Quiet in the earth a drop of water came,
and the little seed spoke: "Sequoia is my name."

A Family Turn

1
All her Kamikaze friends admired my aunt,
their leader, charmed in vinegar,
a woman who could blaze with such white blasts
as Lawrence's that lit Arabia.
5
Her mean opinions bent her hatpins.

We'd take a ride in her old car
that ripped like Sherman through society:
Main Street's oases sheltered no one
when she pulled up at Thirty-first
10
and whirled that Ford for another charge.

We swept headlines from under rugs, names
all over town, which I learned her way, by heart.

and blazed with love that burns because it's real.
With a turn that's our family's own,
15
she'd say, "Our town is not the same"—

Pause—"And it's never been."

The Stick in the Forest

1
A stick in the forest that pointed
where the center of the universe is
broke in the wind that started
its exact note of mourning
5
when Buddha's mother died.

Around us then a new crystal
began to form itself, and men—
awakened by what happened—
held precious whatever breathed:
10
we are all gestures that the world makes.

"Be, be," Buddha said.

Report from a Far Place

1
Making these words things to
step on across the world, I
could call them snowshoes.

They creak, sag, bend, but
hold, over the great deep cold,   5
and they turn up at the toes.

In war or city or camp
they could save your life;
you can muse them by the fire.

Be careful, though: they   10
burn, or don't burn, in their own
strange way, when you say them.

Interview

EC: Bill, I want to talk about how you work when it is necessary to write under particular constraints. For instance, I would like to know if the piece you wrote for *Field* was commissioned or just how it came to be written. I would like to know what kind of magazine *Field* is and how that affected your writing of the piece.

WS: All right, sure. The editors of *Field,* David Young and Stewart Friebert, wrote me a note and said either that they were planning to or were already publishing a set of articles from writers about how they went about writing. So they did set a kind of constraint on me, that is, they aimed me toward letting others know how the writing process seems to me. As soon as I got that, as is my custom, I wanted to respond in a hurry. So I got my typewriter out, and I sat there, and I thought a few minutes, and I began to write, and the thing that came out was very close—I mean *right* out of the typewriter, peeled out of the typewriter—to the way it appears in *Field* magazine.

EC: When you did this essay and it just peeled out of the typewriter, then did you have any concerns about whether it had the right number of words or would fit their editorial expectations—things like that?

WS: Yes. Well, I believe they probably gave me some idea of how long they wanted it. At least, I'm pretty sure that's the way it was, but I can tell you pretty easily how it felt to me as I started to write it. I felt, I'm going to have a rub at this, and they're giving me a number of paragraphs, so I can make two or three turns in this thing I'm writing.

EC: Great.

WS: The essay was probably developing ahead of me because I knew by the time I got going that I was going to make several points in succession. And those points do show up in the article. I even remember a kind of feeling at the last of picking up momentum and making an affirmation about what this process will do for you, or something like that.

EC: So you were actually not only at that moment writing *about* the process, you were literally *in* the process.

WS: That's right. I felt that the article itself was a manifestation of the process I was explaining.

EC: I see.

WS: So, there's another thing I think of, Elizabeth, that I want to put in here. It occurred to me a little bit earlier. And that is that the feeling I have about writing is that I'm not alone when I'm writing—that the language itself, like a kind of trampoline, is there helping me.

EC: How?

WS: Well, there's a bounce in the wording, the phrasing. It's even fun to do long and short sentences. There are all sorts of feelings of a reaction from the medium.

EC: I see.

WS: And I felt that while I was writing.

EC: Yes, so does that actually keep you from living that myth of how terribly lonely writing is?

WS: Yes. When you write you are accompanied by all the people who ever talked. Their ghosts and their feelings are there in the language.

EC: Yes. [Long pause]. I remember, Bill, that you said once that you write for the bonuses that you get out of the experience yourself and that you do not want to learn what other people want in order to supply them that. How do you line that attitude up with the demands of a particular audience for a particular magazine. Or do you even attempt to do this? Where *is* the reader when you write?

WS: In general, if we were on a panel or something and I was talking, I would expect to find myself sort of lonely among other writers by my saying something like, "No, no, I don't think much about a reader." And now with you I want to get into a little bit more than I probably would on a panel, and that is that, no, it's not that I'm aiming for a particular reader. But as a matter of fact, any engagement with the language seems to me to occur in the presence of those who have worked with the language, and so by implication those who represent the language. I'm not sharply aware of a limited audience, usually—certainly not when I'm writing poetry. But when I was writing this article, I guess I assumed I was in the presence of people who are actually engaged in this kind of activity, or at least sympathetic to conversing about it. So I was writing my article to people who would be responsive to the kinds of issues I was raising. I think I sort of assumed that many of my readers would be either surprised or startled or even offended by what I was saying.

EC: Yes.

WS: Because, you know, my article does take a certain definite tack.

EC: Yes.

WS: So I was feeling delight about that. And . . . yes, I even remember that I put in parentheses, "danger here," or something like that — something to spur the readers.

EC: So you were spurring intentionally?

WS: Yes. I was deliberately egging those people on because I wanted to emphasize the delight that there is in your feelings about the language while you write it, being ready to go where you're signaled to go by the adventures you're having right while you're writing.

EC: Bill, you remind me, when you talk about this liveliness of language, of Jung's statement in *Dreams, Memories and Reflections* that he has as companions all those ghosts of everyone who has ever lived.

WS: That's right.

EC: And *you* actually find those people in the very words.

WS: Yes, phrases, associations, maybe even syllables.

EC: How is that?

WS: Syllables have cousins in other words. The family of syllables inhabit the language like some kind of gleam that goes from word to word, phrase to phrase.

EC: Yes.

WS: I have a great sense of luxuriously inhabiting echoes in language.

[Discussion follows of Leonard Bernstein's Charles Eliot Norton lectures in relation to what WS has just said]

WS: While you were talking, I noticed when I was responding I was saying, "mm-hmm" (yes). Even that is significant to me because, for instance, I have a poem called, "The Farm on the Great Plains." In that poem, there are many words that have these cousin syllables that say, "farm," "hum," "home," "a-om," "a-oh."

EC: Yes, I understand what you're saying.

WS: I was using that syllable, which comes from the center of the being;

millions of people even meditate on it, "om," "om," "om."

EC: Right.

WS: So, I have a feeling that there is something that is like life or liveliness waiting in the language for us. And you need to be free enough to welcome those signals, and let the signals that are waiting in the language help you when you're writing. So I have this harmonious feeling with what you're saying about Bernstein.

EC: Bill, could we talk for a minute about writing that is required? My feeling, Bill, is that to have to write is actually an opportunity because it's like an encounter, or—a word I've started using with myself this week—"episode." (I actually looked that up and found that the origin of "episode" is a Greek word which means "following upon the entrance into the road or the way." And it comes from Indo-European, where it means "to go, whence?") So it's as though anything you need to write is an opportunity for a completion of an episode of the moment—that you delve into that live place of language and find the connections, or have them happen to you, or be receptive to them. Of course, this doesn't take away all the craft of shaping it later, making it less wordy, or whatever. But it actually is much more than a pedestrian task, this opportunity to go into that place of liveliness which is language, and come back out with a thing that you are then offering to another person. And it does make an episode amongst the big episode of one's own life.

WS: Yes, well, now you made me think of several things, and it's going to converge with what you are saying. It's almost as if when I start to write, I'm saying, "World, tell me some more, tell me more."

EC: Yes.

WS: And then you may be—think of this—it's almost as if you consult an oracle when you write, but the oracle you consult is the whole world.

EC: Yes.

WS: See, I've often thought of it like this. When you do creative writing, when you do art in language, you are, in effect, writing the research paper, but the research is your whole life.

EC: Yes, I really see that. Well, you would hold also, then, that writing that people ordinarily do not call "creative" is actually creative.

WS: Right, I would hold that. It's got to be creative if it's got some authenticity in it. I mean, otherwise, you're faking it; you're not really writing it. You're just putting some pieces together.

EC: Yes.

WS: So, when you put yourself into the writing, then you are listening to the signals, the oracle, that the world is giving you.

EC: I see. Bill, thank you for talking with me today.

WS: Thank you, Elizabeth. I enjoyed it.

Annie Dillard Talks about Writing

Annie Dillard grew up in Pittsburgh. Her first book was a collection of poems, Tickets for a Prayer Wheel *(1974); she won the Pulitzer Prize for* Pilgrim at Tinker Creek *(1974), a collection of essays. She is also the author of a number of other books, including* Living By Fiction *(criticism, 1982),* Holy the Firm *(1977), and* Teaching a Stone to Talk *(1982). Dillard is currently Writer in Residence at Wesleyan University in Connecticut, where she teaches Creative Writing.*

On the next few pages you will find a selection from Pilgrim at Tinker Creek, *followed by an interview with Dillard.*

from Pilgrim at Tinker Creek

Yesterday I set out to catch the new season, and instead I found an old snakeskin. I was in the sunny February woods by the quarry; the snakeskin was lying in a heap of leaves right next to an aquarium someone had thrown away. I don't know why that someone hauled the aquarium deep into the woods to get rid of it; it had only one broken glass side. The snake found it handy, I imagine; snakes like to rub against something rigid to help them out of their skins, and the broken aquarium looked like the nearest likely object. Together the snakeskin and the aquarium made an interesting scene on the forest floor. It looked like an exhibit at a trial—circumstantial evidence—of a wild scene, as though a snake had burst through the broken side of the aquarium, burst through his ugly old skin, and disappeared, perhaps straight up in the air, in a rush of freedom and beauty.

The snakeskin had unkeeled scales, so it belonged to a nonpoisonous snake. It was roughly five feet long by the yardstick, but I'm not sure because it was very wrinkled and dry, and every time I tried to stretch it flat it broke. I ended up with seven or eight pieces of it all over the kitchen table in a fine film of forest dust.

The point I want to make about the snakeskin is that, when I found it, it was whole and tied in a knot. Now there have been stories told, even by reputable scientists, of snakes that have deliberately tied themselves in a knot to prevent larger snakes from trying to swallow them—but I couldn't imagine any way that throwing itself into a half hitch would help a snake trying to escape its skin. Still, ever cautious, I figured that one of the neighborhood boys could possibly have tied it in a knot in the fall, for some whimsical boyish reason, and left it there, where it dried and gathered dust. So I carried the skin along thoughtlessly as I walked, snagging it sure enough on a low branch and ripping it in two for the first of many times. I saw that thick ice still lay on the quarry pond and that the skunk cabbage was already out in the clearings, and then I came home and looked at the skin and its knot.

The knot had no beginning. Idly I turned it around in my hand, searching for a place to untie; I came to with a start when I realized I must have turned the thing around fully· ten times. Intently, then, I traced the knot's lump around with a finger: it was continuous. I couldn't untie it any more than I could untie a dough-nut; it was a loop without beginning or end. These snakes *are* magic, I thought for a second, and then of course I reasoned what must have happened. The skin had been pulled inside-out like a peeled sock for several inches; then an inch or so of the inside-out part—a piece whose length was coincidentally equal to the diameter of the skin—had somehow been turned right-side out again, making a thick lump whose edges were lost in wrinkles, looking exactly like a knot.

So. I have been thinking about the change of seasons. I don't want to miss spring this year. I want to dis-tinguish the last winter frost from the out-of-season one, the frost of spring. I want to be there on the spot the moment the grass turns green. I always miss this radical revolution; I see it the next day from a window, the yard so suddenly green and lush I could envy Nebuchadnezzar down on all fours eating grass. This year I want to stick a net into time and say "now," as men plant flags on the ice and snow and say, "here." But it occurred to me that I could no more catch spring by the tip of the tail than I could untie the apparent knot in the snakeskin; there are no edges to grasp. Both are continuous loops.

Interview

EC: Annie, as you know, I will be using an excerpt from *Pilgrim at Tinker Creek* in a collection of readings for college students.

AD: Yes. I am pleased.

EC: Well, I would like to begin by asking you this question, "What motivated you to write that book? How did the book come about?"

AD: I read a lot. After I got out of college, I settled down to educate myself. I read books and read books. Then I started keeping notes on my reading, because like any normal human being I can't remember what I read. So I started taking notes on my reading in little spiral notebooks.

EC: What exactly would you put in those notebooks from the books?

AD: Well, I would put interesting facts. I would put quotations I liked. And I would also put my own observations down in writing.

EC: The idea, then, was to write down everything you didn't know that you wanted to know.

AD: Yes. And that turned out to be just about everything! In no time at all I had volumes and volumes of notebooks. It became hard, finally, to find information in them, so I had to index them. Then I had a notebook that was a guide to a notebook.

EC: Did you keep a list of the books you read, too, in addition to the notes?

AD: Yes. I wrote down a list of all the books that I had read—a list that I still keep; when I finish a book I write down the name and author and the date that I read it. So if I want to find a piece of information, I consult the book list first, see when I read it, find the appropriate journal, and there will be all the information.

EC: So, this reading was the first stage of your writing *Pilgrim at Tinker Creek?*

AD: The great French naturalist of the eighteenth century, Buffon, said, ''Let us gather facts in order to have ideas.'' What I was doing was gathering facts; and when you gather enough facts, you will start to have ideas about those facts. When you have material, you will automatically shape. The facts in this case were just like the potter's clay. They were material. You can't do art without material. It turns out that when you have a lot of material, you just automatically sort of organize it.

EC: Were you reading nature books then?

AD: In the course of my reading, I had read a lot of nature books. I read a lot of good ones and then a very bad one. And when I read the bad one, I thought, ''I can do better than this. There are things in that book that the guy didn't know about, and I know. So,'' I thought, ''I should be writing this book instead of reading it.''

EC: Did you start *Pilgrim* at that point?

AD: Oddly enough, the first time I wrote *Pilgrim at Tinker Creek* I set it in the state of Maine, which was where I was when I read the bad book. And I made it, the first time, a fiction book with a young man as the main character. It was all completely different in that first version. After a while I decided I had more material on Virginia than any other place, so I wrote it about Virginia, and changed all of it around.

EC: How did you get the information from your notebooks into the book?

AD: Well, I knew I had a gold mine in my journals. So I copied all the information from the journals that I thought would be pertinent—which was just about everything. A lot of quotations from the Bible and theology, a lot of ideas I had had about art, about poetry. I copied all these on four-by-six index cards.

EC: And how long did this take you?

AD: It took me a month or so. At the end of that time, I had 1,003 four-by-six index cards.

EC: What did you do with these cards?

AD: Then I put them into piles—which anyone can do. You know, if you think about writing a book, you think it is overwhelming. But, actually, you break it down into tiny little tasks that any moron could do. A pile of index cards divides itself into categories; it is very easy to divide things into categories. Oranges here. Apples and peaches there.

EC: And then . . .

AD: The question was how in the hell to write about it! I went back to the good nature books that I had read. And I analyzed them. I wrote outlines of whole books—outlines of chapters—so that I could see their structure. And I copied down their transitional sentences or their main sentences or their closing sentences or their lead sentences. I especially paid attention to how these writers made transitions between paragraphs and scenes. (This convinced me, by the way, that you do not have to lead the reader by the hand, out the door, into the street, to the car. You can just skip from scene to scene. It is, after all, a twentieth-century convention! The reader is sophisticated enough to jump from one subject to another.)

EC: And after analyzing these books?

AD: Then I put all these index cards into a filing cabinet, arranged by chapter, and started writing. I would take out one chapter's worth, lay it on the table, look at it, and start writing. And, of course, I would immediately get carried away. The chapter would just develop itself. In fact, the stuff on the index cards actually occupied only about a quarter of the material of the chapter. But the cards anchored, gave me something to start with, a direction to go in. I had an outline.

EC: After the writing?

AD: No. Before.

EC: When you put the cards on the table?

AD: Yes. I would put the cards on the table, write an outline, and start writing. And almost instantly depart from the outline. And you want to curse yourself. "Oh, shoot, I have departed from the outline once again!" Or you write yourself into a corner, refer back to the outline, try to see where you have gone wrong, write a new outline or whatever you have to do, decide you can afford to keep this side-branch, and go on. You are always going back and forth between the outline and the writing, bringing them closer together, or just throwing out the outline and making a new one.

EC: You said, Annie, that one-fourth of a chapter would come from the notes and three-fourths would just happen spontaneously while you were writing.

AD: Yes, that's right.

EC: Well, how do you teach about the three-fourths? Is it even teachable?

AD: Yes, it is teachable. I teach it myself. But you can't break it down that way. You don't teach the three-fourths. What you do is give the students assignments in which you identify the material they will use in their writing. Beginning writers have enough trouble writing without having to worry about what their facts are going to be. They simply can't write every week—which I require them to do—and gather material and have enough time to organize the whole thing and then write about it. They just can't do this every week.

EC: Can you give an example of what you mean by "giving them their material"?

AD: Yes. I might say, "Go over to the library, and get this book which I have placed on reserve. Read about the Franklin expedition to the North Pole. And that's your assignment." Then when they come to write, I say something like this, "Write a narrative account of the Franklin expedition to the North Pole as though it were going to be printed in x magazine."

EC: You not only then give them the subject to study, but you require them to write as if they are writing for a certain and particular audience.

AD: Yes, I talk quite a bit about this audience. I might say, "Write for readers of the *Atlantic*. Your readers certainly have a bachelor's degree, probably a master's. They have probably read much more than you have read yet. So don't announce to these readers something they already know." I always tell students not to tell the reader something the reader already knows.

EC: Do you ever write to order, or to fit the requirements of a particular publisher or magazine?

AD: No. I'm asked to do it quite a lot. And what I do is say to the people, "If I ever write anything that looks like it might be suitable for you, I'll have my agent try you."

EC: So, you don't ever have to write toward a deadline?

AD: It's just because I have been lucky. I would if I had to, to keep the roof over my head. There's nothing wrong with it. I've just been lucky. I know that.

EC Annie, thank you very much.

AD: I would like to say one more thing about teaching writing. My students are always so grateful—and they fight to get into my classes—because I go through their writing inch by inch. I think some teachers think that if the students have a good heart that is enough. But it isn't. Students want both positive and negative reinforcement. So what I do is mark them black and blue and then say, "Very good!" Instead of confusing them, somehow it works.

EC: Annie, thanks again.

INDEX

American Space, Chinese Place   169
Andersen, U. S.   396
Anderson, Chuck   308
Angelou, Maya   282
Aristotle   93

Baker, Russell   177
Bane, Michael   194
Barbed-Wire Memories   298
B.C.   417
A Beach Cure That Works in Mysterious
   Ways and Lasts Forever   18
A Beautiful Building Enhanced by
   Bach   263
Being a Secretary Can Be Hazardous to
   Your Health   67
Berry, Wendell   173, 246
Beyond the Garden Wall   56
Bird, Isabella   379
Body Surfing   36
Bulliet, Richard W.   97
Buying a Pickup Truck   20

Capturing the Beat of the Beach   199
Carl Jung to His Wife, Emma   367
Cawley, Rusty   292
Charlie Daniels: In Celebration of the
   Things We'd All Like to Believe
   In   194
Chief Seattle   362
Classical vs. Introspective Ballet   259
Colligan, Douglas   88
Colman, Bruce   184
The Country Diary of an Edwardian
   Lady   377

Davidson, Joan   18
Death   314
Declaration of Independence   249
Dickey, James   114
Dickinson, Emily   405
Didion, Joan   102
Digging into the Past; Seventeenth
   Century Virginia   186
Dillard, Annie   423
A Disagreeable Defender of the
   Prairie   184
Drewes, Caroline   63
Dubos, René   56

E. B. White to His Brother   368
Eckhart, Meister   393
Eiseley, Loren   80
An Eschatological Laundry List   370

A Family Turn   418
Faulkner, William   361
Forster, E. M.   171
For You, Julie, February 27, 1982   308

Fowler, Booth and Brenner, Saul   147
Fowler, H. W.   345
Friends Between a Rock and a Hard
   Place   53

Georgia O'Keeffe   102
Giddins, Gary   191
God Laughs and Plays   393
Goodman, Ellen   67
A Good Scythe   173
Graduation in Stamps   282
Guthrie, Woody   406

A Handsome Dance Company Hits Its
   Stride   261
Hartford, John   407
Hays, H. J.   106
High Notes: The Five Best Recent
   Releases   191
Holden, Edith   377
Holmes, Oliver Wendell   360
How Flowers Changed the World   80
How to Bake on a Boat   28
How to Catch Speckled Trout   38
How to Enjoy Poetry   114
How We Can Help Children Learn to
   Write   48
Hunger of Memory   325

In Defense of Literacy   246
In Defense of Optimism   147
In Favor of the Sensitive Man   339
Introduction to Some Poems   416
Is Honesty Still the Best Policy?   63
I Sing the Editor Electric   179
I Wandered Lonely As a Cloud   404
Iwata, Edward   298
I would not be here   407

Jefferson, Thomas   249
Jones, C. C.   365
Joseph, Jenny   407
The Journals of Lewis and Clark   372
Jung, Carl   367

Keller, Helen   331
Kimmel, Stephen   179
King, Martin Luther, Jr.   209
Kopp, Stephen   370

A Lady's Life in the Rocky
   Mountains   379
Lake Maker   242
Leonardo da Vinci   386
Lerner, Max   349
Let's Hear It for the Camel!   97
Letter from Birmingham Jail   209
Lewis and Clark   372
Life in Zero Gravity   88

Listen, and Listen Good: How to Attend a Concert 32
Lucksted, Sue 28

Mandelberg, Cynthia 271
Mann, Thomas 237
Marlowe, John 188
Mayer, Henry 186
McBrearty, Paul 227
Mead, Margaret 48
The Meanings of the Kiss 84
Mentor and Friend: Memory of John Lennon 292
Merriman, Paul 38
Mobil Oil 398
Mozisek, Scott 314

Nin, Anaïs 339
Ninth Meditation 396

On Being a Possibilist 349
An Open Letter to the President and Congress 271

Pease, Roland 408
Perlman, Eric 53
Perrin, Noel 20
Pilgrim at Tinker Creek 423
Plato 222
The Poet 406
Professions for Women 232
Profiles in Eating 156

Reed, Linda 107
Report from a Far Place 418
Reverend C. C. Jones to His Son 365
Rewards of Living a Solitary Life 323
Rodriguez, Richard 325
Rosenwald, Peter 259
Rudner, Ruth 36

Sadalla, Edward and Burroughs, Jeffery 136
Sailing Alone Around the World 302
Sarton, May 323
Schools, Learning, and the Quality of Life 188
Schumann, Robert 403
Sea Sculpture 403
Seeds of Man 406
Selvin, Joel 199

Shadows 416
Shakespeare, William 403
Simmons, Edgar 406
Slocum, Joshua 302
Socrates' Defense 222
Solving the Problem at Dettmers' Greenery 70
Sonnet 116 403
Split Infinitive 345
Spring Scene 403
Stafford, William 412
Stern, Barbara Lang 134
The Stick in the Forest 418
Strehlo, Kevin 142
Swan Lake/Nixon 262

Talk to the Animals 142
Tavris, Carol and Tiefer, Leonore 84
Tears Can Be Crucial to Your Physical and Emotional Health 134
Three Days to See 331
The Three Stages of Man 93
A Tribute to Mahatma Gandhi 171
Tuan, Yi-Fu 169
Twain, Mark 295
The Two Ismo's 177

Uncle's Farm 295
United Technologies 392

VanCaspel, Venita 120
Vocation 417
Von Rhein, John 32

Wall, Don 242
Warning 407
A Way of Writing 412
We Should Abolish Anonymous Evaluations of Teachers by Their Students 227

What Is an Essayist? 86
White, E. B. 86, 368
White, Vicki 70
Widmung 403
Will of Leonardo da Vinci 386
Woolf, Virginia 232
Wordsworth, William 404
The Work Ethic Is Underemployed 136

Yankelovich, Daniel 136
You Can Become a Millionaire 120

ACKNOWLEDGMENTS

Edith Holden, *The Country Diary of an Edwardian Lady*. New York: Holt, Rinehart & Winston, 1977, p. 25. From *A Lady's Life in the Rocky Mountains* by Isabella L. Bird. New edition copyright © 1960 by the University of Oklahoma Press. Reprinted by permission. "High Society Glamour Girl of the '30's, Brenda Frazier" by Paul L. Montgomery in *The New York Times*, May 6, 1982. Copyright © 1982 by The New York Times Company. Reprinted by permission. "Will of Leonardo da Vinci," cited in *The Notebooks of Leonardo da Vinci*, edited by Pamela Taylor. New York: The New American Library, Inc., 1960, pp. 234–237. "World Without End." Copyright © 1982 by Mobil Corporation. Reprinted by permission. "It's What You Do—Not When You Do It," "This Will Make You Feel Better," "Keep It Simple," and "Stop Screaming." Copyright © 1982 by United Technologies Corporation. Reprinted by permission. "God Laughs and Plays" (pp. 143–145) in *Meister Eckhart: A Modern Translation*, by Raymond B. Blakney. Copyright 1941 by Harper & Row, Publishers, Inc. Reprinted by permission of the publisher. "Ninth Meditation" from *Three Magic Words: The Key to Power, Peace and Plenty* by U. S. Andersen, Wilshire Books, Publisher, 1979. Reprinted by permission of the author. Number 47 from *The Way of Life According to Laotzu*, translated by Witter Bynner (John Day). Copyright 1944 by Witter Bynner. Reprinted by permission of Harper & Row, Publishers, Inc. "The Metta Sutra" from *Three Ways of Asian Wisdom* by Nancy Wilson Ross. Copyright © 1966 by Nancy Wilson Ross. Reprinted by permission. Daisetz Teitaro Suzuki, *Essays in Zen Buddhism* (3 vols.). London: Luzac and Company, 1927–1933, 1934. From *The Rig Veda*, translated by Wendy O'Flaherty (Penguin Classics 1981), pp. 57–58. This selection first published in this translation 1981. All rights reserved. Reprinted by permission of Penguin Books Ltd. From *Prayers and Thoughts from World Religions* by Sid G. Hedges. Copyright © 1970 by Sid G. Hedges. Reprinted by permission. From *High Holiday Prayer Book* by Rabbi Morris Silverman. Copyright 1951 by Prayer Book Press, 1363 Fairfield Avenue, Bridgeport, CT 06605. Reprinted by permission. Daniel T. Politoske, *Music*, second edition, © 1979, p. 261. Reprinted by permission of Prentice-Hall, Inc., Englewood Cliffs, New Jersey. Reprinted by permission of the publishers and the Trustees of Amherst College from *The Poems of Emily Dickinson*, edited by Thomas H. Johnson, Cambridge, Mass.: The Belknap Press of Harvard University Press, Copyright 1951, © 1955, 1979 by the President and Fellows of Harvard College. "The Poet" by Edgar Simmons. Reprinted by permission of Jes Simmons. From *Seeds of Man* by Woody Guthrie. Copyright © 1976 by Marjorie Guthrie. Reprinted by permission of the publisher, E. P. Dutton, Inc. "Warning" from *Rose in the Afternoon and Other Poems* by Jenny Joseph. Copyright © 1974 by Jenny Joseph. Reprinted by permission of John Johnson. "I Would Not Be Here" by John Hartford. Reprinted by permission of the author. "Sea Sculpture" by Roland Pease in *The New York Times*, July 22, 1981. Copyright © 1981 by The New York Times Company. Reprinted by permission. "The Way of Writing" and "Shadows" by William Stafford in *Field* Magazine, Spring 1970. Reprinted by permission of Field Magazine. "An Introduction to Some Poems" from *Stories That Could Be True* by William Stafford. Copyright © 1968 by William Stafford. Reprinted by permission of Harper & Row, Publishers, Inc. "Vocation" from *Stories That Could Be True* by William Stafford. Copyright © 1962 by William Stafford. Reprinted by permission of Harper & Row, Publishers, Inc. "B.C." from *Stories That Could Be True* by William Stafford. Copyright © 1957 by William Stafford. Reprinted by permission of Harper & Row, Publishers, Inc. "A Family Turn" from *Stories That Could Be True* by William Stafford. Copyright © 1966 by William Stafford. Reprinted by permission of Harper & Row, Publishers, Inc. "The Stick in the Forest" from *Stories That Could Be True* by William Stafford. Copyright © 1969 by William Stafford. Reprinted by permission of Harper & Row, Publishers, Inc. "Report from a Far Place" from *Stories That Could Be True* by William Stafford. Copyright © 1970 by William Stafford. Reprinted by permission of Harper & Row, Publishers, Inc. Specified excerpts from pp. 72–74 in *Pilgrim at Tinker Creek* by Annie Dillard. Copyright © 1974 by Annie Dillard. Reprinted by permission of Harper & Row, Publishers, Inc.

Thank you to the following students for the use of their essays: Paul Merriman, Vicki White, Linda Reed, Chuck Anderson, and Scott Mozisek.